VAN POL

Directors: E. L., B. J. & F

1 OLD LODGE
PURLEY, SUF

Telephone: 01–668 6~~~

COMPLETE CHURCH FURNISHERS

As the bulk of our business is transacted by mail we have a number of publications available to help you.

GENERAL CATALOGUE.

PART 1 (44 Pages Price 50p).
of Textiles and Textile Goods, Vestments Clothing etc.

PART 2 (64 Pages Price 50p).
of all other Church Furnishings, Wood, Brass, Silver, Carving, Furniture etc.,
SEPARATE PRICE LISTS FOR THE ABOVE ARE PUBLISHED BIANNUALLY.

COLOURED BROCHURE (64 Pages free of charge).
Selection of new and modern designs in both textiles and metal, published annually. Normally posted to all churches in the Spring.

CANDLE PRICE LIST (for Candles, Wafer, Incense etc).

SALE LIST (32 Pages free of charge, January only).
Goods offered at reduced prices in January only.

Westminster Cathedral Bookshop

Opening hours: Monday- Saturday 9.30-5.00
Late Night Thursday till 7.00 p.m.

Morpeth Terrace
Victoria, London SW1
01-828 5582

The Pontifical Mission Aid Societies

Pontifical Association for the Propagation of the Faith (APF)

is the Pope's principal society through which financial aid is given to the missions. It prays for the missions and seeks to arouse interest in them at home. In 1985, the APF in England and Wales contributed £877,000 to the world total. From this fund help is given to all the 910 missionary dioceses of the world. Each bishop receives a regular grant of up to £20,000 to help him in the running of his diocese, and additional grants for churches, schools, convents, etc. on application.

Pontifical Society of St Peter Apostle (SPA)

is concerned with the training of local priests, sisters and brothers in the mission lands. In 1985 the SPA in England and Wales contributed £314,000 to the world total. From this help is given to the missionary bishops to assist them in the training of their own priests etc.

Pontifical Society of the Holy Childhood (SHC)

has as its aim to help spread the Gospel of Christ among the children of mission lands through the prayers and donations of boys and girls at home. In 1985 the children of our primary schools contributed £83,281 for this purpose.

Pontifical Missionary Union (PMU)

tries to stimulate the interest of priests, religious and laity in the missionary work of the Church. In England and Wales this is done mainly through the review, *The Outlook*, which is published four times per year. Annual subscription (inland post free) £4.00.

23 Eccleston Square, London SW1V 1NU

What is the goal of a pastor?

To work with apostles, prophets and evangelists, "to prepare God's people for works of service, so that the body of Christ may be built up until we all reach unity in the faith and in the knowledge of the Son of God and become mature, attaining to the whole measure of the fullness of Christ."

Ephesians 4.12 - 33

Thirty years of service

That goal of maturity among God's people touches upon all aspects of life, both in the parish and in the work of the Catholic Housing Aid Society, which this year celebrates thirty years of service to anyone in housing need.

We need your help

Because so many people are in housing need, trying to find the right place to live, CHAS faces an uphill struggle.

Please consider making a donation to CHAS today. Your money would be well spent. CHAS also welcomes interest-free loans (or loans up to 5%). The interest which these loans then earn for CHAS is used to help the homeless and support local housing advice groups.

So ...

So think about that goal of maturity among God's people; and how we might work together to help the homeless.

Room 39
CHAS
189a Old Brompton Road
London
SW5 0AR

The Pastoral Handbook

COMPILED AND EDITED BY
TONY CASTLE

GEOFFREY CHAPMAN
LONDON

A Geoffrey Chapman book published by
Cassell Ltd
1 Vincent Square, London SW1P 2PN

© 1986 Compilation and editorial material Geoffrey Chapman, a division of
Cassell Ltd

First published 1986

ISBN 0 225 66475 5

British Library Cataloguing in Publication Data

The Pastoral handbook.
  1. Pastoral theology
  I. Castle, Tony
  253   BV4011

Printed and Bound in Great Britain
by Biddles Limited, Guildford

CONTENTS

Contents

INTRODUCTION

The idea for this book came from a reviewer in the *Catholic Herald* who mentioned the need for a reference book of 'everything you need to know to run a parish'. This seemed a good idea and after a certain amount of discussion with parish priests in town and country, in the North and in the South and in Scotland, we set about gathering information.

In the process the original brief widened. The book is not only for parish priests. We hope it will be valuable to all who find themselves with a role to play in any aspect of parish life. It is compiled by a Catholic and is most detailed on the Catholic church, but it includes much specific information on other churches and many sections which are of common relevance. It is about parish life, but that has to lead on to national life and to world churches. Indeed, the breadth of the *Pastoral Handbook* has surprised us and surely indicates the vitality of the parish system in Britain.

Perhaps a word or two about the arrangement is in order. The reader will see from the Contents that the book moves in widening circles from the parish priest himself – to the Universal Declaration of Human Rights. Within each chapter, sections are organised fairly loosely in a combination of short articles followed by useful addresses and book lists. Thus we hope that the user who comes to the book with a question or a problem will find some general advice as well as suggestions on where to get more help. As well as a subject index there is an index of nearly 1000 organisations and suppliers.

Inevitably there are gaps. There were sections we wanted to include but could not deal with adequately in the space and time available. In addition we have not duplicated much material already available in diocesan directories. We have made every effort to give accurate and up-to-date information, but many items in the book, especially names and addresses, will need to change. Therefore we plan to issue new editions regularly. This will give an opportunity to include new articles and we would appreciate hearing from any organisation who would like to be included.

Finally we wish to thank all those who provided articles, advice or information.

Tony Castle
Pentecost 1986

ACKNOWLEDGEMENTS

The editor and the publishers would like to thank the following for their contributions to this book.

Part I

Chapter 1. Rev. Gerald T. Burke, Rev. Bertram Griffin and Chicago Studies, Michael A. Barry, Westminster Diocese East Area Team, Sr Margaret Mary McGrath.

Chapter 2. Robert Kelly, Rev. Michael Perham, Tony Barr, Rev. Edward Matthews, Bernadette Farrell, Rev. David Wilson, Sister Stephanie Clifford, Rev. Michael Shaw, Rev. John Glynn.

Chapter 3. Westminster Diocese East Area Team, Peter N. Cooke, Philip Henwood, Canon Peter Elvy, the Independent Broadcasting Authority and the BBC.

Chapter 4. Rev. Johnny Doherty, Rev. Michael Hickey, Rev. John Redford, John O'Toole, Michael Foley.

Chapter 5. Austin Winkley, Winifride Pruden, Christine Kirby, Dr John Rowntree, William Thwaite.

Chapter 6. Brother Wilfrid Benning, Martin Pendergast, Rev. N. Brown, Marjorie Mason, Rev. Peter Sharp, Rev. David Wilson and CAMD, Sister Stephanie Clifford, Rev. Dunstan Thill, Rev. P. O'Donoghue, Mgr Richard Atherton, Dom Philip Jebb, the Compassionate Friends.

Chapter 7. George O. Capper, Peter Eckersley, Rev. John Glen.

Chapter 8. C. A. James, Rev. John Marsland, Rev. Roger Barralet.

Chapter 9. Mgr Michael Quinlan, Catholic Truth Society, Catholic Marriage Advisory Council, Rev. F. O'Sullivan, Philip Henwood, Catholic Social Welfare Commission.

Part III

Chapter 1. Our Sunday Visitor for material from *The Catholic Almanac 1985*, Peter Bander van Duren.

Chapter 2. Ruth Reardon, Canon Dennis Corbishley, Canon Martin Reardon and Derek Palmer, The British Council of Churches, the World Council of Churches.

Chapter 3. Stuart Polak, The Institute of Ismaili Studies.

Part IV

Chapter 1. David Amess MP.

Chapter 3. Church Action with the Unemployed, Brian Davies, Dan Marlin, Rev. J. Brankin.

PART ONE

The Parish

CHAPTER ONE

The Pastor

The Role of the Priest Today

In recent years the demands made upon the priest, in our changing times, have vastly increased. In order to identify the role of the priest today we need to isolate what is *constant* in the Church's official ministry through the centuries and what *developments* have been necessitated in changing historical situations. Then we may be able to suggest how the priest should react to the challenge of our present situation.

Four Constants in the Church's Ministry in History

1. The first and most important constant is that the purpose of all ministry is to help others to live out the values of our Christian tradition. Those values must be internalised – accepted with one's whole being, with the head, the heart and the hand – so that they transform the lives of the members of the Church and are radiated to the surrounding world. For such a task the Church has therefore always demanded sound doctrinal formation for its ministers.
2. Secondly, ministry in the Church has historically always been diversified and has led to specialised services (e.g. caring for the poor, the sick, the uneducated) as the needs arose.
3. One ministry has always remained a constant whatever the circumstances of time and place. This is the overseeing ministry, the ministry of leading and unifying the Christian community; it coordinates, facilitates, gives common direction and purpose to all other ministries and to the actions of the faithful. Classically, the bishop ('the overseer') has been this minister *par excellence*, but the pastor for centuries, in the parish, has this role in the bishop's name. Other ministries will come and go as needs demand, but the need will always be there for someone to be responsible for the internal unity

of the local church, for community unity and for leading it towards a unity with other local churches and with the universal Church.
4. A final constant in the history of ministry is that there has always been an intimate relationship between the role one exercises in daily life and the role one has in the liturgy. Liturgy is the celebration of the whole life of the Church: it is to the life of the Church what sexual intercourse is to marriage. Hence from early times, the bishop as leader of the life of the Church has presided over the liturgy. In parallel fashion the leader of the local community's liturgy has been the leader of the local community life. We should look with scepticism at the tendency in some quarters to split these two functions: having one person acting as overseer in the local Church community and someone else presiding over the liturgy.

Developments in the history of ministry

Within these four constants, ministry has developed in its service of different people at different times. The original team of twelve apostles was soon dispersed – and already in Titus and Timothy we have examples of roving bishops over particular territories. Towards the end of the first century the roving leader became a thing of the past, as residential leaders took charge of established communities. Gradually too the presbyters, the council of elders which had ringed the resident bishop, were dispersed as priests in the modern sense to missionise outlying areas and in turn become local overseers. All these moves sprang from a single source: the obligation of the Church to adapt its ministry of spreading the Gospel to different circumstances. But all these changes grew out of and promoted the four constants outlined above.

The Present Pastoral Situation

If we consider the present situation of the Church in the light of the four constants and the history of development in ministry, a number of points now may become more clear.

We can project that in our time an increase in specialised ministries will be required to keep pace with modern needs and to utilise the expertise which can be made available today to meet those needs.

This will lead to a shift in the role of pastor. Others will be available to take over many of his former duties, and his task will increasingly become one of orchestrating the activities of others.

Instead of being a one-man band, he will become an orchestra leader who teams up with other orchestral leaders to produce sound for the whole diocesan Church under the bishop. Rather than attempting an all-embracing ministry to individuals, he will need to focus on the traditional role of overseer. This will create human problems for many priests. At the same time respect for the needs of the Church indicates that priests who cannot adapt to this role should not continue in parishes where there is a genuine need for an overseer to stimulate and coordinate specialised ministries among the laity. (See pages 46–9.)

Thirdly, in selecting and preparing persons for various ministries we need to acknowledge structurally the distinctiveness of the priest's role. He is the one who will lead the liturgy and oversee the life of the community – in accordance with the ancient constant that these two functions belong together. The specialist does not lead the community and in general, therefore, such specialised persons should not be ordained to the pastoral priesthood. It follows that appropriate criteria are needed for selecting and training those who are to undertake the overseeing pastoral ministry. Until recently one could be ordained a priest if one was a good Christian man, had an adequate conceptual knowledge of theology and was ready to obey the bishop. The overseeing pastoral ministry requires more specific qualities: a practical, operational group of theological values, and the capacity to lead the community towards a deeper conversion in cooperation with others in the diocese.

A fourth requirement today is that people should recognise that pastoral priesthood is not simply one ministry among many others. The one who organises, facilitates and gives direction to the community around the values of the tradition has the most important ministry. This needs to be said, not to heap glory on pastors, but to encourage those with the ability to prefer the overseeing ministry as the one which, other things being equal, can contribute far more good in the Church than other ministries.

The prime importance of having good overseeing ministries suggests that the Church must make every effort to secure a sufficient number of priestly pastors. If, as seems to be the case, the number possessing the qualities of an overseeing pastoral ministry are small, we shall have to question a policy which restricts candidates to celibates. To allow lay-people to assume overseeing roles with a priest coming to celebrate the liturgy occasionally is to fly in the face of one of the great constants of the history of ministry. It is better to face the question of ordaining married persons than to sanction a practice that goes against so important an aspect of our tradition.

Pastoral Planning by Objectives

Did St John continually remind his followers to love one another because he foresaw the permanent danger of the Church becoming bureaucratic and authoritarian? The 'Servant' Christ gives us a high ideal for the Church when he washes the feet of his disciples and says 'you should wash each other's feet' (John 13:14). For all sorts of reasons that made sense at the time, the Church has developed a management system in which power is centralised. Sadly some members of the Church still live and act in such a way that they 'lord it over others'.

Pastoral planning by objectives is an attempt to develop a sort of institutional incarnation of the principle of not lording it over each other; a model of the 'Servant' Church. If we love one another we should seek to serve, to respect, to listen to one another. So our ecclesiological structure should not be one in which some people tell others what to do, and it should be totally consistent with the mission of the Church.

How can this be achieved? In pastoral planning by objectives we can distinguish two types of decision-making: *policy* decisions are arrived at by consensus after prayer and discussion involving the whole people of God, and *practical* decisions are taken by those who have the personal responsibility of carrying them out. *Unity* is sought at the level of shared policies, and at the same time encourages the widest possible range of practical initiatives.

Experience shows that shared discernment draws people closer together in Christ, but for it to work, a real act of faith is required from all. Guided by the Spirit, priests and bishops have to agree openly to subject themselves to a collective policy-making procedure, which entails the laity, open to the same Spirit, agreeing to take on responsibilities.

Pastoral Planning Method

1. *Discovery* List the *real* local needs. What is specific to this neighbourhood? What could the Church do? (Be clear about basic aims of the Church.)

2. *Choosing Priorities* We cannot meet every need. Which are we realistically going to tackle?

3. *Planning* How are we going to go about it? For every action be clear about what resources are available.

4. *Into Action* Keep on target, remember WHY a particular action is being taken.

5. *Evaluation* Has it worked overall? Did we meet the needs we chose? What needs do we now have to look at? (Back to 1.)

The above is the fruit of the pioneer work of the East London Area Team (Westminster Archdiocese), 117 Bow Common Lane, London E3, Tel: 01 987 1706.
Also Social and Pastoral Action, 73 St Charles Square, London W10 6EJ, Tel: 01 969 9073.
Fuller information and resource material will be readily available from the above addresses.

Peter Clifton Research

This is a full-time agency offering, at modest cost, professional opinion research. PCR specialises in advice, analysis and assistance to parishes, dioceses and organisations who want a factual basis for decisions on projects. The importance of basing plans for pastoral action on a well-informed view of a situation is obvious. For details contact:

Peter Clifton
146 Coombe Lane
London SW20 0BA
Tel: 01 947 0678

In-Service Training

Ministry to priests programme

Most dioceses now have a Director of In-Service Training, and a few a Director of Continuing Education for clergy. Interest in the subject is, however, patchy, and financial provision often inadequate. The diminishing number of active clergy means also that finding a 'supply' or 'locum' during in-service training becomes increasingly difficult. Yet increased demands on clergy, a rapidly changing environment, and confusion about identity and role all combine to make this a time when continuing education is more necessary than ever.

The Ministry to Priests Programme was developed, along with similar programmes for other groupings, to answer the contemporary needs of the clergy. Originally designed for Roman Catholics, it is now used by a Methodist Conference in America, several congregations of male and female religious and groups as diverse as teachers, military chaplains, groups of laity, missionaries and diocesan clergy. The Programme is available in French and Spanish as well as English, and is now operating in Scotland, Ireland, England, Canada and the United States.

Continuing adult education is more than in-service training. The adult develops as he becomes aware of his needs and takes steps to meet them, whether they be intellectual, spiritual, emotional or physical. To attend to one and disregard the others is to grow deformed. The task of personal development has four characteristics: it is never-ending, it is unique to each, it is relational, and it is holistic. The Ministry to Priests (and others) Programme offers groups of people a carefully designed system by which these criteria for continuing education can be met. The Programme originates from the Center for Human Development, with whom a group of people (a diocese, a conference, a congregation, etc.) contract for two years to have the Programme established. Once set up, client groups are urged to make it their own, so that it becomes permanent and self-resourcing. Further information from:

The Center for Human Development
Rev. Gerard T. Burke, Associate
Director
23 Kensington Square
London W8 5HN

Other useful addresses:

AVEC
155a Kings Road
Chelsea
London SW3 5TX
AVEC comes from the French 'with',
signifying the thrust of the agency,
which is to train people to work *with*
others.

Richmond Fellowship
8 Addison Road
Kensington
London W14 8DL

Westminster Pastoral Foundation
23 Kensington Square
London W8 5HN

Training courses for priests are integral parts of the two renewal programmes of which details are given on pages 104–9.

The following addresses may be useful:

Advent Group
New Bearings Secretary
c/o Rt Hon. N. St John-Stevas MP
House of Commons
London SW1A 0AA
A support group for former active
priests and religious now involved in
secular pursuits.

*Movement for the Ordination of
Married Men*
Details from Rev. M. B. Gaine
Liverpool Institute of Socio-Religious
Studies
Christ's and Notre Dame College
Woolton Road
Liverpool L16 8ND

New Bearings
Rt Hon. N. St John-Stevas MP,
Chairman
House of Commons
London SW1A 0AA
Counselling and help are available for
priests and religious in difficulties over
their vocation. New Bearings is
supported by the Bishops' Conference
but the service is totally independent
and confidential.

Vocations to Priesthood and Religious Life

In addition to the Director for Vocations and promotions teams that most Catholic dioceses have, there are other agencies that can be called upon.

National Religious Vocations Centre
Secretariat
114 Mount Street
London W1Y 6AH
Director:
Sr Margaret M. McGrath, MMM

The NRVC coordinates the ever-increasing efforts by religious institutes and the Caring Church Week Movement in schools and parishes in England and Wales. New vocations projects and initiatives are communicated via the NRVC to all principal vocations promoters and others involved in the vocation ministry.

Efforts to determine the result of vocations promotion is also part of the task of the NRVC, thus allowing more objective planning by the major religious superiors of England and Wales for future apostolic ventures in collaboration with the hierarchy of England and Wales.

*The Association of Religious Vocations
Promoters (ARVP)*
c/o NRVC
114 Mount Street
London W1Y 6AH
Chairperson:
Susan Clarkson, SC
436 Altrincham Road
Wythenshawe
Manchester M23 9AB
Secretary:
Sr Patricia Donlan, VS
Gothic House
High Street
Angmering
West Sussex BN16 4AH

The Association aims to advance the work of fostering vocations in England and Wales, to serve as a forum for communication of ideas and information, and to provide religious vocations promoters with such advice and assistance as they may from time to time require. It does this by promoting cooperation between promoters of vocations from the various institutes among themselves and with diocesan promoters, by undertaking appropriate projects and publicity for the fostering of religious vocations.

The ARVP is accountable through its Executive to the Conference of Major Religious Superiors of England and Wales.

Vocation Sisters
House of Prayer for Vocations
Norfolk Drive
Mansfield NG19 7HG
Tel: 0623 21164

Syon House
High Street
Angmering
West Sussex BN16 4AG
Tel: 0903 783315

Serra International (England and Wales)
'Courtfield'
43 Green Lane
Formby
Liverpool L37 7BH
A voluntary organisation of Catholic laypersons whose main object is to foster vocations to the priesthood, permanent diaconate and the religious life.

Serra International (Scotland)
Area Trustee for Gt Britain:
Mr Noel Rodgers
46 Fernleigh Road
Glasgow G43 2UB
Tel: 041 637 3828

District Governor for Scotland:
Mr K. Robson
32 Wellesley Drive
East Kilbride
Glasgow G75 8TR
Tel: 03552 49428

Vocations Centre, Scotland
Director:
Rev. Hugh J. McEwan
Sal Terrae
1647 Paisley Road West
Glasgow G52 3QT
Tel: 041 883 0139

Caring Church Week

What is it?

Caring Church Week is a method of reawakening in people, especially young people in schools, an awareness of the person of Jesus Christ. It also aims to elicit a response to the call which he makes to each one, through the Church, thereby awakening and encouraging an individual awareness of vocation.

Who Works on it?

Priests, brothers and sisters representing a variety of religious institutes, diocesan clergy and occasionally representatives of lay organisations form a team, and, on the invitation of the Head Teacher, go into a school for a Caring Church Week. Involvement of local clergy and religious is actively encouraged.

How Does it Operate?

The team comes into contact with the young people through assemblies, morning and evening prayer, class periods and a daily, voluntary Mass. There are usually special evenings set aside for the most senior members of the school and for families. There is also an exhibition, showing something of the nature and work of the institutes represented. The pupils visit each exhibition stand in small groups and talk to the team members there. By these various means and others, formal and informal, the team hope to stimulate Christian awareness and encourage those whom they meet to think about their role in the local Church and to consider the calling the Lord has for them, whatever it may be.

Can a Parish have a Caring Church Week?

Several parishes have already experienced a Caring Church Week and there has also been experimentation in tertiary education. Such

Caring Church Weeks are valuable and, of course, the format and presentation are adapted to suit the needs and nature of the parish, college or university concerned.

When did the Caring Church Week Movement start?

In March 1974 the first Caring Church Week took place in Flint in North Wales. It was run on the lines of a careers convention. Sr Margaret Joyce of the Good Shepherd Sisters and Fr Eric Darwell, Salesians of Don Bosco, led it. During that week there were requests for Caring Church Weeks from three other schools. The seed was sown and it has been growing ever since. The work soon spread to Scotland where many schools and some parishes have experienced a Caring Church Week. Recently information has gone out to Australia, the United States and Canada.

Further Information

Contact your Diocesan Director of Vocations or the Vocations Promoter of a religious institute or write to:

The Director
National Religious Vocations Centre
CMRS Secretariat
114 Mount Street
London W1Y 6AH
Tel: 01 493 1817.

The Parish and Lay Ministry in the revised Code of Canon Law

This article by Bertram Griffin first appeared in *The Revised Law of the Church – A Pastoral Guide*, Chicago Studies, 1984 and is reproduced here with permission. The whole publication is available from Chicago Studies, Box 665, Mundelein, IL 60060 USA $5.50 (postage included): International money order or funds drawn on a US bank.

Although it was originally written for readers in the United States the article provides a useful summary of the startling changes in the Church's law relating to parishes. Details of application will vary from country to country but as Griffin says 'we can be proud that the Church has recorded these rights and structures as a task to be achieved'.

I am a presbyter from the Church of Portland, which is in Region XII, which includes five Catholic conferences: Oregon, Washington, Idaho, Montana and Alaska; three provinces: the Provinces of Seattle, Portland and Anchorage; and eleven Particular Churches. All the words in the preceding sentence are Canon Law: 'Presbyter – Church of Portland – Region XII – Catholic Conference – Province – Diocese – Particular Church.' In fact, about all canon lawyers have to deal with are words. This is a far different approach from the kind of Canon Law that I was taught as a seminarian back in the '50s. When I was a seminarian, and studied five hours of Canon Law a week for four years, we were led to believe that Canon Law was a recipe book for moral behaviour – a list of do's and don'ts. Since the Second Vatican Council and particularly since the revision of the new Code, it has become clear to all of us that Canon Law is basically a 'naming process'. It does not deal with recipes for behaviour; it names structures like Church of Portland and Region XII and Province and Diocese and Particular Church. It names rights and obligations; it names relationships and roles; it names offices and ministries. Canon Law is closer to ecclesiology, a study of the church, than it is to moral theology, a study of behaviour.

If canon law is about naming, then it also is about words; and words are blessings and curses. Since canon lawyers deal with words, in our history as canonists we have both been blessed and cursed. We have been at times in the forefront of church renewal; and we have also laid burdens on people's shoulders and refused to lift them with the smallest finger. Words, canonical words even, can be curses as well as blessings.

Canonical words are sometimes viewed negatively. This is because in the naming of something with a word, one controls and defines it. When we name structures, rights, obligations in the parish, in a sense we are taming the multiplicity of charisms and gifts, the richness of church life, by actually naming and defining the rights and obligations. Hence, the naming of rights and obligations can be somewhat uncomfortable to some people because it is a taming process. When Adam named the animals in the Book of Genesis he tamed them. He demonstrated his superiority over them. When Moses wanted to know God's name, he wanted to tame the fire in the bush. That is why God told him, 'My name is *"Ehyeh asher Ehyeh."* I will be who I will be.'

At the same time, words and the naming of rights and obligations, and the naming of structures in the church, also can be a freeing experience and a blessing. The Northwest Indians say that the most important ceremony in a person's life is the 'naming ceremony'. Because if a person does not have a name, he will not know it when God calls him. So the naming of rights and obligations and structures in the church is a way of freeing us so that we can respond to God and God's mission in the church.

Canon Law, therefore, is not only an attempt to structure the church itself, but it also ought to provide us with an instrument, a tool, for mission. So we ask: how does the revised Code, particularly on the parish level, both structure the parish church and provide the parish church with those tools necessary to carry on the mission of the church? In this article Canons 515 to 552 on parish structures and ministries will be reviewed in order to answer those questions.

In considering these canons we should recall what Pope John Paul II said when he presented the revised Code to the church in February 1983: In order to understand the Code, we should think of a triangle. The top of the triangle is the Word of God. That is the most important word: the Bible – the Word of God. That is the constitution of the church. That is our fundamental law. The words of the Second Vatican Council are at one corner of the triangle. The 16 documents of Vatican II are essential for understanding the meaning of the Code. At the other corner of the triangle is the revised Code of Canon Law. In order, therefore, to understand the revised Code and understand the revised law regarding the parish, we have to keep in mind that the primary word is the Word of God – the Bible, the secondary word is the 16 documents of the Second Vatican Council. And it is only within that context that we can begin to understand the words in the revised Code.

The words which this paper discusses are: parish, parishioner, pastor, lay ministry, pastoral council, and finally some implications for the future.

The Parish: 1917 Code
First, the word *parish*. There is a tremendous difference between the 1917 Code definition of the parish and the definition of the parish in the present Code. Perhaps the definition of the parish in the 1917 Code will seem like a caricature to some because in the American Church the 1917 definition of a parish wasn't totally verified. In the 1917 Code a parish was two essential elements: a territory and an endowment. A parish was essentially defined as a territory with people attached. Saul Olinsky once said how he

envied the Catholic Church because of its territorial divisions. The entire planet Earth was divided into squares called dioceses, and each square was divided into other squares called parishes, and there was somebody responsible for every square inch of turf. And for a community organiser, that was a marvellous way to organise the planet Earth. Saul Olinsky was basing his appreciation of Catholicism on the pre-Vatican II way of organising the Church: namely, in terms of territory. It was a feudal concept. The parish was a territorial division of the church and the people were assigned to that territory. Those who are my generation and older remember how important parish boundaries were at one time in the church. It was extremely important to know which side of 45th Street you lived on because if you lived on one side, you belonged to one parish; if you lived on the other side, you belonged to another parish. There is a section of Portland, my archdiocese, called Willamette Heights. In order to get from Willamette Heights to Cathedral Church, you have to pass through another parish. The legend is that the pastor of the neighbouring parish lost that territory to Cathedral in a poker game. The territorial lines were changed. In Portland our Catholic newspaper is called the Catholic Sentinel. Every time the morale of the clergy hits a new low, someone publishes an underground newspaper called the Catholic Senile. In one recent edition, in the question and answer column, someone asked, 'Is it a sin to cross a parish boundary?' The answer was, 'The gravity of the sin depends upon the number of boundaries you have to cross. If you cross a diocesan boundary it is a mortal sin.' I know people of my generation who actually thought it was equally a mortal sin to divorce, to murder, to eat meat on Friday and to cross parish boundaries.

The second essential concept in the 1917 Code concerning the parish was the concept of endowment, or as we called it in Canon Law a 'benefice'. The parish was an endowed office and the pastor was the holder of the benefice or endowment. There were two kinds of office holders: tenured, or as we called them, irremovable pastors, and non-tenured office holders. Pastoral care was attached to the benefice. Theoretically, all of the income from the vineyards and the olive orchards and everything else that the parish owned belonged to the pastor. His responsibility was to repair the roof of the church, pay the organist, pay the assistant, pay the housekeeper out of the income; anything left over belonged to him. As a result, particularly in Spain and Italy where the benefice system was still in effect, in order to obtain a parish you had to pass a 'civil service exam' called the *concursus*. The score you received on the exam determined what kind of benefice you received and, therefore, what your income was. There developed a tremendous competitiveness to pass the civil service exam and obtain a better parish. If you were transferred, you had to be transferred to an equal, or better benefice. You could not be transferred freely by the bishop, since every time you moved, the endowment, or the income, would change; and your rights as a pastor would be damaged if you were transferred to a lesser parish. You could not hold more than one parish because each parish was a benefice, and collecting benefices was a scandal. In this country, the pastor's income was determined by a salary scale, but we had remnants of the benefice system. The stole fees went to the pastor. When I was a young assistant, I performed all the marriages and funerals, and the pastor got all the stole fees. (At least that's the way it seemed.) The Christmas collection went to the pastor, the All Souls day collection, the Easter collection and any other special collection that he could think of went to the pastor.

The Pastor and Parishioner: 1983 Code
The 1983 Code has turned all of that upside down. In the revised Code, the two essential elements of a parish are not territory and benefice, but rather 'community' and 'pastoral care'. Community is now primary in the revised Code, not only in the parish, but on every level of the church. The church is no longer a series of squares drawn on the planet Earth.

To understand the parish, first it is necessary to look at the diocese in the revised Code. Canon 369 defines the diocese: 'A diocese is a portion of the people of God' (not a territory). It is a portion of the people of God entrusted for pastoral care not to a bishop only, but to a bishop with his presbyters. It is a 'bishop with his presbyters' who are in charge of the pastoral care of that portion of the people of God called a diocese. This portion of the people of God is gathered in three ways: in the Holy Spirit, in the Gospel, and in the Eucharist. And by being gathered in the Spirit, by the Gospel and by the Eucharist, that portion of the people of God becomes a particular church in which the one, holy, Catholic and apostolic Church of Christ is truly present and operative. So the one, holy, Catholic and apostolic Church of Christ is truly present and operative in the particular church of Chicago. (We did not talk that way when I was a young priest. Chicago was a territorial division of the Universal church.)

The Revised Code even permits *personal* dioceses. Besides defining a diocese as a portion of the people of God in Chicago, you could also define a diocese as a portion of the people of God who speak Spanish, for example.

Similarly, Canon 515 defines the parish as a defined and stable community of the Christian faithful in a particular church. Territory is not the primary concept in the new Code. The primary concept is that of the parish as a community. Canon 518 says that the ordinary way to define a parish community is by geographic boundaries. The ordinary way would be to define a parish as a neighbourhood group. But the community is still primary and territory is secondary. In the 1917 Code, if a bishop wanted to create a national parish, he had to write to Rome for an indult. Now, if a bishop wants to create a national parish, a university parish, a parish for Southeast Asians, or a parish based on some other personal quality, all he must do is consult with the Priests' Senate. He no longer has to ask Rome.

The community is primary. People are no longer tied to the land as people were in the old Code. In the 1917 Code a member of the parish was attached to the land almost like a serf. It was a feudal concept. In the new Code it is far easier to have cumulative membership in several parishes. I know someone in Portland who lives on 24th Street near Fremont and, therefore, belongs to the territorial parish of The Madeleine. Because he is Spanish speaking, he also belongs to the personal parish of San Juan Macias and has cumulative membership in both parishes. Because he also attends the University of Oregon in Eugene and, therefore, lives in another city for at least three months out of the year, he has a quasi-domicile and proper parish in Eugene. Because he is Spanish speaking he also has the right to belong to a Spanish-speaking parish in Eugene. Because he attends the university, he also belongs to the university parish. And since a person can be married now in either the parish of the groom or the parish of the bride, if he falls in love with a Polish girl it would be possible for them to be married in any one of ten parishes.

My friend actually crosses his proper parish boundaries and attends a sixth parish where he enjoys the liturgy. Such *de facto* affiliation is not recognised in the revised Code. However, a parishioner is not nearly as tied to a single parish as previously. For example, Canon 857 states that infants should be baptised in the parish church of their parents, but can be baptised anywhere else for a just reason. Canon 1115 says that the proper parish for marriage is the parish of either party, not only the parish of the bride. Proper parish includes a month's residence. Canon 1177 states that the parish for a funeral is generally the parish church, but the funeral can be celebrated elsewhere with the consent of the rector of the church and after informing the proper pastor. Naturally, reception of penance, Communion and anointing of the sick are not limited to a proper parish. Canon 1248 says you can attend Mass anywhere. Territory now fixes the pastor's responsibility, but the people of God are no longer tied to the territory the way serfs are tied to the land in the feudal system. The people of God are attached to a community rather than a territory.

The Parish and Pastoral Care
Canon 529, paragraph 2, states that the pastor has the obligation to build a sense of community in the parish community, the diocesan community and the universal church community. Moreover, pastoral care now takes precedence over the benefice system. The system of endowed offices, or benefices, has been abandoned by the revised Code. From now on the clergy throughout the world, not just in American and other Anglo-Saxon countries, are to be supported by a salary rather than by a benefice. The stole fees, or offerings people give at the time of a wedding, funeral or a baptism belong to the parish. Now all parishes are equal canonically, since the benefice system disappears. Now it is possible for a pastor to pastor more than one parish since parishes are no longer benefices. Hence, the organisation of parish life is no longer tied to the concept of benefice, but to the concept of pastoral care and mission. In terms of organising parish life, there are a lot of possibilities in the revised Code one may not see in a large urban diocese but which are certainly occurring out West where vocations are minimal and where the territory is vast. It's now possible to have non-residential parishes. A pastor may live in one parish and pastor three or four parishes. In the old Canon Law the problem was solved by calling the other communities missions. The pastor would live in one parish and would serve two or three missions. We were forbidden to have more than one parish so we served several missions. Now, if a mission is mature enough to be created a parish, there is no reason why it could not be raised to the status of a non-residential parish. However, if communities are not stable enough and mature enough to be created as a mission or parish, they are still given pastoral care.

This new flexibility is evident in the fact that parishes based on nationality or language can be created; university parishes can be created. And a parish can be entrusted to a team of priests who serve *in solidum* as pastor either of a single parish or of a group of parishes. Because of the shortage of clergy out West, one probably will not see team parishes except in some religious parishes where community life is important and the religious institute sends a community of priests. In diocesan parishes, however, a team of priests acting as pastor probably would serve several parishes. A parish without a resident pastor also may be directed by a deacon, a lay person, or a team of lay people, under the leadership of a priest with pastoral faculties. This is already quite prevalent in western Canada, in Alaska, and in a few dioceses in Oregon and Washington.

Several years ago I had the opportunity of setting up a church court in Samoa. I discovered that much of the new Canon Law had already been lived in mission territories. In Samoa every pastor usually had five or six villages in his parish. The Samoan word for parish is *matagaluego* which means 'ministry centre'. The parish where the priest lived was the ministry centre, but all the other villages had a separate church building and a full-time married catechist who resided in the parish and led Sunday services each Sunday. Every week the pastor would call the catechists from the other villages into the central parish. Together they would study the scriptures and prepare the Sunday sermon and discuss the pastoral problems in the area. Each week the pastor would celebrate Mass in a different parish and do the necessary parish visiting. On all the other weeks the Sunday service was led by the catechist.

The parish vicar, or as we call him, the associate pastor, is now parallel to the episcopal vicar on the diocesan level. The bishop can appoint a parish associate as a general vicar for the entire parish, or as a vicar for a distinct part or territorial section of the parish, or for the Spanish speaking or other language group in a parish, or as an associate for youth ministry in several parishes at once. Whether or not this particular way of appointing assistants occurs in our churches is not the point; law is now flexible enough for whatever missionary situation the church may face. Finally, there is ample opportunity for the appointment of deacons, lay staff, especially catechists, liturgical ministers and pastoral visitors to parishes in the revised Code.

Lay Ministry and the Parish
The parish is a community of the people of God. Because it is a portion of the diocesan people of God, it, too, is called together in

the spirit by the Word and by the Eucharist. From the standpoint of the parishioner the important renewal is in the modern phenomenon of lay ministry. Lay ministry is the new 'word'. When I was ordained 26 years ago, the only ministers we could name were Protestant ministers. We did not talk about lay ministry in the Catholic Church. Ministry is an explosive word that has caught the imagination of people throughout our church. The word 'minister' includes pastoral ministry, the ministry of priesthood, all the possible ministries we see occurring in the church. For example, I have a friend in Portland who says that he belongs to the restaurant ministry. He means that by running a restaurant, he sees God present in his life and is attempting to use Christian principles in the way he provides service. The word ministry is evocative to him; he is using the word for what we called in my generation, 'apostolate'. The word 'apostolate' has disappeared almost totally from American church English although it is in the Vatican Council and the Code. Previously the Catholic action of the laity was defined as 'the participation of the laity in the apostolate of the hierarchy'. The hierarchy had the apostolate and the laity participated in it. Then we began to say that the laity had an authentic apostolate of their own in the world. But apostolate of the hierarchy was the spiritual apostolate in the church and the apostolate of the laity was the temporal apostolate in the world. The Second Vatican Council, of course, went far beyond that concept. As a result, the word apostolate has a confused meaning in popular church language and seldom is used.

The Second Vatican Council in the decree on the laity mentioned several levels of lay ministry, or lay apostolate. The revised Code of Canon Law refers to these levels as well.

The first level is evangelisation. Canon 211 states that all the Christian faithful have the right and duty to work for evangelisation so that the divine message of salvation may reach the whole of humankind in every age and in every land. The Great Commission, therefore, at the end of Matthew's Gospel to make disciples of all nations, baptising them in the name of the Father, the Son and the Holy Spirit and teaching them all that Christ commanded, is a general commission to all the Christian faithful. Canon 225, paragraph 1, repeats the Great Commission for the laity. Not only are the Christian faithful in general commissioned to evangelise the nations, but in a very special way the laity have a right and duty to evangelise.

The next level of ministry is sanctification. Canon 210 states that all members of the Christian faithful have the obligation to lead a holy life and to promote growth and sanctity *in the church*. The vocation of the people of God is not just temporal service to the world, but all of us together are called, laity and clergy, to promote the sanctity of the church. In that context, Canon 214 mentions the right of everyone in the church to our own proper form of spirituality provided it is consonant with church teaching. And Canon 836 refers to the 'common priesthood of the faithful'. When I was in the seminary it was considered heretical to refer to the 'priesthood of the laity', if not heretical, at least Lutheran. The Second Vatican Council used the expression 'common priesthood of the faithful' and so does the revised Code.

The third level of lay ministry is the works of charity called by many pastors the most important precept of the church: the precept to support the church financially. The schema of the new Code states that everybody is obliged to support the church financially. Pope John Paul II added two other paragraphs to that canon after the consultation process had been completed: not only do we all have an obligation to support the church financially, we also have an obligation 'to support social justice' and to 'support the poor from our own resources'. Hence, the works of charity, helping the poor from our own resources, and the promotion of social justice, or renewal of the social order, are authentic lay ministries of the people of God. *Gaudium et Spes* describes five areas in the modern world where the renewal of the social order is particularly needed: marriage and family life; culture and education, or literacy; labour and economic justice; politics and freedom; and the area of international order and world peace.

Canon 222 says that it is the obligation of all the people of God to promote social justice and Canon 225, paragraph 2, says the laity in particular are to imbue the *temporal* order with the spirit of the gospel.

Freedom and Autonomy

Now these four levels, or areas of ministry; evangelisation, sanctification, works of charity and the transformation of the social order are authentic and autonomous ministries of the laity themselves. Vatican II recommends that they occur in the parish, or use the parish as a base. Nevertheless, the laity and the members of the people of God are free and autonomous in these four ministries.

There are several canons which speak to this freedom:

– Canon 215 verifies the freedom of all Christians to found and direct associations for charitable, religious and spiritual purposes and guarantees freedom of assembly for these purposes.

– Canon 216 guarantees the right to promote and sustain lay ministry.

– Canon 275, paragraph 2, imposes on all clerics the obligation to recognise and to promote the mission of the laity in the church and in the world. Canon 529, paragraph 2, reminds the pastor of his specific obligation to recognise and promote the mission of the laity.

– Canon 204 is one of the constitutional canons on lay ministry. It defines the people of God, the Christian faithful, as those who are incorporated into Christ through baptism and thereby become the people of God. Because of our baptism, we share in Christ's priestly, prophetic and royal office. All of the baptised share in the priestly, prophetic and royal office of Christ and are called to exercise the mission which Christ has entrusted to the church.

– Canon 208 talks about the equality of all the baptised in dignity and action. These four ministries flow from our dignity as baptised Christians and our share in the mission and office of Christ.

Besides these four levels of lay ministry there is the fifth level of 'participation in pastoral care'. Some people think the laity are only ministers if they read from the pulpit or distribute communion. Vatican II has a much broader concept of lay ministers, a part of which is participation in pastoral care. Pastoring is the profession of the ordained priest; that's why the priest is ordained, to pastor. In the new Code, the word pastor has three levels of meaning. The Bishop of Rome is called the pastor of the universal church. The diocesan bishop is the pastor of the particular church, and the parish priest is the pastor of the parish church. Canon 150 says that the office of pastor involving the full care of souls can only validly be conferred on a priest. Canon 521, paragraph 1, says that the parish pastor must be a priest. The priesthood is basically a pastoral profession – either pastoring a local parish church, or assisting the bishop in the super-parochial pastoring of the diocese, or the Holy Father in his pastoral concern for the universal church. However, Canon 517, paragraph 2, says that lay people can *participate* in the exercise of pastoral care. As an historic canon, Canon 517 is ex-extremely important. Although our canonical tradition implies that the priest is ordained for the profession of pastoring, lay people now can participate in the exercise of pastoral care. In fact, if there is a shortage of priests, as there is out West, the parish can be committed for pastoral care to a deacon or to a non-ordained person, a sister, a lay person, or to a team under the direction of a priest who has the actual pastor's faculties.

This sense of participation is found in other canons. Canon 519 says a pastor's obligation is to teach, to sanctify and to govern the parish community. But he is to do that with the cooperation of the Christian laity as ministers. Canon 228, paragraph 1, says the laity are eligible for appointment to ecclesiastical office and ministry in accordance with law. The 1917 Code forbade lay people to be appointed to church office.

As a result, on the parish level there are a lot of ministries that can be performed by lay persons. Canon 230, paragraph 2, says that the laity can serve as readers, commentators and cantors. Paragraph 3 says that when other ministers are lacking, the laity can exercise the ministry of the Word. They can preside over liturgical prayer, confer solemn baptism and distribute Holy Communion.

Regarding ministry of the Word: Canon 759 says the laity can be called to cooperate with the bishop and his presbyters in exercising the ministry of the Word. Canon 766 mentions lay preachers. Canon 776 mentions lay people acting as parochial catechists; Canon 784, as missionaries; and Canon 785, as missionary catechists.

Regarding sacramental ministry, the ordinary minister of baptism is the deacon or priest; the extraordinary minister would be the catechist or lay person deputed by the bishop. Canon 910 refers to a lay person as an extraordinary minister of communion. Canon 1248, paragraph 2, makes provision for 'priestless Sundays'. In France now there are over 2,000 parishes without a priest. Over 2,000 parishes without a priest! We have many parishes in the West without a priest where the liturgy is celebrated by a lay person. According to Canon 1248, if because of a lack of a sacred minister participation in Mass is impossible, it is recommended that the faithful take part in a liturgy of the Word celebrated in the parish church . . . or in another sacred place . . . or in a group of families at a Sunday service presided over by a lay person who could preach and distribute communion.

Canon 1063 discusses marriage preparation. It does not say that it is the pastor's obligation to prepare people for marriage; it says that the pastor's obligation is to assist the Christian community to prepare people for marriage.

Canon 1112 even says that in certain circumstances lay people may act as official witnesses of marriage (in mission situations if the Episcopal Conference and Rome were to permit it). Canon 231, paragraph 2, talks about the right of lay people who work for the church to a living and family wage and to health insurance benefits and social security benefits.

To conclude, the parish community's ministry includes the ministry of evangelisation, sanctifying, works of charity, and renewal of the social order. These four ministries are authentic and autonomous ministries supported, recognised and facilitated by the pastor. But, in addition to these four, the laity cooperate in the ministry of the pastor himself; the ministry of the Word and the ministry of the sacraments.

Pastor and Parish

The pastor's ministry also involves five levels.

Canon 528, paragraph 1, says the first and primary ministry of the pastor is preaching. The church is created by the Word and only after the church is created can the church celebrate Eucharistically. The ministry of the Word is the primary task of the pastor, and he does this in five different ways: by preaching from the pulpit, by catechetical instruction – or at least by overseeing it, by promotion of evangelical and social justice programmes, by promoting Catholic education of children and youth, and by evangelisation of inactive Catholics or the unchurched non-Catholic.

The second and co-primary job of the pastor is his sacramental duties. He is to see that the Eucharist is the centre of church life. He is to be concerned that the people are informed in liturgical piety and in frequent reception of the sacraments. He is to teach individual and family prayer and is to supervise the liturgy in accordance with liturgical norms.

Thirdly, Canon 529, paragraph 1, talks about pastoral care in the strict sense, and the pastor's specific responsibilities: parish visitation, or sharing the life of the people; ministering to the sick and dying; special ministerial care to the poor, the afflicted, the lonely and migrants, exiles (four groups are specifically named in the Code); and finally, family life ministry.

The fourth duty of the pastor is leadership development. Canon 529, paragraph 2, mentions his obligation to recognise and promote lay ministry and his obligation to build a sense of community on the parish level as well as on the diocesan and universal church level.

The fifth obligation of the pastor is administration. The pastor represents the parish in legal matters, signs contracts and oversees the proper administration of church finances and property with the cooperation of the people.

As a result, particularly in parishes where there is only one pastor, it is clear that the pastor must involve other priests and deacons assigned to the parish, religious and, above all, lay people in the ministry of the church.

The Pastoral Council

The parish pastoral council is a new structure in the 1983 Code (Canon 536). To understand the parish pastoral council, it should be compared with the diocesan pastoral councils which are described in Canons 511 to 514. I maintain that the parish pastoral council presented in the revised Code is a very new concept for the American church. This may seem surprising, but my reasons for saying this are several. First of all, there is a very strong commitment to consultation and to consensus in the new Code. Canon 127 says that if the Code requires a bishop or a pastor to consult, his action is invalid if he fails to do so. It also goes on in the same canon to say that if the consultation reaches a consensus, the superior, the bishop or the pastor is technically still free to act as he best sees fit, but the presumption is in favour of the consensus. And the pastor should not act against that consensus without an overriding reason. Hence, the presumption of the revised Code is that the church is a consultative and consensus form of church government. This presumption certainly is at variance with the 'majority wins' approach operative in many existing parish councils.

This perspective is reinforced by Canon 212, paragraph 2, which talks about the right of the faithful to make known their needs and desires to pastors and, therefore, implies the correlative obligation on the part of pastors not only to listen to people, but also to create structures which will facilitate this. Paragraph 3, of the same canon, talks about the right and duty of the faithful to advise pastors regarding the good of the church and to participate in the formation of public opinion.

Secondly, the parish pastoral council is a planning council not a coordinating council. When the American church, after the Second Vatican Council, began parish councils, we went to the wrong document. Most guidelines on parish councils refer to the document on the laity, paragraph 26, which talks about a coordinating council on the parish and diocesan level. The purpose of the coordinating council is to coordinate lay ministry respecting the autonomy of various apostolates. However, the guidelines should have quoted paragraph 27 of *Christus Dominus* which mentions a pastoral planning council on the diocesan level. It does not mention the parish level, but subsequent documents apply this concept to the parish level. It's this pastoral planning council which the Code refers to when it refers to a parish council. The purpose of the pastoral planning council is to study the life and activity of the people of God; that is, to research the needs, the ideas, the hopes of the people of God, their actions and so on; secondly, to evaluate the parish in conformity with the gospel; and thirdly, to recommend policies, procedures and programmes. The job of the parish council, therefore, is not to decide whether our flag will be in or out of the sanctuary, or whether coleslaw will be served at the parish dinner. The job of the parish council is to deal with the mission of the church, long-range and short-range goals and objectives, and to design those procedures and processes by which the pastoral work of the church is to be accomplished. It does not coordinate the work of the church. You do not have to attend a boring meeting once a month to hear what everybody else is doing. That is not the idea of a parish council in the revised Code.

Likewise, the parish council in the revised Code is not supposed to pit the pastor, the staff, and the people against each other. In fact, the canon says specifically that the staff and leadership from the parish should serve together on the pastoral council. It is a council where cooperative planning occurs and where the old distinction between policy and administration, directors and staff, is not implied. The pastoral council is not a board of directors for a school or a non-profit corporation. It is a consultative planning group, planning the mission of the parish church. The Holy Spirit has given a multitude of charisms to the church. The way those charisms can be heard is through such structures as a planning council.

It is for these reasons the pastor presides at the parish council (that doesn't mean that he chairs permanently). He presides as the pope presides over the episcopal synod, or the bishop over the diocesan council, or the presbyteral council. The church's role is a ministry of reconciliation. It is not a division of the house or rule by majority or minority. The church's role is to gather people in the Spirit, the gospel and the Eucharist, not to create boards of directors and parliaments. In the revised Code we have to take seriously the partnership between pastor, staff and parish leadership. Community organisation is fond of defining a community as a group of people who support and challenge one another to work individually and corporately to realise their values and self-interest. The pastoral council is a way in which the values and concerns of the people of God including the staff and the pastor can work together in partnership for the Kingdom.

I will not develop here the parish finance council; this is demanded in the revised Code. The pastoral council is recommended but can be demanded by the bishop after he consults the Priests' Senate. The finance council is a group of lay people who assist the pastor in administration of the parish, preparing budget, financial statements, making investments, overseeing property and facility management, fund raising, church building and so on. The finance council does not make priorities or set policy. It is the pastoral council in cooperation with the staff and pastor that sets policy for the parish.

Implications

Let me conclude with some implications for the future. These rights and obligations and structures are not all new; we have experienced many of them in the post-Vatican II church. Remember, it has been twenty years since the Second Vatican Council. However, some of these rights, obligations and structures are tasks to be achieved. Alexander Hamilton says that the rights of humankind are not to be rummaged among old parchment and musty records. The rights and obligations of the pastor on one hand and the rights and obligations of the people of God or the parishioner on the other hand are not to be rummaged among the books and pages of Canon Law. Many of the things mentioned in the Code haven't occurred yet. People will read the revised Code and say, 'that's not true, the church doesn't operate that way'. We have to remember that when our forefathers wrote the founding documents of our nation, they stated 'all men are created equal'. But it has taken over 200 years to spell out the meaning of that phrase. When they wrote 'all men are created equal' they meant 'all men', not *women*. Women did not have suffrage at the time that statement was made. They meant 'white males', not Indians or blacks. Slavery was still permitted and broken treaties were still a common occurrence. They meant 'propertied men', not poor men. Poll tax was necessary in order to vote. They meant 'Anglo-Saxons', not immigrants. In many places, 'Irish need not apply' signs occurred. They meant 'Protestants' and not Catholics. We have forgotten that it was as late as the time of Kennedy's campaign that we still debated whether a Catholic could be president of the United States. And we still have not lived out the meaning of that phrase, 'all men are created equal' in this nation. But I am proud as an American that our founding fathers wrote that as a task to be accomplished. Similarly with the Code; although many of the rights and structures in the new Code are not yet lived out in the church (we do not yet have a truly consultative style of church government, and many of the rights of the laity are still not respected), I am proud that the church records these rights and structures as a task to be achieved. These now are criteria for decision making. They require conditions for their exercise. It is useless, for example, to say that the laity have a right to theological education if they are denied access to theological universities. These rights have correlative obligations and limitations. The laity have a right to be consulted; hence, my 'right' to act arbitrarily without a compelling reason is limited. If there are frequent violations of these rights, then it is up to the church to design, not only a due process, but a prior process to correct these abuses.

The pastor's role in this document is complex. In a way, no one priest can have all of the skills required of a pastor. Hence, the importance of a multiplicity of ministries on the parish level. Similarly, the charisms of the laity are gifts of the Holy Spirit and they, too, need to be facilitated and organised on the parish level. Above all, we have to keep in mind the basic message of the revised Code. The parish is not a political convention. It is not a school board or social agency. It is not a non-profit business, or a club or an association. The parish is a community of the people of God entrusted to an ordained priest for pastoral care under the authority of a bishop; and his ministry is to gather people in the Spirit by word and Eucharist for the sake of the Kingdom.

B.G.

The Parish and the Law

Whatever our religious beliefs, as citizens, we are all under the law. Those in pastoral roles should take great care to comply with the law and set a good example to other citizens by avoiding any infringement. There are a number of commonplace areas where care should be taken.

Employees

The parish priest may employ people: a housekeeper, a gardener, a club steward. The housekeeper and gardener may be 'casual' workers, or the housekeeper may 'live in'. The club steward may be employed full time and provided with accommodation. The parish priest is an 'employer' in these situations and will, when payable salaries reach the required level, be responsible for PAYE and National Insurance deductions and accounting.

In granting 'tenancies' or 'service occupancies' to housekeepers and club stewards the parish priest is an employer and, perhaps, a landlord. Obviously many arrangements of this nature work very well on an amicable basis. However, the parish priest may be well advised to seek legal advice and ask himself certain questions.

Has he a clearly defined, written contract of employment with his employee (a legal requirement)?
What 'security of tenure' does the club steward have?
Has a tenancy been created?
Will the steward vacate the premises when the employment comes to an end?

These are only a few of the issues which need to be considered and to which the law applies. It is foolhardy, and perhaps illegal, to rely upon amicable agreements. Always get things right from the start with proper legal advice. There are many books now available on running small businesses; parish priests would do well to acquire one and study the sections relating to employment.

Raffles and Draws

Raffles are a well-established source of fund-raising but can be illegal unless certain requirements are met. First, there must be a named 'Promoter' and his/her address must appear on each ticket. The promoter must be registered under the Gaming and Small Lotteries Legislation. The local authority will provide a form for this licensing on request. Secondly, at the conclusion of the raffle, or draw, the returns must be filed with the Local Authority who will provide the requisite form.

An on-the-spot raffle at the parish dance with cloakroom tickets should, strictly speaking, also comply, but the long-established practice seems to be accepted.

The Sale of Alcohol

The Social Club will require a licence and most parishes appreciate that. But what about the parish social, where drinks are to be sold, or the fund-raising dance where a bar is requested? One way is to ask a local publican to arrange this and obtain the necessary licence. This takes away the work involved but greatly reduces the profit!

Another long-established method is to sell raffle tickets which entitle the purchaser to a share in a raffle but the ticket can also be surrendered at the bar in exchange for a drink. A clever device, but it is illegal! There have been a number of successful prosecutions arising from this type of event.

Another way is to apply to the local Magistrates Court, attend on a fixed date, and obtain an 'occasional licence'. But there is no need to go to that trouble and inconvenience. An application form can be obtained from the local police station; this, when completed, will enable the police to issue a licence. This licence has to be displayed over the bar. Such licences can be granted up to four times a year.

Motor Vehicles

A parish or school mini-bus needs to be licensed, taxed and insured. If it is to carry passengers who pay to be transported it becomes classed as a 'public service vehicle' and must have a special licence. The driver too will require a special licence. Details of what is involved can be obtained from the local authority.

Even if the passengers do not pay a fare, if the vehicle carries more than eight people the special licence is required. The 'operator', usually the parish priest, is responsible in law for the condition of the vehicle, its tyres, brakes, lights, silencer, etc. The parish or community should make sure that the law is complied with, and passengers kept safe, by regular and thorough servicing.

M.B.

Insurance

Insuring against Accidents

Every year thousands of churches are robbed by thieves and spoiled by vandals. Storms take their toll; fires accidentally or deliberately started are an ever-present risk. Repair and replacement costs escalate. A parish cannot ask 'Can we afford to have proper cover?' It must ask 'Can we afford not to?'

A useful and practical approach to insurance is to divide possible happenings into three categories: material loss and damage, legal liabilities and personal accidents.

Material loss and damage
An adequate insurance against fire is essential. If it is possible, a policy should pay for a proper scheme of repairs. Churches are

seldom totally destroyed, but partial damage restoration can be very expensive in matching what remains. The Ecclesiastical Insurance Office, address below, which insures most Anglican churches, has a very favourable scheme which provides for such eventualities.

Good stewardship demands that the following should also be covered: Storm and floods; bursting and overflowing water from tanks, pipes, etc.; impact from road vehicles, aircraft and aerial missiles; malicious damage. The last takes into account the ever-increasing incidence of vandalism. Cash, often taken from church boxes, can also be covered but it will need to be specifically mentioned.

Legal liabilities
Claims can be made against the parish by members of the congregation, passers-by, neighbours or employees. At a modest cost cover can be included in the policy.

Personal accidents
Personal accident insurance will provide for those who work in or for the church if they are faced with extra expense as a result of accidents for which no one is to blame. Such insurance is usually on a 'group' basis, for example the sanctuary guild.

Order of priority
For financial reasons a full scheme of insurance may be impracticable. If that is the case, due consideration must be given to degrees of priority. Two priorities are basic fire cover and cover against public liability and employers' liability in view of the large awards which can be made these days following serious cases of bodily injury.

Insurance is a complicated business. There are those who, over many years, have specialised in meeting the needs of churches. One such is the Ecclesiastical Insurance Office, Beaufort House, Brunswick Road, Gloucester GL1 1JZ; Tel: 0452 28533, whose regional surveyors are prepared to advise on the subject of church insurance, at no cost to the parish.

Further reading
It won't happen to us, CIO Publishing, Dean's Yard, London SW1P 3NZ.

The Parish Council

A Parish Council is made up of members of the local church formed into a group to assist and advise the parish priest. The operative words are 'assist and advise'. The final decision on any issue rests with the parish priest. However, a Parish Council, by representing the views of the parishioners on particular issues, can have a positive influence on the final decision. The legal requirement, Canon 536, is that 'In this council, which is presided over by the Parish Priest, Christ's faithful, together with those who by virtue of their office are engaged in pastoral care in the parish, give their help in fostering pastoral action.' Starting a Parish Council may mean that, initially, most of the members are appointed by the parish priest whilst others are elected by the parishioners. The ultimate objective must be an elected Council.

Organising Elections

First, find your candidates. This can be done by asking those willing to serve to write their names on a tear-off slip on the parish newspaper or newsletter. The parish priest may ask people to put their names forward.

The number of people comprising the Council is a matter for each parish to decide. It will largely depend on the number of committees the Council will have. For example, it may be decided that there will be seven committees: liturgical, education, ecumenical, finance, development, social welfare and entertainment. A good number for a committee is five, so the full Council could comprise thirty-five people. Each member will serve on a committee and each committee will elect its own chairperson. In this situation thirty-five nominations or appointments are needed.

In subsequent years Council members will offer themselves for re-election and, if the Council is seen to be doing things, other parishioners will also put their names forward. Voting can take place on ballot papers provided outside church on a Sunday, and ballot boxes can be arranged. The parish priest can act as 'Returning Officer' and publish the results.

What does the Council do?

The Council will work through its committees and through its council meetings. The function of the committees is defined by their names and in the case of those listed would be:

Liturgical: Help in the planning of the community's worship and ensure full lay participation.

Education: Maintain an overview of local and national education plans and proposals that affect Catholic education; propose adult education schemes.

Ecumenical: Liaise with other local churches and religious bodies. Plan joint activities with them.

Finance: Assist and advise on the financial affairs of the parish. Fund-raising projects and parish budgeting (see Canon 537).

Development: Help in the care of the buildings of the parish – the church, the presbytery, the church hall and/or club premises, their maintenance and development.

Social Welfare: Assist in Christian action at local and national level and, as necessary, at international level.

Entertainment: Organise the social life of the parish.

Committees meet regularly and make proposals for action, report on progress and raise matters for consideration by the Council. The Council meets at regular intervals, say quarterly, and considers committee reports. It then makes recommendations to the parish priest.

The Chairman of the Council

The chairman may be elected, from their number, by the Council at its annual meeting, or appointed by the parish priest. The chairman has a major role to play in the operation of the Council. He or she needs to liaise with committee chairpersons and the parish priest and to generate interest in and enthusiasm for the work of the Council. A good secretariat is important, to ensure that agendas, reports and minutes are circulated and that the administration is good.

The Parish Priest and the Council

The parish priest is, *ex officio*, a member of all committees, and is President of the Council. Apart from listening to issues raised by the Council he will, of course, play a major role in getting the committees working by putting specific projects to them.

The Council and the Parish

The Council must keep the parish informed of its activities, and encourage parishioners to raise issues with Council members. The parish newsletter should contain regular reports, and the Parish Council should be a 'public' meeting, which parishioners are encouraged to attend.

The Council Constitution

The Council should have a written constitution, setting out, in simple terms:

1. *Its name*, i.e. 'The Council shall be known as The Parish Council of St — Church.'
2. *Membership*, i.e. The Council shall consist of X number of members, elected annually by the parishioners of St — Church.
3. *Committees*: What they are, what their function is, and the numbers serving on them.
4. *Meetings*: When the committees will meet, when the Council will meet.
5. *Powers* and *Duties*: What the Council will do, i.e. 'Advise and assist the parish priest on matters relating to the life and work of the parish and the community.'

Will it Work?

It will, if the parish and the Council members want it to. It will, if it is seen as a Council that does things – gets things done. It will fail if it is just a forum for discussion. Properly organised it can be a source of growth and development for the parish and the parishioners.

M.B.

Recommended books

Catholic Truth Society, *Principles of Liturgical Design and Reordering*, 1984.
CIO Publishing, *It Won't Happen to Us – Insurance*.
  A Guide to Church Inspection and Repair.
  Stonework Maintenance and Surface Repair.
  Heating Your Church.
  Lighting and Wiring.
Mowbray's Parish Handbooks, *A Handbook of Parish Finance.*
  A Handbook of Parish Work.
  A Handbook for Council and Committee Members.
St Andrew's Press, *Care for your Church*, 1983.
St Michael's Abbey Press, *Planning for Liturgy: Liturgical and*

Practical Guidelines for the Re-ordering of Churches, S. and C. Johnson, 1983.

Pilgrimage and Tour Operators

Albron Travel
100 Langworthy Road
Salford M6 5PN
Tel: 061 743 1702

Cathedral Pilgrimages
11 Stanley Street
Liverpool L1 6AB
Tel: 051 236 1219

Saint Catherine Air Ltd
50 Bury New Road
Prestwich
Manchester M25 8JU
Tel: 061 798 7807

The Catholic Touring Association Ltd
122 Coombe Lane
London SW20 0BA
Tel: 01 947 6991/2

Christian Fellowship Travel
62 St Andrew's Avenue
Ashton
Preston
Lancashire PR2 1JN
Tel: 0772 728117

Christian Holidays and Tours
PO Box 67
Stockport SK4 3BJ
Tel: 061 483 9328 and 061 431 9663

Christian Travel International Ltd
76 Church Road
Upper Norwood
London SE19 2EZ
Tel: 01 771 5141/4

Fatima Travel
500 Bromley Road
Downham
Bromley
Kent
Tel: 01 698 1234

Fellowship Travel
162 Westcombe Hill
Blackheath
London SE3 7DH
Tel: 01 853 5151 or 01 853 4909

Highway Holidays Ltd
30 Sackville Gardens
Hove
East Sussex BN3 4GH
Tel: 0273 738821

Holy Land Fellowship Tours
118 High Street
Dover
Kent CT16 1ED
Tel: 0304 204404

Inter Church Travel (part of Thomas Cook Group)
45 Berkeley Street
London W1
Tel: 01 734 0942

Kestours Ltd
Travel House
Elmers End
Beckenham
Kent
Tel: 01 658 7316

Leahy's Travel Ltd
116 Harpenden Road
St Albans
Herts AL3 6BZ
Tel: 0727 52394

Lionheart Tours
Desk CU
15 Maddox Street
London W1R 9LE
Tel: 01 629 2898

Mancunia Travel Limited
2–14 Oxford Street
Manchester
Tel: 061 228 2842;
213 Piccadilly
London W1V 0HN
Tel: 01 734 6286;
130 Bridgegate
Glasgow G1 5HZ
Tel: 041 552 1449

Orientours
Kent House
87 Regent Street
London W1R 8LS
Tel: 01 434 1551

Raymond Cook Holidays
118 High Street
Dover
Kent CT16 1ED
Tel: 0304 204404

Spes Travel Ltd
18 Churton Street
London SW1
Tel: 01 821 5144

St Peter's Pilgrims (for Lourdes)
4 Penerley Road
Catford
London SE6 2LQ
Tel: 01 698 3788

Tangney Tours Ltd
496/500 Bromley Road
Downham
Bromley
Kent
Tel: 01 698 1234

Tangney Tours North
Jackson House
23–34 Northumberland Road
Newcastle-upon-Tyne
Tel: 0632 611144

West Country Christian Holiday Fellowship
95 Hillview
Bristol
Avon BS6 4QQ
Tel: 0272 622525

Worldwide Christian Travel and Olympic Coachways
95 Hillview
Bristol
Avon BS6 4QQ
Tel: 0272 622525

Catholic Peoples' Weeks

CPW is a national Catholic organisation, registered as a charity. CPW has run over 150 Weeks since its foundation in 1945. It operates on a voluntary basis, funded by members' subscriptions, keeping charges for the Weeks as low as possible.

The Weeks are an opportunity for people to combine study of their faith, a thoughtful and joyous daily liturgy and a holiday. Talks and discussions are normally held in the mornings and during a short early evening session. During the mornings and evenings, children are looked after by helpers and have their own programme of activities. Every Week has a chaplain and in some cases also a children's chaplain.

For further information write to:

Patrick Cusack
Hon. Secretary
31 Lime Grove
Kirby Muxloe
Leics LE9 9DF

CHAPTER TWO

The Parish Liturgy

Liturgy as Summit and Source

This book covers a wide range of activities in which practising Christians might find themselves engaged and in all this work they could, justifiably, claim to be giving glory to God: in St Benedict's classic phrase, *laborare est orare*. But there is a special sense in which liturgy and worship have to be regarded as the summit, the highest form of our activity as Christians. This is not just because it is in the liturgy that we specifically and explicitly dedicate our time and thoughts to God; to giving him glory; to listening and responding to his word. More than that, it is the liturgy which most perfectly shows Christ to the world of today and continues his redeeming work.

God loves the world, and wants all people to be saved and to come to him; this reaches its climax in the sending of Christ his Son, so that by spreading the Good News, all might be drawn through him to the Father. This mission of Christ reaches its fullest expression in the paschal mystery, his death, resurrection and glorification; we are invited to share in this mystery and so to share in the mission of Christ himself and continue his work in the world of today.

It is through the liturgy that this happens: baptism is a personal sharing in the paschal mystery, whereby we die to sin so as to live anew in Christ; it is in the eucharist that the Good News is proclaimed and the paschal mystery celebrated. More than that, in baptism we are quite literally made into Christ (literally we are *anointed* or in the more traditional English expression *christened*). Thereby, we accept the responsibility and privilege of continuing Christ's work. By baptism we are made members of God's royal and priestly people (the Old Testament symbolism of anointing) and so given the responsibility for the worship of the Father and proclaiming the Good News.

Each of us may have different ways of fulfilling that mission as Christians – traditionally those different ways are known as 'ministries', i.e. the form of service we are able to offer to the community. But precisely because we each have different ministries, the liturgy becomes the summit of our activity, that is where all ministries come together, however symbolically, so that as we act together Christ continues his work in the world of today. The Church is the sacrament of Christ, the sign of his presence alive and working in the here and now: the liturgy itself is the sacrament of the Church – it is where the Church can be seen most clearly for what it is.

To say that the liturgy is the summit of Christian activity, then, is to make an essential theological point about the nature of the Church and its mission and our sharing in that mission through baptism. That is not to denigrate the value of other Christian activity: on the contrary, it should lead to a serious re-evaluation of all else we do!

The fundamental interplay between worship and life is summed up in the traditional phrase that liturgy is the 'source and summit' where the one is the expression of the other, where the one influences and inspires the other. One of the greatest temptations always confronting the Church is to over-evaluate one at the expense of the other: where Christians submerge themselves in a frenzy of activity at the expense of prayer and worship; where Christians are content to pay lip-service during Sunday worship with no attempt to provide real service Monday to Saturday. When liturgy is source *and* summit the balance between worship and life is a happy and fruitful one.

The Priestly People in Action

All have a part to play

To say, as we have, that liturgy is the responsibility of all who are baptised is not just an important theological principle. Yes, it is an essential part of our Christian belief, but it is a belief that should be taught less by sermon and more by the way we celebrate. Or to put it negatively, there is no point in clergy preaching the priesthood of all believers to a church full of believers who are not allowed to exercise that priesthood. The first principle is to let the liturgy be the summit for those taking part. That is to say, in organising liturgy we should try to ensure or facilitate the greatest possible participation by everyone in that particular celebration. This is not out of some sense of 'democracy' or simply to make things easier by sharing the load (one soon discovers it is more difficult!). Rather, it is because the liturgy should be allowed to be what it really is: the sacrament of the Church, where the Church can be most clearly seen. Therefore, each member ought at least occasionally to be allowed to contribute as a sign that through their own particular ministry, they contribute to the activity of the whole body.

But not necessarily the same part

However, this does not mean that everyone has to do everything in the celebration! The classic expression of what should happen is found in Paul's writing to the noisy, vibrant church at Corinth: he stresses the variety of gifts which all have their origin in the same Spirit, that there are all sorts of services but always the same Lord (Christ, the Son); working in different ways in different people, it is the same God (Father) (1 Corinthians 12). There is the unity of one body, but each member contributes to that in a different way, according to their gift; their service/ministry is exercised according to whatever talent or natural gift they have been given. The secret is in recognising what natural ability or aptitude church members have and then allowing those gifts expression in worship. Some of the traditional gifts are easy to accommodate: those with musical talent can express that through voice or instrument. But whatever the gift, remember:

1. They must never supplant the role of the congregation as a whole. Continuing the music example, we are *all* called to sing the glory of God, and our liturgy must allow us *all* the opportunity to do that. Within that, some may have the special role of facilitating or enhancing our singing – but not simply doing it for us.
2. Remember the essential connection: liturgy and life. As St Augustine once put it, in a sermon on the Psalm 'Sing a new song to the Lord': 'by all means sing a new song, but make sure that your life sings the same song as your mouth'.

Do not confuse 'participation' with 'activity'

One of the most often voiced complaints against liturgical renewal and reform is that we risk losing the 'sense of mystery'. Such a complaint is based on a wrong notion of 'mystery' (it literally means 'sacrament'), but it does express a valid fear. Our liturgies can be too full of activity, a constant bombardment of sound, albeit in

prayer, scripture readings, sermons and hymns. We can also participate by being silent together. For example, in the restored Prayer of
the Faithful in the Roman rite, the moment of silence is the heart of
the Prayer, but it is most frequently rushed past without allowing
the faithful that solemn, silent prayer time before we make our
intercession together.

A sense of balance is needed. Moments of silence can highlight
moments of 'noise', whether sung or spoken; absolute silence can
be empty and oppressive – the right spoken word can fill the 'empti-
ness', the right background music can make the silence more bear-
able, less threatening. Similarly, moments of movement need to be
balanced by moments of physical stillness (and vice versa). Like a
skilful artist who uses light and shade, we need to have sound,
silence, stillness and activity on our liturgical palette.

R.K.

The Parish Liturgy Group

It is not advisable, nor even possible, to dictate here what kind of
structure is needed for a parish liturgy group. However, it must be
kept in mind that this is a planning and coordinating group, so one
does not need, for example, all the altar servers, or all the choir.
The key members and leaders of all those with a clear participatory
role need to be included. Each community must evolve the structure that suits the temperament and competence of those who will
make up that group. But since the task facing such a group, however
constituted, is a common one, here are some thoughts that ought to
be relevant.

Learning and teaching

The group may need to function on two levels. It is not enough to
meet and plan practicalities. Especially in the early days, the group
members ought to be aware of their own lack of liturgical knowledge and expertise. Therefore, the group meetings ought to serve
explicitly as opportunities for *learning*. Plan ahead items for common study, so that everyone comes prepared to contribute to the
discussion: invite 'experts' from the diocese or neighbouring
parishes to share their insights.

The second level at which the group has to operate is that of
teaching. Remember, though, that the best teacher will be a good
celebration. The aim should be to let the liturgy itself speak to the

people. In all of this teaching and learning, resist the temptation to 'leave it to the professionals'! Without a doubt, the group will look to the clergy for a great deal of input (and this implies that the clergy ought to be members of the liturgy group) but theirs should not be the only, or even last, word. Their input, as with that of any individual, should be shaped by group discussion.

Personal experience suggests that our worship may be clerically dominated, less because of a dictatorial mentality among the clergy than because of a too ready acceptance by lay people of 'whatever Father says . . .'. Liturgy belongs to us all by right and we have all to find our right expression.

Evaluation and assessing past celebrations

A lot of thought is given in liturgy groups to planning celebrations and rightly so. Because of the continual unfolding of the Church's year a 'post mortem' on a previous celebration might seem a waste of time. Not at all: such an appraisal – well conducted – is the most effective springboard to improved future celebrations. Certainly, it could easily degenerate into a grousing session, an opportunity for people to rehearse their particular liturgical prejudices. To avoid this, encourage everyone to say succinctly

1. what they liked about the celebration and why, and only then move on to
2. what they thought did not work and why.

It is very important to spend time on the 'why' they did or did not like whatever; i.e. the time should be spent not on likes and dislikes as such, but on analysing the causes.

Planning celebrations

Apart from the fundamental theological principles, there are a couple of practical principles which can guide any planning. The group ought to ask itself the following key questions:

1. 'What is the overall meaning of the celebration?' Or to phrase it in a more personal way, 'Are the worshippers going to leave with a single clear idea of what they have been celebrating?' 'Have we helped the liturgy to speak to them?'
2. Once we are clear on the central meaning we must also ask 'What is the meaning of the various parts of the celebration?' and 'How do these parts contribute to the overall meaning?'. It could be that the

parts of the celebration are working against each other – and if we judge that that is happening we can strive to remedy it.

3. 'What is the relative importance of the various parts?' Remember that not everything in a celebration is of equal worth: some parts are essential, others are not. This can be measured partly by reference to tradition (what has always and everywhere been thought essential) and partly by reference to what each part contributes to the meaning of the celebration.

Let me give an example – a real one, as it happens, of how the liturgy group in one parish planned part of the Easter Vigil, and in particular the Liturgy of Light. They decided that the overall meaning of the Vigil is to celebrate Christ's passover;

in the Liturgy of Light this passover is expressed symbolically through the passing from darkness to light;
it was essential, then, to ensure for the people the physical sensation of passing from darkness to light; further they thought that the candle, as a sign of the Risen Christ, was essential;
however, a fire as such was not considered essential; and given the layout of the church entrance, they could not have an orderly procession; the candle inasmuch as it gave light was essential but not in itself symbolic, and therefore the ritual of marking the year, and inserting the grains of incense was not essential. And so on.

A final word or two. I have no doubt that as a group works together as a team, it will become more proficient in the mechanics of planning celebrations. That is very necessary – but it is only half of the task! The 'mechanics' are only the means: try always to keep sight of the end – which is to leave everyone enriched by a fruitful and meaningful celebration. The task of liturgy-planners is more than being stage-managers of worship: they must facilitate the liturgical expression of everyone in the celebration – it is theirs by right.

R.K.

Building a parish liturgy library

I. Source Books

Documents of Vatican II, Dominican Publications.
The official texts of all the rites revised by Vatican II contain important introductions, which should be essential reading for all

liturgy planners. They are found at the beginning of their respective official liturgical book, but also (and more conveniently for study purposes) in collections:

Instructions on the Revised Roman Rites, Collins.

The Rites, Pueblo/T. Shand.

II. Commentaries

A. G. Martimort, *The Church at Prayer*, Geoffrey Chapman.
A four-volume edition, probably the most authoritative commentary on liturgy.
J. D. Crichton, *Christian Celebration*, Geoffrey Chapman.
This presents the previously published *The Mass*; *The Prayer of the Church*; *The Sacraments* in a single volume.
Bishops' Conference of England and Wales:
The Parish Mass, Catholic Truth Society.
Music in the Parish Mass, Catholic Truth Society.
Sean Swayne:
Communion: the new rite of Mass, Veritas.
The sacraments, Veritas.
Tom Coyle, *This is our Mass*, Collins.

III. Reviews

Liturgy, published six times per annum by the Bishops' Conference of England and Wales Liturgy Office.

R.K.

Anglican Sunday Liturgy

For the Anglican priest today, there is very often a problem in providing a stable pattern of worship in each of his churches in such a way that congregations are not confused by varieties of time, form and style, or even spiritually undermined by this unpredictability. Though a congregation needs to be helped towards the freedom that responds positively to the sort of varieties and special ingredients that can bring freshness to worship, they need first to be given a sense of security, which comes through feeling at home within a given, though not rigid, structure in which there is much that is familiar and reliable. In planning the liturgy of his church, the parish priest needs to have in mind this need for security as the base out of which experience can grow. Where he has to vary times of services, or follow a pattern that moves from eucharist one week to family service another, and so on, this need for security needs to be developed in other ways, not least by the continuity that he himself can bring to every service and celebration.

If the parish uses the calendar and lectionary of *The Alternative Service Book*, the priest is presented each week with a theme that runs through the collect and readings at both eucharist and offices. These themes (*ASB*, pp. 1092f.) help to ensure a unity to each service and to each Sunday, but they are not to be followed narrowly and slavishly. It is the readings that are the starting point for the emphasis of any particular service, and there is always a variety of themes to be drawn from any set of lections. The *ASB* allows the Sunday eucharistic lections to be used at other Sunday services and, for continuity's sake, they should usually be followed at the principal service of the day, whether the form be eucharistic or not. In preparing for Sunday, it is also important to guard the pattern of the Christian year against too many intrusions in the form of special Sundays for particular causes. Though these have their place in relating Christian life and worship to the contemporary world, they can obscure the carefully planned liturgical cycle which meets a very deep need within people. This is especially so between the Ninth Sunday before Christmas and Pentecost.

Although the *Book of Common Prayer* provision is not so explicitly thematic or its liturgical cycle so developed, to a limited extent these same considerations apply for those who use the older material.

M.P.

Recommended books

L. Dakers, *Church Music in a Changing World*, Mowbray, 1984.

A. Dunstan, *Interpreting Worship*, Mowbray, 1984.

R. Jasper (ed.), *Getting the Liturgy Right*, SPCK, 1982.

R. Leaver, *Hymns with the New Lectionary*, Grove, 1980.

M. Perham, *The Eucharist*, SPCK, 2nd edn, 1981.

M. Perham, *Liturgy Pastoral and Parochial*, SPCK, 1984.

D. Silk, *Prayers for Use at the Alternative Services*, Mowbray, 1980.

K. Stevenson, *Family Services*, SPCK, 1981.

Grove Books publish a very comprehensive list of booklets on ministry and worship. A full list is obtainable from Grove Books, Bramcote, Notts NG9 3DS. Tel: 0602 251114.

Liturgical Ministries

The General Instruction on the Roman Missal provides a starting point for a consideration of liturgical ministries.

> The celebration of Mass, is the action of Christ and the people of God hierarchically assembled. (GIRM 1:1)

This does not mean that the one body of Christ must, when it gathers for eucharist, divide into various groups according to particular skills or merits, but that each member of the assembly has his or her own ministerial role to fulfil. Applying this principle means that one person will not take over a role which is appropriate to another. The first and second readings belong to the reader; normally the celebrant would no sooner assume this role than the reader take over the collect.

It is also important that those who carry out particular actions should be part of the assembly. To bring someone into the liturgical celebration in order that they can carry out a task and then depart shows little regard for the praying church. Those who minister to the assembly must be part of the assembly.

Ministry is the privilege of all who are baptised; all are called to share in the ministry of Christ. This fact needs to be borne in mind when organising training sessions for ministers. Sessions which focus almost exclusively on the 'how to' of a particular ministry will produce ministers who are active yet who do not participate in the prayer of the community. People who are preparing for a particular liturgical ministry should be helped to see that if they are to assist the community in its prayer, they must be people of prayer who are willing to place their gifts at the service of the community. The question that needs to be tackled is: 'How can this liturgy be for me an experience of prayer when I have to do all these things and do them well?' It is never enough simply to train people in the practicalities of a ministry.

Some Liturgical Lay Ministries

Hospitality

This is the basic ministry of the whole celebrating community. It is not just a question of a few people standing at the door greeting the stranger and handing out hymn-books, or about ushers ensuring that each pew is full to capacity. The task of the whole community is to 'come alive' for worship. This process requires hospitality.

Gathering, speaking, singing, paying attention and silence are the activities of hospitality and of the celebrating community which extends this hospitality to all.

Lesson reader
Within the liturgy the lesson reader may carry out the following functions:

1 Read the lessons (not the Gospel)
2 Announce the petitions during the Prayer of the Faithful.

It is not simply a matter of 'getting' the reading a few minutes before Mass begins. The reader needs to know what is being read and how to read the particular passage. Many people who have responsibility for reading in church have had little or no formation. This is often apparent in the way they read – with much hesitation and little understanding. Possibly the reluctance of many people to enter this ministry is because there is no time given to formation between volunteering, or being volunteered, and appearing at the lectern.

Three essential elements in the training of readers are:

1 *Why?* This ministry belongs to all the baptised.
2 *What?* The reader has to make the Word come alive for the community. This demands not just a familiarity with the different literary forms present in the Old and New Testaments, but also a willingness to allow the Word of God to speak in their own lives. The reader is called to be a receiver of the Word even as he or she proclaims it.
3 *How?* We speak with our bodies as well as our voices. Movement and posture as well as voice production need to be dealt with. Readers begin to 'speak' to the community from the moment they begin to approach the lectern.

Music Ministers
This title can encompass a great many people – choir director, organist, instrumentalists, cantor, animator. The basic qualities that we should look for can apply to all these people. We need to ensure that the people who are called to this ministry are assets and not liabilities. Mediocrity has no place in ministry.

Two basic qualities are required:

Musical competence: Some would say that only professionals can fulfil this requirement. The problem here is that there are not enough available and, if there were, the money is not available to pay them. The solution is possibly to find a minimum competence and then ensure that adequate training through music lessons, summer schools, etc., is made available. Education may be an acceptable substitute for remuneration. It is also important to ensure that the instruments that musicians are asked to play are of a standard which shows respect for their ability.

Liturgical competence: All musicians are not automatically ministers of music. More is required of a minister. Coupled with an awareness of their relationship to the whole community should be the ability to make various judgements with regard to the music suggested for a particular liturgy. These judgements are:

1 Musical: Does a piece exhibit musical craftsmanship regardless of its date of composition?
2 Theological: Does the text express the faith of the Church?
3 Liturgical: Does it support the liturgical season and moment when it is to be used?
4 Pastoral: Will it support and enhance the prayer of this community gathered in worship?

We must at all times ensure that music does not become the ammunition for liturgical warfare!

Ministers of Communion

The minister of communion carries out one part of the ministry of acolyte, that of distributing communion either in church or in the homes of the housebound. It is not a clerical ministry but a ministry of the people. This is why it is important that those who carry out this ministry should be seated in the midst of the community until they come forward during the communion rite. It is important to ensure that there are sufficient ministers within a community especially as the practice of communion under both kinds is once again being restored to the liturgy. Normally these ministers are commissioned for a fixed period. This principle may be usefully adopted with regard to other ministries as it enables people to move into other areas of ministry and prevents groups of ministers becoming an established clique within the parish. The commissioning must be preceded by a period of formation and any re-commissioning by a time of renewal. Those who take communion to the housebound may need training in counselling, coping with bereavement, and also an awareness of the various social services which can be provided for the housebound.

Environment

The church building provides the environment for the worshipping community. Its layout, order and decoration can support or hinder the activity which takes place there. Those who have responsibility for the building and its decoration need to understand the relationship between their activity and the act of worship. The creation of a worship space is prerequisite for any act of worship.

There are many other opportunities for ministry within the liturgical life of a community. The important question to ask is not, 'Where will I find the people?', but 'How do we help all who are baptised recognise that ministry is an integral part of the Christian life?'

Ordained Ministries

Priest/Presider

In the early history of the Church, priests and other ministers fulfilled their specific functions. By the Middle Ages, however, the priest had effectively taken over the tasks of many other ministries, which then fell into disuse. In recent times the Church has restored a variety of ministries which are proper to all the baptised. The function of the presider is that of enabling the different ministries to flourish within a community and to witness to this by the manner of his presiding at the liturgical celebrations. In order that this can be done effectively, attention needs to be paid to the development of particular skills, the principal ones being speech and gesture. Also important is a careful use of words; a criticism of contemporary liturgy is that often too many words are used.

Deacon

The restoration of the permanent diaconate is part of the Church's restoration of a variety of ministries. The liturgical functions of a deacon are:

1. To assist the bishop and priest during liturgical services in those matters assigned to the deacon by the liturgical books.
2. To administer baptism solemnly and to supply the ceremonies that were omitted in either an infant or adult baptism.
3. To reserve the eucharist and give communion to himself and others; to give viaticum to the dying; to give benediction with the monstrance or ciborium.
4. To assist at marriages in the name of the Church.

5. To administer sacramentals and preside at funeral and burial rites.
6. To read the books of Scripture to the faithful, to instruct and exhort the faithful.
7. To preside at offices of worship and at prayer services when no priest is present.
8. To lead celebrations of the Word, especially in places where there is a lack of priests.

(Sacrum Diaconatus Ordinem n. 22)

Care must be taken to see that the deacon is not restricted to a liturgical role alone. In his ministry the deacon witnesses to the link between daily life and the worship of the Church.

M.S.

The Permanent Diaconate

The document entitled *Sacrum Diaconatus Ordinem*, promulgated by Pope Paul VI on 18 June 1967, authorised the restoration of the permanent diaconate in the Roman Rite. This made it possible for men to become deacons permanently without going on to the priesthood.

The action of the Pope implemented the express desire of the Second Vatican Council for the re-establishment of the diaconate as an independent order in its own right. Since the fourth and fifth century the Western Church had followed the practice of conferring the diaconate only as a sacred order preliminary to the priesthood. However the Eastern Church had retained the older practice. The Pope's document provided that

qualified unmarried men of 25 years of age or older may be ordained permanent deacons. They cannot marry after ordination.

qualified married men of 35 years of age or older may be ordained permanent deacons. The consent of the wife of a prospective deacon is required. A married deacon cannot remarry after the death of his wife.

preparation for the diaconate includes a period of study and formation of not less than three years.

candidates who are not members of a religious order must be affiliated to a diocese. The re-establishment of the permanent diaconate among religious is reserved to the Holy See.

deacons will practise their ministry under the direction of a
bishop and with the priests with whom they will be associated.

Music

When you praise God, praise him with all your being: May your
voice sing, may your heart sing, may your deeds sing, may your life
sing.

St Augustine

Why Music?

Music plays a vital and immediate role in worship. If we give it the
thought and care it merits, it can help build community and act as a
unique vehicle for prayer. An assembly which sings wholeheartedly
is one which participates fully and actively, and which therefore has
the capacity to be renewed and changed by the liturgy. This affects
the whole life of the parish.

A word of encouragement to the tone-deaf! Whether or not the
priest can sing – or indeed is interested in music at all – is of little
importance compared to his responsibility to help generate an
atmosphere which inspires and encourages people to pray through
singing.

Starting-points

Priests and musicians working together need common priorities.
The place of music in the Sunday eucharist is fundamental. The
Church sees music not as an optional extra, but as part of the *action*
of the Mass itself; in fact, as *integral* to every rite we celebrate. Some
parts of the liturgy are actually conceived as song and can only be
fully and effectively expressed when they are sung.

Absolute priorities are those 'shouts of praise' which are the
acclamations of the whole assembly: Gospel acclamation (Alleluia)
and eucharistic acclamations (Holy, holy; Memorial Acclamation;
Great Amen). These must be sung if the sense and meaning of what
we celebrate is to be made manifest: our greeting of Christ present
in his Word and through the eucharist. Other parts of the liturgy,
too, are designed to be sung and are considerably less effective
when not sung – for example, the Responsorial Psalm, Gloria and
various litanies (Penitential Rite, *Lamb of God* accompanying the
breaking of bread, etc.).

It is temptingly easy to think in terms of hymns only, but then we risk ensnarling ourselves in the 'hymn-sandwich' approach to music in the liturgy. A very limited number of hymns, based around the scriptures of the day, *can* help proclaim the message, but too many overload the liturgy and obscure its very structure.

However carefully chosen our words and songs, they will only be able to take root if there is some space and stillness in the liturgy. Here we can think about using both silence and music of a different kind. The wordless, mood-setting capacity of purely instrumental music should not be forgotten. A sensitive player can make a major contribution to the liturgy.

Discovering your Resources

Resources naturally vary from place to place. But *central* and common to every situation is the liturgical assembly itself: the 'priestly people' who come together to give praise to God. The presence of a choir or folk-group will not always be sufficient in itself to encourage the people to raise their voices in praise! *Music in the Mass* told us as long ago as 1969 that 'some form of leadership is indispensable'. Experience also proves that the most essential minister of music in the parish is:

The Cantor

He or she may have a number of different roles to fulfil, but most important will be to relate to the people and encourage them in their response. This may involve singing, animating and rehearsing the congregation.

A few moments spent with the people before Mass begins not only helps to involve them and facilitate their fuller participation, but coordinates them so that they can pray *together* through song. It shows that what is happening is an action of the whole community; not just the prerogative of a few, nor something which will 'happen' irrespective of their presence and participation.

Certain qualities are called for in the cantor: someone whose ministry is to pray, inspire and encourage. A reasonable voice needs to combine with belief and commitment, and a personality which is confident but not over-assertive. All the rest will be down to training and experience: remember that cantors are made, not born!

The Choir

A good parish choir does not mean that a cantor or animator is unnecessary – often the reverse. It is easy for a congregation to become lazy in the presence of a disciplined body of singers, and easier still for them to feel superfluous if the choir have not properly assimilated their role. Two points should be borne in mind. The choir should see themselves as the 'yeast' of the congregation, leading and encouraging them in their response: they should not function as 'a race apart'. Their secondary role of singing 'for' the people, where appropriate, means that they must know their own limitations. To inspire and lead to prayer requires a certain competence, and in most cases excellence will mean simplicity. Too many choirs attempt to sing music which is far beyond them.

Hitting the Right Note

However varied or limited musical resources, what counts above all is the spirit in which things are done. Where there is common vision, much can be achieved. We should strive to ensure that what has the power to bind and unite does not, through neglect or lack of communication, become a source of tension and thus lose its effectiveness. The following points may be helpful.

It is very worthwhile setting aside time(s) in the year for the parish musicians and clergy to meet together – preferably away from the presbytery (and its telephone!). This can be a time of prayer, perhaps a time to invite an 'expert' in to encourage and inspire, a time to exchange ideas.

It is most desirable to have a single mind, one person, to coordinate and channel the various musical activities – perhaps a parish music director/coordinator, who would emerge after a period of time and training. It is always problematical having different groups of music resources run by different people for different celebrations. A single person – perhaps not always the choirmaster – can effectively oversee the entire musical life of a community and help the celebration of the whole parish family at times such as Holy Week and Christmas. Obviously such a person needs an open mind and heart, and it is important that there be a relationship of mutual trust and an ability on both sides – pastor and musician – to talk things through with honesty and to pray together about them if problems arise. Equally obviously, if the person is well qualified, experienced, and satisfactory in his/her work, adequate remuneration is a matter of common justice.

Another thing to remember: in the same way that every parish has a budget for liturgy, there should also be proper provision for liturgical music. In this connection, the following resource list may prove useful.

B.F.

Organisations and Centres Offering Information and Assistance

St Thomas More Centre for Pastoral Liturgy
9 Henry Road
London N4 2LH

Music Committee of the Bishops' Conference of England and Wales
General Secretary
39 Eccleston Square
London SW1V 1PL

Society of St Gregory
Secretary
St Thomas More Centre (above)

Composers Group of the SSG
Secretary: Mr G. Boulton Smith
66 Belmont Road
Portswood
Southampton

Organ Advisory Group
Secretary: Mr J. Rowntree
2 Burys Bank Road
Greenham Common North
Newbury
Berks RG15 8BZ

Royal School of Church Music
Addington Palace
Croydon
Surrey CR9 5AD

Panel of Monastic Musicians
Chairman: Dom R. Simpson
Douai Abbey
Upper Woolhampton
Reading
Berks RG7 5TH

Publishers and Distributors of Liturgical Music

Asterisks indicate smaller publishers specialising in liturgical music.

*AMP Music
Cathedral House
Parsons Hill
Arundel
Sussex BN18 9BA

Chapman, Geoffrey
1 Vincent Square
London SW1P 2PN

*Chiswick Music
Malting Cottage
Church Road
Peldon
Colchester
Essex CO5 7PU

*Clifton Music
Clifton Cathedral
Bristol BS8 3BX

Collins Liturgical Publications
8 Grafton Street
London W1X 3LA

Fowler Wright Books Ltd
Burgess Street
Leominster
Hereford

Grail Publications
Grail Centre
Pemberton Street
Nottingham NG1 1GS

*Jabulani Music
c/o St Thomas More Centre

*Magnificat Music
St Thomas More Centre

Mayhew, Kevin, Ltd
The Paddock
Rattlesden
Suffolk IP30 0SZ

McCrimmon Publishing Co. Ltd
(formerly Mayhew-McCrimmon)
10–12 High Street
Great Wakering
Essex SS3 0EQ

*Parish Music
Cathedral Precinct
Mount Pleasant
Liverpool L3 5TQ

*Portsmouth Publications
66 Belmont Road
Portswood
Southampton SO2 1GE

Royal School of Church Music
Addington Palace
Croydon
Surrey CR9 5AD

St Thomas More Centre
9 Henry Road
London N4 2LH
Stocks a large range of recently composed liturgical music, specialising in
the smaller imprints, on display and to
order.

Veritas Publications
7–8 Lower Abbey Street
Dublin 1
Eire

Copyright

For information and details of the National Copyright Licensing
Scheme, contact the St Thomas More Centre.

Resource Books of Liturgical Music: General Collections/Psalmody

Alleluia, Amen, ed. Margaret Daly, Veritas
Biblical Hymns and Psalms, Lucien Deiss, World Library Publica-
tions, 3815 N Willow Road, Schiller Park, IL 60176, USA
Music for the Mass, ed. G. Boulton Smith, Geoffrey Chapman
Music from Taizé, Volumes 1, 2, Jacques Berthier, Collins
Lord, by Your Cross and Resurrection, Celebrating Holy Week, St
Thomas More Centre
He Comes to set us free, Celebrating Advent and Christmas, St
Thomas More Centre
Focus on Holy Week, Kevin Mayhew Ltd
A Responsorial Psalm Book, ed. G. Boulton Smith, Collins
Psalms for Sundays, 3 volumes, Mayhew-McCrimmon
Psalms for Parishes, comp. J. H. Fitzsimmons, Glasgow Church
Music Association and St Thomas More Centre
Responsorial Psalms for Singing, Joseph Gelineau, Grail

Ways of Singing the Psalms, ed. Robin Leaver, Collins
Psalms for the Eucharist, 3 volumes, Mayhew-McCrimmon
A large collection of hymn-books is currently available and further editions are appearing all the time. Any list would be out of date almost immediately.

Visual Images

Worship, in a Catholic tradition, is a highly visual experience. People meet to call to mind an ancient story, to give thanks for the deeds and promises brought to life by a retelling of that story and to pray for God's continued presence in our day.

That story is handed down in word and symbol, both of which rely heavily upon the visual and the imaginative to engender a response. The quality of the art-form in which the story is retold very often shapes not only the quantity but also the quality of the participation. For a story to be creative in the lives of people, it must engage the participants' response. Visual images, therefore, serve a two-fold purpose. First they clothe, or present to the people, the story about God's dealings in human history. Secondly, they become both the invitation to, and the means of, responding to that story.

The visual image can take many forms. At the basic level it embraces the gestures, the clothing and the decoration of the occasion of worship. The various 'rituals' or cultic activities are highly instructive if carried out sensibly and sensitively; the style and colour of the vestments can have an immediate impact on the participants, and the furnishings and embellishments of the place of worship likewise engage participation, even before any liturgical celebration has begun.

At a deeper level the visual carries the story, the invitation and the response. This is the level of the symbol. The book containing the word is seen to be the Book in which can be found the living Word. The symbols of bread and wine are recognised as food and drink which nourishes far more than bodily needs. Water is seen to be a statement about life which survives death. Candles are acknowledged as being more about enlightenment than illumination. Even perfumed smoke is endowed with analogous meanings, such as the rising of prayer before the Lord and the cloud within which God's glory may never be seen but is known to be present.

Additionally, there are other areas of the visual which foster varying levels of participation, both reflectively and dynamically. At the reflective level there is all that makes up 'sacred art', that is, paintings, statues, stained glass, etc. These provide food for thought and encourage prayerful piety.

At the dynamic level, which touches both mind and heart, participants are stimulated by images which are direct statements about the world and the time in which we live. Posters can very dramatically present the living word, using, for example, a powerful photograph coupled with a challenging text from scripture, classical or contemporary literature. (Also at the dynamic level, as well as the reflective level, is the 35 mm slide. We shall return to this.)

Drama, dance and mime are highly visual art forms for use in celebration, and are much more than merely decorative. Lighting, for example, to highlight areas of the assembly in which the celebration is currently taking place, deserves very serious consideration. A solitary red lamp in a darkened church is no less eloquent than a stronger light around the ambo and subdued light around the altar during the liturgy of the word.

Filmstrip or slide can be useful in worship. Slides can be used to attract attention to the beauty of life, and so focus our sense of wonder, a faculty so often crushed by life's brashness. Slides may also be used to illustrate Scripture or some other text or occasion of worship. Perhaps the most challenging, slides may be presented as an interpretation, an exegesis in modern terms.

Reflective slides are used frequently for depicting the creation story, conveying a visual narrative of the beauty of this earth. A danger to be avoided is that those responsible for compiling such sequences can be self-indulgent; a subdued balance of emotive pictures can celebrate (and so communicate) more effectively than a barrage of powerful images. The purpose is to arouse a sense of wonder and thanksgiving, not to stun by over-emphasis.

Illustrative slides present images which reflect the details and events of a story. This kind of presentation is like a documentary or travelogue. The danger to be avoided here is banality. For example, when describing Jesus' entry into Jerusalem on a donkey, it is not necessary to show a picture of a donkey! Let these pictures be gentle illuminative accompaniments to the story.

Interpretative slides need extreme sensitivity, both of the issues being described and of the levels of receptivity of the audience. Absolute honesty must be the guideline for the compiler. Slides of violence and images of hope are valid here, but always bearing in mind that the visual serves the Gospel; the message is more basic and important than its visual presentation.

In mixed-media presentations, it is important to preserve a

balance between the art-forms used, be they slides, poetry, dance or drama. It is even more important to provide opportunities for participants to respond – in song, psalm, silence, etc. The purpose is not to entertain. The congregation is a 'performing audience' and must be given a level of responsibility, an opportunity to articulate its response.

Without the visual, we lose interest, with too much visual, we are numbed into insensitivity. A careful, balanced visual presentation is a great treasure, and, as with every treasure, we must constantly seek it.

T.B.

Posters for worship

'Window on the World' series; published by USPG, 15 Tufton St, London SW1P 3QQ, tel: 01 222 4222. They also produce an excellent book, *Living with Posters*.
Liturgical seasons, and a good set of Stations of the Cross, from McCrimmons, 10–12 High St, Great Wakering, Essex, tel: 0702 218956.

Posters on development issues

Catholic Fund for Overseas Development (CAFOD), 2 Garden Close, Stockwell Rd, London SW9 9TY, tel: 01 735 9041.

Posters for Children

Palm Tree posters from Kevin Mayhew Ltd, The Paddock, Rattlesden, near Bury St Edmunds, Suffolk IP30 0SZ, tel: 04493 7978.
Veritas Visual Aids, available from Fowler Wright Books Ltd, Leominster, Herefordshire, tel: 0568 4561.

Slide sets and film strips

St Thomas More Centre for Pastoral Liturgy, 9–11 Henry Rd, London N4 2LH, tel: 01 802 1485. They have an expanding catalogue of ready-made slide sets for use in worship.
Upholland Northern Institute, College Rd, Skelmersdale, Lancs WN8 0PZ, have a good collection of catechetical, homiletical and liturgical slide sets.
The St Paul Book Centres in London, Birmingham, Liverpool and Glasgow all carry a good range of visual aids, many imported from USA and Italy (see pages 115–22).

The Eucharist

The Mass Filmstrip, notes, slides and cassette, by R. Bulbeck SJ, St Paul Audio Visual Productions.

Exploring the Mass Filmstrip, cassette and guidebook, written and narrated by Bishop David Konstant, McCrimmons.

The Mass and Daily Living Filmstrip, cassette and guidebook written and narrated by Bishop David Konstant, McCrimmons.

Eucharist Filmstrip, cassette and notes, produced by TeleKetics of USA.

I am Bread 45 slides, cassette and guidebook, produced by CAVC of Australia.

The Supper at Emmaus 18 slides, cassette and guidebook, written and presented by Frank Topping and produced by SIF, Upholland.

Let the Children Come Video tape, audio tape, 6 charts, 2 leader's handbooks, prepared and produced by Veritas Publications as an outline programme for parents whose children are preparing for First Communion.

Baptism

The Veritas pre-Baptism programme A kit for 36 parents includes all the material necessary for beginning the pre-baptism programme in the parish.

Baptism Filmstrip or slides (34 frames) with cassette and notes by R. Bulbeck SJ, produced by St Paul Audio Visual Productions.

Belonging to Christ Filmstrip or slides (34) on the sacrament of Baptism with cassette and notes by DSP of USA.

Confirmation

You will be my witnesses Video tape and other material for a parish-based programme for parents whose children are preparing for Confirmation. Prepared and produced by Veritas Publications. Published in the UK by Geoffrey Chapman.

Confirmation Filmstrip (18 frames) and notes by St Paul Filmstrips.

Confirmation Filmstrip, or slides, cassette and notes by R. Bulbeck SJ, produced by St Paul Audio Visual Productions.

Reconciliation

Forgiveness and Reconciliation Filmstrip (48 frames) and notes produced by St Paul Filmstrips.

Penance Filmstrip, or slides, cassette and notes prepared by R. Bulbeck SJ, produced by St Paul Audio Visual Productions.

The above titles are only a small selection of a wide range of audio-visual aids available from the St Paul Book Centres (see pages 115–22 for addresses). A full catalogue is available on request.

Celebrating the Eucharist with Children

Adapting the Mass is not an end in itself. Rather, 'full and active participation by all the people is the aim to be considered before all else' (*Constitution on the Liturgy*, n. 14). We adapt the Mass for young children so that they may more fully participate in the Church's worship.

The adaptations suggested here are derived from *The Directory for Masses with Children* (Congregation for Divine Worship, 1 November 1973) and from the *General Instruction on the Roman Missal* (4th edition, 27 March 1975). Those adaptations actually used will depend upon particular needs and circumstances. Little is said here about music and the place of the celebration; these are best left to the good sense of those responsible for the celebration.

Mass in which the majority of participants are children, e.g. school

The *Opening Song* and *Priest's Greeting* are followed by:
Introduction: this may be done by a child.
Penitential Rite: can be prepared by the children (remember, this rite should proclaim the forgiveness of God, rather than produce a list of sins). A child, or children, may lead the rite, in place of the priest. Occasionally, the rite may be omitted altogether.
Glory be to God on high: essentially a hymn whose text may be adapted to facilitate children's singing.
Opening Prayer, Prayer over the Gifts, Prayer after Communion: any suitable prayer may be selected from the Roman Missal, and if none is suitable, then a specially composed prayer may be used which is faithful to the customary literary style and is not 'childish' or moralising.
Liturgy of the Word: better a little the children can understand than much which is incomprehensible. The number of readings may be reduced to one, but that one must be a Gospel reading. The text may also be simplified; this would mean the restructuring of sentences and the choice of words more suited to the age-level of the

children. Obviously a complete rewriting of the substance and the cultural style of the passage would not be acceptable because we are dealing with God's inspired word. Dramatised and dialogued reading can be of great help. A non-biblical reading may not take the place of the biblical reading; nevertheless such a reading may be used as a sort of commentary on the biblical reading.

The homily may be given by a lay person if the priest feels himself unable to do this adequately.

Prayers of Intercession (Bidding Prayers) are best composed by, or at least with the help of the children. Even so, childishness should be avoided; it should be remembered that ideally each petition is addressed to the participants, not to God, inviting them to pray in their hearts for some particular intention (e.g. 'Let us pray for . . .'). After a short pause, each petition is concluded with a regular phrase such as, 'Lord, hear us. Lord, graciously hear us.' In any instance of specially composed texts we are helping form styles of praying of future adult communities.

Preparation of the Gifts: children may prepare the altar, bring up the bread and wine and other gifts, for example for the poor. However the latter should not overshadow the former.

Eucharistic Prayer: three prayers, specially composed for children, have been published by the Roman authorities and should be used in preference to the adult prayers. Though following the traditional pattern, they are simpler in language and ideas and call for greater participation by the children. Musical participation is by far the best and settings are available. Where space allows, it is helpful to have the children gathered around the altar.

Communion Rite: the three essential and invariable elements are the Lord's Prayer, the Breaking of Bread and the invitation to Communion, as well as the moment of Communion itself. A corollary is that all other elements of the Communion Rite may be omitted, if this would facilitate the children's participation.

Mass in which children are not in the majority, *e.g. Sunday parish Mass*

A separate Liturgy of the Word for children in an adjoining hall or room is both popular and helpful. The children assemble either at the beginning of Mass, or just before the first reading of the adult Mass, and rejoin the adults for the Preparation of the Gifts. The separate Liturgy of the Word is naturally adapted to the children's needs.

The priest should address the children directly at various points in the Mass, *viz.* the Introduction, after the homily, at the dismissal.

Children's choirs, or music groups, young readers and cantors all assist children in regarding themselves as an essential part of the local community. Adults, too, become aware of the contribution children can make to the worship of the community.

All the adaptations outlined in this section respect and highlight the essential elements of the eucharistic celebration and aim at the more conscious, fruitful and active participation of the children. This will lead, in due course, to better adult participation.

E.M.

Celebrating the Eucharist with Mentally Handicapped People

When the celebration of the eucharist is based almost exclusively on the use of words, mentally handicapped people are not only at a disadvantage but are also prevented in many respects from participating in the liturgy. When the celebration takes full advantage of all that is non-verbal, and the rites are distinguished by a 'noble simplicity', those for whom words are a barrier are drawn more fully into that movement of praise which is essential to worship.

In many areas groups meet for the eucharist outside the times normally used for Mass or other services, Sunday afternoons for example, and sometimes in a place other than the church. Here it is possible to experience the richness of a small community where the atmosphere is relaxed and parents with their sons and daughters feel at ease. There is also the practice of what is called in some places 'a special family Mass', which takes place at an ordinary service time in the church. This is where the worship is made more accessible, with a deliberate focus on the non-verbal, and a more appropriate liturgy of the Word. This means that mentally handicapped people can participate more fully, and it also can be of benefit to many others for whom a 'less intellectual' approach to the Sunday eucharist will be useful.

Key Principles

There are a number of principles to bear in mind:

Make full use of non-verbal elements
Christian worship, especially in the Catholic tradition, contains many elements that are non-verbal, including gesture, movement,

objects, clothing, colour, song, music, lighting, setting and smell – incense especially. However we tend to focus on words and these other aspects are neglected. Non-verbal elements should always be as large as possible: gestures need to be generous, the lectionary, candles, banners, and so forth should be big. They should be beautiful, and clean – especially all the altar linen. In worship everything is significant and all must direct people's minds and hearts towards the Holy God whom we worship.

Never use more words than necessary
Words are a barrier for many mentally handicapped people. Use only those that are essential. No explanations are necessary, if the action is done properly. If the meaning is not clear without words, then look at the way the action is performed. It is not necessary to speak as if to children when reading or praying. Clear unhurried diction is all that is required. Announcement of hymns can be done in a prayerful way with a minimum of words.

Concentrate on the essentials
Mentally handicapped people often find it hard to focus for any length of time and are easily distracted. This means removing anything that is not essential, and carefully planning the celebration so that there are no hitches, technical or otherwise. Examples of things that distract are: altar boys moving or looking about unnecessarily, surplus books on the altar or in the sanctuary, surplus furniture around the altar, microphones not correctly prepared, lengthy searching in a missal or lectionary for the place, etc. All this indicates the importance of planning with all those involved. To have everything ready half an hour before the service is to begin, with the altar candles lit and lights on, is a wonderful preparation for those involved in the ceremony. It is also a sign of welcome to people. Concentrating on the essentials also means allowing those parts of the liturgy which are important to stand out over and above the less significant. Worship has its 'highs and lows', and this needs to be taken into account.

Music and song
These are vital elements in all celebrations. Many mentally handicapped people know a repertoire of songs, but it is not necessary to keep to these just because they are well known. A medley of the well known joyful ones may be an excellent way of ending the

celebration. Good tunes are important and songs with a refrain are specially useful. A good group of musicians and singers to lead is most helpful and they can introduce suitable new or less well known songs.

Music without singing can be helpful. It creates a sacred atmosphere and can accompany an action. It may be provided by the organ, folk-group or use of recorded tapes. If the last are used then the volume needs turning up and down gradually.

When the music and songs blend harmoniously into the words and action of the service there is a sense of movement and wholeness which will draw everyone present into the heart of worship. Once again careful planning is most important.

A useful guide is the *Directory for Children's Masses* published by the Catholic Truth Society. This is not to say that the mentally handicapped are always children. It means that the principles for simplifying and adapting the liturgy are presented in this document (DCM 6).

Preparation

Preparation of any liturgy begins with a prayerful reflection of the Gospel of the day. What is the heart of the passage, the essential message as expressed in the words of the text? Everything then will focus on just one point. If the Gospel brings together two or more passages each with its particular message, then just take one passage for this celebration. Then look again at the text and see what is essential to the meaning of the message and what is non-essential. The latter may only add to the weight of words and may be omitted (DCM 43). There is of course the danger that such a practice may make the reading too short. In this instance the judicious use of repetition, perhaps of a key verse, can be useful.

On most Sundays of the year the first reading is a preparation for the Gospel. Treat it in the same way as the Gospel. What if it is felt that the readings given are totally unsuitable? As a last resort it is permissible to make a change (DCM 43). But it is important to keep in close harmony with the liturgical life of the Church.

The Jerusalem Bible version is usually quite adequate. Sometimes sentences require dividing into two or the replacement of 'he' by 'Jesus'. In preparing the rest of the celebration it is important to try to allow the message of the Gospel to find an echo in the different changeable parts.

Introductory Rites

The welcome is most important. It should have begun with the priest vested at the door of the church well before Mass is due to begin. At the altar the word 'Welcome' can be repeated two or three times.

The penitential rite can consist of just the 'Lord have mercy' said with head bowed and beating the breast.

The Glory to God can be sung and the Peruvian version lends itself to gestures.

The prayer of the day may need a word or phrase altered to be made more straightforward.

The Liturgy of the Word

The way that the Liturgy of the Word is celebrated is particularly significant. The whole presentation of this part of the Mass or service requires especially a 'noble simplicity' and that demands careful preparation. The readings if different from the appointed text should be written out and inserted in the lectionary which should be as big and as beautiful as possible. Meaning is given by the way the book is used. God's Word is a treasure and should be moved and treated with reverence. Never allow the readings to be given from a piece of paper held in the hand.

The Liturgy of the Word can begin with a procession moving slowly through the congregation accompanied by beautiful music. It could consist of a banner bearer, a reader holding the book up high, acolytes and others. The book can be shown to the people before the reading commences.

The way the reading is carried out is important, for unless God's Word is clearly heard by all it cannot nourish hearts and minds. A few mentally handicapped people are excellent and thoughtful readers. But it is usually better not to use this part of the service as the opportunity for involving the handicapped person, at least as a reader. Nothing should detract from the power of the message.

Unless the passage is a story, it is often better *proclaimed* rather than merely *read*. This approach adds authority to the Word and attracts the listeners. The book should be raised at the end of the reading for all to see. At some celebrations it may be possible to mime the Gospel, during the reading or afterwards. Organising this is a skill which not all will have.

The homily can take the form of a short story with a simple

message. An alternative is for the priest to take the key phrase of the Gospel and proclaim it in a personal way to each part of the congregation, making eye contact as he speaks.

Jesus says to you today
  Ask my heavenly Father and he will give you the Holy Spirit (17th Sunday Year C).
Jesus says to you today
  I am the bread of life (18th Sunday Year B).

Sometimes it is hard to use so few words and the priest will be tempted to embellish, to exhort his listeners, to comment on what he is doing. Such practices must be avoided as they will immediately detract from what he really wants people to hear.

Preparation of the Gifts

If the creed and intercessions are omitted there is a natural flow from the Liturgy of the Word to the offering of the gifts. The procession of gifts can be given a certain solemnity if not too many people are involved, and if the bread, wine, and water are held up for all to see. Music can focus attention on the action. Let the music continue until the washing of hands. Significance can be given to this action if bowl, jug and towel are large and the hands are really washed. We wash our hands before we do something significant and so it highlights the importance of the Great Prayer.

Eucharistic Prayer

The preface can be adapted to include certain phrases from the Gospel and thus give motives for the praise and thanks offered to God our Father.

The second Eucharistic Prayer is probably more appropriate than the Eucharistic Prayers for Children which are much longer. The sung refrain, however, is a useful addition for involving the people at a time when the emphasis is on words. The host should be as large as possible, and at the doxology lifted above the chalice to make it clearly visible.

Communion Rite

As the priest receives communion, music is appropriate, or the music group could sing something meditative. Communion can be a stressful moment for mentally handicapped people – or maybe more for parents. All however are helped by the prayerful atmosphere engendered by beautiful music or song. This however does not preclude a time of silent prayer after Communion.

Conclusion

The end of the Mass is the time when there can be an explosion of joy and celebration. Singing and dancing with clapping of hands brings at this time a wonderful sense of release and if it can lead to continuing the celebration in a nearby room or hall so much the better.

Through the power of a truly harmonious celebration, it is not only mentally handicapped people who benefit, but the whole congregation. In worship,

our hearts and minds should be raised to that which lies beyond and above us. I mean by this that we must be led to perceive, albeit in a glass darkly, the mystery which God is. The longing in all of us to know that which is most lovable and beautiful must, so I believe, be awakened when we attend Mass (worship). We must sense we have been in the presence of the holy (Cardinal Hume, *One Heart and One Mind*, Meditation for 4th Sunday of Advent 1979).

D.W.

Further Reading

Response to Worship, Fr David Wilson, 6 pp., 1983. Obtainable from MENCAP, 17 High Street, Taunton, Somerset TA1 3PJ.
'Liturgical Integration of the disabled person', Sr Mary Therese Harrington, *DocumenCap* No 1, January 1978, pp. 8–14. Obtainable from Pastoral Office for Handicapped People, St Joseph's Centre, The Burroughs, London NW4 4TY.
'Thoughts for the Preparation of Special Liturgies', Malcolm Williamson, *DocumenCap* No 4, October 1978, p. 6. Obtainable from Pastoral Office for Handicapped People (address above).
'Mentally Handicapped People and Forming the Parish Community', Anthony Gibbings *All People* No. 18, April 1982, pp. 5–7. Obtainable from Pastoral Office for Handicapped People (address above).
'The Liturgy for Handicapped People', A. J. McCallen, *Pastoral Liturgy, A Symposium*, pp. 140–6, edited by Harold Winstone, Collins Liturgical Publications, London 1975.
'Handicapped People and Sunday Mass' *The Parish Mass*, pp. 89–96, Catholic Truth Society, London 1981.

Preparing People with a Mental Disability for the Sacraments

Introduction

Initiation of people who are mentally handicapped into the sacramental life of the Church is not only possible but is their right as baptised persons. This initiation, however, is in no way to be seen as the aim of any catechetical or religious education programme which may be available to them. Rather is it seen more as a consequence than as an end. The reception of the sacraments is a means for the mentally handicapped person to enter into a deep relationship with God through Jesus and through his Church.

The Reception of Communion

All members of the Church who are baptised have the right to make their first communion. There is no particular age laid down at which this must take place. Because mentally handicapped children develop at a much slower rate, they may be 9 or 10 years of age before they are ready to receive Holy Communion. For such a child, immediate preparation begins with a question: 'What is the best way for *this* child to approach the sacrament?'

The Church asks from each what they are capable of giving. At its most elementary, this means a certain devotion, that is a reverence, and a desire to receive Communion. This devotion is not an intellectual thing. It springs more from the heart than from the head. It is not necessarily detected in words or replies to questions, but in attitudes and the look in the eyes. Devotion will grow through example.

The Importance of the Family

The need for the child who is mentally handicapped to experience living faith is no different from that of his normal counterpart. The Christian family is the place where he will catch his first glimpse of the mystery of God among us. The faith of the family is of primary importance as the child prepares for first Holy Communion. This living faith is transmitted by attitudes, behaviour, feelings and not through formal teaching or instruction.

Relationships

The heart of our religion is a relationship with a person – Jesus. Faith is to do with welcoming a person. Mentally handicapped people are at the level of relating to a person rather than knowing doctrine. The mentally handicapped child who is capable of forming a relationship, however primitive, is capable of faith, faith that can grow. Some children need more help than others to form and sustain relationships. However, the mentally handicapped child's capacity to relate in friendship is basic to his or her personal growth and development. When the child can form relationships, he can participate sacramentally in the life of the Church. Parents play a vital role in this developing of relationships. The sacraments are not a reward for relationships achieved as much as they are the source of relationships to be developed. It is Christ who, through the Church, offers the invitation and fosters growth.

Experience of Worship (see pages 38–41)

The Church is larger than the family. The mentally handicapped person needs to experience faith in this wider context. Going to Mass with a handicapped person every Sunday can sometimes be quite difficult for a number of reasons. But perhaps it may be possible to take him or her to Mass, if not every week, then maybe on a weekday during holiday time. Take the handicapped person to a Mass with singing where the congregation is allowed to participate, rather than to one monopolised by the choir. Draw his or her attention to something specific within the Mass. This could be to the gestures used by the priest – gestures of welcome, of prayer, of praise or of offering. At other times draw his or her attention to the congregation and what you do – 'now we stand to listen to God's word. The priest is reading from the Holy Book. Jesus is with us.' Be attentive to what is happening yourself.

When you go to Communion take the handicapped person with you for a blessing. Receive Communion with reverence. When you return to your place, give him or her a sign of this gift of love which you have just received in Communion, such as a warm gesture of affection with a phrase 'Jesus loves you too' or 'Jesus says "I am coming soon"'.

Our attitude at Mass will transmit more to the handicapped person than words or gestures. How we pray, how we prepare for and receive Jesus in Holy Communion will lead the handicapped person to know intuitively the reality of what is being presented to him or her. He or she too will want to share with all God's people the Bread of Life.

Involvement in the Parish Sacramental Programme

Unless it is absolutely impossible, it is best to bring the handicapped child, teenager or adult to all the meetings with the first communion or confirmation people. Being with the others is step one to creating an awareness of their presence in our parishes, of their right to receive the sacraments and to be 'involved' in the local church community.

The format of involvement in the catechetical sessions is as follows: Bring the handicapped person to the general gathering for ALL sessions. That he understands what is happening is less important than that he is present with others. He will benefit from this contact and the other candidates will also benefit from the handicapped person's presence.

It is good to ask one or some of the 'normal' children to be his or her friend. The only time when it will be necessary to introduce 'the special' is for the moment of catechesis.

During the group sessions it is advisable to have a catechist to work with the handicapped person following the method and using the materials (with adaptability and flexibility to suit the particular person) suggested at St Joseph's Centre. For the final part of the meeting ALL come together again. The same applies to the liturgical celebrations.

It is up to each team to decide how much or how little participation there is to be by the mentally handicapped persons. Invite the parents to be involved just as you do the other parents.

In this way parish catechetical teams are making a valuable and visible contribution towards integrating the mentally handicapped person into the life and worship of his or her local parish.

S.C.

The Reception of Holy Communion: Guidelines for Priests

All who are made sons of God by faith and baptism should come together to praise God, in the midst of his Church, to take part in her sacrifice, and to eat the Lord's supper. (*Constitution on the Sacred Liturgy*, n. 10)

As members of God's family, people who are disabled are equally called to union with God through their growing friendship with Christ. For this reason they 'must be made welcome in the liturgical life of the Church, especially at Mass, where the community of the faithful gather'. (*All People Together*, n. 18)

Mentally handicapped people have the potential to grow in faith and have therefore the right to all that will enable them to do so. They can often intuitively grasp their relationship with Christ, without necessarily being able to express their understanding in words.

The eucharist is the supreme sign of unity with Christ and his Church, and is the particular means by which an individual grows in holiness. Moreover Holy Communion is the climax of those sacraments which initiate the individual into membership of the Church. Provided an appropriate faith can be discerned, mentally handicapped people should be admitted to this sacrament of unity.

The discernment of faith belongs first of all to parents who 'must be acknowledged as the first and foremost educators of their children' (*Declaration on Christian Education*, n. 3; also *Rite of Infant Baptism*). They also have a primary responsibility for the preparation of their children for Holy Communion. In both the discernment and the preparation they need the advice and support of priests, teachers, catechists and others.

In reaching a decision about the readiness of a mentally handicapped person to receive Holy Communion the priest, as pastor of his people, has a special responsibility. By visiting the family he strengthens their sense of belonging within the parish, especially when they come to Mass, and he becomes a special friend to the mentally handicapped person. By knowing the family he is in a position to assist the parents to come to a right judgement in the matter. Through such contacts and developing relationships the mentally handicapped person can share in and contribute to the faith and life of the parish.

Where mentally handicapped people reside in schools, hospitals, or other establishments, the parish has a special responsibility to ensure that these places are visited and that the handicapped people are welcomed into that parish and prepared for Holy Communion.

The readiness of a mentally handicapped person to receive Holy Communion for the first time may not necessarily be indicated by his or her ability to answer questions (cf. *All People Together*, n. 19). Those who know the mentally handicapped person are frequently able to understand signs and sounds which show appreciation and reverence for the mystery of the sacrament and a desire to share in it. These signs and sounds may be unusual but are nevertheless genuine and adequate (cf. *All People Together*, n. 16). Such experience and knowledge is of great value in assuring the priest that the mentally handicapped person is ready to receive Holy Communion (cf. *All People Together*, n. 19).

The family or caring group is the focus and support for the mentally handicapped person. It is this group of believing and loving people who make possible his or her proper preparation for the sacrament and who are able to affirm his or her readiness to receive the body of the Lord. Their advice must always be sought.

The pastoral care of the family or caring group needs also to be attended to. There are two matters of particular importance. First, the support and encouragement given to this group in their demanding task when the mentally handicapped person receives Holy Communion. Secondly, the support that needs to be given to this family or caring group when they judge that the mentally handicapped person is either not able or not ready to receive Holy Communion.

Some handicapped people find the actual receiving of Holy Communion difficult because of the nature of their disability. If this is the case, parents should talk to the priest about this beforehand. The priest may need to ask the parent to give Holy Communion to the handicapped person. Where necessary he or she may receive from the chalice only.

The mentally handicapped person is usually ready to receive Holy Communion earlier than he or she is capable of grasping what is involved in the Sacrament of Reconciliation. It is up to parents, priests, teachers and catechists to decide whether Reconciliation before Holy Communion is appropriate or not.

As far as the profoundly handicapped are concerned there is no doubt that they belong to a special portion of the People of God, and they do need special attention on the part of parents, pastors and educators, who should ultimately decide whether the children are ready to approach the sacraments or not. (Letter of Cardinal John Wright, 23 November 1978, Prot. 159082/11)

The spiritual life of mentally handicapped people is nourished in a special way by their receiving Holy Communion within the loving, praying family of the Church. The Church needs to welcome them into this union, for 'how can she contribute to the integration of the handicapped into modern society, if she does not endeavour to have them recognised as full members of her own?' (Pope Paul VI, *Pastoral Care of Handicapped and Maladjusted Youth*, October 1973)

(Guidelines approved by the Bishops' Conference of England & Wales, April 1983)

Preparing people with a mental disability for Confirmation

Introduction

Today discussion continues on the most suitable age for receiving this sacrament, but there is a tendency towards seeking greater maturity. Mentally handicapped people can only benefit from this trend. For those whose intellectual development has been slowed down, receiving confirmation at a later age means that it will have a deeper significance in their lives, and therefore in the lives of their families and the parish community. It also provides better opportunities for an appropriate catechesis. Further, although those who were confirmed at birth or at an early age are not eligible to receive the sacrament again, they would clearly benefit from sharing in the preparation with others.

Confirmation, like first Holy Communion, needs to be seen within the context of an ongoing relationship with the Lord. There is a great temptation, especially with mentally handicapped people, to just 'do the confirmation bit' and 'the First Communion bit' and to isolate these significant events in the life of the person and the Church from the wholeness of our religion.

Useful Principles

People who are mentally handicapped need a small group of believing adults who are willing to build a welcoming and supportive community in which they can prepare to receive the Spirit of Jesus in confirmation. They find it difficult to communicate in large groups. For them the concept of community means intimacy, nearness. In this situation they need to belong, to fit in, to be known by name. About 10 to 12 people should be the maximum in a group made up of catechists and handicapped people. Within the group each handicapped person has a sponsor, a friend. This sponsor relates to his or her friend as a godparent to a godchild rather than as a teacher to his pupil. Invite friends, parishioners, young people to share in the preparation of mentally handicapped people for the sacrament of confirmation. It may be that you are in a situation where there is only one mentally handicapped person to be prepared for the sacrament of confirmation. A group can be very small, perhaps just three or four people. Maybe two families could link up. Mentally handicapped people who have already been confirmed could be in the group also. The possible combinations are numerous.

Through baptism we belong to the Church. But this idea can too easily remain notional and abstract. The small community of believing people makes the sense of belonging real and concrete. Such a supportive group provides the contact for our people to agree to belong.

Membership of the Church implies a decision. The decision to belong to this small community of faith united to the larger church family of the parish may be the most concrete way a person who has a mental disability can commit herself or himself to the Church. It is the bishop who affirms this commitment when he confirms the person. Through the sacrament of confirmation he says to the person 'Yes, you belong to the people of God.'

The bishop, if he is to be significant in forming this sense of belonging, must be seen more as a friend than as a stranger – someone who just appears for the ceremony. It is important for the group to have met him before the actual celebration of confirmation.

We are confirmed in the Spirit to exercise a ministry within the local parish. We need to discover ways of allowing our people who are disabled in any way to exercise this ministry. There are many ministries open to them.

Parents and Parish

The introduction to the rite of confirmation states: 'The initiation of children into the sacramental life is for the most part the responsibility and concern of Christian parents', and it goes on to say they are expected to play an active part in the celebration of the sacrament. The parents should therefore be part of any group that is set up.

From the parish point of view, such parents must not become separated from the regular group of parents whose children are preparing for confirmation. They need to be invited to parents' meetings and to receive all necessary information about the nature of the sacrament of confirmation and how it is to be fully celebrated. The parents could also be involved in helping to develop some service programmes which would involve their children in parish activities. The regular group of parents would profit from hearing about the approach to confirmation for the mentally handicapped young people. For the confirmation service itself it is only right that mentally handicapped people, who have been prepared within the small community, join the larger parish community wherever practicable as regards numbers, time and place of the liturgical celebration.

Sponsors

The Praenotanda to the Rite of Confirmation say:

Ordinarily there should be a sponsor for each of these to be confirmed. The sponsor brings the candidate to receive the sacrament, presents him to the minister for anointing, and will later help him to fulfil his baptismal promises faithfully under the influence of the Holy Spirit.

It is suggested in the rite that if possible the sponsor should be the baptismal godparent. This shows the unity between the two sacraments. However, a special sponsor for confirmation may be chosen provided that they are sufficiently mature for this role, and that they belong to the Catholic community and have received all three sacraments of initiation, baptism, confirmation and the eucharist. The revised Rite of Confirmation originally allowed parents themselves to be sponsors, but the new Code of Canon Law of 23 January 1983 has revised this, and parents can no longer request or be invited to be their son's or daughter's sponsor.

Conclusion

The challenge for those concerned with the preparation of people with a mental disability for confirmation is to build small faith communities into which they can be welcomed and in which they feel a sense of belonging. We need to create communities which become, not isolated ghettos, but stepping stones for integration into the larger faith community of the parish.

S.C.

Reading list

Called to Belong, A guide to preparing the mentally handicapped person for confirmation. Sister Stephanie Clifford, Kevin Mayhew, 1983.
The Church's Ministry in Mental Retardation, H. W. Stubblefield, Broadman, 1965.
Helping the Retarded to know God, H. R. Hahn and W. H. Raasch, Concordia, 1969.
I am with you, David G. Wilson, St Paul Publications, 1975.

Invitation to Communion, A guide to preparing the mentally handicapped child for Communion. Sister Stephanie Clifford, Kevin Mayhew, 1982.

Partners in Life, G. Muller-Fahrenholz, World Council of Churches publication, 1979.

Pastoral Care of the Mentally Handicapped, J. Browning, Free Church Chronicle, 1971.

'Pastoral Care to the Mentally Handicapped', L. Turner, in *Religion and Medicine* Volume 3, SCM, 1976.

Preparing the Mentally Handicapped for Confirmation, J. Bradford, Church of England Children's Society.

Liturgy: Some useful addresses

Catholic

Archconfraternity of St Stephen
St Joseph's High Road
Wembley
Middlesex HA9 6AG
Tel: 01 902 0081
Secretary: A. J. Hawes
Guild for altar servers.

Association for Latin Liturgy
29 Boileau Road
London W5 3AP
Secretary: Mr Martin Lynch
To promote the use of Latin and of Latin church music in the approved rites of the Church.

Catholic Liturgy Office
39 Eccleston Square
London SW1V 1PL
Tel: 01 821 0553
Secretary: Rev. E. Matthews

Pueri Cantores
Presbytery
Rant Meadow
Hemel Hempstead
Herts HP3 8PG
Tel: 0442 55471
National president: Rev. D. Higgins
An international organisation to promote music in the liturgy and choirs of boys and men.

Society of St Gregory
110 Minster Court
Crown Street
Liverpool L7 3QD
Secretary: Clare Faux
To promote full active and conscious participation in the liturgy.

St Thomas More Centre for Pastoral Liturgy
9–11 Henry Road
London N4 2LH
Tel: 01 802 1485
Director: Rev. M. Shaw
Good resource centre for advice, visual and cassette library, supplier of liturgical music, and a developing copyright clearance agency. (See page 87 for more details.)

Anglican

The Gregorian Association
Epsom College
Surrey KT17 4JQ
Secretary: R. M. Bennett
The Association was founded to demonstrate the suitability of plainchant to the English language and to promote its use by means of lectures, services and conferences.

The Guild of Church Musicians
Hillbrow
Blechingley
Surrey RH1 4PJ
Tel: 0883 8431 68
General Secretary: John Ewington,
ACertCM
Examining body for Archbishop of
Canterbury's Certificate in Church
Music. Trains church musicians in
music and liturgy.

Guild of Servants of the Sanctuary
8 Dalefields
Roebuck Lane
Buckhurst Hill
Essex IG9 5QT
Secretary: H. S. Gadd
This is a Guild of Altar servers and
Acolytes which seeks to deepen their
spiritual life.

Plainsong and Medieval Music Society
46 Bond Street
Egham
Surrey TW20 0PY
Secretary: Dr David Hiley
Publication of music and studies of
music, organisation of lectures,
sponsorship of recordings, etc.

Royal School of Church Music
Addington Palace
Croydon
Surrey CR9 5AD
Tel: 01 654 7676
Director: Lionel Dakers
The School exists to further the study
and practice of music and singing,
principally for the Church of England
but there are relations too with the
World Council of Churches and the
Roman Catholic Church.

The Parish Prayer Group

A request for a prayer group from a number of his parishioners
should be a moment of great encouragement for a pastor. It reveals
both a thirst for prayer and a future spiritual support for the whole
community. A desire to pray together does not mark people out as
holier than others, but the recognition of a need.

Careful planning for the group's meetings is important. First the
place of the meeting: this should be relaxed and welcoming, and of
course of an appropriate size to accommodate the group. Chairs
should be arranged in a circle, if possible around a lighted candle
and a simple flower arrangement; this creates a prayerful atmosphere.

Secondly, the meeting itself: this should be regularly once a
week. Most meetings take place in the evening and should last at
least an hour but rarely longer than two. Each meeting must have a
leader although this does not have to be the same person each week.
He or she should ideally spend some time in prayer before the
meeting seeking God's guidance and help.

What actually happens at a prayer meeting? Unlike the liturgy or
more formal prayer, the emphasis is on the participants' sharing of
their own life of prayer in a spontaneous way. Priests especially may

feel threatened and insecure if they are not accustomed to praying in this way. However, in spite of the informal nature of the gathering, there *is* a loose structure which most groups employ.

Five elements usually make up the structure: they are welcome, praise, teaching, sharing and petition. There should always be a word of *welcome*, especially for newcomers, because it is important from the start to make people feel accepted and relaxed, which prepares them to be open to God in prayer.

As a Mass without the Eucharistic Prayer would be no Mass, so a prayer meeting without *praise* is empty. Praise puts the emphasis firmly upon God; as one song puts it, 'forget about yourself, and concentrate on him, and worship him'. Songs and hymns, especially those based upon Scripture, are helpful in creating this spirit. These may be interspersed with spontaneous prayers of praise and thanksgiving and short readings from Scripture.

After a generous time given to praise, a short *teaching* is appropriate. When the priest is present it is an especially fitting ministry for him, but the leader or another capable person should also have an opportunity to do this. A period of silence is often helpful after the teaching.

A time of *sharing* or personal testimony, may follow, during which some members of the group may wish to share an experience or event which has occurred since the last meeting and in which they have seen the hand of God. This might be anything from a cancer cure to a little act of kindness by a stranger. Such sharing is very helpful because our own faith is built up as we experience faith in action.

The meeting draws to a close with a time of *petition* or intercession. While spontaneous bidding prayers come more easily to us than praise, it is important not to prolong them. A good ABC for this final part of the meeting is Audibility – make sure the whole group can hear your prayer; Brevity – no comment required; in Christ – prayer should be directed to the Father in and through Christ.

Praying can be hard work so, after a concluding song that all can join in, a cup of tea and biscuits can round off the evening with a social touch.

One final note: do not give up if the first meeting or two is a little awkward and faltering, perseverance will be rewarded.

J.G.

Further reading

Not Mad, Most Noble Festus, David Parry OSB, Darton, Longman
and Todd, 1979.
Ten Minute Teachings for Prayer Groups, Sister Josephine OSU,
Brentwood Diocesan Service Team, obtainable from the Ursuline
Convent, Queens Road, Brentwood, Essex CM14 4EY.

CHAPTER THREE

Parish Communication

The Parish Magazine

The role of the parish magazine is probably far more complex than most editors or contributors imagine – or admit. At one end of the spectrum, it can bear a strong religious message, it can report on parish events past and future, it has a role as parish communicator and gossip column in the nicest possible way, and finally, and probably most important of all, it can be the only contact the parish has with at least a part of the potential congregation.

Editorial Content

In starting a parish magazine, as distinct from a weekly newsletter, other magazines can give a clue to structure. A well-produced magazine will follow a definite 'house-style' – perhaps beginning with advertisements, then news, an editorial column, some feature articles and finally a close-out, followed by closing advertisements. A well-planned parish magazine should follow a similar type of structure both to give it a feel of professionalism and also to enable its editor to attract interesting pieces, advertisements and, most of all, make potential readers open it rather than throw it away.

Thus, with the parish magazine, you may decide to follow a strategy of, for example, advertisements, editorial comment – the pastoral piece – followed by the report of parish events. You might then decide to include a couple of articles, the first on one of the parish groups or societies and a second on the wider aspects of the church, then some closing advertisements. A lot to put in a single magazine, certainly, but, with careful planning and financial management, quite feasible.

A twelve-month editorial plan for contents is strongly recommended. The plan needs to be pushed forward every six months, and articles and writers pencilled in well ahead. Editorial planning, and achieving the agreement of prospective writers, is a sadly neglected discipline in all too many cases – and it shows! Within the twelve-month plan, it can be beneficial to allocate a feature spot to each parish or diocesan activity and to warn the leader of that group when their spot will be. There are few things more frustrating than being told, 'If only we had had a few more days warning we would have had the pictures too.'

Crisp, clear writing, even if it has to be achieved through careful editing, is essential if the magazine is to be read. The role of editor is clearly a task a competent layperson can take on and make their own.

Sales, Controlled Circulation or Subsidised Production?

A fundamental decision needs to be made early as to whether a parish magazine should be sold, and so reach a small audience, or given away to every home in the parish free. If the latter, then the parish will have to enter into commerce or subsidise it from parish funds.

If people pay for the magazine they are more likely to read it – or it may be 'conscience-money' – but the circulation will be small with a lot of effort in collecting payments. A freely distributed magazine can be a drain on funds and, to be financially manageable, would probably only be distributed to active members of the parish. A third option is to give the magazine free of charge to every household in the parish, and recoup the costs through advertising. A controlled circulation magazine (considered below) distributed to every household in a parish can make an attractive advertising proposition for local businesses and services.

Advertising

The ideal parish magazine would probably carry no advertising at all. However, the economics of the situation make it almost mandatory. With a well organised circulation, a magazine can be attractive to local businesses. Rates for pages, half pages or quarter pages can be calculated to cover the costs of the numbers of copies it is planned to produce. The first time you make the circulation, it is worthwhile asking a member of the congregation who is financially oriented to check the calculations because it is of some importance later.

Perhaps the best advertising plan is to determine how many pages need to be sold at an acceptable rate to cover the cost of production. As a rule of thumb, do not have more than half the magazine as advertising, and base your advertising rates on that level of charge. Try to sell advertising on six or twelve month agreements; however retain about two pages for new customers or companies and businesses that only want a single advertisement.

Presentation, Production and Printing

Perhaps unfairly, the parish magazine has the popular image of being typed and run off by the clergy, containing typographical and literary gremlins which are the joy of journalists and comedians. Provided that funding is properly organised, generally through advertising, there is no reason why parish publications should appear anything less than professional.

Typed pages are quite acceptable, provided that the typing is done on a good machine, and preferably by a professional. If the material is typed, it should be done on the type of machine which can justify both margins.

Printing of parish magazines may well be arranged through small independent 'jobbing printers' with suitable offset litho equipment. An agreement for six or twelve editions, to be delivered on specified dates, is attractive to such printers and good rates should be available.

Financial Aspects

It is strongly recommended that separate accounting books and a separate bank account is retained for the parish magazine. A tight financial control should be kept to monitor costs against expenses. Try to get advertising rates right at the beginning because they cannot be adjusted too frequently.

The Controlled Circulation Magazine

The principle of the controlled circulation magazine is simple. A magazine is distributed, perhaps twice a year, unsolicited and free to every household in a given specific area – the parish – between certain dates. Advertising space is sold to local organisations interested in reaching such a specific audience through a magazine which is likely to be read, and better still, retained by the recipients.

The level of profitability depends upon the quantity printed and distributed, the mix of advertising to editorial content and the advertising rates charged. With careful budgeting and a small amount of good salesmanship, the magazine is not printed until it has moved to break even or into profit.

To produce a professional-looking and beneficial controlled circulation magazine is quite a big undertaking, and the final magazine must look good, both to attract readers and sell the advertising for the next edition. However, this type of project may be sufficiently different to the normal parish project that one can attract new talent to assist with such a scheme. The amount of work involved, and advertising potential, might suggest that such an undertaking could be made once or twice a year.

The controlled circulation magazine is, by definition, a publication which will reach a wider readership than just the congregation. Its potential as a communication medium should therefore not be underestimated.

Conclusions

The parish magazine has more competition than ever before, yet it is an element of parish life that can valuably be used to keep people in touch with the Church and help spread word of parish activities. A professional approach to the magazine, to get it away from the bumbling image, to produce a magazine that people wish to read, is within the reach of practically every parish.

P.C.

The Parish Newsletter

Keeping the weekly newsletter bright and attractive is a demanding task; the following information and addresses may help. Those parishes that like to purchase a 'cover' (one side prepared with picture or instructional material, the other blank for parish news) can chose from a number of suppliers.

Sunday Bulletin is one of the longest established 'notice sheets' in this country. It provides clear, simply expressed teaching attractively designed, and is published by Redemptorist Publications
Chawton
Alton
Hants.
Tel: 0420 88222

Also available from Redemptorist Publications, *Sunday Plus* is a fuller instruction sheet based upon the liturgical theme of the Sunday. It offers a varied selection of material on the scriptures, the teaching and laws of the Church, all in a lively digestible form.

Beautiful *full-colour covers* – as above
but with a picture instead of text – are
available from Concordia Publishing
House Ltd
Hothorpe Hall
Theddingworth
Lutterworth
Leics LE17 6QX
Tel: 0858 880860.
Particularly suitable for special
occasions, e.g. weddings.

Home Words and Church News
PO Box 44
Guildford
Surrey GU1 1XL
Publishers of a range of covers and
other stationery for the parish
newsletter or magazine.

Church News Service
37a New Cavendish St
London W1M 8JR
Provides a monthly supply of Christian
news items, articles, extracts, quotes,
cartoons and humour all ready for
'instant' reproduction in your
newsletter or magazine.

Churchmouse Publications
102 Oxford Road
Clacton-on-Sea
Essex CO15 6LX
Tel: 0255 421295
Churchmouse specialise in the pre-
printing of 'personalised' parish
magazine covers of good quality at
competitive prices.

Other stationery requirements

Allen Press Ltd
Martins Town
Enfield
Co. Meath
Ireland
Tel: 010 353 405 41215
Suppliers of In Memoriam and
Acknowledgement cards. Samples on
request.

Church Finance Supplies Ltd
Radley Road Industrial Estate
Abingdon
Oxon OX14 3SE
Suppliers of offering envelope sets
(weekly or monthly) and allied
literature: pledge cards, thank you
cards, reminder cards, record cards and
ledgers.

Christian Graphic Arts Ltd
29 Freemantle Road
Gosport
Hants PO12 4RD
Tel: 0705 525132
CPF is a small group of Christian
printers who print for Christian groups
and churches.

Pharos Press
87 North St
Great Wakering
Essex SS3 0EL
High-class book-binding of breviaries,
lectionaries, altar missals, etc., by an
experienced craftsman at very
competitive prices. Details on request.

Powell Agency
137 Wicklow Drive
Leicester LE45 4EL
Suppliers of In Memoriam cards.
Samples on request.

Social Service Supplies
Stepfield
Witham
Essex CM8 3BY
Tel: 0245 380465
Social Service Supplies provides
everything used in the office, producing
standard printed matter or items
printed to specific instructions.

The Copyright Law

The word 'copyright' means *having the right to copy* someone else's work for your own purposes. For various reasons, but mainly it would seem through ignorance, the copyright law, which protects the rights and livelihood of writers, composers and artists, is being continually broken in parishes and schools. The ease of access to photocopiers and the economics involved blind many people to the immorality and illegality of their actions. It should always be remembered that once an individual's idea has been put down in a tangible form, for example as a hymn or a recorded song, then the owner alone has the right to copy it unless he gives that right to another person. A copyright work is the personal property of the owner.

A legal description

A copyright can briefly be described as the exclusive right to do and to give permission for other people to do, in the United Kingdom (or any other country to which the Copyright Act of 1956 extends) certain acts in relation to literary, dramatic and musical works and also in relation to other works such as artistic works and sound recordings, films and television broadcasts and published editions of works. The 1956 Copyright Act extends to the United Kingdom. There can be an infringement of copyright if a person does anything which can be construed as being a restriction under the 1956 Act and if that particular person does not hold a copyright which is breached. It follows, therefore, that the composers of hymns can claim the copyright in the words and music (if they are the authors of both) or there can be more than one copyright in a particular hymn i.e. the author of the words can be the holder of the copyright in those words and the person who composed the music can be the holder of the copyright in the musical composition. There can also be a copyright in a particular typesetting of a hymn or work if this is distinctive.

If anyone is in doubt as to whether a breach of copyright is likely to occur by the publication of existing material (where the proposed publisher does not know if there is a copyright in that particular work) then careful enquiry should be made. As regards copyright in books, for example, enquiry could be made of the British Library Board. Furthermore, most publishing houses will also have records and/or details of copyright works and the authors of such works.

The general rule therefore is to avoid the publication of 'in-house' service sheets or hymnals without first carefully checking whether the copyright of the contents of any such service sheets or hymnals is vested in a third party. Recent cases in the law courts would indicate that courts are awarding substantial damages where there have been breaches of copyright.

P.H.

Photocopying

Photocopying of certain material is permitted by the 1956 Copyright Act, but only when it amounts to *fair dealing*. This is understood to mean only one copy of any item for the purpose of research, private study, judicial proceedings, etc., but credit acknowledgements are still required. Multiple copying without specific permission is always illegal.

Applying for copyright permission

Let us take one of the most common examples of a desire to reproduce copyright material. A number of hymns are to be printed in an order of service for a wedding. Before a printer is in any way involved, the compiler must first consult the acknowledgements page of the hymnal from which the material is being taken. This page will give the information of who owns the copyrights to the hymns printed in the book. (It is worth remembering that the publisher of the hymn book has had to seek permission himself from the copyright owners and pay for the privilege of reproducing their work.) Take careful note – jot it down – of the actual wording regarding the hymns you wish to reproduce; that is the form of the acknowledgement you will have to print on the order of service once you have gained permission.

Write now to the publisher whose name is given against the hymn in the acknowledgements (see pages 54–5 for a list of publishers). If it is an American or foreign copyright holder and there is no address given, write to the publisher of the hymn book from which you are taking the material. You also only write to the publisher of the hymn book if it is their copyright you seek, otherwise they will refer you to the copyright holder. Some hymns are now considered 'traditional' and are out of copyright. If you search the acknowledgements page and there is no reference to the hymn, that may mean no acknowledgement has to be made because the item is out of copyright. You are free to reproduce it. If you can double check this with another hymn book which carries the same hymn, that will make quite certain you are correct in your findings. If in doubt check with the publisher.

In your letter to the copyright holder you must state quite clearly which hymn or hymns you wish to reproduce, by name and composer, what you wish to reproduce it for, whether it is a once only occasion (as with a wedding) or if you are intending to print something more durable (a parish's own hymn collection). You should also declare how many copies you intend printing, whether they will be for sale and by what date you would like permission. You can add that you are very happy to make the usual acknowledgements of composer, publisher and source from which the material comes. If you do not add the latter the copyright holder will make it a condition of permission anyway.

Allow plenty of time for the copyright holder to reply; however if time does become pressing do not hesitate to telephone and enquire. The copyright holder will decide whether a charge is applicable. If you are confused about the ownership of a copyright, telephone a hymn-book publisher who uses it in his hymn-book and ask to speak to the copyright dept. They will be pleased to help you if they can.

Central Clearing of Copyright

Two Christian organisations are seeking to help pastors and teachers troubled by the copyright problem. Both, with certain limitations, can offer to clear permissions for you.

St Thomas More Pastoral Centre
9a Henry Road
London N4 2LH
Tel: 01 802 9910.
The Centre is endeavouring to set up a comprehensive licensing system to enable parishes, schools, etc., to have the requisite permission on payment of an annual fee. More details are available direct from the Centre.

Jubilate Hymns Limited
61 Chessel Avenue
Southampton SO2 4DY
Tel: 0703 30038
This organisation is only concerned with music of a Protestant origin.

The Publishers Association can always be approached in the last resort.
Publishers Association
19 Bedford Square
London WC1B 3HJ
Tel: 01 580 6321–5

Further Information

A Question of Copyright, Eric Thorn
Third Day Enterprises
PO Box 3
Maidstone
Kent ME14 1AP

An Introduction to Copyright and Christian Music Publishing
Kingsway Music
Eastbourne
Sussex

A User's Guide to Copyright
Butterworth
London

Some organisations concerned with copyright

Authors' Lending and Copyright
Society
7 Ridgmount Street
London WC1E 7AE

Music Publishers' Association
Kingsway House
103 Kingsway
London WC2B 6AX

British Academy of Songwriters,
Composers, Authors
148 Charing Cross Rd
London WC2H 0LB

Performing Right Society
29/33 Berners St
London W1P 4AA

British Copyright Council
29 Berners Street
London W1P 4AA

Video Copyright Protection Society
Visnews House
Cumberland Avenue
London NW10 7EH

Mechanical-Copyright Protection
Society
Elgar House
41 Streatham High Rd
London SW16 1ER

The Local Press

There is nothing secret or sophisticated about good press relations.
It is a matter of communicating clearly and effectively with local
journalists and supplying them with the sort of material they can
use.

The majority of a parish community probably see a local
newspaper regularly, or, at the worst, intermittently. To feature
regularly in those pages can be highly beneficial to the parish and
the Church in terms of telling people where you are and how you
can be of benefit to them. Favourable press comment can only help
attract people to your church.

The first and obvious task is to find out who owns the local press, what range of subjects interest it and which journal may be the most sympathetic to you. You need to know what sort of approach the press takes – pop or serious – do they have a local religious column, if so, who writes it.

Get to know the editor and key members of his staff, treat them as intelligent people with an important task to perform. Make sure you know the crucial timings in the publication's cycle – when do they need information for normal news and what is the absolute deadline for late news. If there is a local daily paper, check if there is a flat day during the week when a weak story may have more chance of being published.

A newspaper has to be fresh, interesting and readable; imagine you are the editor – what would you publish? There are no best stories, but guidelines can be useful: always look for human interest, is there a picture in the story you have? Do you have a celebrity, even a minor one, attending something in the parish? Do not be afraid to encourage healthy controversy, but be sure of your facts.

Press releases are a normal channel of information to the local press. Such a release should be short – few stories warrant more than two pages. There are some basic rules which should always be followed in a press release:

they should be written on paper specially headed 'Press Information' – make the headed paper through your local copyshop and have a dozen sheets copied.
give information factually and concisely with the main facts first. All the major facts should be in the first paragraph.
leave space top and bottom for the sub-editor to write printing instructions and always type double space. Only use one side of the paper.
keep paragraphs and sentences short and do not split between pages.
try to have at least one quote in every press release.
at the end of the piece, give a name and a phone contact for further information.

Wherever possible, provide a black and white glossy picture, in focus, to illustrate the story. Avoid wasted space on the picture and submit a typed caption, stuck along one edge, to the back of the picture. Submit, if you can, both horizontal and vertical pictures so the editor can choose. Not every story is suitable for a press release, so establish links with a friendly reporter to whom you may pass on leads.

Finally, we all know just how annoying newspapers can be. They often get the facts wrong, put totally the wrong emphasis on a story and regularly misquote. However, don't try to enter a running battle – you will not win as they control the copy – and always remember, the story may be wrong because you did not communicate it clearly enough to the journalist who wrote it.

P.C.

Broadcasting

The value we attach to broadcasting is important and it almost defines our objectives as Christians. Do we identify ourselves as broadcasters too, concerned with the whole world and with anyone who will listen? Or would we rather narrowcast, preferring the telephone with our listener 'targeted' before we start? What of broadcasting itself? Is it the greatest formative influence in the western world with an immense power to change religious responses? Or is it a disappointment and a cause of ever lower standards? How important is religious broadcasting? This particular question can have a straightforward answer. Church news, ecumenical arrangements, worship and even gospel music are simply minority interests. Religious controversy on the other hand is newsworthy especially when it leads to violence; but religious comedies (*Bless me Father*) and even scandals (*Thorn Birds*) become mass entertainment and have an immense influence on religious perceptions.

Some Christians have been disappointed because in 'Religious Broadcasting' they hoped for an extension of the Church public address system. In Britain, up to now, no one has been able to buy time on the airwaves. Following Lord Reith, religious programmes have tried to 'educate, inform and entertain' – and be ecumenical. But all is changing. In many parts of western Europe, the state broadcasting monopolies are breaking down. In Britain, broadcasting has been in the hands of two public-service and essentially Reithian institutions – the BBC and the IBA. This cosy condominium is now threatened. In the BBC's case the threat is financial but no sum of money would stave off the change in broadcasting that is bound to occur in the next decade.

Satellites above Europe are already reflecting back to earth, with complete disregard for frontiers, a multitude of new television channels. Linked into cable communications systems, a much greater choice of programming is becoming available to a growing number of people. And it will not all be soap operas and quiz shows. Local programmes produced by local people will also be on offer. Cable is only part of the story. The government has accepted the need for community broadcasting, and the first licences to community, special interest and ethnic radio stations are just the tip of the iceberg. Among the unlicensed radio stations – the pirates – religious broadcasting is emerging. One pirate radio ship has an annual budget for its religious output of over £100,000.

Add to all this the established national and regional television and radio services and two competing local radio networks, to say nothing of the largest proportion per head of video recorders in the world, and it is obvious that the Christian Church in the UK must – to quote a recent book by Colin Evans – *Communicate or Die.*

Priests ought to be skilled communicators. Every time he presides at the altar and 'communicates' his people, every time he preaches before his congregation, every time he declares the forgiveness of God, the priest is engaged in the most significant communication of all. But of course his is a stylised, formal liturgical task involving special buildings, special clothes and furniture and (dare it be said) special people. The priest spends much of his time preaching to the converted and this is a very necessary task. But a lifetime communicating with fellow Christians, taking for granted the shared expectations, culture and technical terms, will turn the priest into a good church communicator, but little else.

The evangelist has to be a skilled communicator. His task is to take the good news to the whole world which God loved so much, but there can be no contradiction, for it is for the world that the Church exists. There can be no inward-looking Christianity. A priest cannot be just a servant to the Church. His has to be a concern for the world and he has to speak the language of the world.

P.E.

Local Radio Stations

Local radio stations have been a growth industry in the last decade. But those stations operate generally with a very small staff and, even after the time for music has been taken out, have a lot of air time to fill. Finding enough good material to fill that time is a constant headache, and producers are always grateful for a good story. However, they are unhappy with a bad story.

There are many ways in which you might be able to work with local radio – religious programmes, parish activities, comments on national and local events which call for a 'church comment', as a 'stringer' with unparalleled local contacts, and through keeping them informed of local church events for diary type programmes.

While you are not trained to spot a story, producers and reporters are. Get to know a local reporter or producer – you may even have one in the congregation – and simply tell him or her what you want to do. If you need a name, listen to the credits for a particular programme and call the local station and ask to speak to the producer. Talk to the reporter and give them an idea of the type of story which comes your way, and tell them you would like to do something for the local audience. Also tell them you want to be as professional as possible. Given that interest on your part, the local reporter will generally be glad to tell you the type of material they feel is of interest to their programme. He may also tell you about particular policies the station likes to follow – it could save you a lot of time and frustration!

Do not try to pull any 'religious superiority' on the reporter; your story will have to stand on its own merits, although the religious or moral slant may give it additional interest.

Make sure you always invite your local radio contact to any interesting parish functions – give him plenty of warning – and make sure they have details of any special interest stories of tasks or studies being undertaken by the Sunday School, choir, etc. Beware of trying to give an 'exclusive' story to two organisations.

Reporters are busy people, so do not be afraid to call and check how they are progressing with a story you have passed to them. It may have to be discussed with the editor before they take it further. Be prepared to put yourself out for the radio reporter. If she asks for a quiet room, find one, even if it is your study. The church may be suggested as it could 'exude atmosphere' – arrange for somebody to watch the door so you are not disturbed. Even a short interview may take a couple of retakes, even if only a very short comment is finally used. Don't worry if what you consider a very good piece is dropped for a sudden local news story.

Over a period of time, as you develop your relationship with the local radio station, establish your willingness to offer sensible and clear comments on local and national news stories and events – perhaps even develop a personal style. Not every comment for which you are asked will be positive. You may be asked to defend a case or point of view. A well-ordered argument or debate makes good broadcasting, so be willing to defend positively as well as comment when the media are on your side.

If you are invited to appear on a live show, or even one which is to be pre-recorded, try to find out who will be doing the interview, who will be the other people in the discussion and the broad direction of questions. You should be able to answer the questions thrown at you to present your case or attitude in the best possible light. Arrive at the studio at the time requested, listen to the questions and answer them clearly and naturally. If you do not know the answer, say so. Speak up, and talk slowly. Do not try to be funny, you are invited as a serious contributor so be yourself and keep your answers short.

Finally, don't try to fool the media – you can't.

P.C.

Local Radio Stations

Although developments in local radio are likely, at present stations are provided by one of two authorities, the BBC or the IBA (Independent Broadcasting Authority). Enquiries of a general nature can be directed to the authority concerned:

BBC Local Radio Publicity
Broadcasting House
Portland Place
London W1A 1AA
Tel: 01 927 5887

IBA Information Office
70 Brompton Rd
London SW3 1EY
Tel: 01 584 7011
Religious Broadcasting Officer:
Rev. E. M. Shegog

BBC Local Radio Stations

BBC Radio Bedfordshire
PO Box 476
Luton LU1 5BA
Tel: 0582 459111
Religious Producer:
Vacancy

BBC Radio Bristol
3 Tyndalls Park Road
Bristol BS99 7QT
Tel: 0272 741111
Religious Producer:
Margaret Collingwood

BBC Radio Cambridgeshire
Broadcasting House
104 Hills Road
Cambridge CB2 1LD
Tel: 0223 315970
Religious Producers:
Canon D. Thomas/Ms Pat Heap

BBC Radio Cleveland
PO Box 1548
Broadcasting House
Newport Road
Middlesbrough
Cleveland TS1 5DG
Tel: 0642 225211
Religious Producer:
Bill Hunter

BBC Radio Cornwall
Phoenix Wharf
Truro
Cornwall TR1 1UA
Tel: 0872 75421
Religious Producer:
Nicki Julien

BBC Radio Cumbria
Hilltop Heights
London Road
Carlisle
Cumbria CA1 2NA
Tel: 0228 31661
Religious Producer:
Norman Ivison

BBC Radio Derby
PO Box 269
56 St Helen's Street
Derby DE1 3HY
Tel: 0332 361111
Religious Producer:
Ivan Gatford

BBC Radio Devon
PO Box 100
St David's Hill
Exeter
Devon EX4 4DB
Tel: 0392 215651
Religious Producer:
Rev. Chris Cheeseman

BBC Radio Furness (Radio Cumbria)
Broadcasting House
Hartington Street
Barrow-in-Furness
Cumbria LA14 5FH
Tel: 0229 36767

BBC Radio Humberside
63 Jameson Street
Hull HU1 3NU
Tel: 0482 23232
Religious Producer:
David Taviner

BBC Radio Kent
30 High Street
Chatham
Kent ME4 4EZ
Tel: 0634 46284
Religious Producer:
Pam Gillham

BBC Radio Lancashire
King Street
Blackburn
Lancs. BB2 2EA
Tel: 0254 62411
Religious Producer:
John MacBryde

BBC Radio Leeds
Broadcasting House
Woodhouse Lane
Leeds LS2 9PN
Tel: 0532 442131
Religious Producer:
Rev. Steve Jarrett

BBC Radio Leicester
Epic House
Charles Street
Leicester LE1 3SH
Tel: 0533 27113
Religious Producer:
Janet Mayo

BBC Radio Lincolnshire
Radion Buildings
PO Box 219
Newport
Lincoln LN1 3EU
Tel: 0522 40011
Religious Producer:
Rev. J. Hawthorne

BBC Radio London
PO Box 4LG
35a Marylebone High Street
London W1A 4LG
Tel: 01 486 7611
Religious Producer:
Ron Aldridge

BBC Radio Manchester
New Broadcasting House
PO Box 90
Oxford Road
Manchester M60 1SJ
Tel: 061 228 3434
Religious Producer:
Ralph Birtwistle

BBC Radio Merseyside
55 Paradise Street
Liverpool L1 3BP
Tel: 051 708 5500
Religious Producer:
John Thompson

BBC Radio Newcastle
Crestina House
Archbold Terrace
Newcastle upon Tyne NE2 1DZ
Tel: 091 281 4243
Religious Producer:
Francis Wood

BBC Radio Norfolk
Norfolk Tower
Surrey Street
Norwich NR1 3PA
Tel: 0603 617411
Religious Producer:
Graham Humphries

BBC Radio Northampton
PO Box 1107
Abington Street
Northampton NN1 2BE
Tel: 0604 20621
Religious Producer:
Rev. David Saint

BBC Radio Nottingham
York House
Mansfield Road
Nottingham NG1 3JB
Tel: 0602 415161
Religious Producer:
Jeremy Younger

BBC Radio Oxford
242/254 Banbury Road
Oxford OX2 7DW
Tel: 0865 53411
Religious Producer:
David Lawrence

BBC Radio Sheffield
Ashdell Grove
60 Westbourne Road
Sheffield S10 2QU
Tel: 0742 686185
Religious Producer:
Jack Shaw

BBC Radio Shropshire
2–4 Boscobel Drive
Shrewsbury
Shropshire SY1 3TT
Tel: 0743 248484

BBC Radio Solent
South Western House
Canute Road
Southampton SO9 4PJ
Tel: 0703 31311
Religious Producer:
Fr Michael Henesy

BBC Radio Stoke-on-Trent
Conway House
Cheapside
Hanley
Stoke-on-Trent
Staffs. ST1 1JJ
Tel: 0782 24827
Religious Producer:
Stephen Lynas

BBC Radio Sussex
Marlborough Place
Brighton
Sussex BN1 1TU
Tel: 0273 680231
Religious Producer:
Rev. Michael Bootes

BBC Radio WM (West Midlands)
PO Box 206
Pebble Mill Road
Birmingham B5 7SD
Tel: 021 472 5141
Religious Producer:
Rev. Michael Blood

BBC Radio York
20 Bootham Row
York YO3 7BR
Tel: 0904 641351
Religious Producers:
Michael Nokes/Bernadette Burbridge

Two Stations outside the UK
BBC Radio Guernsey
Commerce House
Les Banques
St Peter Port
Guernsey
Tel: 0481 28977
Religious Producer:
Rev. Gibson Nelson

BBC Radio Jersey
Broadcasting House
Rouge Bouillon
St Helier
Jersey
Tel: 0534 70000
Religious Producer:
Rev. Bob Delap

Independent Local Radio

The name of the independent local radio producer for religious programmes is only available on application to the individual station.

LBC
Communications House
Gough Square
London EC4 4LP
Tel: 01 353 1010

Capital Radio
Euston Tower
London NW1 3DR
Tel: 01 388 1288

Radio Clyde
Clydebank Business Park
Clydebank
Glasgow G81 2RX
Tel: 041 941 1111

BRMB Radio
Radio House
PO Box 555
Aston Road North
Aston
Birmingham B6 4BX
Tel: 021 359 4481/9

Piccadilly Radio
127/131 The Piazza
Piccadilly Plaza
Manchester M1 4AW
Tel: 061 236 9913

Metro Radio
Radio House
Long Rigg
Swalwell
Newcastle upon Tyne
NE99 1BB
Tel: 091 488 3131

Swansea Sound
Victoria Road
Gowerton
Swansea SA4 3AB
Tel: 0792 893751

Radio Hallam
PO Box 194
Hartshead
Sheffield S1 1GP
Tel: 0742 71188

Radio City
PO Box 194
8–10 Stanley Street
Liverpool L69 1LD
Tel: 051 227 5100

Radio Forth
Forth House
Forth Street
Edinburgh EH1 3LF
Tel: 031 556 9255

Plymouth Sound
Earl's Acre
Alma Road
Plymouth PL3 4HX
Tel: 0752 27272

Radio Tees
74 Dovecot Street
Stockton-on-Tees
Cleveland TS18 1HB
Tel: 0642 615111

Radio Trent
29–31 Castle Gate
Nottingham NG1 7AP
Tel: 0602 581731

Pennine Radio
PO Box 235
Pennine House
Forster Square
Bradford BD1 5NP
Tel: 0274 731521

Radio Victory
PO Box 257
247 Fratton Road
Portsmouth PO1 5RT
Tel: 0705 827799

Radio Orwell
Electric House
Lloyds Avenue
Ipswich IP1 3HZ
Tel: 0473 216971

Radio 210
PO Box 210
The Filberts
Bath Road
Calcot
Reading
Berkshire RG3 5RZ
Tel: 0734 413131

Downtown Radio
PO Box 96
Newtownards
BT23 4ES
Northern Ireland
Tel: 0247 815555

Beacon Radio
PO Box 303
267 Tettenhall Road
Wolverhampton WV6 0DQ
Tel: 0902 757211

Red Dragon Radio
Radio House
West Canal Wharf
Cardiff CF1 5XJ
Tel: 0222 384041

Mercia Sound
Hertford Place
Coventry CV1 3TT
Tel: 0203 28451

Hereward Radio PLC
PO Box 225
114 Bridge Street
Peterborough PE1 1XJ
Tel: 0733 46225

Two Counties Radio Limited
5–7 Southcote Road
Bournemouth BH1 3LR
Tel: 0202 294881

Radio Tay
PO Box 123
6 North Isle Street
Dundee DD1 9UF
Tel: 0382 29551

Severn Sound
PO Box 388
Old Talbot House
67 Southgate Street
Gloucester GL1 2DQ
Tel: 0452 423791

DevonAir Radio
The Studio Centre
35–37 St David's Hill
Exeter EX4 4DA
Tel: 0392 30703

Northsound Radio
45 Kings Gate
Aberdeen AB2 6BL
Tel: 0224 632234

Radio Aire
PO Box 362
51 Burley Road
Leeds LS3 1LR
Tel: 0532 452299

Essex Radio
Radio House
Clifftown Road
Southend-on-Sea
Essex SS1 1SX
Tel: 0702 333711

Chiltern Radio
Chiltern Road
Dunstable
Bedfordshire LU6 1HQ
Tel: 0582 666001

West Sound
Radio House
54 Holmeston Road
Ayr KA7 3BD
Tel: 0292 283662

GWR
PO Box 2000
Watershed
Canons Road
Bristol BS99 7SN
Tel: 0272 279900

Moray Firth Radio
PO Box 271
Inverness IV3 6SF
Tel: 0463 224433

Radio Wyvern
5/6 Barbourne Terrace
Worcester WR1 3JS
Tel: 0905 612212

Red Rose Radio
PO Box 301
St Paul's Square
Preston
Lancashire PR1 1YE
Tel: 0772 556301

GWR
PO Box 2000
Lime Kiln Studios
Wootton Bassett
Swindon
Wiltshire SN4 7EX
Tel: 0793 853222

Saxon Radio
Long Brackland
Bury St Edmunds
Suffolk IP33 1JY
Tel: 0284 701511

County Sound
The Friary
Guildford GU1 4YX
Tel: 0483 505566

Southern Sound
Radio House
Franklin Road
Portslade BN4 2SS
Tel: 0273 422288

Marcher Sound
The Studios
Mold Road
Gwersyllt
Wrexham
Clwyd LL11 4AF
Tel: 0978 752202

Signal Radio
Studio 257
67–73 Stoke Road
Stoke-on-Trent
Staffordshire ST4 2SR
Tel: 0782 417111

Viking Radio
Commercial Road
Hull HU1 2SG
Tel: 0482 25141

Invicta Radio
37 Earl Street
Maidstone
Kent ME14 1PF
Tel: 0622 679061

and

15 Station Road East
Canterbury
Kent CT1 2RB
Tel: 0227 67661

Radio Mercury
Broadfield House
Brighton Road
Crawley RH11 9TT
Tel: 0293 519161

Leicester Sound
Granville House
Granville Road
Leicester LE1 7RW
Tel: 0533 551616

Radio Broadland
47–49 St George's Plain
Colegate
Norwich NR3 1DD
Tel: 0603 630621

Hereward Radio
PO Box 1557
73 Abington Street
Northampton NN1 2HW
Tel: 0604 29811

Religious Advisers to Independent Television Companies

ANGLIA
Rev. Philip Graystone SM, MA
41 High Street
Walsingham
Norfolk
Tel: 032872 567

BORDER
Very Rev. David Murphy, VF
The Presbytery
Whinlatter Road
Whitehaven
Cumbria CA28 8BN
Tel: 0946 2083

CENTRAL
Rev. Geoffrey Tucker BA
Harvington Parish Church
Harvington Hall Lane
Harvington
Kidderminster DY10 4LR
Tel: 056 283319

CHANNEL
Mgr Canon W. Raymond Lawrence
St Joseph's
Amphill House
Cordier Hill
St Peter Port
Guernsey C.I.
Tel: 0481 20196

GRANADA
Rev. T. Vincent Whelan
St Mary's
Chipping
Preston
Lancs.
Tel: 09956 238

GRAMPIAN
Very Rev. Charles McGregor
St Columba's
Banchory
Kincardineshire
Tel: 03302 2885

HTV WEST
Rev. Michael House
St George's
31 Boreham Road
Warminster
Wilts. BA12 9JP
Tel: 09859 212329

HTV WALES
Very Rev. Canon Edwin Regan
The Presbytery
Court Road
Barry
S. Glamorgan CF6 7EP
Tel: 0446 735051

LONDON WEEKEND
Rev. George Stack
92 Station Road
Wood Green
London N22 4SY
Tel: 01 888 2390

THAMES
Rev. Michael Hollings MC, MA
St Mary of the Angels
Moorhouse Road
Bayswater
London W2 5DJ
Tel: 01 229 0487

TSW
Very Rev. Canon A. Bede Davis
Cathedral House
Cecil Street
Plymouth PL1 5HW
Tel: 0752 662537

TVS
Rt Rev. Cormac Murphy-O'Connor
St Joseph's Hall
Greyfriars Lane
Storrington
Pulborough
W. Sussex RH20 4HE
Tel: 09066 2172

Sr Immaculata
1 Magazine Road
Ashford
Kent TN24 8NH
Tel: 0233 38620

TYNE TEES
Rev. Thomas Towers MA
60 Cockerton Green
Darlington
Co. Durham DL3 9EU
Tel: 0325 464848

ULSTER
Very Rev. Joseph Maguire PP, VF
Parochial House
Downpatrick
Co. Down
Northern Ireland

YORKSHIRE
Very Rev. Michael J. Buckley DD
St Joseph's Church
St Joseph's St
Tadcaster
N. Yorks LS24 9HA
Tel: 0937 833105

S4C
Dr Harri Pritchard Jones
9 Wingfield Road
Whitchurch
Cardiff CF4 1NJ
Tel: 0222 611170

BBC and training

Catholic assistant to the Head of Religious Broadcasting: Miss Frances Gumley
Room 312
BBC Yalding House
152–156 Great Portland Street
London W1N 6AJ
Tel: 01 580 4468, ext. 8078

Chief Broadcasting Officer for the Church of England
Rev. John Barton
Church House
Great Smith Street
Westminster
London SW1P 3NZ
Tel: 01 222 9011, ext. 260

National Catholic Radio and Television Centre
St Gabriel's
Oakleigh Road
Hatch End
Middlesex HA5 4HB
Tel: 01 428 1198
Director: Very Rev. Canon Peter Bourne. Courses organised in all forms of media presentation. Application to the Centre for details.

Churches TV Centre (its former title, now known as *CTVC*)
Hillside
Merry Hill Rd
Bushey
Watford
Hertfordshire WD2 1DR
Tel: 01 950 4426
Director: Rev. Leslie Timmins. Training available in radio and TV techniques. Details available from the Centre.

CHAPTER FOUR

Parish Education and Renewal

(The section 'Pastoral Planning by Objectives', pages 6–7, should be taken account of with this section.)

Building the Parish through Small Groups

One of the more encouraging features in the life of the Church today is the steady growth of small, apostolic groups, or basic Christian communities as they are sometimes known. Although these groups take various forms – family groups, house or neighbourhood groups, common interest groups such as those for one parent families – they are united by a common objective. They exist to help ordinary people to relate the truths of the Christian faith to their everyday life. Based on the belief that the Church is a living Christian community in which all are called to share fully, they offer a practical means of helping people to carry out the mission they received at baptism.

The groups are designed to build up stage by stage a living Christian community which can provide an ideal basis on which the parish is restructured for its mission to the wider community. Some parishes have as many as 20 groups based on different districts and localities. In this way even a large urban parish can be broken down into small missionary units in which a genuine spirit of Christian love and service is fostered.

Value of the groups

The groups are not merely discussion groups, neither are they concerned only with activities. Their prime aim is to promote Christian growth in individuals and in the parish. Among the benefits which these groups bring are the following:

they provide people with real friends and help them to overcome the modern problems of loneliness and isolation

married couples find a new source of strength which is reflected in their marriage and family life

parishioners find a practical means of really getting to know each other and of making their parish into a real community centred around the eucharist

men and women acquire the confidence to become involved in social, civic and community life

through the work of these groups, parish structures such as parish councils are more representative and have an apostolic and missionary character rather than a purely administrative or legalistic approach.

How the groups work

They normally consist of about 6 to 12 people; large enough for the group to feel a sense of identity but small enough for each member to participate fully. They usually take turns to meet in each other's homes fortnightly or monthly depending on the circumstances of the members. Where this is not practical, a comfortable parish room is used. Although there is a great flexibility and variety in these groups many of them find it helpful to follow a simple pattern based on a combination of the following items:

Gospel Enquiry
A discussion from a text of Scripture in an attempt to relate the Gospel to daily life.

Social Enquiry
An examination of some aspect of everyday life – family relationships, neighbours, education, housing, social pressures.

Review of Life
An exchange of experiences in which group members discuss together ways in which they are trying to live their Christian life in the different situations which confront them each day.

Priests and People

Above all, the groups provide an easy contact between priests and people which can develop a great spirit of collaboration. Although the groups are designed to develop lay leadership, the involvement of a priest or religious can be vital. In many cases it is they who take the initiative in forming the groups but as the group develops they recede from a leadership position and adopt the role of spiritual animator. Where a number of groups exist within a parish it is normal to form some kind of central group which helps to relate the life and activity of the various individual groups. Normally it is in this group that the priest plays his most effective role.

Family and Social Action

Although these groups have various approaches and styles, they often welcome ideas and support. Family and Social Action provides a comprehensive service to promote and sustain small groups in parishes. This consists of practical discussion programmes, advice on how to run groups, suggestions on organising parish study days, training sessions for group leaders and a bi-monthly Newsletter, *Parish and Community*, which provides a forum for groups throughout the country.

M.F.

Further information can be obtained from:

Family and Social Action
120B West Heath Road
London NW3 7TY
Tel: 01 458 7485

Book List

Cells for Life, Ron Trudinger, Olive Tree Publications, England. While this book is for Baptist groups and by a Baptist minister, it is full of good practical advice and points.
Building Small Groups, John Mallison, Scripture Union. Creative ideas from a Methodist background in Australia.
Parish Renewal, George Martin, Word of Life of USA. This book tries to integrate the Charismatic renewal with the growth of small groups, and hence renewal, in the parish.

RENEW: Diocesan renewal – the Newark programme

Five English bishops, with accompanying staff, have recently travelled to Newark, New Jersey, to experience at first hand the remarkable success of a programme for renewal initiated there.

Many American dioceses have already adopted the programme and in the United Kingdom the diocese of Galloway has led the way in launching the three-year programme, followed by Glasgow. In the United States the course of events is as follows:

> The RENEW service team is invited to meet the bishop and members of his staff; this is followed by one or two members of the team spending a week in the diocese to present the process to priests, religious, pastoral and deanery councils.
>
> Once a diocesan decision to proceed has been made, a person or persons is appointed to manage the RENEW effort in the diocese with the establishment, if possible, of a diocesan RENEW office.
>
> The local newly appointed diocesan staff either visit Newark for a full day or a RENEW member of staff comes to the diocese for a full day's consultation, leaving written guidelines for office procedures.
>
> The RENEW staff also assist in the thorough planning of the initial parish recruitment phase.
>
> There will be on-going personal support and literature available from the RENEW team.

Brief description of RENEW

RENEW is a parish-based programme for the revitalisation of parishes. It has three goals:

> Fostering witness to the message of the scriptures.
> Forming vibrant faith communities.
> Promoting responsibility for action towards social justice.

The programme runs for three years with an initial year of leadership training, followed by five six-week periods of programme planning and activity in the parishes. It should be the coordinated effort of all diocesan offices and agencies, and allow for maximum participation of parish personnel in its development and implementation.

Initial Leadership Training

Each parish which is interested in learning about parish renewal is invited to send a team of people to an initial, overnight training session. In most cases this team consists of the pastor, or one of his associates, a man or woman religious working in the parish, and one or two lay readers.

During this session, participants are urged to look at the need for renewal and redirection in their own lives, their own parishes, and their own communities. Having prayerfully and reflectively explored the basis for the need for change, the different aspects of the RENEW programme itself are explained to the teams and they are invited to participate in its implementation in their own parish.

Most teams involved with the initial sessions make a commitment to work for renewal and agree to participate in further training which takes place in four three-hour workshops at a later date.

The Programme

The programme provides parish teams with a variety of options for use in their parish. Written material that may be used as it is, or adapted to a particular parish stituation, gives ideas for five six-week periods of special homilies, Sunday liturgies, home activities, large group activities and small discussion groups.

All of the options tie into the goals and central themes of the programme, which are:

'The Lord's Call': a look at the needs people have and how the Lord seeks to answer those needs.

'Our Response to the Lord's Call': a look at the need to make a choice for Christ in one's life.

'Empowerment by the Spirit': the segment that deals specifically with the Gospel-based concern for social justice.

'Discipleship': a segment that provides for increased lay ministry formation based upon the Gospel call for everyone to take responsibility for ministry.

'Evangelisation': a period in which the newly revitalised Christian communities reach out to others with the Gospel message they have received.

Parish Involvement

Following the initial overnight session, the parish team, who have made a commitment to work towards the renewal of their own parish, meet in prayerful reflection to select a wider team of people (usually about twelve) to join them in being responsible for the parish's implementation of the programme. The expanded team meets for several months to develop plans with their own parishioners for:

A network to pray for RENEW.

Committees to be responsible for coordinating Sunday liturgies, paraliturgies, small group meetings and the home materials that will be used during the actual six-week implementation period of the programme.

Home visits of parishioners.

Recruitment of participants through a telephone campaign, publicity campaign, and 'sign-up' Sunday.

Evaluation.

Further Leadership Training

In the months following the initial overnight session, skill workshops are provided for the core leadership team from each parish. These teams in turn return to their own parishes and train the expanded parish team. Key to the training is the motivation of people to seek renewal, specific skills and the idea that parish teams must adapt what they have learned and the materials received to their own particular parish situation and people.

Among the specific skills included in the training are those of group leadership, committee organisation, home visiting, personal communication, group dynamics, telephone campaign, and the creation of an atmosphere in which people are encouraged to develop their own thoughts and skills.

Many pastors participated as team members for RENEW, but in addition, a special workshop can be made available to them to help further in familiarising them with the programme.

Further information may be had from:

Deirdre Collins	Galloway RENEW Office
Central Area Office	8a Corsehill Road
73 St Charles Square	Ayr KA7 2ST
London W10 6EJ	Director: Rev. Archie Brown
Tel: 01 960 4029	Tel: 0292 289888

RENEW – above – is distinct from the following section in that RENEW seeks for a diocesan renewal programme for all parishes in the diocese. 'Parish Renewal' is a more localised programme.

Parish Renewal

Introduction

Parish Renewal, begun in 1977, has never been envisaged as a movement in the Church. Rather it is an attempt to open up the main directions in which we, the people of the Church, need to be moving if the Church is to be built as the sacrament of Christ in the world. Many programmes have been developed by the initiators of this project in order to facilitate our moving in these directions and to link in with the various movements and other programmes which are developing in the Church.

Origins

Fr Chuck Gallagher SJ, of New Jersey, is mainly responsible for this Parish Renewal thrust. Together with laity, religious and other priests in America and Ireland, he set out to develop programmes which would make the teaching of the Church a lived experience for people within the setting of the parish community. The main documents were those of Vatican II and *Evangelii Nuntiandi* of Paul VI.

The first weekends took place in New Jersey in late 1977 and in Ireland in early 1978. Since then thousands of parishes throughout the English-speaking world and in other languages and cultures have benefited from the work begun then. Parish Renewal was started in Britain in 1980 and has been developed here mainly by Fr Johnny Doherty CssR, and Fr Michael Hickey, a priest of the diocese of Hexham and Newcastle.

Available Programmes

The general title given to the programmes is 'Working at a Parish Spirituality'. This title is deliberately chosen both as a statement that the list is not complete and as a recognition that the various movements and the other programmes that are developing in the Church should be given their rightful place.

Training course for priests
This is a Monday to Friday course on the spirituality of the priest in his call to be a leader of his people.

Parish Renewal Weekend
This is a retreat experience for parishioners, given by the priests and other leadership in the parish. Its aim is to acquaint people with their dignity and call them to their responsibility as Catholics.

Parishioner Empowerment
This is a weekend retreat experience which is best given by the bishop but may be given by others who are trained for it. Its purpose

is the personal missioning of parishioners for various vital growth points in the life of the parish.

Towards a Community Spirituality
This is a programme for religious communities. It is aimed at helping to integrate religious more fully in the life of the local church while preserving the special prophetic role of belonging to the universal Church. It is generally a ten-day course.

Other programmes include
Single young adults; healing through forgiveness; family renewal through reconciliation; parish mission week; sacramental catechesis; evenings for engaged; evenings for parish ministers; study guide for sacrament of matrimony.

J.D. and M.H.

For further information

Fr Johnny Doherty CssR
Clonard Monastery
Clonard Gardens
Belfast BT13 2RL
Tel: 0232 241044

Fr Chuck Gallagher SJ
67 Prince Street
Elizabeth
New Jersey 07208
USA
Tel: 201 353 8640

Setting up RCIA

The Roman 'Rite of Christian Initiation of Adults' (RCIA), first published in 1972, is one of the most important Church documents since the Second Vatican Council. It revives the *catechumenate*, the process whereby a person is gradually introduced into the life of the Church, as a preparation for full membership by initiation.

The full 'Rite of Catechumenate Received in Stages' envisages an *unbaptised* person making a journey of faith by celebrating the Rite of Becoming a Catechumen, then proceeding to the Rite of Election, then going through a Period of Purification and Illumination, before finally receiving baptism, confirmation and eucharist at the Easter Vigil. Today, many more people in Britain than previously are not baptising their infants; so the full Rite is itself becoming more and more relevant to our situation.

However, the Rite can and must be adapted to suit the needs of other than the unbaptised. For instance, the preparation for baptised Christians of other denominations to be received into full communion with the Catholic Church should now follow an adapted RCIA Catechumenate model. This is because, using this model, a person begins better to sense being a member of the *Church* during this period of preparation.

Also, many baptised Catholics who have lapsed from the practice of their faith could be brought back much more effectively to the life of the Church after sharing in the process of the RCIA-type catechumenate. They can discuss their problems within the community of the Church, and grow in their own faith and understanding. Their return to the practice of the liturgy will thereby become conscious and active participation in all aspects of the Church's life.

The setting up of the RCIA process within the parish can itself be a spark to renew all believers: since in all there are areas of lives that have not been touched by Christ and his Gospel. The RCIA foresees involvement of all the ministries within the Church, the whole body, in the formation of catechumens. The whole Church becomes missionary, not just the priest and the deacon.

Catechists must be trained in order to help the catechumen grow as a whole person. They are not to be transmitters of doctrine to a passive receiver. They are fellow pilgrims on that road. They should be aware, therefore, not only of their own faith, but also of recent insights into the way in which faith develops in a person. Their catechesis should be in shared dialogue, being prepared to 'learn' as well as to 'teach', since Christ is our one and only teacher (Matthew 23:10). It is particularly in the training of catechists, and in helping to devise programmes to meet local situations, that the diocesan and national catechetical centres can help most effectively.

Sponsors, those who accompany the enquirers on their journey, have a much more personal role even than the catechist. Their role is to make the enquirers feel increasingly that the Church is their home; because that is what it is. Thus the person chosen to sponsor an enquirer should be able to relate to that particular person, should share the enquirer's 'journey' by regularly attending all the meetings, and above all should be an *encouragement* to the one preparing to play a full part in the body of Christ.

Usually, the setting up of an 'Enquiry' class is the most effective beginning for an enquirer. This should have no 'strings attached', catechists and sponsors being present and available, but not pressurising the enquirers by their presence. Those who are enquirers will be at various stages of faith, and will be encouraged to 'tell their story'. The programme will therefore need to be flexible enough to meet the questions and needs of the enquirers, rather than following a pre-established scheme.

As time goes on, different groups may emerge. Some may wish to go on further, to become *catechumens* ('Yes, I think I want to become a member of the Church'). There should be a joyful ceremony to celebrate this decision, with all involved, and led by the priest as celebrant. On the other hand, those who do not wish to go on any further at this stage must not be made to feel guilty. They have made their journey thus far, and God is with them on the next stage, wherever that might be, for them.

As the catechumenate proceeds, an important stage is reached with the 'election' of the catechumen; i.e., 'the choice and admission of those catechumens who have the dispositions that make them fit to take part, at the next major celebration, in the sacraments of initiation' (RCIA: Roman 22; ICEL 106). It is most appropriate that these candidates, who by now have some good awareness of what it is to become a member of the Church, should be 'elected' at a ceremony presided over by the bishop.

The parish should be made aware at regular stages of the progress of the catechumens. The candidates should be made welcome most of all at Sunday Mass. The catechumens might ceremonially leave the liturgy at the Preparation of the Gifts as a sign that they are still catechumens. If done tactfully and with preparation, this will by no means make the catechumens feel inferior. Rather, it will emphasise the importance of the choice they are contemplating, and will also remind the congregation of how precious is their own relationship with Christ and his Church, and of what a tremendous privilege it is for us to celebrate the eucharist.

In this whole process, the priest will find his own role not diminishing, but rather increasing in significance, as the encourager and overseer of the whole body of Christ, representing the bishop in his own parish. He will find his own role as helping others to find their role. In this way, the RCIA becomes not just a formula for receiving new converts, so much as a living model for adult formation in the Church.

Points to get Started

Get started. Don't wait for everything to be perfect before you begin.

Get a small group of four or five 'good Catholics' in your parish and
discuss the meaning and implications of the RCIA in their own lives
and the life of the parish.
Start with the date of the Easter Vigil and work backwards to plan
the programme.
Invite enquirers to approach the Catholic Church, by way of sermon, newsletter, local press and, above all, by encouraging
parishioners to invite people personally.
Contact a diocesan Catechetical Centre for advice.

J.R. and J.O'T.

The stages and rites of Christian Initiation:

	Stage 1	*Stage 2*	*Stage 3*	*Stage 4*
WHAT?	Evangelisation & pre-catechumenate	Catechumenate	Purification & enlightenment	Post-baptismal catechesis or mystagogy
WHO?	Enquirers	Catechumens	The Elect	Neophytes
WHEN?	Any time	As necessary	Lent	Eastertide
WHY?	Establish trust and foster initial conversion	Thorough formation in Christian faith and living	Spiritual preparation for Easter Sacraments	Integration into wider community
HOW?	Listen to enquirers' questions: introduction to Gospel values	Catechesis, community life, worship and Christian service	Lenten reading, liturgical rites, fasting, almsgiving	Easter Gospel and Eucharist, works of charity
RITES	Acceptance as catechumens		Election or enrolment of names	Initiation through Baptism, Confirmation & Eucharist at Easter Vigil

Book List

Rite of Christian Initiation of Adults, CTS. Provisional text.
New Wine, New Wineskins, James B. Dunning. Pastoral implica-
tions.
A Journey in Faith, Raymond B. Kemp. An experience of the
catechumenate.
Becoming a Catholic Christian, William J. Reedy, ed. Symposium.
A History of the Catechumenate, M. Dujarier. First six centuries.

Creating a Living and Missionary Parish, Office of Evangelisation.
A brief guide to the Rite of Christian Initiation of Adults.
On Becoming a Catholic Christian, Office of Evangelisation. An
introduction to the Rite of Christian Initiation of Adults.
The Rites of Christian Initiation, Michael Dujarier. Historical and
Pastoral Reflections. Sadlier (1979).
Christian Initiation of Adults, Living Parish Pamphlets, Ealing
Abbey.

The Parish Library

The desirability of adult education in the faith conducted in and
through the parish is not in question; the problem of the 'how' of it
all faces enthusiastic pastors. Experience shows that there is no one
single way, many contributory and complementary methods must
be sought, aware all the time that the task of raising the understanding and appreciation of any community is going to be a gradual and
uphill task. One method worthy of consideration is the community
library.

As with so many other projects, the key to success lies in finding
an imaginative and enthusiastic librarian. No previous experience is
required because the titles for the library will in most cases be
chosen or vetted by the priest. The very practical problems of
storage, cataloguing, display, etc., will fall to the librarian.

The period of preparation is all important; it is imperative not to
make a start until there are enough books available and the planning of when they will be available to view, how they will be
returned, how displayed, etc., has been satisfactorily sorted out.
Some parishes have found that a good time to have the books on
display is during the morning coffee after the principal Sunday
Mass. This allows interested parishioners the leisure time to browse
– return books and select fresh ones. The librarian needs to think
out carefully the method of display; the front covers of all books
should be clearly visible.

A bright popular image is very important, otherwise people will
not even look and be attracted to take the books home with them.
No one will make time to read if they are not motivated, and we live
in a world that places much store by the attractive packaging of
products. This principle must not only be kept in mind in the display
of the books but also when one is adding to their number.

Books to launch the library can be had in various ways. A regular
appeal, perhaps for a period of a month, through the parish newslet-

ter has two advantages: it may produce a number of books but it also acts as an advertisement for the proposed opening of the library. A kind begging letter to all local convents, religious houses, etc., asking them for any Christian books, particularly popular paperbacks, that they have finished with will produce a few more. In appealing to parishioners for any books they have finished with, it is not unknown for generous benefactors to donate money towards the project! A courteous letter to each of the Christian publishing houses (see page 122) asking if they have any slightly damaged or imperfect books, or 'returns' that are unsaleable (offering to pay the postage) could turn up further copies. In the weeks prior to the launch of the library (the beginning of Lent or Advent is a good time), the librarian might visit any local book sales that are run for funds by voluntary organisations; Christian paperbacks often turn up at these.

It is quite reasonable, in fact very necessary for the stocking of the library, to make a nominal charge for the loan of a book for, say, a three-week period. Every few weeks a book list could be produced and either made separately available or reproduced in the parish newsletter as 'Recommended Reading for Lent', etc. The library must be continually kept bright and attractive and before the public gaze.

Book Agents

There are large areas of the British Isles where there is no bookshop providing books of Catholic and Anglican interest. To offset this problem there is no reason why all parish churches, schools and church groups cannot set up bookstalls, making a wide range of Christian books readily available to their members.

It is not difficult to set up as a book agent. The first step, if there is a Christian bookshop in the vicinity, is to call and talk it over with the manager. He will probably already have some book agents and will be pleased to help. If he is not in a position to help, he can supply the address of the Publishers Association, who will send the forms necessary to register. Some distributors, for example RP Bookservice, run a complete service for book agents. A letter to them (addresses below) will bring all the details you require to proceed.

Any adult who is in a position to offer books to a group for resale can be a book agent. These days there are many parish priests, curates, parish sisters, teachers and leaders of prayer and study groups offering books to their members for sale.

Once you have registered with the Publishers Association you can buy books from your supplier at a discount not usually less than 10 per cent, for resale at a fixed net price. Your local bookshop or distributor may impose a lower limit under which you may not order. You should check with the supplier but usually, if the books are kept clean and in a resaleable condition, you will be able to return those which do not sell when you make your next selection. The acceptance back of 'returns' depends upon two factors, the good condition of the books and the period of time that has elapsed; this should be as short as is reasonable.

If you have no method of display – and effective selling does depend largely upon good display – do not hesitate to ask your supplier for help. It is in his interest for your efforts to be successful because he benefits from every book you sell.

Advice and assistance in setting up is available from the following who have much experience in helping book agents.

RP Bookservice
Alphonsus House
Chawton
Alton
Hants. GU34 3HQ
Tel: 0420 88222

Christian World Centre
PO Box 30
123 Deansgate
Manchester M60 3BX
Tel: 061 834 6060

Celebration Services (Post Green) Ltd
57 Dorchester Rd
Lytchett Minster
Poole
Dorset BH16 6JE
Tel: 0202 623651

The Christian Bookstall Managers'
Association
Secretary: Leslie B. Gunn
9 Trystings Close
Claygate
Esher KT10 0TF
Tel: 0372 78 65826
Set up in 1970 to help and support those who run church bookstalls.

Christian Bookshops

The number of stockists of Catholic and Anglican books is limited, but most Christian bookshops will order titles for customers and be pleased to register a church bookstall as a book agent. The following selection of bookshops is not exhaustive but should prove useful.

London

Catholic Truth Society Bookshop
25 Ashley Place
Westminster Cathedral Piazza
London SW1P 1LT
Tel: 01 834 4392
Wide range of devotional objects and books.

Church House Bookshop
Great Smith Street
London SW1P 3BN
Tel: 01 222 9011
Wide range of books, cards and music.

Church Lit. Association Bookshop
Faith House
7 Tufton Street
London SW1P 3QN
Tel: 01 222 6952
Books, devotional objects; specialises in Anglo-Catholic material.

Damascus House Bookshop
The Ridgeway
Mill Hill
London NW7
Tel: 01 959 8971
Selection of books and RE material.

Mothers Union Bookshop Ltd
Mary Sumner House
24 Tufton Street
Westminster
London SW1P 3PR
Tel: 01 222 5533
Books of special interest to mothers and families.

A. R. Mowbray & Co. Ltd
28 Margaret Street
London W1N 7LB
Tel: 01 580 2812
Church requisites, books and devotional objects.

SPCK Bookshop
Holy Trinity Church
Marylebone Road
London NW1 4DU
Tel: 01 387 5282
Wide range of books, RE material and music.

St Paul Book Centre
199 Kensington High Street
London W8 6BA
Tel: 01 937 9591
Wide range of books, music and visual aids.

Westminster Cathedral Bookshop
Morpeth Terrace
Victoria
London SW1
Tel: 01 828 5582
Specialises in more substantial books of theology and spirituality.

SE England

Bernadettes
29 Bristol Road
Brighton
Sussex BN2 1AP
Tel: 0273 680829
Catholic parish shop, devotional objects, books and cards.

Church Shop
222 Leigh Road
Leigh-on-Sea
Essex SS9 1BP
Tel: 0702 710409
Catholic parish shop, range of books, cards and devotional objects.

DABCEC
1 Southgate Drive
Crawley
Sussex RH10 6PR
Tel: 0293 515 666
Centre for RE material and books.

The Friars Bookshop
The Friars
Aylesford
Kent
Good selection of books and
devotional objects.

Southend Christian Bookshop
57 London Road
Southend-on-Sea
Essex SS1 1PF
Tel: 0702 44008
Selection of Christian books, cards and
music.

SPCK Bookshop
Chapel Royal
North Street
Brighton BN1 1EA
Tel: 0273 28767
General books and wide range of
Christian books, cards, etc.

SPCK Bookshop
7 St Peters Street
Canterbury
Kent CT1 2EF
Tel: 0227 462881
Christian and general books, cards, etc.

SPCK Bookshop
St Mary's Church
Quarry Street
Guildford
Surrey
Tel: 0483 60316
General books, range of Christian
books, cards, etc.

South Coast
Castle Books
82 High Street
Newport
Isle of Wight PO30 1BH
Tel: 0983 525885
General range with Christian titles,
cards, etc.

Keith Jones Bookseller
2–3 Hinton Road
Bournemouth
Dorset BH1 2EE
Tel: 0202 292773
Wide range of books, music, cards, etc.

Portsmouth Diocesan RE Centre
La Sainte Union
The Avenue
Southampton SO9 5HB
Tel: 0703 31194
Centre for RE material, visual aids,
books, etc.

SPCK Bookshop
St Olave Church
North Street
Chichester PO19 1LQ
Tel: 0243 782790
Small shop, books of general Christian
interest.

SPCK Bookshop
24 The Square
Winchester SO23 9EX
Tel: 0962 66617
General books and range of cards and
Christian books.

SPCK Bookshop
51 High Street
Salisbury SP1 2PE
Tel: 0722 4535
General books, good selection of
Christian books, cards, etc.

West Country
The Catholic Bookshop
Church of Christ the King
Armada Way
Plymouth PL1 2EN
Part-time Catholic parish shop;
devotional objects, cards, books, etc.

Downside Abbey Bookshop
Stratton-on-the-Fosse
Bath
Avon BA3 4RH
Good range of books, devotional
objects, etc.

ECL Bookshop
60 Park Street
Bristol
Avon BS1 5JT
Tel: 0272 24426
Large evangelical bookshop, some
books of Catholic and Anglican
interest.

Emmaus House Bookshop
Diocesan Retreat and Pastoral Centre
Clifton Hill
Clifton
Bristol BS8 4PD
Centre for RE material, books of
spirituality, etc.

*La Sainte Union Pastoral and Book
Centre*
33 Pulteney Road
Bath
Avon BA2 4EY
Centre for RE material, visual aids,
books, etc.

SPCK Bookshop
8 Park Street
Bristol BS1 5HT
Tel: 0272 23461
General books and cards, Christian
paperbacks, cards, etc.

SPCK Bookshop
1–2 Catherine Street
Cathedral Yard
Exeter EX1 1EX
Tel: 0392 73640
General books and cards, Christian
paperbacks, cards, etc.

SPCK Bookshop
Bishop Phillpotts Library
Quay Street
Truro TR1 2HF
Tel: 0872 2771
General books and cards, Christian
paperbacks, cards, etc.

SPCK Bookshop
27 Southgate Street
Gloucester GL1 1TP
Tel: 0452 22805
General selection of books, cards, etc.

East Anglia
The Guildshop
Mrs Barling
Walsingham
Norfolk
Tel: 032872 387
Gifts and devotional objects; few
books.

A. R. Mowbray & Co. Ltd
14 Kings Parade
Cambridge CB2 1SR
Tel: 0223 358452
General books, cards, posters, wide
range of Christian books.

SPCK Bookshop
19 Pottergate
Norwich NR2 1DS
Tel: 0603 27332
General books and cards, Christian
paperbacks, cards, etc.

Home Counties
All Saints Pastoral Centre
London Colney
Herts. AL2 1AF
Centre with RE resource material,
books, etc.

Aslan Books
6 Duncombe Street
Bletchley
Milton Keynes MK2 2LY
Tel: 0908 644313
General bookshop with religious dept.

Newman-Mowbray Bookshop
87 St Aldates
Oxford OX1 1RB
Tel: 0865 244654
Wide-ranging specialist shop in
theology, scripture and spirituality.

St Andrew's Bookshop
126A High Street
Maidenhead
Berks. SL6 1PT
Tel: 0628 21985
Good range of Christian books, cards
and music.

St Andrew's Bookshop Ltd
16 Garden Court
Wheathampstead
Herts. AL4 8RF
Tel: 058 283 2460
Wide range of Christian books, cards
and music.

SPCK Bookshop
7 Castle Street
Reading RG1 7SB
Tel: 0734 53716
General selection of books, cards, etc.

Midlands
Book Room
7 Carrs Lane
Birmingham
West Midlands B4 7TG
Tel: 021 643 9235
Good range of general (esp. children's)
books, Christian books, cards and
music.

Catholic Truth Society Bookshop
St Chads
Queensway
Birmingham B4 6ET
Small shop with devotional objects and
a few books.

Christian Bookshop
70 Chilwell Road
Beeston
Nottingham NG9 1FQ
Good selection of Christian books,
cards and music.

The Bookshop
Mount St Bernard Abbey
Coalville
Leicester LE6 3UL
Books and quality devotional objects.

A. R. Mowbray & Co. Ltd
St Martin's Bookshop
The Bull Ring
Birmingham B5 5BB
General books, cards and Christian
titles.

SPCK Bookshop
68 High Street
Leicester LE1 5YP
Tel: 0533 26161
General selection of books, cards, etc.

SPCK Bookshop
105 High Street
Worcester WR1 2HS
Tel: 0905 24396
General selection of books, cards, etc.

St Paul Book Centre
133 Corporation Street
Birmingham B4 6PH
Tel: 021 236 1619
Wide-ranging selection of theology,
scripture and spirituality.

NW England
T.D. Carroll
15 Talbot Road
Blackpool
Lancs.
Tel: 0253 21142
Mostly devotional objects and books.

Catholic Truth Society Bookshop
11 Roe Street
St John's Precinct
Liverpool L1 1HH
Tel: 051 709 5208
Mostly devotional objects and books.

Catholic Truth Society Bookshop
8 South King Street
Manchester M2 6DW
Tel: 061 834 1301
Good range of Catholic titles,
devotional objects, etc.

Christian Book Centre
4–6 Fox Street
Preston
Lancs. PR1 2AB
Tel: 0772 59279
Wide range of Christian books and
cards.

Christian World Centre
123 Deansgate
Manchester M60 3BX
Tel: 061 834 6060
Wide range of Christian titles, visual
aids, paperbacks, cards, etc.

Methodist Book Centre
Bemersley House
Gitana Street
Hanley
Stoke-on-Trent ST1 1DU
Tel: 0782 22146
General titles, cards and Christian
paperbacks.

Metropolitan Cathedral Bookshop
Cathedral Precinct
Mount Pleasant
Liverpool L3 5TQ
Tel: 051 709 9222
General books and good range of
Christian titles.

Our Lady Star of the Sea
71 St Davids Road South
St Annes-on-Sea
Lancs. FY8 1TY
Tel: 0253 726253
Parish bookshop with a good selection.

St Paul Book Centre
82 Bold Street
Liverpool L1 4HR
Tel: 051 709 1328

SPCK Bookshop
Cathedral Close
Blackburn BB1 5AA
Tel: 0254 60973
General books, cards and Christian
paperbacks.

SPCK Bookshop
14–16 Bold Street
Liverpool L1 4DS
Tel: 051 709 4999
General titles, cards and Christian
paperbacks.

SPCK Bookshop
14–16 St Mary's Street
Deansgate
Manchester M3 2LA
Tel: 061 834 0257
General titles, cards and Christian
books.

SPCK Bookshop
7–11 St Werburgh Street
Chester CH1 2EJ
Tel: 0244 23753
General titles, cards, Christian
paperbacks.

NE England
Advance Bookshop
17 Monks Road
Lincoln LN2 5HL
Tel: 0522 25898
General titles and cards, selection of
popular Christian titles.

The Carmel Bookshop
33 Cookridge Street
Leeds LS2 3AQ
Tel: 0532 450850
Catholic shop with a wide range of
theological works, popular and
devotional books.

Catholic Truth Society Bookshop
Princess Square
Upper Level
Newcastle upon Tyne NE1 8ER
Tel: 0632 321169
Good range of Catholic books and
devotional objects.

Christian Books
17 Byram Street
Huddersfield HD1 1DR
Tel: 0484 34377
Good selection of Christian titles.

Christian Centre
Ice House
Victor Street
Grimsby
South Humberside DN32 7QN
Tel: 0472 49917
Wide range of Christian books, cards
and music.

The Grapevine
29 Church Street
Keighley
West Yorkshire BD21 5HT
Tel: 0535 606666
General titles with popular Christian
paperbacks.

Hallam Book Centre
22 Norfolk Row
Sheffield S1 2PA
Tel: 0742 78225
Catholic parish bookshop with a good
selection of popular titles.

Hazlewood Castle Bookshop
Hazlewood Castle
Tadcaster
North Yorks LS24 9NJ
Tel: 0937 832738
Centre bookshop with wide selection of
Catholic books.

Our Lady's Bookshop
102 Swanland Road
Hessle HU13 0NJ
Tel: 0482 644209
Catholic parish shop with a good
selection of books.

SPCK Bookshop
14 North Parade
Bradford BD1 3HY
Tel: 0274 728669
General titles, cards and Christian
books.

SPCK Bookshop
36 Steep Hill
Lincoln LN2 1LU
Tel: 0522 27486
General titles, cards and popular
Christian titles.

SPCK Bookshop
42 Stonegate
York YO1 2AT
Tel: 0904 54716
General titles, cards and popular
Christian titles.

SPCK Bookshop
8 Ridley Place
Newcastle upon Tyne NE1 8LP
Good, well-stocked shop.

Wales
Catholic Truth Society Bookshop
27–31 High Street
Cardiff CF1 2BB
Good selection of Catholic books and
devotional objects.

Noddfa Retreat Centre
Conway Old Road
Penmaenmawr
Gwynedd LL34 6YF
Centre with good selection of Catholic
titles.

SPCK Bookshop
20 The Friary
Cardiff CF1 4JA
Tel: 0222 27736
General titles and cards with popular
Christian selection.

Scotland
Goodliffe Neale
122 Clyde Street
Glasgow C1
Mostly devotional books and objects.

A. Harkins & Bros
4–6 North Bank Street
The Mound
Edinburgh EH1 2LP
Tel: 031 225 6209
Catholic books, devotional objects,
church furnishings.

St Paul Book Centre
5A Royal Exchange Square
Glasgow G1 3AH
Tel: 041 226 3391
Good wide range of books, music,
visual aids and RE material.

SPCK Bookshop
St John's Church
Princes Street
Edinburgh EH2 4BJ
Tel: 031 229 3776
Good selection of Christian titles.

Book distributors

Fowler Wright Books Ltd
Burgess Street
Leominster
Herefordshire HR6 8DE
Tel: 0568 4561
Chief Executive:
Nigel Fowler Wright.
Will supply shops, book agents and
personal customers. Stockists of all
British Catholic and Anglican
publishers and some Irish and
American publishers.

R.P. Bookservice
Chawton
Alton
Hants.
Tel: 0420 88222
Chief Executive:
James McKell.
Serves a network of book agents and
also personal customers. A catalogue is
available on request, showing the wide
range of British and American books
available.

Valley Books
Hadnock Road
Monmouth
Gwent NP5 3NQ
Tel: 0600 2402

Christian Publishers

Burns & Oates Ltd
Wellwood
North Farm Road
Tunbridge Wells
Kent TN2 3DR
Tel: 0892 44037/8

Canterbury & York Society
Borthwick Institute of Historical
Research
St Anthony's Hall
Peasholme Green
York
North Yorks. YO1 2PW

Celebration Services
57 Dorchester Road
Lytchett Minster
Poole
Dorset BH16 6JE
Tel: 0202 623651

Geoffrey Chapman
1 Vincent Square
London SW1P 2PN
Tel: 01 630 7881

Catholic Truth Society
38–40 Eccleston Square
London SW1V 1PD
Tel: 01 834 4392

Church House Publishing
(formerly *CIO*)
Church House
Great Smith Street
Westminster
London SW1P 3NZ
Tel: 01 222 9011

Anthony Clarke Books
16 Garden Court
Wheathampstead
Hertfordshire AL4 8RF
Tel: 058 283 2460

Collins Liturgical Publications
8 Grafton Street
London W1X 3LA
Tel: 01 493 7070

William Collins Sons & Co. Ltd
8 Grafton Street
London W1X 3LA
Tel: 01 493 7070

Concordia Publishing House Ltd
28 Huntingdon Road
Cambridge CB3 0HH
Tel: 0223 65113

Darton, Longman & Todd Ltd
89 Lillie Road
London SW6 1UD
Tel: 01 385 2341

Epworth Press
Room 195
1 Central Building
Westminster
London SW1H 9NR
Tel: 01 222 8010, ext. 276

Fowler Wright Books Ltd
Burgess Street
Leominster
Hereford & Worcester HR6 8DE
Tel: Leominster (0568) 4561

C. Goodliffe Neale Ltd
Arden Forest Industrial Estate
Alcester
Warwickshire B49 6ER
Tel: 0789 763261

Grove Books
St John's College
Chilwell Lane
Bramcote
Nottingham NG9 3DS

Highland Books
6 The White House
Beacon Road
Crowborough
East Sussex TN6 1AB
Tel: 089 26 2364

Hodder & Stoughton Ltd
PO Box 700
Mill Road
Dunton Green
Sevenoaks
Kent TN13 2YA
Tel: 0732 450111

Hughes and Coleman Ltd
Delta Close
Norwich
Norfolk NR6 6BG
Tel: 0603 46159

Hulton Educational Publications Ltd
Raans Road
Amersham
Buckinghamshire HP6 6JJ
Tel: 024 03 4186

Inter-Varsity Press
30 De Montfort Street
Leicester LE1 7GP
Tel: 0533 551700

Kingsway Publications Ltd
Lottbridge Drove
Eastbourne
East Sussex BN23 6NT
Tel: 0323 27454/6

Kevin Mayhew Ltd
The Paddock
Rattlesden
Nr Bury St Edmunds
Suffolk IP30 052
Tel: 04493 7978

Lion Publishing PLC
Icknield Way
Tring
Hertfordshire HP23 4LE
Tel: 044 282 5151

Lutterworth Press
7 All Saints' Passage
Cambridge CB2 3LS
Tel: 0223 350865

Marshall Pickering
3 Beggarwood Lane
Basingstoke
Hampshire RG23 7LP
Tel: 0256 59211

McCrimmon Publishing Co. Ltd
(formerly *Mayhew-McCrimmon*)
10/12 High Street
Great Wakering
Essex SS3 0EQ
Tel: 0702 218956

Methodist Publishing House
Wellington Road
Wimbledon
London SW19 8EU
Tel: 01 947 5256

Mirfield Publications
House of the Resurrection
Mirfield
West Yorkshire WF14 0BN
Tel: 0924 494318

A. R. Mowbray & Co. Ltd
Saint Thomas House
Becket Street
Oxford OX1 1SJ
Tel: 0865 242507

The Paternoster Press Limited
Paternoster House
3 Mount Radford Crescent
Exeter
Devon EX2 4JW
Tel: 0392 50631

Religious and Moral Education Press
Hennock Road
Exeter
Devon EX2 8RP
Tel: 0392 74121/5

Salvationist Publishing and Supplies Ltd
117/121 Judd Street
King's Cross
London WC1H 9NN
Tel: 01 387 1656/5621

SCM Press Ltd
26–30 Tottenham Road
London N1 4BZ
Tel: 01 249 7262

Search Press Ltd
Wellwood
North Farm Road
Tunbridge Wells
Kent TN2 3DR
Tel: 0892 44037/8

Sheed & Ward Ltd
2 Creechurch Lane
London EC3A 5AQ
Tel: 01 283 6330

Stainer & Bell Ltd
82 High Road
East Finchley
London N2 9PW
Tel: 01 444 9135

St Michael's Abbey Press
Farnborough
Hampshire GU14 7HQ

Henry E. Walter Ltd
26 Grafton Road
Worthing
West Sussex BN11 1QU
Tel: 0903 204567

Also useful:
Christian Booksellers Association
PO Box 30
123 Deansgate
Manchester M60 3BX
Tel: 061 834 6060

Guidelines on Submitting a Typescript

If you are considering submitting a typescript to a publisher for possible publication there are certain basic guidelines to keep in mind.

Publishing is a business and like all businesses must make a profit. Your typescript may be very worthy but unless it is marketable a publisher cannot accept it.

Publishers specialise both in what they publish and to whom they sell. For example, it is futile sending an erudite work on the history of the liturgy to Salvationist Publications; however, a folk group's music might well be seriously considered by the same publisher. Before submitting a typescript to a publisher inspect their catalogue (which they will supply on request).

Never send a complete finished typescript to a publisher. First write, giving an outline idea of the book, with a synopsis and, if possible, a sample chapter. Always retain a photocopy of whatever you send to a publisher. Enclose a stamped addressed envelope with the material you submit.

Expect it to be returned! But don't give up, believe in what you have written and try again with another publisher. Many great works have been refused many times before finding a publisher.

Your submission to the publisher must be clearly typed with double line spacing. Publishers are busy people who warm to those who make their life easier; on the other hand, a messy manuscript may be returned uninspected.

If the publisher is interested and wants to proceed, confidently ask for a contract and what advance on royalties will be made. (This is standard practice.)

Undertake no work, even for the most seemingly respectable publisher, without a contract which spells out clearly the terms. This is particularly important for commissioned work.

Never submit a typescript to publishers who advertise for typescripts. It will cost you a lot of money. Vanity publishing is not interested in your literary work, only your money.

Christian Newspapers, Magazines and Journals

Africa
Buchlyvie
St Patricks
Buchlyvie
Stirlingshire FK8 3PB
Tel: 036 085 274

Magazine to stimulate and sustain interest in the missions, particularly in Africa.

Ampleforth Journal
Ampleforth College
York YO6 4EN
Tel: 04393 206
Quality journal of academic interest.

Baptist Times
4 Southampton Row
London WC1B 4AB
Tel: 01 405 5516
Weekly newspaper of the Baptist
Church.

A Bookstalls Newsletter
11 Thorpe Chase
Ripon
North Yorkshire HG4 1UA
Tel: 0765 2907
Occasional newssheet for book agents
and bookshops.

Braille Theological Times
Braille House
338–46 Goswell Road
London EC1V 7JE
Tel: 01 837 9921
Specially produced for the blind
Christian.

British Weekly & Christian Record
Livingstone House
11 Carteret Street
London SW1H 9DJ
Tel: 01 222 3464
Weekly newspaper for evangelical
Christians.

Buzz Magazine
37 Elm Road
New Malden
Surrey KT3 3HB
Tel: 01 942 9761
Lively monthly Christian music
magazine.

Catholic Gazette
CMS
114 West Heath Road
London NW3 7TX
Monthly magazine of the Catholic
Missionary Society.

Catholic Herald
Herald House
Lambs Passage
Bunhill Row
London EC1Y 8TQ
Tel: 01 588 3101
Weekly Catholic newspaper.

Catholic Pictorial
Media House
34 Stafford Street
Liverpool L3 8LX
Weekly Catholic newspaper.

Christian Activity
The Old Mission Hall
Cedars Road
Colchester
Essex CO2 7BS
Tel: 0206 560435
A new monthly ecumenical magazine.

The Christian Bookseller
Grafton Place
Worthing
Sussex BN11 1QX
Tel: 0903 209983
A quarterly round-up of news and
reviews for Christian booksellers.

The Christian Herald
27 Chapel Road
Worthing
West Sussex BN11 1EG
Tel: 0903 212171
Weekly newspaper for evangelical
Christians.

Christian Update
Grafton Place
Worthing
West Sussex BN11 1QX
Tel: 0903 209983
Quarterly news and reviews of
Christian books for book agents.

Christian Woman
27 Chapel Road
Worthing
West Sussex BN11 1EG
Tel: 0903 212171
Quarterly glossy magazine specially for
Christian women.

Church Observer
Church Union
Faith House
7 Tufton Street
London SW1P 3QN
Tel: 01 222 6952/3/4
Magazine of the Church Union's
Anglo-Catholic readers.

Church of England Newspaper
Livingstone House
11 Carteret Street
London SW1H 9DJ
Tel: 01 222 3464
Weekly newspaper for Church of
England membership.

Church Times
7 Portugal Street
London WC2A 2HP
Tel: 01 405 0844
Weekly newspaper for Church of
England membership.

Churchman
Church Society
Whitefield House
186 Kennington Park Road
London SE11 4BT
Tel: 01 582 0132
Magazine reflecting the aims of the
Church Society.

Concilium
T. & T. Clark Ltd
36 George Street
Edinburgh EH2 2LQ
Tel: 031 225 4703
Quality theological journal reflecting
developments in theology.

Doctrine and Life
Dominican Publications
St Saviours
Dublin 1
Eire
Review of theological developments
and their application to life.

Downside Review
Downside Abbey
Stratton-on-Fosse
Bath BA3 4RH
Tel: 0761 232295
Quality journal of academic interest.

Expository Times
T. & T. Clark Ltd
36 George Street
Edinburgh EH2 2LQ
Tel: 031 225 4703
Theological journal.

Faith
2 Redford Avenue
Wellington
Surrey SM6 9DP
Tel: 01 647 8919
Monthly magazine concerned with
maintaining traditional Catholic
orthodoxy.

Family
37 Elm Road
New Malden
Surrey KT3 3HB
Tel: 01 942 9761
Glossy monthly magazine prompting
Christian family life.

The Friend
Friend Publications Ltd
Drayton House
30 Gordon Street
London WC1H 0BQ
Tel: 01 387 7549
Magazine for the membership of the
Society of Friends.

The Furrow
St Patrick's College
Maynooth
Co. Kildare
Eire
Monthly journal for the clergy on
theological and pastoral matters.

The Heythrop Journal
Heythrop College
University of London
11–13 Cavendish Square
London W1M 0AN
Tel: 01 580 6941
Quality theological journal.

Intercom.
Catholic Communications Centre
169 Booterstown Avenue
Blackrock
Dublin
Eire
Magazine of the Communication
Centre especially on Christian
communication matters.

The Irish Catholic
55 Lower Gardiner Street
Dublin 1
Eire
Tel: 0001 747538/742795
Weekly newspaper for Irish Catholics.

Irish Theological Quarterly
St Patrick's College
Maynooth
Co. Kildare
Eire
Tel: 0001 285222
Quality theological journal.

*Journal for the study of the New
Testament*
c/o Dept of Biblical Studies
Sheffield University
Sheffield
South Yorks. S10 2TN
Tel: 0742 78555 ext. 4615
As the name suggests.

*Journal for the study of the Old
Testament*
c/o Dept of Biblical Studies
Sheffield University
Sheffield
South Yorks. S10 2TN
Tel: 0742 78555 ext. 4615
As the name suggests.

Journal of Ecclesiastical History
St John's College
Cambridge CB2 1TP
Tel: 0223 61621
As the name suggests.

Journal of Theological Studies
Oxford University Press
Walton Street
Oxford OX2 6DP
Tel: 0865 56767
As the name suggests.

Methodist Recorder
122 Golden Lane
London EC1Y 0TL
Tel: 01 251 8414
Weekly newspaper for Methodists.

The Month
114 Mount Street
London W1Y 6AH
Tel: 01 491 7596
A monthly quality journal published
under the auspices of the Society of
Jesus.

New Blackfriars
Blackfriars
Oxford
Tel: 0865 57607
A monthly review of theological and
related matters.

New Life
106 Clapham Road
London SW9 0JX
Tel: 01 735 7031
Magazine of young Christian workers.

New REview
c/o 39 Eccleston Square
London SW1V 1PD
Journal of the National Catechetical
Association, appears three times a
year.

New Testament Studies
King's College
Strand
London WC2R 2LS
Tel: 01 836 8454
Quality journal of New Testament
studies.

Renewal
6 The White House
Beacon Road
Crowborough
East Sussex TN6 1AB
Tel: 089 26 2634
Monthly magazine reflecting the
interests and concerns of the
Evangelical Movement Renewal.

Restoration Magazine
Harvestime House
136 Hall Lane
Bradford
West Yorkshire BD4 7DG
Tel: 0274 729752
A renewal magazine of evangelical
appeal.

Scottish Catholic Observer
19 Waterloo Street
Glasgow G2 6BT
Tel: 041 221 4956
Catholic weekly newspaper for
Scotland.

Scottish Journal of Theology
33 Montgomery Street
Edinburgh EH7 5JX
Tel: 031 556 2796
As the name suggests.

The Sower
The Huddleston Press
Marston House
Priors Marston
Rugby
Warwickshire
Quarterly magazine for those engaged
in catechetics.

The Tablet
48 Great Peter Street
London SW1P 2HB
Tel: 01 222 7462
Quality international weekly Catholic
newspaper.

Theology
SPCK
Holy Trinity Church
Marylebone Road
London NW1 4DU
Tel: 01 387 9761
Review of developments in theology.

Today
37 Elm Road
New Malden
Surrey KT3 3HB
Tel: 01 942 9761
Glossy monthly magazine reflecting
current concerns for Christians.

Together
Church House
Dean's Yard
London SW1P 3NZ
Tel: 01 222 9011
Magazine for teachers and others
involved in Religious Education;
appears nine times a year.

The Universe
33–9 Bowling Green Lane
London EC1R 0AB
Tel: 01 278 7321
Catholic weekly newspaper.

The Way
114 Mount Street
London W1Y 6AH
Quarterly journal of theology and
spirituality.

See the following pages for publications
available for research at Catholic
Central Library.

The Catholic Central Library

Situated in Francis Street, just behind Westminster Cathedral, the
Catholic Central Library acts as a lending and reference library. It
stocks over 55,000 volumes and adds 800 or more titles a year
including the latest religious and ecumenical literature, theology,
ecclesiastical history, biography and liturgy. The reference facilities
are excellent. A very willing and able staff in the person of Mrs Joan
Bond, the librarian, and the Franciscan Friars of the Atonement,
who are responsible for the library, are always happy to advise. The
subscription, per annum, for one-book borrowers is £4.00. The
library is open from 10.00 a.m. to 5.00 p.m. Monday to Friday, and
10.00 a.m. to 1.30 p.m. on Saturdays. Postal service available.

For further details, write, phone or call:

Catholic Central Library
47 Francis Street
London SW1P 1GR
Tel: 01 834 6128

Journals available at the library (these cannot be borrowed):
Acta Apostolicae Sedis 1909–
Acta Sanctae Sedis 1865–1908
African Ecclesiastical Review 1962–
America 1961–
American Ecclesiastical Review 1889–1975
Ampleforth Journal 1944–80
Analecta Bollandiana 1882–1913; 1945–70
Archivum Franciscanum Historicum 1910–
Archivum Historiae Pontificiae 1963–
Art D'Eglise 1961–9
L'Art Sacre 1951–69
Ateismo E Dialogo 1976–
At-One-Ment (complete)
Ave Maria 1961–70
Aylesford Review 1962–8
Beda Review 1956–72
Bible Today 1962–
Biblica 1920–
Biblical Theology Bulletin 1971–
British Journal of Religious Education 1978–
Brownson's Quarterly Review 1845–59
Buckfast Chronicle 1931–70
Bulletin (CMAC) 1970–

Bulletin of the B'Ham Diocesan Ecumenical Commission 1966–70
Bulletin: Secretariat for Non-Christians, 1968–
Canon Law Abstracts 1958–
Catholic Biblical Quarterly 1939–
Catholic Citizen 1963–
Catholic Education Today (& Catholic Teachers Journal) 1958–
Catholic Gazette 1923–
Catholic Historical Review 1915–
Catholic Institute for International Relations 1976–
Catholic International Outlook 1955–62
Catholic Luminary and Ecclesiastical Repertory 1840–1
Catholic Magazine 1839–42
Catholic Magazine and Review 1831–5
Catholic Medical Quarterly (& Guardian) 1923–
Catholic Mind 1934–57; 1963–73
Catholic Miscellany 1822–30
Catholic Progress 1880–1
Catholic Pulpit c. 1848
Catholic Spectator 1823–6
Catholic World 1865–
Centro Pro Unione Bulletin 1969–
Chesterton Review 1974–
Chicago Studies 1976–
Chiese Orientali 1976–
Christ to the World 1962–70
Christian 1973–
Christian Attitudes on Jews and Judaism 1968–79
Christian Century 1966–
Christian Democrat 1921–66
Christian Jewish Relations 1980–
Christian News from Israel 1973
Christus Rex 1964–70
Chrysostom 1960–
Church Alert (Sodepax) 1976–80
Church and World (& Bulletin) 1947–64
Church Music 1959–74
Church Observer 1962–
Churchman 1973–
Cistercian Studies 1983–
Civiltà Cattolica 1947–
Clergy Review 1931–
Commonweal 1961–

Communicationes 1970–
Communio 1974–
Community 1971–
Concilium 1965–
Confraternity of Unity, Bulletin of the, 1927–33
Contact 1975–
Critic 1962–78
Cross Currents 1966–
Diaconal Quarterly 1976–
Diakonia 1966–
Dialog 1978–
Doctrine and Life 1961–
Doctrine and Life Supplement 1963–79
Documentation Catholique 1919–
Dominican Studies 1948–53
Downside Review 1883–
Dublin Review 1836–1968
Eastern Churches Newsletter 1981–
Eastern Churches Quarterly 1936–64
Eastern Churches Review 1966–78
Ecew Bulletin 1967–
Ecumenical Press Service 1972–
Ecumenical Review 1948–
Ecumenical Trends 1972–
Ecumenism 1968–
Ecumenist 1963–
Edinburgh Catholic Magazine 1837–8
Encounter Today 1966–79
Epworth Review 1974–
Espirit 1961–70
Essex Recusant 1959–
Etudes 1931–
Face to Face 1978–
Faith and Unity 1962–78
Farm Street Calendar 1920–38
Franciscan 1972–
Franciscan Studies 1959–
Furrow 1950–
Gregorianum 1946–
Hallel 1975–
Heythrop Journal 1960–
Homiletic and Pastoral Review 1921–

Hopkins Quarterly 1980–
Informations Catholiques Internationales 1961–
Innes Review 1952–
Insight 1982
Interface 1979–
International Review of Mission 1973–
Irénikon 1952–
Irish Ecclesiastical Record 1887–1968
Irish Theological Quarterly 1951–
Islamochristiana 1975–
Istina 1959–
Japan Missionary Bulletin 1968–81
Jesus Caritas 1958–
Jews and Ourselves 1959–65
Journal for the study of the OT 1981–
Journal of Biblical Literature 1977–
Journal of Ecclesiastical History 1950–
Journal of Ecumenical Studies 1964–
Journal of Medical Ethics 1975–
Journal of Theological Studies 1900–
Jurist 1941–
La Vie Spirituelle 1932–65
Laity Today 1969–
Lamp (Graymoor NY) 1903–74
Lamp (York) 1850–95
Life and Worship 1970–4
Life of the Spirit 1946–64
Liturgical Arts 1938–71
Liturgy 1976–
Liturgy (Pershore) 1947–69
Liturgy (Washington DC) 1981–
Liturgy Bulletin 1971–
London & Dublin Orthodox Journal of Useful Knowledge 1835–45
London Recusant 1971–
Lumen Vitae 1949–
Lumière Et Vie 1952–67
Masses Ouvrières 1945–52
Midstream 1976–
Missionary Research, International Bulletin of, 1977–
Modern Liturgy 1975–
Month 1864–
Monthly letter on Evangelism 1974–

Moreana 1963–
Music and Liturgy 1974–
New Blackfriars (& Blackfriars) 1920–
New Covenant 1971–81
New Life 1950–
New REview 1982–
New Sower 1975–9
New Testament Abstracts 1956–
New Testament Studies 1969–
Newman 1965–70
Northern Catholic History 1975
Notitiae 1965–
Nouvelle Revue Théologique 1910–
Oecumenica: revue de l'Anglicanisme et des Questions Oecuméniques 1934–40
Old Testament Abstracts 1978–
One in Christ 1965–
One World 1974–
Outlook 1972–
Pastoralia 1891–1908
Pilot (SPCU) 1933–50
Pope Speaks 1954–
Prism: An Anglican Monthly 1961–5
Pro Mundi Vita Bulletin 1972–
Quis Custodiet? 1964–73
Rambler 1848–62
Ransomer 1962–
Recherches De Science Religieuse 1951–65
Recusant History (& Biographical Studies) 1951–
Religion in Communist Lands 1975–
Religious Life Review 1980–
Religious Studies 1965
Re-Union 1934–65
Review for Religious 1945–
Review Biblique 1898–1978
Revue D'Histoire Ecclésiastique 1922–59
Revue Des Sciences Philosophiques et Théologiques 1951–65
Revue Thomiste 1949–67
Risk 1973–7
Scottish Journal of Theology 1963–
Scripture Bulletin (& Scripture) 1946–
Scripture in Church 1971–

Search 1962–8
Secretariat for Promoting Christian Unity: Information Service 1967–
Sicut Parvuli 1955–
Sidic 1967–
Sixteenth Century Journal 1975–
Slant 1966–70
Sobornost 1951–
Social Compass 1965–77
Sourozh 1980–
Sower 1962–75, 1979–
Speculum 1964–8
Staffordshire Catholic History 1961–
Stimmen Der Zeit 1958–70
Studia Liturgica 1962–
Studies 1912–
Study Encounter 1970–6
Tablet 1841–
Teilhard Review 1966–
Theological Studies 1962–
Theologie Und Glaube 1968–78
Theology 1920–
Theology Digest 1953–
Theology Today 1958–
Thomist 1959–
Thought 1951–69
Together in Christ 1983–
Truthteller 1826–9
Twentieth Century 1946–64
Una Sancta 1966–
Unitas 1949–68
Unité Chrétienne 1942–
Unité Des Chrétiens 1972–
Unity Trends 1967–9
Vers L'Unité Chrétienne 1950–63
Vision 1971–
Way 1961–
Way Supplement 1965–
Westminster Cathedral Chronicle 1908–67
Woodstock Letters 1948–69
Worcestershire Recusant 1963–
World Justice 1959–71
Worship 1956–

CHAPTER FIVE

Parish Property

How to Commission an Architect

It is not difficult to find an architect. Wherever you live in the UK there is a list in the Yellow Pages Classified, with a boxed entry from the Clients Advisory Service of the Royal Institute of British Architects. This will give the address and telephone number of the local architects' chapter, and the address of the RIBA Headquarters. Either of these can help you select an architect.

The advisory services, both in London and the regions, understandably deal with enquiries primarily on a local basis. Always direct a general enquiry to the Advisory Service at the starting point. You may be recommended to an architect at some distance from yourself. Clients recognise that travelling expenses represent a fraction of building costs and that previous experience, knowledge of the Church and liturgy could override local considerations. A client's aim must be to find the right architect for the particular commission. However, if the local practitioner is a match for the brief, his sense of what is indigenous to the neighbourhood, knowledge of local contractors and materials can be of great value.

For Catholic church projects there is frequently an established diocesan procedure and an enquiry to the chairman of the Art and Architecture Committee or the financial secretary of the diocese should lead to a list of architects who have carried out work in the diocese or who are known to the diocesan trustees. Few dioceses have a formally approved list of architects but a parish should draw on the experience of diocesan officers in this area. Since the Second Vatican Council, and the revision of Canon Law, it is clear that the parish priest, with representatives of the parish community, should decide on such a matter as the choice of architect because he or she has to enter into a very close working relationship with the commissioning church, learning about the people's material and spiritual needs which are to be expressed in built form. Trust is required which is unlikely to come from an outside appointment.

The Parish Church, a booklet published by the Liturgy Commission of the Bishops' Conference, reminds us that architecture, though incorporating the science of construction, is primarily an art. The architect's role is that of an interpreter, reflecting people's aspirations born from a deep understanding of functional requirements and of the spirit which underlies the less definable.

In many parishes some people will be eager to defend the values they recognise in the existing fabric and furnishings, others will remind their community of the spirit of poverty to which we are committed. We do not live at a time when the Gothic style vies with the Classical for the label 'Christian architecture', but aesthetics are still debated, particularly since the post-war years have generated many buildings of impoverished artistic merit. Because there is no stylistic formula, the role of the client in first choosing and then working confidently with an architect is as important now as it has ever been.

The potential clients should make a short list of architects who have demonstrated by quality in design and construction the experience needed to undertake the commission. They can be asked to provide illustrations or articles about their work. Where the project relates to an existing building, particularly one of special historic interest or architectural merit, the architect should also have experience in the philosophy and techniques of conservation. The practitioners' potential for working sympathetically and creatively with the client in its broadest sense will become clear from a short list, interviews, and if possible visits to previously executed commissions.

The client has a particular responsibility for providing the architect with a brief. However, it is unnecessary, and perhaps unwise, to consolidate the brief before commissioning the architect, because his skills can assist in preparing the brief, in case a lack of realism frustrates the end in view. A brief contains a schedule of accommodation, guidance on the budget and as many considerations as possible which evoke the activities and aspirations of the client and all future users of the building.

In church architecture a substantial part of the brief should deal with liturgical renewal and the place of the sacraments. The architect should talk at length with his clients about these areas in the search for challenging plans and a creative ambiance for worship and parish life. *The Parish Church*, subtitled *Principles of Liturgical*

Design and Reordering, referred to above, will be an invaluable reference. If design problems linked with liturgy arise, either the diocesan Art and Architecture Committee should be consulted or the Liturgy Committee of the Bishops' Conference.

The formal relationship between client and architect, their respective duties and responsibilities, the project work stages and bases for the architect's remuneration are most readily found in an RIBA publication called *Architect's Appointment* which is obtainable from the Institute.

Publications dealing specifically with church architecture are few and have diminished internationally with the recent demise of *Art D'Eglise* from Belgium and *L'Espace* and earlier *L'Art Sacre* in France, but back numbers can be found in selected libraries and they provide the most searching reference to post-conciliar churches. *Kunst & Kirche* is still available from Austria. In England we have a promising successor to the *Catholic Building Review* in the joint Roman Catholic/Church of England publication, *Church Building*, published twice yearly from 1984. (Copies can be inspected at Catholic Central Library.) For the re-ordering of churches, *Planning for Liturgy* by Stephen Johnson and Cuthbert Johnson, published by St Michael's Abbey Press, Farnborough, Hants., can be highly recommended.

A.W.

For further information consult:

The Royal Institute of British Architects
66 Portland Place
London W1N 4AD
Tel: 01 580 5533

The Royal Incorporation of Architects
in Scotland
15 Rutland Square
Edinburgh EH1 2DE
Tel: 031 229 7205

The Liturgy Committee
The Bishops' Conference of England &
Wales
38–40 Eccleston Square
London SW1V 1PD

Austin Winkley AADipl. RIBA Dipl.
Conservation AA
Williams & Winkley
Chartered Architects
40 Linhope Street
London NW1 6HW

How to Commission Paintings and Sculpture

The most important points when commissioning any work of art are to know what you want and to know how much you are prepared to pay for it. It is absolutely fatal to say to the artist: 'You're the expert. I leave it all to you.' An artist needs discipline, and he needs to know what is expected of him. Most of the greatest works in the history of art have been executed in the service of a demanding patron, in response to an exacting brief, in struggling with an intractable medium, or in following the rigid dictates of a traditional canon.

Make up your mind what you want, and ask the artist if he can produce it. If, as often happens, your idea is not technically feasible, it doesn't matter. The artist will tell you so, and will suggest alternatives or modifications, and between you a compromise can be worked out.

If you are not knowledgeable, how can you choose the right artist? Look at work in galleries, and consult art books in your local reference library. Talk to someone on the staff of an art school, museum or art history faculty. You can approach organisations such as the Arts Council, the Crafts Council and the Council for the Care of Churches, which maintain libraries of photographs and slides and lists of competent artists and craftsmen.

It is a good idea to tell the artist at the outset roughly how much you want to spend. This saves a great deal of time which can be wasted in the preparation of sketches or maquettes that may be much more or much less ambitious than you planned. It cramps the artist's creativity if he has to work in the dark. Clients are often unwilling to put their cards on the table, perhaps because they imagine that artists operate a variation of Parkinson's Law – the more money they know you have to spend, the higher they will price the job. It doesn't really work that way. Few artists are good at managing their own money affairs and are certainly not market manipulators.

Having found an artist whose work appeals to you, consider, or ask your consultant, if he or she is the right person for the job. It may seem elementary to say that the best miniaturist in the world is not likely to paint a bold and effective stage-set, or that a carver of ivory netsuke is not the ideal choice to produce a monumental equestrian statue; but mistakes of this kind are often made. The fact that Graham Sutherland was a famous painter was no guarantee that he would design a good tapestry. The fact that Chagall was a lyrical colourist did not necessarily qualify him to design stained glass windows. Ideally, a work of art should be designed and made by the same person, who knows the scopes and the limitations of the medium. Of course, he may have skilled assistants whom he can supervise in his studio – most of the great masters have had large workshops – but he must not separate design from execution.

The average layman is understandably confused by technical

terms. He may find himself in deep water if he asks an artist to paint a fresco on his wall when all he wants is a simple mural painting; or to make an etching of his wife when what he really means is a pen-and-ink portrait. He is inclined to think that watercolour is an easier medium than oil and that wood is easier and probably cheaper to carve than stone, whereas the reverse is usually true. So be sure to ask the artist to explain anything about which you are uncertain. He will not be flattered if you describe his work as Futuristic, when what you mean is *avant-garde*. (Futurism was a style which flourished briefly from about 1910 until the First World War. The term should be confined to this usage, but journalists continually misapply it.)

Do not expect a work which is modelled and cast to look like a carving, or vice versa; though nowadays, fibreglass and various resins can be made to imitate almost any natural material.

The patron must also consider the setting for which the work is intended. It may look wonderful in the artist's studio, but in a different space and with the light falling from a different angle, it may appear less effective.

If the materials with which the artist is working are costly, the patron should be prepared to advance a proportion of the fee as soon as the design is finally approved.

The time factor must not be ignored. An artist who is in demand will probably have a waiting list. Be suspicious of anyone who offers to make something in a week – suspicious, not dismissive, for some painters in oils work very quickly; but most media impose more patience on both artist and patron. It is best to follow the advice given by gardeners to those who wish to grow asparagus: start four years ago.

W.P.

Reading list

Articles

'Symbol and Art in Worship', in *Concilium* **132**, 1980.
.'The Church, Patron of the Arts', J. Crichton, in *Liturgy* **33**, 1964.
'The Image Maker in the House of Liturgy', O. Ellis, in *The Furrow*, 1965.
'Design as Worship', E. Fischer, in *Worship* **48**, 1974.
'Liturgy as Visual Experience', J. Fitzer, in *Worship* **48**, 1974.

Books
Early Christian and Byzantine Art, J. Beckwith, London, 1979.
Christianity and the Visual Arts, G. Cope, ed., London, 1964.
Traditional Symbols and the Contemporary World, F. W. Dillistone, London, 1973.
Fundamental Questions on Ecclesiastical Art, K. B. Franks, Collegeville, Minnesota, 1962.
Modern Art in English Churches, Michael Day, Oxford, 1984.

How to Commission Stained Glass

When a stained glass commission is being proposed, there are many things to be aware of, and a few of the main ones are outlined here. I write as a stained glass artist who works to commission, and so have first-hand experience of the process. The fundamentals are as follows.

The 'brief' needs to be worked out together with the budget at an early stage and before contacting an artist.

Who to commission the work from? Because stained glass is not a catalogue item, but a creative medium through which many fine artists are working today, it is important to invite several artists to become involved at the early stage in order that the client can see how they would each interpret the brief. One of the popular ways of going about this is to invite the artists to submit a selection of slides (which are returned in due course) showing examples of previous work. The second stage is to invite those artists whose work looks most promising (in terms of the proposed project) to submit a preliminary design to the prepared brief. A nominal fee should be allowed to cover some expenses involved in the preparation of such a design. At this stage full discussion should be made possible between all parties involved.

After these initial designs have been submitted it is hoped that it will be apparent whose work is most promising, and that artist can then be asked to submit a more developed or detailed design.

A relationship will by now have been established with the artist, and methods of working from this stage onwards can be agreed between the parties concerned.

The societies to contact who can advise on an initial list of stained glass artists are as follows.

The British Society of Master Glass
Painters (BSMGP)
Hon. Sec. Mrs S. Mole
115 Woodwarde Road
London SE22 8UP
This society will send you on request a
catalogue of practising stained glass
artists/craftsmen, listed by county. Do
not feel restricted to only invite those
local to you, you are reducing your
options unnecessarily. The extra
expense incurred at the initial stages
will be repaid in the long term when the
best and most appropriate artist has
been found.

The Crafts Council
12 Waterloo Place
London SW1Y 4AU
The Council have an index of artists
working in stained glass.

For further addresses see page 146.   C.K.

How to Choose or Restore an Organ

Church Organs – General Principles

Preference is to be given to the pipe organ, for it is the traditional musical
instrument which adds a wonderful splendour to the church's ceremonies
and powerfully lifts up man's mind to God and to higher things (*Constitution on the Liturgy* vi:120).

The organ is a musical instrument and should always be a work of
art. It should have an artistic appearance and produce a beautiful
sound. Well-built pipe organs are long lived. Some of the finest
organs in the world are over 200 years old, and still function day by
day in the liturgy. In the main, however simple or small, they have
the following characteristics, as do the best of contemporary instruments:

An appropriate tonal and spatial disposition
A responsive mechanical action
Straight registers
Slider windchests
Appropriate casework and console
A position from where it can support the singing of congregation
and choir, being clearly heard by all.

An organ for church use today should embody these characteristics.
If it is well made by craftsmen and properly maintained it will have a
very long life.

Choosing an Organ

It is essential that informed advice, free from commercial interest, is sought before any approach is made to commercial firms. (See page 145 below, on Organ Advisory Group.) The role of an adviser or advisory body is to ensure that the church gets an organ suited to its needs, and to ensure that the organ builder is given due opportunity to fulfil these needs by his artistry. The organ builder is, or should be, both a craftsman and an artist – he should not be deprived of his initiative and responsibility. The recent extant work of an organ builder should be the criterion for choosing an organ. It should be stressed that *quality* of work, not size or quantity, is of paramount importance.

Electronic Instruments

Electronic instruments can hardly compare in terms of tonal quality, tonal variety or effectiveness with a pipe organ, or in terms of cost/life/investment in terms of a craft-built pipe organ. From a liturgical point of view the difference between the real sound of a pipe organ and sound reproduced in a loudspeaker should not be overlooked, nor the matter of obsolescence. It is worth recalling that the noblest task of the organ is the accompaniment of congregational and choral song – the music of voices. The pipe organ, which is a wind instrument, is particularly well suited to the accompaniment of voices, which are of course wind instruments themselves.

Restoring or rebuilding old organs

Before deciding to restore or rebuild an old organ informed advice should be sought. Inexpert 'restoration' can result in irreparable loss. Although there are relatively few fine old organs in Britain it should be stressed that within the Catholic Church in England there is a heritage of fine historic organs. These should be safeguarded and cared for. Such organs can play a very practical and beautiful role in the liturgy today. Grant aid may be available for the restoration of historic organs.

Secondhand Pipe Organs

The greatest caution should be exercised and expert advice sought before obtaining and installing a secondhand pipe organ. In too many instances in the past Catholic churches have acquired large, indifferent, secondhand organs which have become a financial and liturgical liability, as well as being unsatisfactory architecturally. The credentials and craftsmanship of anyone offering secondhand organs for sale/installation should be very carefully checked. This said, there are a number of fine instruments from the past which are well worth consideration and if one of suitable quality, size and appearance can be obtained this can, on occasion, be a very satisfactory course of action.

Maintenance

Regular maintenance by a reliable craftsman should be a normal arrangement on the part of a parish.

Insurance

Organs should be *fully* insured for their total loss/replacement value: this should be periodically reviewed.

Heating and Ventilation

As with any timber furnishings, an organ can be damaged if the air in a church is overheated, or if excessively rapid temperature changes occur. Care should be taken when heating systems are installed or improved. The relative humidity in a church should not be allowed to fall below fifty per cent or rise above eighty per cent.

Acoustic

It should be remembered that a rich, reverberant acoustic is important for music, song and speech and is a *vital* factor in encouraging corporate liturgical activity. A dead acoustic means a dead liturgy.

Conclusion

The Liturgy is the peak towards which the Church's activity tends, just as it is the fountainhead from which all its vitality flows (*Constitution on the Liturgy* 1:10).

Such activity demands an organ of musical integrity. Here is no place for ostentation, pretension or extravagance, but rather a place for a simple wind instrument of noble simplicity, the well-crafted and artistically voiced work of human hands. Such a pipe organ encourages and enriches congregational and choral song, helping the community in its singing of acclamations, psalms and hymns to rejoice, weep, unite, be converted and pray.

J.R.

Sources of information

Advice

The Organ Advisory Group of the Society of St Gregory offers informed advice, free from commercial interest, on the installation, restoration, renovation and maintenance of organs. The services of the Group are available to parishes, communities, schools, etc. Contact:

The Hon. Secretary
Dr John P. Rowntree
The Cottage
2 Bury's Bank

Greenham Common North
Newbury
Berks. RG15 8BZ
Tel: 0635 44630

Literature

Choosing an Organ, a booklet available from the Organ Advisory Group – see above.
The Classical Organ in Britain Volume I 1955–1974, Volume II 1975–1978, Volume III 1978–1985, by J. Rowntree and J. Brennan, Positif Press, 140 Southfield Road, Oxford OX4 1PA.
The British Organ, by C. Clutton and A. Niland, Methuen, 1982.
The Organs of Britain, by J. Norman, Allen and Charles, 1984.
A New History of the Organ, by P. Williams, Faber, 1980.

Organ Builders (a representative list)

Church & Co.
Nesbitt Hill Head
Stamfordham
Newcastle upon Tyne NE18 0LG
Tel: 06616 305

W. Drake
Chapel Street
Buckfastleigh
Devon TQ11 0AB
Tel: 0364 42623

P. D. Collins
Northcote
South Common
Redbourn
St Albans
Herts AL3 7NB
Tel: 058 255 2060

Goetze & Gwynn
Gardens House
Welbeck Abbey Estate
Worksop
Notts S80 3LW

Harrison & Harrison
Hawthorn Terrace
Durham DH1 4EW
Tel: 0385 43115

Hill and Son & Norman and Beard
134 Crouch Hill
London N8 9DX
Tel: 01 340 2271

N. P. Mander
St Peter's Organ Works
St Peter's Close
London E2 7AF
Tel: 01 739 4747

J. W. Walker
Wimbledon Avenue
Brandon
Suffolk IP27 0NF
Tel: 0842 810 296

Music Manuscripts and Published Works

It is all too rarely realised that in Catholic churches, especially those founded in the eighteenth and early nineteenth centuries, or which have descended from such foundations, there is a heritage of music of significance. The greatest of care should be taken before throwing out or disposing of any choral or instrumental music from parish, community or school libraries or choir lofts. Any manuscript or printed music (or service books), especially from the eighteenth century or earlier, should be carefully safeguarded and advice sought as to its proper housing. Sometimes a University Library or local Record Office may be an appropriate location, but expert musicological advice should be sought before any action is taken. All such collections should be catalogued.

J.R.

Suppliers

Stained Glass

Contemporary Stained Glass Art
28 West Field Road
West Green
Crawley
West Sussex
Tel: Crawley (0293) 36188

Bronson Shaw Design
40 Acton Lane
Chiswick
London W4 5ED
Tel: 01 994 3212

Cox and Barnard (Hove) Ltd
58 Livingstone Road
Hove
Sussex BN3 3WL
Tel: 0273 734906

Goddard & Gibbs Studios Ltd
41–49 Kingsland Road
Shoreditch
London E2 8AD
Tel: 01 739 6563

G. Maile & Son
10–12 The Borough
Canterbury
Kent CT1 2DT
Tel: 0227 61296
Also church furniture and engraving.

Church Furniture

James Chase & Son (Furnishings) Ltd
14a Pears Road
Hounslow
Middlesex TW3 1SY
Tel: 01 570 9601 or 9602
Speciality: manufacture and sale of all
church furnishing.

A. Edward Jones Ltd
St Dunstan Works
Pemberton Street
Warstone Lane
Birmingham
West Midlands B18 6NY
Tel: 021 236 3762 or 1451
Speciality: silver and metal work.

Gopack
Range Road
Dept CD
Hythe
Kent CT21 6HG
Speciality: folding tables for halls.

Ormsby of Scarisbrick
Woodland Works
542 Southport Road
Scarisbrick, Ormskirk
Lancs. L40 9QQ
Tel: 0704 880294
Speciality: woodwork, especially
statues.

Philip N. Irvine
25 Carlisle Road
Southport
Merseyside PR8 4DJ
Tel: 0704 60221
Specialists in high quality traditional
and modern church ware.

F. Restall Ltd
Great Hampton Street
Birmingham B18 6AG
Tel: 021 551 6051
Speciality: furniture.

Silvercraft & Design Studios
14a Pears Road
Hounslow
Middlesex TW3 1SY
Tel: 01 570 9601/2
Speciality: church silver and plate.

Stonford Design Ltd
The Manse
Stamfordham
Northside
Northumberland NE18 0LA
Tel: 066 16 340
Speciality: fine quality wood altar
tables, folding pulpit, font, candle-
holders designed and manufactured in
Sweden.

Godfrey Syrett Ltd
Eagle Works
Killingworth Township
Newcastle-upon-Tyne NE12 0RJ
Tel: 0632 681010

Tracery
Unit L4
Liver Industrial Estate
Aintree
Liverpool L9 7ES
Tel: 051 521 3847
Speciality: church seating and cabinet
makers.

Tysons (Joinery) Ltd
PO Box 93
Dryden Street
Liverpool L69 5AA
Tel: 051 207 4949
Speciality: church benches and
woodwork.

Stonework and Bells

John Lowes & Sons Ltd
T/A Morris's Marbleworks
Market Lane
Whickham
Newcastle upon Tyne NE16 4TH
Tel: 091 488 7289
In business for the past 150 years,
experts in the use of marble, stone and
granite.

John Taylor & Co (Bellfounders) Ltd
The Bell Foundry
Freehold Street
Loughborough
Leicestershire LE11 1AR
Tel: 0509 212241
Deals with all aspects of church bell
work.

Whitechapel Bell Foundry Ltd
32–34 Whitechapel Road
London E1 1DY
Tel: 01 247 2599
Speciality: church bells.

The Handchime Company Ltd
Unit 4
Industrial Estate
Newton Abbot
Devon TQ12 6RF
Tel: 0647 40800

Heating

*Flo Rad Heating Systems (Underfloor)
Ltd*
Pipeline House
18 Theobald Street
Borehamwood
Herts. WD4 4OZ
Tel: 01 953 4065
Speciality: Underfloor heating.

Church Heating Services
Chilton Hall Farmhouse
Bury Road
Stowmarket
Suffolk IP14 3QA
Tel: 0449 612118
Supply tailor-made low-level radiant
heating panels to provide economic,
responsive comfort for the whole
congregation.

Drugasar Ltd
Deans Road
Swinton
Manchester M27 3JH
Tel: 061 793 8700
Installers of Drugasar heaters.

Frederick Greenwood and Sons Ltd
Belfield
Rochdale
Lancs.
Tel: 0706 38271
Installers of 'Quartz Ray' high efficient
radiant heaters.

Shelbourne Letheby & Co Ltd
154 New King's Rd
Fulham
London SW6
Tel: 01 736 4211/2
also 200 Trafford Rd
Eccles
Nr Manchester
Tel: 061 789 3850
General heating, ventilating engineers.

Clerical Outfitters and Vestments

Academic Robe and Gown
Manufacturers Ltd
201 Victoria Road
Lockwood
Huddersfield HD1 3TT
Tel: 0484 545459
Speciality: choir and servers robes and
cassocks.

Hayes and Finch
Hanson Road
Aintree
Liverpool L9 7BP
Tel: 051 525 7201
Other offices:
London 01 701 4186/7
Birmingham 021 773 9213/4
Huddersfield 0484 32778
Coatbridge 0236 27457
Gateshead 0632 402129
Also general church supplies.

House of Vanheems
Broomfield Works
6 Broomfield Place
Ealing
London W13 9LB
Tel: 01 567 7885
Speciality: clerical outfitters and church
suppliers.

McCauls
13 & 14 Cathedral Street
Dublin 1
Tel: Dublin (0001) 740460
Speciality: clerical tailors and
outfitters.

St Martin Vestment Ltd
Lutton
Spalding
Lincs. PE12 9LR
Tel: 0406 362386
Speciality: vestments and frontals.

Vanpoulles Ltd
1 Old Lodge Lane
Purley
Surrey CR2 4DG
Tel: 01 668 6266
and
1–6 Chalice Close
Lavender Vale
Wallington
Surrey SM6 9RU
Tel: 01 669 3121
Speciality: clerical outfitters and church
furnishings.

J. Wippell & Co Ltd
PO Box 1
88 Buller Road
Exeter EX4 1DG
Tel: 0392 54234

11 Tufton Street
London SW1P 3QP
Tel: 01 222 4528

24 King Street
Manchester M2 6AG
Tel: 061 834 7967
Speciality: clerical outfitters.

Church Supplies

J. Chandler & Co. Ltd
Abbey House
26a Peterborough Road
London SW6 3BP
Tel: 01 736 2185/6
Speciality: altar wine.

Delaunay & Co. Ltd
Marley Lane
Battle
East Sussex TN33 0RE
Tel: 0424 87602
Speciality: charcoal and incense.

Dumont Altar Breads
F. A. Dumont Ltd
High Steet
Lyminge
Folkestone
Kent CT18 8EL
Tel: 0303 863193
Speciality: altar breads and wine.

Eiren Candles Ltd
7 Union Drive
Boldmere Road
Sutton Coldfield
West Midlands B73 5TE
Tel: 021 355 4241
Speciality: candles, altar wine, incense, charcoal.

Exon Associates Ltd
Barclays Bank Chambers
22–23 Wellington Street
Teignmouth
Devon TQ14 8LP
Tel: 06267 3629/79277
An independent, clergy-run purchasing scheme for churches, which has made a breakthrough in sacristy supplies. The country's top three manufacturers/distributors of candles, wine and communion wafers are now working together to provide clergymen of all denominations with a comprehensive range of best quality products at a new low price.

Charles Farris Ltd
Bishopsgate Candle Works
Staines Road
Hounslow
Middlesex TW4 5DN
Tel: 01 570 1161
Speciality: church supplies, candles, wine, etc.

J. G. Ford & Son
Waterloo House
228–232 Waterloo Station Approach
London SE1 7BE
Tel: 01 928 9541 & 01 928 4851
Speciality: altar wine.

Hayes & Finch Ltd
Head Office: Hanson Rd
Aintree
Liverpool L9 7BP
Tel: 051 525 7201
General suppliers of church requisites.

E. Stafford & Co.
Lords Meadow
Crediton
Devon EX17 1ES
Tel: Crediton (03632) 2333
Suppliers of altar wine.

Tower Lamp Co. of London Ltd
Unit 4
St Margarets Way
Huntingdon
Cambs. PE18 6EB
Tel: 0480 50871
Manufacturers of liturgical candles.

Suppliers of Devotional Objects

CBC
Greenbank Industrial Estate
Newry
Co. Down
Northern Ireland

Goodliffe Neale
Arden Forest Industrial Estate
Alcester
Warwickshire
Tel: 0789 763261

Gortings of Ludlow Ltd
St Stephen's Hall
Upper Galdeford
Ludlow
Shropshire SY8 1QQ
Tel: 0584 2453

Ormsby of Scarisbrick
Woodland Works
542 Southport Rd
Scarisbrick
Ormskirk
Lancs. L40 9QQ
Tel: 0704 880294

Useful Publication
Church and School Equipment News
Crown House
London Road
Morden
Surrey SM4 5EW
Tel: 01 540 3897

Publications and Further Useful Addresses

General fabric
How to look after your Church, published for the Council for Places of Worship, 83 London Wall, London EC2M 5NA, by CIO Publishing, Church House, Dean's Yard, London SW1P 3NZ.
Stonework: maintenance and surface repair, A. D. R. Caroe and M. B. Caroe, published by CIO, as above.
The conservation of brick buildings, T. G. Bidwell, published by Brick Development Association 1977.

Heating
Heating your Church, William Bordass, CIO Publishing, Church House, Dean's Yard, London SW1P 3NZ.
Indoor Climate, D. A. McIntyre, Applied Science Publishers, 1980.
Heating and Air Conditioning of Buildings, O. Faber, J. R. Kell and P. L. Marting, Architectural Press, 1979.

Lighting and Wiring
Lighting and Wiring of Churches, L. King, P. Jay and R. Macdonald, CIO, Church House, Dean's Yard, London SW1P 3NZ.

Church Building Magazine
33–39 Bowling Green Lane
London EC1R 0AB
Tel: 01 278 7321
The object of the magazine is to provide a service to Roman Catholic and Church of England parishes giving them reference material where their building restoration, maintenance and alteration requirements are concerned, not only for their church structure but also for associated parish buildings.

Dial Publications Ltd
PO Box 249
Ascot
Berkshire SL5 0BZ
Tel: 0990 26394
Publishes *Maintenance and Equipment News*, giving updated news to church and school markets on these two areas.

Administry
69 Sandridge Road
St Albans
Herts. AL1 4AG
Tel: 0727 56370
The church administrator's resource centre.

Campbell, Smith & Co. Ltd
9/11 Cowper Road
Stoke Newington
London N16 8NY
Tel: 01 254 8551
Specialised in all aspects of
ecclesiastical decoration and period
restoration for over a century.

Churches Purchasing Scheme
Beaufort House
Brunswick Road
Gloucester GL1 1JZ
Tel: 0452 28533
The CPS is an interdenominational
body which publishes annually a
comprehensive purchasing and
information guide for Christians. The
objective of the CPS is to seek out
responsible suppliers of goods and
services who may be approached with
confidence in the knowledge that their
goods or services will be of a
satisfactory standard and that prices
charged will be fair.

Co-Aid Limited
Capital House
20/22 Craven Road
London W2 3PX
Tel: 01 723 1255/1276/1504
Co-Aid offers charities and Christian
organisations two differing services:
1. A buying service which considerably
reduces the cost of Charity
Administration. 2. By consolidating the
buying power of supporters of a
Charity, Co-Aid is able to increase the
level of donations.

Fellows and Ballard
37 High Street
Huntingdon
Cambridgeshire PE18 6AQ
Tel: 0480 53896
A partnership providing a consultancy
service offering advice on the financial
aspects of church buildings.

Public Address systems and Video equipment

Each church building is unique in its requirements. This makes it
virtually impossible to install a sound system as a do-it-yourself job;
the assistance of a local specialist for advice and a quotation, is
essential. If you have difficulty in locating a local person or require a
second opinion, the addresses below may prove useful. The listing
of a specialist company in no way constitutes a recommendation of
its services.

Amdio Ltd
Progress House
Albert Road
Aldershot
Hampshire GU11 1SZ
Tel: 0252 334121
Free advisory service on sound
reinforcement systems. Specialists for
sound in churches.

Centres for Audio-Visual Education
The Vicarage
Swine
Hull
North Humberside HU11 4JE
Tel: 0482 815250
Offers to local churches a newsletter,
working papers on local AV production
and presentation.

Christian Audio Vision Services Ltd
1 St Michael's Terrace
Wood Green
London N22 4SJ
Tel: 01 889 9371/2/3
Sound specialists, for discreet and
effective sound reinforcement in
church.

Christian Video Experience
6 Cecil Way
Hayes
Bromley
Kent BR2 7JU
Provides one of the largest selections of
Christian video programmes available
in the UK – for hire by mail order.

Christian Video Ventures
10 Weymoor Road
Harborne
Birmingham B17 0RY
CTV is a production organisation
making Christian video programmes
from concept to cassette.

*Coomber Electronic Equipment
Limited*
Croft Walk
Nr. Pitchcroft
Worcester WR1 3NZ
Tel: 0905 25168/9
One of the leading specialist
manufacturers of audio. Supply
equipment to the majority of education
authorities in the United Kingdom and
many in Europe.

*Creative Vision Productions and Gospel
Vision*
The Showroom
143 Toller Lane
Bradford
West Yorkshire BD8 9HL
Tel: 0272 41437/306089
Offers a postal Christian video library.

CTVC
Hillside
Merry Hill Road
Bushey
Watford
Herts WD2 1DR
Tel: 01 950 9426
Secretary:
Jack Allan.
Training in radio and TV techniques,
video production, studio facilities –
suitable for educational/discussion
groups.

*Cunnings Recording Associates/
Playbacks*
Broderick Hall
Broderick Road
London SW17 7DY
Tel: 01767 3533
Suppliers of video, audio and public
address equipment.

Delta Sound
Delta House
Levens Road
Newby Industrial Estate
Hazel Grove
Stockport SK7 5DN
Tel: 061 456 7171
Sound specialists in church and school
PA systems.

ICC Studios
Silverdale Road
Eastbourne
Sussex BN20 7AB
Tel: 0323 26134
This company provides a prompt and
personal service for record companies
and computer software houses and
smaller runs for schools and churches,
etc.

Keith Monks Ltd
Progress House
Albert Road
Aldershot
Hampshire GU11 1SZ
Tel: 0252 334121
Keith Monks, established in 1968, are
manufacturers, distributors and
installers of sound equipment.

Sound and Vision
1 Oldershaw Mews
Maidenhead
Berks. SL6 5HB
Tel: 0628 33011
A specialist team supplying expertise in the field of Christian technical communications, who are able to offer a free independent consultancy service.

Sound Cassette Services Ltd
PO Box 2
Chard
Somerset TA20 1LR
Tel: 0460 20988
Main dealers for cassette fast copying and recording equipment.

Trinity and Bagster Video
Westbrook House
76 High Street
Alton
Hants. GU34 1EN
Tel: 0420 89141
Trinity Video is a Christian video production-duplication house.

West London Electric (Acton) Ltd
9–11 High Street
London W3 6NQ
Tel: 01 992 2155
Wholesale distributors of public address equipment.

Further reading

Highly recommended is *Sound Amplification in Churches*, Jennifer Zarek, CIO Publishing, Dean's Yard, London SW1P 3NZ.

Other books which might be of value:
Acoustic Treatment for Places of Worship, William Allen, Ecclesiastical Architects' and Surveyors' Association, 1981.
Public Address Handbook, Vivian Capel, Keith Dickson Publishing.

Other Useful addresses

Association of Sound and Communication Engineers Ltd
47 Windsor Road
Slough
Bucks. SL1 2EE

Institute of Acoustics
25 Chambers St
Edinburgh EH1 1HU

Parish Planned Giving Campaigns

There are very few work activities in which the total novice is able to match, or even improve on, the results achieved by the professional. Yet this can certainly be the case today when a member of your church, known to the congregation, undertakes to conduct a Covenant Funding programme to increase your parish's Planned Giving income. There is much published material available to assist the novice campaign director, and the church member now has not only the support and understanding of the congregation but the best advice on what to do, how and when.

By far the most helpful development over the past decade has been the provision of financial and organisational models which allow the campaign director to plan the logistics of the seven-week exercise meticulously in advance and to predict with accuracy how the financial equation will be resolved. These models, with guidance of unusual precision for method and presentation, are contained in step-by-step guidebook form which is available to parishes of most denominations, from the address given below.

The Financial Model

One of the most significant planning tasks will be to identify policies and priorities and to define the consequent total financial need of the parish over the next four to five years. An average yearly direct-giving income requirement for the church can then be estimated. This forward budgeting needs to be very thorough and take full account of all regular outgoings, envisaged capital expenditure and/or reserves, outward giving to missions, charities, etc., and must, of course, include provision for year-by-year inflation.

The new parish income requirement figure and the size of your church membership can then be applied to one of the covenant programme's appropriate financial models. An accurate profile of the numbers/sizes of covenanted and pledged contribution needed will then be seen. Published as part of your campaign brochure, this 'giving profile' tells the membership exactly what they need to know and assists them to make an informed decision about the levels of their giving that will combine to achieve the new parish income requirement.

At the conclusion of the programme it will be found that the pattern of giving achieved reflects closely what was depicted in the parish's own financial model. Approaching the whole matter of giving/parish requirement in this way has brought new understanding and remarkable increases in planned giving incomes to parishes of every kind and size. Parishes undertaking the covenant funding programme find that approximately eighty per cent of those who participate in the scheme covenant their giving as a matter of course and that over ninety-two per cent of the parish's new planned giving income is covenanted. In the context of total direct-giving income, parishes should expect to receive at least twenty-five per cent of that amount in the form of reclaimed Income Tax.

It is essential that the parish keeps accurate records of every net payment received under deed of covenant so that the Treasurer is able to certify, when making the Tax claim to Inland Revenue, that the due sum has been received. This means that contributors under deed of covenant must use either identifiable Offering Envelopes, a Bankers' Standing Order or cheques when making their contributions – not loose cash in the collections.

The Organisational Model

It is necessary in the pre-campaign stage to prepare a plan of action, the detail of which will be sufficient to convey, first to the body of helpers who will implement the programme and later, by letter, brochure and home visit to all members of the congregation, why the programme is necessary, what it aims to achieve and how the campaign is to be run. Every aspect of the undertaking is expressed in brief subject papers: the organisation of helpers required; the sequence of meetings and their purpose; details of the forward budget and assessment of target; the pre-campaign and envisaged post-campaign giving situations; a detailed timetable of the activities by which at any time progress can be measured and monitored. In short, a purposeful coordinated effort with economy of time. In this way, even the largest parish can complete the exercise within the seven weeks of the programme.

Despite its title, increased covenanting is not the sole aim of the exercise. It is simply a part of an integrated method which reshapes the giving in a parish and which, simultaneously, increases the number who participate in planned giving, increases the standard of giving and increases the proportion of income which is covenanted. It sets the parish on a newly confident path of planned activity, unhampered by unstable or inadequate giving.

Further information is available from:

Mr W. G. Thwaite
Thwaite Funding Consultants
Mill Lane
Collingbourne Kingston
Marlborough
Wiltshire SN8 3SD
Tel: Collingbourne Ducis 617

The Registration of Charities

To qualify as a charity an organisation must be for the relief of poverty, the advancement of education, the advancement of religion, or for other purposes beneficial to the community, not falling under any of the preceding heads. The four heads enumerated above have been the subject matter of extensive judicial interpretation. Legal advice therefore is essential in the formation of any trust or organisation which it is intended to register as a charity.

Over 148,000 charities have registered with the Charity Commission. Charities, registered or not, are entitled to certain fiscal benefits such as relief from income tax, corporation tax, capital gains tax and rates. Applications and enquiries regarding relief from income tax, corporation tax or capital gains tax should be addressed to:

The Chief Inspector of Taxes (Claims)
Charities Division
Magdalen House
Stanley Precinct
Bootle 20
Lancs.

Rating relief application should be addressed to the relevant rating authority. More information may be obtained from the *Charities Digest* published by the

Family Welfare Asociation
501–505 Kingsland Road
Dalston
London E8 4AU
Tel: 01 254 6251

or from the

Charity Commission
14 Ryder St
St James's
London SW1Y 6AH

Grant Aid for Voluntary Organisations

Virtually every single government department is funding some part of the voluntary sector, which provides services or runs programmes relevant to its departmental policy concerns. For help consult *Government Grants, a guide for voluntary organisations*, obtainable from

NCVO
Bedford Square Press
26 Bedford Square
London WC1B 3NU

See also *The Directory of Grant Making Trusts*, Anne Villemur, 1985: Charities Aid Foundation Publications, 48 Pembury Road, Tonbridge, Kent TN9 2JD.

CHAPTER SIX

Pastoral Care

Pastoral care of the sick

Jesus, rich in mercy, identified himself with the poor and the sick. In the Incarnation Jesus became one with all humankind. It is an act of the love of God by which he wishes to draw near and make real a wonderful intercommunion of himself with us. It is the oneness with our wretchedness, our sinfulness that unites us to sanctify (2 Cor. 5:21). In the Beatitudes Jesus listed the poor, those who weep and who are persecuted, as the first in his kingdom (Luke 6:20–6, Matt. 5:3–12). The picture of Jesus with the sick is surprising and full of expression, of continuous acts of salvation.

The Gospel tells us that Christ went through all Galilee teaching and healing every sickness and pain. And this fame went before him and they brought to him all those who were suffering; those stricken by illness and pain, and those possessed by demons, the mentally ill and the paralysed, and he cured them (Matt. 4:23–5; 9:35). People wondered at him and exclaimed: 'Behold he has done all things well: He has made the deaf to hear and the dumb to speak' (Mark 7:37).

Yes, of course, the cures were many, but we also do well to consider the attitude of Jesus to the sick: gestures, words, silences. Jesus also felt emotion for his friends – Peter's mother-in-law (Luke 4:38); for Lazarus (John 11:3): 'Lord, he whom you loved is sick.' Then consider how Jesus stimulated faith and gathered people to him (Luke 5:17; 8:2): 'Several women who had been cured of their sickness followed him.' Jesus is attentive. He sees, touches, takes their hand, walks, halts (John 9:1–40). Ponder on how Jesus respects each one at his own level. The temperament of each one, and the sins of each (Luke 24:13–35). He does not judge, but welcomes all, he converts, encourages to change, helps to live (John 8:1–11; Matt. 9:18–26; 8:5–13).

Jesus cures, but to do it, to share, to make the sick whole, he meets them anew in their own place (Mark 1:40–5). Every cure is a promise from Jesus because it is a manifestation of his love and mercy (Matt. 11:28; John 5:5–9). Each cure is a sign of the coming of the kingdom, making its message ever clearer to us, each is a step forward to a total freedom, to when sickness will be no more (Apoc. 21:3–41). Always hope.

Jesus is not only attentive to the sick but also to their families. 'Do not weep', he says to the mother of the young man who has died (Luke 7:13), and to Jairus whose daughter was sick, 'Fear not, but believe' (Luke 8:50). 'Woman, your faith is great' to the Canaanite woman (Mark 15:28), and to Martha and Mary on the occasion of the death of their brother, 'Where have you laid him?' (John 11:34).

The Church is the continuation of the words and acts of Christ. It must fill the vacuum, go where nobody else goes. Where the state plays a role the Church must offer its collaboration in the field of health to bear witness to its presence alongside the sick. It must always remain its indispensable duty to carry out its specific pastoral role in continuing the work of Christ, to say a word, to make a gesture to all, but especially to the weak, the old, the sick. The whole history of the Church is marked by the care of the sick – saints, institutions, unknown individuals. And everyone has a responsibility – bishops, priests, religious, laity.

In 1985, Pope John Paul II set up a Commission for pastoral health care. It will be presided over by a cardinal. At the moment the pro-President is Archbishop Angelini. (See the Document below, page 160.)

Deeply involved in pastoral health care are, or should be, doctors, nurses, medical technicians, hospital administrators, and countless others. Besides the pastoral health care of the sick, the dying, the handicapped both physical and mental, and the aged, the pastoral health care of those employed in hospitals and health services in general must also receive proper attention.

Pastoral health care needs to be well organised with teams to deal with its various aspects. Training is necessary and today there are courses available. In hospitals a pastoral health care department should not be seen as something fitted into a makeshift office. It is just as important as the other departments.

W.B.

Further Reading

What is Pastoral Care of the Sick?, International Secretariat of Pastoral Care of the Sick.
Pastoral Care of the Sick in Hospital and in the Parish, Sick Order of St John of God.

For these and further information contact:

The Hospitaller
Order of St John of God
St Cuthbert's Hospital
Hurworth Place
Darlington
Co. Durham DL2 2BP

Christian Ministry to the Sick, Tom Coyle, ed., Geoffrey Chapman.
Pastoral Care of the Sick, Rites of Anointing and Viaticum, Geoffrey Chapman.
Prayer in Pain, Ian Williams, Grove Books. Explores how Christians pray in pain – a journey through despair to faith.
Prayer of the Sick, Joseph O'Mahony, ed., Geoffrey Chapman.

The Pontifical Commission for Pastoral Health Care

Document of Constitution by Pope John Paul II:
1. The keen interest the Church has always shown to those who suffer is well known. In this it has done nothing else but follow the example of its Founder and Master. In the Apostolic Letter *Salvifici Doloris* of 11 February 1984 I pointed out that 'In his messianic activity in the midst of Israel, Christ drew increasingly closer to the world of human suffering. He "went about doing good" and his actions primarily concerned those who were suffering and seeking help.' (No. 16)

The Church through the centuries has, in fact, strongly adverted to service of the sick and suffering as an integral part of its mission, and has not only favoured amongst Christians the various works of mercy but has also given birth to many religious institutes with the specific end of promoting, organising, improving and extending the care of the sick. Missionaries, too, in their work of evangelising, have constantly associated the preaching of the Good News with the assistance and care of the sick.

2. In its approach to the sick and the mystery of suffering the Church is guided by a precise conception of the human person and

its destiny in the plan of God. It insists that medicine and other curative therapies have as their aim not only the well-being and health of the body, but the whole sick person. Disease and suffering are experiences which concern not only the physical part of man, but man in his totality, in his psycho-somatic unity. It is a fact that sometimes diseases which are manifested in the body have their origin and true cause in the depths of the human psyche.

Disease and suffering are phenomena which, at their deepest level, always challenge medicine to reach the essence of humanity in this world (cf. G.S. 10). From this one can easily understand the importance in social/health services not only of the presence of pastors of souls but also of therapists who are guided by an integrated human vision of disease, and know how to approach in a thoroughly human way the sick person who is suffering. For the Christian, the redemption of Christ, and his saving grace, reach all of humankind in their human condition and therefore also redeem illness, suffering and death.

3. In civil society the social/health services have known, in recent years, an important and significant evolution. On the one hand, the recognition of the right of every citizen to adequate health services has become more widespread and as a consequence the structure of the services has been extended. On the other, countries, in the face of these exigencies, have set up ministries, passed legislation and adopted policies to aid health services. The United Nations has set up the World Health Organisation.

This vast and complex area directly concerns the well-being of the human person and of society. Precisely for this reason it also poses delicate and elusive questions which enquire not only into social and organisational aspects, but also ethical and religious aspects, because these connect fundamental events such as sickness, suffering and death with questions about the function of medicine and the doctor's mission as it affects the sick person. The new frontiers opened by scientific progress, and their possible technical and therapeutic applications, touch the most delicate limits of life at its source and in its most profound significance.

4. On the part of the Church, a profound and searching study of the ever more complex problems health workers have to face seems important, in the context of a greater collaboration between groups and their corresponding activities. Today there exist many organisations which engage Christians directly in the area of health care. Beside the religious congregations and institutes with their specific apostolate in health care there are organisations of Catholic

doctors, of para-medics, nurses, pharmacists, volunteers, etc., diocesan and interdiocesan, national and international, formed to face the problems of medicine and health.

There is a need for a better liaison between these organisations. In my Allocution to Catholic Doctors on 3 October 1982 I underlined this necessity: 'To do this an individual action is not enough. It requires a work which is at the same time intelligent, planned, constant and generous, not only in the framework of single countries, but also on an international scale. A coordination on a world level could, in fact, be considered a better announcement and defence of your Faith, your culture, your christian duty in scientific research, and your profession.' (*Teachings*, 1982, **3**, p. 674)

5. This coordination is to be understood in the first place as favouring and spreading a better ethical-religious formation of Christian health workers in the world, taking account of different situations and specific problems which they have to face in developing their profession. It will, then, better sustain, promote, and intensify the necessary studies, and thus improve the ability to deal with the specific problems of health care mentioned above, in the context of the true good of humankind. In this field there are many delicate and grave problems of an ethical nature, about which the Church and Christians everywhere should courageously and lucidly intervene in order to safeguard the values and rights essentially connected with the dignity and supreme destiny of the human person.

6. In the light of these considerations and supported by the opinions of experts, priests, religious and lay people I am disposed to constitute a *Pontifical Commission for the Pastoral Care of Health Workers*, which will act as a coordinating agent for all Catholic Institutes, religious or lay, which have as their apostolate the care of the sick. It will be associated with the Pontifical Council for the Laity, of which it will form an integral part while maintaining its own individual character and work.

The Hospital and the Parish

The parish as a community overlaps with many other communities within its midst. One such is the hospital community. If any priest or minister is serving a hospital as part of his/her duties it is important to hold constantly in mind that this ministry is done in the name of the Christian community and not as an individual. The Christian community is among other things a healing community and expresses this in a twofold way in hospital ministry. It does so by immediate service to those who are sick, through visiting, through specific sacramental ministry and simply by solidarity with those who are sick, handicapped or vulnerable in other ways that require some form of hospital treatment. The minister, ordained or lay, also has a ministry to those who are directly involved in treatment, research or ancillary support for those who are patients. This can be done by regular contact with those who work in the hospital system. It can be done by posing questions about ethical or industrial issues within the health context. Just as the hospital chaplain allocates time for those who are sick, so it is imperative to build into hospital ministry time for the support of those who work in the system.

Practical expressions

One way of expressing the sense of a community ministry can be through enlisting lay ministers. The chaplain becomes animator for these, their support and encouragement. If the hospital is serving a particular community – this is perhaps easier in rural areas than in the larger cities – then lay persons can be enlisted from the various localities from which patients come. They can be alerted when a patient from their 'patch' is in hospital and can act as a link between hospital and local Christian community, often not the same thing. How many patients see a chaplain while in hospital but have no follow-up ministry after discharge? Such lay ministers can visit in the name of the Church, bringing sacramental support where appropriate. They can be a support also to relatives and can enlist support within the community during hospitalisation and after discharge.

One way of expressing support for hospital workers, including nurses, ancillary staff, doctors and social workers, is to develop staff groups. Using a SEE-JUDGE-ACT method, questionnaires can be produced for use as discussion papers in workplace or groups, or simply as individual 'prodders' to stimulate people into thinking beyond the immediate problem. A wide range of issues can be covered, not always strictly religious but directed to humanising the health system. A story of a particular real situation – e.g. union dispute or ethical issue – can be given; two or three questions posed and some space for 'what would you do/what do we do now' type of response.

M.P.

Pastoral Care of Blind people

It is very easy when talking of the blind world to fall into the error of making generalisations about 'the blind', imagining that one can classify them as one would classify any other minority group. The only thing which the blind have in common is a negative attribute, the loss of vision. Apart from this one can find blind people in any section of the community. Some are blind from birth whilst others become blind later in life, through disease, accident or old age and of course, people vary enormously in the degree to which they are able to cope with the problem.

Another fact which is not generally realised is that many people who have been classified as blind do have a certain degree of vision, perhaps even being able to read the headlines in a newspaper. The criterion for blindness is that a person does not have that degree of vision which would enable them to do work for which sight is required.

Blindness is a blow, not to the eyes only, but to the whole person and in a sense there has to be a death to the old sighted world, and a resurrection to the blind world. Probably the greatest problem areas lie with the younger newly blind. For the older person blindness is often more easily accepted as part of the process of growing old and its effect is not so traumatic.

When a person in the prime of life goes blind they face a multitude of problems. He or she suddenly finds that they are separated from a great deal of human contact. They can no longer see their family, friends, the smile on a face, the look in the eyes of a loved one, they can no longer recognise people in the street by sight, private correspondence has to be read by another person unless they are writing in braille, and all this tends to isolate them, to make them feel a sense of a loss of human dignity, and a lack of love even by those close to them. The need for mature, understanding love is perhaps the greatest single need of any blind person. They need the assurance of acceptance, that their life still matters to other people, and they need the opportunity to show affection to others if they are not to grow bitter and disheartened.

Emotional insecurity is caused because all the relationships in life seem to be affected, and it is quite probable that it will mean loss of a job and uncertainty about the future. If he or she had been getting a high salary before it may mean a drop in standard of living, at least for a time. Physical insecurity arises because sight is normally the means by which one is orientated to one's surroundings. Sight reaches out to touch the objects around us to tell us where we are and to warn us of danger. It is the primary sense which rules all others, so that a sighted person who selects a coin from his pocket by touch will almost invariably check it by sight. When a newly blind person walks along the street their first impression may well be of disorientation, of not being quite sure where the next step will take them, and matters are not helped by the incredible variety of parking meters, tripods, prams and spiky corners on shops which impede passage along the pavement. It can be quite terrifying for a partially blind person to find hands groping out towards them from some well-meaning person who wishes to guide them across the road and has not taken the trouble to speak first.

Needless to say, one should always speak directly to a blind person and it is particularly important that a blind parishioner should be made aware of the presence of the priest if the priest is talking to others outside the church. 'Good morning, Miss Jones, Father Snooks here.' One cannot presume that the blind person knows of one's presence and a cheerful greeting can help to break that sense of isolation from which so many suffer.

Always treat a blind person as an individual, and if one is visiting regularly it is useful to discover whether they were blind from birth or newly blind, whether they use such aids as a white stick, guide dog or dark glasses to shade the eyes. Some people refuse to use these things because they feel that it marks them out too much, and causes more problems than they solve. Lack of their use may also betray a sensitiveness to his/her state on the part of the blind person, and it is well to be conscious of this. An over-sympathetic and condescending attitude is extremely depressing for a blind person.

Since Vatican II we have established parish councils, and it should not be difficult for a liaison officer to be appointed who would be responsible for the spiritual care of the blind members of the parish. The liaison officer could ensure that the blind parishioners were regularly visited, given guidance if necessary to Mass, and kept informed of meetings within the parish, talks, discussions and so on. He or she could also make sure that the blind parishioners were told of notices in the church porch and read the Catholic papers at the weekend. The liaison officer could be responsible for helping the blind to join such things as a Catholic Action group.

Perhaps this sounds rather a lot to demand, but there are likely to be only three or four blind people to a parish, and if the number is larger the probability is that they will be together in a hostel and may be dealt with in a small group for such things as the reading of a paper. Some blind people will need no help of this kind where it is already being provided by friends or relatives, but alongside these, there are many living in spiritual isolation, spiritually impoverished for want of a proper understanding of their needs. If the blind person is capable of doing so, he or she might even be encouraged to become a member of the parish council and make a valuable contribution to the life of the parish.

The Crusade of the Blind is a Catholic organisation producing a bi-monthly braille magazine. This is the only Catholic magazine in braille produced in England, apart from *Saint Cecilia's Guild Quarterly*, which contains informative articles of Catholic interest. The Crusade holds an Annual Quiet Day in London, and also a Christmas party.

The Bible Reading Fellowship notes are produced in braille and many Catholics may not be aware of the fact that they are encouraged to use these notes.

There is also an Association of Blind Catholics, which issues a bi-monthly bulletin, included with the *Crusade Messenger*. The objects of the Association are generally to enable blind people to take a fuller part in Catholic life and in particular:

> To supply information as to Catholic literature in embossed type and on what Catholic activities there are in various areas.
> To act as a clearing house for information concerning blind Catholics and their needs.
> To advise publishing houses as to required literature.

There are no special liturgical services for the blind for, on the whole, they are perfectly capable of joining in the usual services provided for the sighted, unless they have the added handicap of deafness, when special provision has to be made for someone to transcribe in the manual alphabet for the deaf-blind.

Let us repeat the warning that only a minority of blind people read braille, so the great need is for individual action within the parishes.

N.B.

The Torch Trust

It was in 1959 that Ron and Stella Heath felt called to bring the Christian message to blind people. Over the years the organisation known as the Torch Trust for the Blind has developed and the headquarters, situated in a large old mansion in Leicestershire, house some forty staff, blind and sighted, all working together to produce Christian literature for the blind worldwide.

Four thriving libraries daily send out all types of Christian material in the different media. There is braille for sensitive fingers which covers about fifteen per cent of the blind population; moon-type, a less widely used system of touch reading; giant print for those with a little sight, and tape, which is a very widely growing medium and is produced on both standard talking book and compact cassette.

Nine magazines are written or compiled, covering every need from children and teenagers to overseas readers and the deaf-blind. All this literature is available free and is sent post-free.

Capital or lower-case letters a quarter of an inch high form the giant print, and the whole of the New Testament and Psalms are available for purchase or loan. Other Old Testament books are being added. *Daily Light* daily readings are available in large print and braille. Also in braille are the hymn books *Keswick Praise* and *Mission Praise*, together with many scriptures. Small devotional booklets and tracts, covering a wide aspect of the Christian life, are obtainable in braille and large print.

Foreign braille is an important feature of the work and scripture portions are produced in many languages including Russian.

Tapes for long loan or purchase include *Daily Light*, much of the Bible, music tapes produced by the Torch Choir (purchase only); and Scripture Union *Daily Bread* readings (on loan only with nominal initial cost).

Together with literature for the blind, Torch Trust also provides fellowship in different ways. Several houseparties are held throughout the year at Torch House in Leicestershire, while 'Little Torch' in Sussex is open most of the year for individual holidays or the opportunity to join in houseparties at Easter or Christmas. The houseparties cater for all ages.

Around the country a growing number of Torch Fellowship Groups meet once a month, where blind and sighted people get together for Christian fellowship. Each group is run by a committee who organise transport, tea and a varied programme. Blind people are visited during the month if there are sufficient sighted helpers in the Fellowship.

At Torch House a year's course exists called Christian Service Training. It is for those blind folk under 30 years old who want to make something of their lives for God. Concentrated Bible teaching, communication and living skills figure prominently on the course with an opportunity to develop musical, craft, drama or writing talents.

Two books have been written by Stella Heath on the growth and work of the Torch Trust, called *The Torch Family* and *Where There is Vision*. These and full details of all the literature and amenities available can be obtained from:

The Torch Trust for the Blind
Torch House
Hallaton
Market Harborough
Leicestershire LE16 8UJ

M.M.

Services for Blind people

The Royal National Institute for the Blind (RNIB)
224 Great Portland Street
London W1N 6AA
Tel: 01 388 1266
The RNIB promotes and facilitates education, training, rehabilitation, employment and welfare of blind people and provides special schools, homes, training establishments, a wide range of industrial and recreational appliances and braille publications.

The Royal Commonwealth Society for the Blind
Commonwealth House
Haywards Heath
West Sussex RH16 3AZ
Tel: Haywards Heath (0444) 412424
Sponsors medical teams to treat eye diseases.

Guide Dogs for the Blind Association
9–11 Park Street
Windsor
Berks SL4 1JR
Tel: Windsor 55711
The Association has 5 training centres where blind people who wish to apply for a guide dog can receive the necessary training.

Association of Blind Catholics
58 Oakwood Road
Horley
Surrey RH6 7BU
Secretary:
Mr P. Questier

British Wireless for the Blind Fund
224 Great Portland Street
London W1N 6AA
Tel: 01 388 1266
Any registered blind person who is in need of a radio can obtain a portable VHF receiver from the above address. A television licence may be obtained by any registered blind person at £1.25 below the standard rate.

St Cecilia's Guild for the Blind
Rosary Priory
Elstree Road
Bushey
Herts WD2 3RJ
Secretary and Librarian:
Sr Perpetua Griffin OP
Cassette lending library.

National Library for the Blind
Cromwell Road
Bredbury
Stockport SK6 2SG
Books may be borrowed free.

The Partially Sighted Society
(incorporating the former Society for
the Visually Handicapped)
Breaston
Derbyshire DE7 3UE
This Society provides information on
aids, careers and equipment available
to partially sighted people.

St Dunstan's for Men and Women
Blinded on War Service
12–14 Harcourt Street
London W1A 4XB
Tel: 01 723 5021
St Dunstan's provides training,
resettlement and after-care for men
and women blinded on active service
with the armed forces, or with civil
defence services, e.g. police and fire
service.

Pastoral care of deaf and hard of hearing people

About one person in twenty suffers a severe hearing loss, for which
a hearing aid can at best only provide a partial solution for some.
The greater handicap, however, is often that this identification of a
person as deaf or hard of hearing tends to distract from the abilities
and attributes which make that person the individual he or she is.
Thus deaf people are frequently overlooked as people who, having
received the gifts of the Spirit at baptism and confirmation, are full
members of the Christian family with a contribution to make as well
as with particular needs. Deaf people do not need to be enabled to
belong; they are already members. However, because deafness
creates problems of communication, we all need help to understand
one another so that we may live and grow together as members of
the Christian family, deaf and hearing.

The difficulties experienced when the deafness is profound and
present before speech is learnt, and those when deafness has occurred later in life, are very different and it is important to appreciate
that there is a very wide range of handicap as a result, for which no
set of guidelines could be exhaustive. For deaf and hard of hearing
people themselves, the communication problems are ever-present,
affecting almost every area of life, and often making solutions very
difficult even to seek. Hearing people suffer the effects of deafness
too, when it is present in relatives, friends, colleagues or in the
community, which may be deprived of the contribution and insights
of hearing-impaired members. The following guidelines, therefore,
are offered as aids for the whole community, deaf, hard of hearing
and hearing.

Parish Worship

Deafness in the community challenges all who are involved in
liturgy and celebration to communicate more clearly for everyone.

Words, of course, play an important part in worship, but the concepts they express are more important and these should be communicated in every possible way, reflected in the setting, the props, movement, gesture and expression of celebrants, readers and assistants. Visual communication, whether intentional or not, often has more impact than words, however well expressed. Whether the Gospel can be heard or not by some of the congregation, it can still be apparent that God's presence through his word is being celebrated. For the hard of hearing, as well as the hearing, a well-designed and maintained public address system is essential, and a loop system will enable hearing-aid wearers to tune in, without the interference of background noise which often makes the use of a hearing aid impossible in a public place. Well-planned lighting can also enhance communication and ease concentration for lip-readers and others. Many profoundly deaf people have associated speech and language difficulties, which make communication a particular problem for themselves and others. There are in some areas and churches special priests or ministers trained in sign language and the problems associated with deafness. Sometimes these services are provided from a Mission for the Deaf and in other places they are developing through the community and structures of the local church. When the eucharist is celebrated in both 'word and sign', enabling deaf and hearing people to worship together, the experience is often both moving and enlightening for everyone. It is then that the rich contribution of deaf people from their life and language is most appreciated.

Parish Life

It is in the community that the effects of deafness are felt most acutely. Meetings of any sort, business or social, tend to emphasise the handicap; isolation or withdrawal alleviates it. There are, however, many activities in which the deaf or hard of hearing person need not be disadvantaged, and it is important that, though he or she may not be able to take an effective part in parish council or similar meetings, someone should represent the contribution and special needs of hearing-impaired people, for the benefit of everyone. Alternative forms of communication should be provided as a matter of course for those who cannot easily follow spoken announcements.

Hearing-Impaired Children

Even children who have the greatest difficulty in communication can be properly instructed and prepared for sacramental life in the church community. Though specialist teachers in this field are not yet available in every part of the country, there has been considerable work and development in religious education for deaf and partially hearing children, and church authorities should be urged to make this provision available wherever it is needed.

P.S.

Useful Addresses

For Catholic services throughout the United Kingdom:

The Association for Catholic Deaf of
Great Britain and Ireland
c/o Henesy House
104 Denmark Road
Manchester M15 6JS

For Church of England services:

The General Synod Council for the
Deaf
Church House
Dean's Yard
Westminster
London SW1P 3NZ

For general information concerning deafness, and national and local social, educational and voluntary services for deaf and hard of hearing people:

The Royal National Institute for the
Deaf
105 Gower Street
London WC1E 6AH
Tel: 01 387 8033
The RNID publish an annual
information directory listing all services
and facilities for deaf and hard of
hearing people as well as leaflets
explaining the Inductive Loop System
and other aids. The Institute also
houses a library service covering all
aspects of hearing impairment.

Services for Deaf and Hard of Hearing people

The Breakthrough Trust: Deaf–Hearing Integration
Charles W. Gillett Centre
Selly Oak Colleges
Birmingham B29 6LE
Tel: 021 472 6447
The aim of the Trust is to integrate deaf with hearing people by means of self-help groups.

The British Association of the Hard of Hearing
7–11 Armstrong Road
London W3 7JL
Tel: 01 743 1110
The Association promotes the formation of local groups. Also provides a wide range of education, cultural and social activities.

The British Deaf Association
38 Victoria Place
Carlisle CA1 1HU
Tel: Carlisle (0228) 48844
The Association organises a variety of group activities for deaf people and is able to advise individuals and parents on development and education.

National Deaf Children's Society
45 Hereford Road
London W2 5AH
Tel: 01 229 9272/6
This is an organisation for parents of deaf chldren which aims to improve and advance the arrangements for the education of deaf and partially hearing children.

The National Deaf-Blind Helpers' League
18 Rainbow Court
Paston Ridings
Peterborough PE4 6UP
Tel: Peterborough (0733) 73511
The League provides social activities for the deaf-blind in local groups.

The National Association for Deaf-Blind & Rubella Handicapped
164 Cromwell Lane
Coventry CV4 8AP
The Association gives advice about financial and educational problems and support to parents.

Pastoral care of physically disabled people

Many people do not grow to their full stature as Christians – because they have never personally realised the challenge of the Gospel and have consistently undervalued their own potential or it has been undervalued by others. This applies especially to groups who are thought to be powerless and frequently includes disabled people, whose handicap may be aggravated by low self-esteem or by the able-bodied underestimating their true ability, combined with a lack of concern about provision of opportunity and equal rights.

It is important to be clear about terms:

To be disabled means to suffer a loss or reduction of functional ability.
A handicap is the disadvantage or restriction of activity caused by a disability.

The distinction between *disability* and *handicap* is important and it is clear that not all disabilities need cause handicap. Handicap simply refers to the impact of a disability on specific areas of functioning.

There are, however, three factors, all capable of some amelioration, which help to turn disability into handicap.

The physically disabled person's own attitude

Disabilities affect people mentally and emotionally very differently, depending upon personality, outlook on life, degree of disability and experiences. One often finds that someone who is only slightly disabled is capable of leading a fully active life, but resentment at being classed as handicapped affects their actual degree of activity unduly. Equally, there are severely disabled people who will rise above their problems and lead a very active life.

The attitude of others

In considering the problems of a disabled person we must be aware that it is often the attitudes of the 'able-bodied' that cause or exacerbate the degree to which a disabled person experiences handicap. Able-bodied people are often embarrassed by disabled people, not knowing how to relate to them and often assuming a greater level of handicap than actually exists. If movements of the person are ungainly or speech is impaired, the assumption that the person is also mentally handicapped is often made.

Practical problems

The range of practical problems experienced by disabled people is vast. There is the whole range of sensory disabilities: people who cannot see what is written, who cannot hear what is said, who cannot say what they feel and know. Problems may be experienced with a whole host of daily activities, such as dressing and eating.

Many disabled people experience difficulties with mobility. Mobility, even when possible, can be difficult, painful and slow, needing enormous effort. The disabled person may be immobilised by the environment, e.g. lack of appropriate access to the church or parish centre. Access, however, is much more than a matter of ramps. Access includes suitable stairs and rails, appropriate floor coverings, bench construction, altar rails, lighting and effective PA and loop systems, as well as handy toilets which have space for a wheelchair.

The emotional impact of disability

There are a number of problems of an emotional nature inherent in disability. The way loss or impairment of functional ability is caused can and does have an impact on the nature of emotional problems. The cause of loss or impairment can usually be placed in one of four categories:

1. Congenital: this refers to those people who are *born* with a physical disability.
2. Traumatic: this refers to the sudden and irretrievable loss of some form of functional ability by a normal healthy individual. Such loss normally occurs as a result of an accident, and less commonly as a result of illness.
3. Progressive: this refers to the slow but nonetheless irretrievable loss of some form of functional ability. The onset can be slow, the progress and extent of the disability uncertain.
4. Old age: this refers to the disability all of us will experience, to a greater or lesser extent, in old age. It may be loss or impairment of sight or hearing, pain or weakness that slows us down, or defects of the heart, lungs, digestion, or other organs which curtail activity.

It is impossible here to examine in detail each and every aspect of the emotional impact of disability. It is however possible to provide an overview using the following three broad headings and relating them to the cause of disability:

1. Coping with loss.
2. Interpersonal relationships.
3. Sexuality.

The emotional impact of disability caused by old age is not mentioned in the following section but is likely to be similar to that caused by progressive disability. The numbers involved however are substantial, since the majority of physically disabled people are 65 or over.

Coping with loss

1. Congenital disability: loss here affects both parent and child. For parents it is the loss of the perfect child they may have been expecting. This sense of loss may manifest itself in feelings of disappointment, anger, guilt, shame, denial and bitterness. Development and increasing awareness may result in the child experiencing an increased sense of rejection and loss with the realisation of what may not be, or might have been – be it freedom, independence, home,

family, spouse, job, etc. Relative to the intensity of these experiences, self-image and self-esteem may be correspondingly low.

Some parents with support and help reach a great degree of acceptance and encourage the children to grow up as normally as possible.

2. Traumatic disability: loss here affects one's self-image and the inability to do things that were once possible, together with the shattering of future plans. All too often there may follow the loss of girl/boyfriend or spouse. Friends and relatives will also experience a sense of loss. There is need to support not only the disabled person but also the whole family.

3. Progressive disability: here the sense of loss is similar to that of traumatic disability, but much more insidious; it is an experience of gradual loss. A gradual loss of hope, of future, of the ability to plan, aggravated perhaps by the fear of losing one's spouse and the loss of self-esteem. The gradual process of erosion of one's previous life, the giving up of job, hobbies and social life. Friends and relatives will also experience a sense of loss and will need assistance to cope with an ever-changing situation.

Interpersonal relationships
This simply refers to the ability and capacity to establish and maintain relationships with other people. Relationships are affected both by the attitudes of the able-bodied to the disabled and by the disabled person's own feelings of self-worth.

For a person suffering from a congenital handicap the early formative years will be critical. It is, however, the early years that are amongst the most difficult for parents of handicapped children. Parents experience a whole range of emotions when confronted with the knowledge that their child is handicapped. Amongst these emotions are feelings of guilt, anger, denial and rejection. Establishing a truly loving relationship with the child may be further hampered by frequent and lengthy periods of separation resulting from the need for regular hospitalisation. Parents may grow to be over-protective of their child or unable to offer sincere warmth and love but nonetheless offering a high standard of physical care. All of these factors will have a profound influence on the child's emotional development and ability to establish and maintain relationships with other people.

For a person disabled by trauma or illness, the emotional impact is just as severe. In particular the assault on one's own self-image can be devastating, placing enormous strains on relationships with friends and relatives. The disabled person's sense of worth will be critical in forming relationships with others.

Sexuality

A disabled child is likely to receive help and support in many aspects of life; however, a young person's sexuality, needs and drives, is an area frequently overlooked. The young person's sexual development will probably be normal, but will bring with it a whole lot of conflicting feelings. In some instances the physical development will be ignored, with other people and even parents believing that the child is younger in terms of physical development than their actual chronological age. There will be feelings such as 'it doesn't happen to disabled people', 'they don't get married', 'it's better not to think about it'.

As the years pass, issues such as the possibility of marriage will arise. Is the ability to engage in normal sexual relationships a pre-requisite to marriage? If child-bearing is impossible, how should a couple cope with this? If physical disability precludes normal sexual activity (deformity or excessive spasm), is there some way to overcome this?

The problems experienced by a person disabled through trauma or illness are equally complex. The disability can bring about impotence, make sexual intercourse physically impossible or difficult, and place a tremendous and often unbearable strain on relationships and remove the possibility of a couple having children.

The challenge of the Gospel

For a variety of reasons the religious formation of a disabled person is often curtailed both by difficulties in participating in the sacramental life of the Church and by difficulties in gaining access to basic religious instruction, spiritual guidance, or formation, or even merely getting to talk to a priest.

Many physically disabled children attend special schools in which they receive little or no religious education. Frequently, but not always, they do not come forward or receive an invitation to partake in parish-based programmes.

Religious formation continues throughout adult life, and this also presents particular difficulties for the disabled person, whether they live in an institution or in their own home. Many disabled people are unable to go on retreats and participate in study groups or prayer groups. This is not just a problem of transport and attitudes. Many disabled people are excluded and do not attend because they cannot hear, speak or see, because of incontinence, the need for a special diet or because of the need for help with washing, feeding, dressing and toileting. There is not only a need to cultivate an attitude of acceptance of the right of the disabled person to become fully involved in the life of the Church, which is passive, but also to cultivate the attitude that the 'able-bodied Church' has an obligation to seek out and involve their disabled brethren, which is active.

Priests and catechists may need to ask about the impact of a specific disability on a person, but the stress should be on a person's individual assets and abilities as opposed to what they cannot do. A disabled person, possibly not used to decision-making and parish involvement, may need warm and friendly invitations to participate in what is going on. A well-organised transport system will offer – maybe for the first time – the opportunity of choice which most able-bodied people accept as a matter of course. Consideration could be given to using a local institution or someone's home as a venue for meetings or talks. With regard to the sacramental life of the Church, one of the biggest difficulties is again the need for transport and subsequently the difficulty of access to some places of worship.

There are certainly no easy answers to achieving the full partition of disabled people in the life of the Church, but there is one point of particular importance. Physically disabled people need the encouragement and support to provide for *themselves* the momentum and the guidance to achieve their full integration within the Church. Living a life in which decisions are often made by others and choice is often absent, many have never been presented with the opportunities of ministering to others, including other disabled people. There is much untapped potential.

D.W.

Useful Addresses

Disabled Christians Fellowship
50 Clare Road
Kingswood
Bristol BS16 1PJ

Westminster Diocese Advisory Group
for Physically Disabled People
c/o Social and Pastoral Action
73 St Charles' Square
London W10 6EJ

Association of Carers
Lilac House
Medway Homes
Balfour Road
Rochester
Kent ME4 6QU

RADAR
25 Mortimer Street
London W1N 8AB

Pastoral care of mentally handicapped people and their families

We begin by imagining that we are giving to them, we end by realising that they have enriched us.

Pope John Paul II

The age we live in is not naturally kind to mentally handicapped people. Their dependence calls for community. Our world is split into little cells in which most prefer 'to keep themselves to themselves'. Mentally handicapped people need time to express themselves and to respond. Our world has little time; there are always so many things to do. Mentally handicapped people sometimes have difficulty in working things out. Our world is sophisticated and complex. Sometimes mentally handicapped people are not worldly useful. Our world thinks 'usefulness' is extremely important, and therefore disabled and sick babies are best left to die, or better, to be aborted if possible.

We are happier on the whole if we categorise and even this can do a disservice to people with a mental handicap, for it hides the richness of individuality among those thus labelled. Those who, with the help of others, have had the chance to speak for themselves resent the term anyway, and it is one we should always use carefully, at least adding the word 'people' to enhance, in a little way, the dignity of those we refer to.

Such people are those who for a variety of reasons have suffered damage to the brain either at conception, in the womb, at birth, or very shortly after birth. Occasionally a mental handicap is caused by illness during childhood or by an accident at any time in life. The damage can vary from the very severe to the negligible, and at this end of the spectrum, individuals blend into the population at large. There is no hard and fast cut-off point. For those who seek a definition one could say that mental handicap is a continuing disability of the intellect which is likely to slow down and interfere with normal growth, development or capacity to learn. It is therefore something quite different from *mental illness* and it is important not to confuse the two. This condition is not a continuing one and can frequently be treated and cured. Mental handicap cannot be treated or cured, but with skilled help a mentally handicapped person can learn and develop skills and talents without ever being able to reach the level of abstract reasoning.

When a child is born, the parents have no other thought than: 'Is the baby all right?' This is their only concern. The announcement then, or maybe later, that 'something is wrong' is a shock that can only be dimly imagined by outsiders. For several months that wonderful baby has been living in the parents' minds, and all the things that child is going to do and become. When the baby is born handicapped that child of the imagination – yet so real – dies, and the shock the parents experience is a type of grief. The mourning period may be long or comparatively short. It is never entirely avoided.

Pastoral care at this stage calls for compassion of the purest kind. There is little to say, but more can be done. The priest or parish worker who can take the baby in their arms, holding him (or her) warmly and lovingly, is speaking a thousand words. To sit with the parents and cry with them is sufficient. You know that that baby, made in the image and likeness of God, has a mission in the Church and in society and a role to play far exceeding his worldly value, but parents are scarcely ready for that yet. What they need is a presence which says 'I am with you' without words. Sometimes it is also a help to know others who have been in the same situation, and parent-to-parent counselling, even of an informal nature, may be most useful.

Today a new situation has arisen. The pregnant mother frequently undergoes pre-natal screening which may indicate that the baby in the womb has some form of impairment or disability. An abortion may be proposed or even recommended. What guidance can be given in this situation? Could you say, 'If your baby comes to term and is born handicapped the Church will be there'? There is a grave responsibility involved in making such a remark, but it pinpoints a crucial response to this dramatic situation. No church can campaign against abortion without living out the serious consequences of such a stand.

At all stages in the life of their son or daughter, parents need to be assured of the presence of the Church. Many say that a handicapped child means a handicapped family. Sometimes the pattern of life is smooth and the family will need no more pastoral care than any other. But more frequently than in other families, there will be crises where a sense of aloneness can arise. It is important therefore that those in a parish responsible for pastoral care know these families well, so that help can come through friendship without increasing the parents' sense of inadequacy and sometimes of guilt.

The pastoral care of the mentally handicapped person begins at baptism. If the baby is thus diagnosed at birth, he or she may well be baptised at the hospital, by priest, parent or nurse, even though there may be no immediate danger of death. If this is so, it is good practice to inform the parish priest of the home parish, to ensure not only appropriate pastoral care for the family, but also that the baptismal ceremony may be completed. The presentation of the baby in the church is a significant moment, and if the family are able for it, completion of the ceremonies at a Sunday Mass would be a wonderful opportunity to call upon the support of the whole parish community. If this is somewhat too ideal, then the ceremony needs to be as carefully celebrated as possible. At this early moment the handicapped baby is often presented as a tragedy and a problem. The priest, carefully using the child's name, needs to say that in the body of Christ every member has a role to play and that the child brings a gift which may only become clearer later on in life. In holding the baby the priest, the representative of Christ in a special sense, speaks a powerful non-verbal message.

Pastoral care is not solely the responsibility of the priest. Lay members can be involved in different ways, but in the early years the presence of the priest has a special significance. His attention to the handicapped child must not overshadow his love for other children in the family. Indeed it is good practice when he enters the home to greet the handicapped child only after greeting the other child first. It is easy for them to be pushed into the background and for resentment to simmer and grow. Through personal contact the handicapped child's relationship with the priest will grow, and this is important for his or her future spiritual development.

The mentally handicapped child will frequently be able to attend school from a very early age, even 2½ years or 3, but this may not be necessarily so. The mother may approach the priest to put the child's name down for the local Catholic school. She is saying that she wants her child to be treated like other children in the parish, and she wants him to receive education in faith. Whether or not the school is able to take this particular child – and there are good examples of such practice – is beyond our scope here. However, even in a special school the handicapped child of believing parents need not be outside the involvement of the Church.

Special schools nearly always welcome visits from the clergy and frequently involve them in assemblies and feast day celebrations. The priest's presence will encourage some teachers to ask about religious education, and children from his parish will identify with him if he has met them at church or in their homes. He will frequently discover after a time Catholic children whose parents may not be known to their parishes for any number of reasons. The fact that the priest goes into the school from time to time is the sign, especially for non-Catholics, of the Church's concern for handicapped people and their development.

In certain situations the priest will be able to initiate or encourage a link between the special school and the local Catholic school, especially if the former is situated in his own parish.

The word 'integration' is frequently heard today but it has many levels of meaning. Any links between the two schools can become part of an integrating process. To enable Catholic mentally handicapped children to share in any way, however small, is to share with them resources established by the Church, and in a sense a response to the call for justice. Coming in for a class Mass or on a feast day or simply to share in activities in class or playground is a part of integration. The priest, in his own right, and perhaps as chairman of governors, may be able to play a significant role in this.

As the mentally handicapped person approaches the teens and enters adolescence (even earlier for some), ways of involvement in parish life can be considered. Looking positively and creatively for opportunities for integration will seldom be ineffectual. Serving on the altar, assisting the ushers, singing in the choir, joining the youth club or other activities for young people have all been successfully undertaken by mentally handicapped people. Involvement may call for extra thought and maybe a friendly companion to walk alongside. It may require preparation so that others involved in the activity are welcoming and supportive.

From early on in their son's or daughter's life parents begin to be concerned about the future. They wonder who will care for their child when they can no longer do so. It is hard for them to be detached from this question. It is the one parents always come back to. At present, provision for residential facilities is provided by the health or social services, or the voluntary sector. It may be in a hostel, or more frequently now a group home, or in a hospital.

Those mentally handicapped people who live in a residential facility are in urgent need of the Church's pastoral care, not only on the level of faith, but also on the level of ordinary human and social interaction. This is especially important today with the government actively pursuing a policy of care in the community.

A local parish is in a unique position to make mentally handicapped people welcome in the local community. This is best done in an inconspicuous way through friendship on a one-family-one-resident basis. Catholic residents need to be invited to Mass and some may need accompanying. They will not automatically become involved in parish life unless invited and befriended. Creating opportunities for people singly or in pairs is much better than group activities. Good practice means enhancing the person's dignity and indicating that they are to be valued.

Some parishes have found it particularly useful to have a small group to coordinate pastoral care with mentally handicapped people and their families. Friendship is the key ingredient. This breaks down isolation and gives support to parents. It gives value and dignity to mentally handicapped people who in a sharing relationship are able to give as well as to receive.

D.W.

Useful Addresses

Faith and Light
Coordinator for England and Wales
Marie Durning
48 Narrow Lane
Hathern
Loughborough
Leics
An international and ecumenical movement with mentally handicapped people, their families and friends which seeks to create small communities where the gifts of each person can be readily shared.

Pastoral Office for Handicapped People
St Joseph's Centre
The Burroughs
London NW4 4TY
Tel: 01 202 3999
Publishes resources and books relating to pastoral care and religious education.

MENCAP (The Royal Society for Mentally Handicapped Children and Adults)
123 Golden Lane
London EC1Y 0RT
Tel: 01 253 9433
The Society aims to improve the provision for mentally handicapped children and adults especially by increasing public knowledge and concern.

The Shaftesbury Society
Shaftesbury House
2a Amity Grove
Raynes Park
London SW20 0LJ
Tel: 01 946 6635
This is an interdenominational Christian caring charity, maintaining eighty caring units. The Society cares for physically and mentally handicapped and those who are socially deprived.

L'Arche Communities

The following extract from the Charter of the Communities of L'Arche, expresses well the spirit and motivation of the L'Arche Communities:

We believe that each person, whether handicapped or not, has a unique and mysterious value. The handicapped person is a complete human being and as such he has the rights of every man; the right to life, to care, to education and to work.

We also believe that a person who has been wounded in his capacity for autonomy and in his mind is capable of great love, which can be called forth by the Spirit of God. We believe that God loves him in a special way because of his very weakness.

Because of his handicap and because he feels rejected, a wounded person may shock or repel. But given an atmosphere of security, where his latent capacities can develop, he can also radiate simplicity, welcome, joy and peace.

The world of suffering and the number of handicapped people rejected, denied work, or shut up in mental handicap hospitals causes deep anxiety. But this anxiety should not paralyse us. It should incite us to work for the rejected by creating communities of peace and to do all we can to encourage our society to develop a greater sense of justice and brotherly concern for all men.

L'Arche communities are havens of peace and security where people with mental handicap, and those society calls normal, live and work together. In each community it is a fundamental belief that each individual has something unique to offer and all can grow to a greater freedom in an atmosphere of love and respect. Neither material success nor intellectual achievement, so valued by the world, have any place in the building up of the L'Arche community.

Around the world there are some sixty communities in fourteen different countries. In each community, varying in size from 400 to a dozen people, approximately half of the residents are handicapped people and the other half are the assistants. These latter come from many countries and although of varying age, they are predominantly young. Some come for short periods but many commit their lives to making L'Arche their home.

There are five communities in the United Kingdom, addresses below, all of whom can supply more information about L'Arche. Or enquiries can be directed to the registered office at:

14 London Rd
Beccles
Suffolk NR34 9NH
Tel: 0502 715329

UK Communities of L'Arche

'Little Ewell'
Barfrestone
Nr Dover
Kent CT15 7JJ
Tel: 0304 830930

'Braerannoch'
13 Drummond Crescent
Inverness IV2 4HD
Tel: 0463 239615

'The Bridge'
127 Prescot Road
Liverpool 6
Tel: 051 260 0422

'Lambeth'
1 Dunbar St
West Norwood
London SE27
Tel: 01 670 6714

'Sea Rover'
4 Argyle Circus
Bognor Regis
West Sussex
Tel: 0243 863426

Some publications about L'Arche
The Challenge of L'Arche, Jean Vanier and others, Darton, Long-
man and Todd, 1982.
Enough Room for Joy, Bill Clarke, Darton, Longman and Todd,
1974.
L'Arche, Ann Shearer, Daybreak Publications, Richmond Hill,
Canada, 1976.
These and books by Jean Vanier, founder of L'Arche, can be
obtained from:

'The Wedge'
11/13 Norwood High St
London SE27
or one of the St Paul Book Centres,
details on pages 115–22.

Pastoral Care of Alcoholics

Of all people who drink alcohol, some ten per cent are likely to
become addicted, that is, to become 'alcoholic'. It follows, therefore, that any member of the clergy engaged in pastoral work will
inevitably come across this distressing illness, either directly,
through contact with the drinker, or indirectly, through the dis-
astrous effects of the malady on the drinker's family.

Pastoral care of the alcoholic will begin with learning about
alcoholism – its symptoms, manifestations, progress, social implications, and so on. Such information is freely available from organisations such as those listed below, and many libraries have useful
books on the subject. Having acquired this basic knowledge, it then
becomes possible to approach the sufferer with genuine understanding and compassion, rather than the frustration and impati-
ence which the alcoholic personality frequently – and understandably – provokes in the less well-informed.

Whilst the clergy can offer spiritual support and general counsell-ing, it should be remembered that alcoholism is a specialist subject, and the sufferer should therefore be directed towards such help as may be available in the immediate locality. Alcoholics Anonymous is the best known and most widely available source of help, but although great numbers of alcoholics have recovered with AA, it should be noted that there are many sufferers for whom AA does not provide the answer, often because the individual is unable to accept group sharing of the problem, as practised by AA. For these people, confidential, one-to-one counselling by trained profession-als is a welcome alternative, and clergy should have to hand in-formation on such services available in their area.

When initial contact occurs between the clergy and anyone with a drinking problem, it is important to remember that the drinker – in whatever light he or she may choose to appear – is a sick, sensitive, uncertain person with very low self-esteem. If this is borne in mind one is more likely to succeed in winning their confidence.

Very often, however, it is the family of the alcoholic who will initially seek help with the problem. Living with alcoholism poses a myriad of problems, ranging from severe financial hardship and its attendant stresses, to social isolation and disturbed children. Here again, spiritual guidance and general support are necess-ary, but preferably with the ultimate aim of finding the most acceptable form of specialised help, either confidential counselling, or the local Al-Anon Family Group; some areas will also have an Alateen Group (for young people who have an alcoholic parent).

In general terms, it is important in dealing with the family of the alcoholic to reassure them that they are in no way responsible for the alcoholic's drinking. Many partners and children of problem drinkers carry an inordinate amount of guilt and anxiety on this score, which only adds to the general stress and confusion. They need, too, to understand that they should not protect the drinker by 'covering up' for him or her, or by paying debts or in any way making it easy and comfortable for the drinker to continue drink-ing.

The following section lists helping agencies from whom informa-tion and advice may be obtained.

Alcoholics Anonymous
Refer to local phone directory or see
list below.

Regional Councils on Alcoholism
These exist in most counties and
Metropolitan areas. Consult your local
directory, e.g.
Avon Council on Alcoholism
14 Park Row
Bristol

*Westminster Advisory Centre on
Alcoholism*
38 Ebury Street
SW1W 0LU
Tel: 01 730 1574
(also at Purley, Kingston and
Guildford)

WACA specialises in one-to-one counselling and therapy, not only
for drinkers but also for their families, the latter often being as much
in need of help as the drinkers themselves. Vitamin therapy is used
to aid and speed up the patient's recovery. Individual needs are
assessed on a basis of detailed investigation with the aid of mineral
analysis. WACA also promotes a Schools' Education Programme
as well as a training programme for those wishing to help in the
counselling of alcoholics.

D.T.

Alcoholism, Drug Addiction and Gambling: Some care services available

Alcoholics Anonymous
Box 514
11 Redcliffe Gardens
London SW10 9BG
Tel: 01 352 9779/9669
or refer to local telephone directories.
This organisation provides anonymous
groups throughout England and Wales
for the mutual assistance of alcoholics
and problem drinkers.

Al-Anon Family Groups
61 Great Dover Street
London SE1 4YF
Tel: 01 403 0888
This organisation offers group support
and friendship for friends and relatives
of problem drinkers.

Alateen
61 Great Dover Street
London SE1 4YF
Tel: 01 403 0888
This organisation is part of Al-Anon
and gives help and support to teenagers
(aged 12 to 18) with a friend or relative
who is an alcoholic or problem drinker.

Alcohol Concern
305 Grays Inn Road
London WC1X 8QF
Tel: 01 833 3471

Alcohol Education Centre
Maudsley Hospital
99 Denmark Hill
London SE5 8AZ
Tel: 01 703 6333, ext. 40 and 01 703
8053

Churches Council on Alcohol and Drugs
4 Southampton Row
London WC1B 4AA
Tel: 01 242 2511
Secretary:
Mrs Beth Smith
The Council is an independent ecumenical forum where churches can exchange information to formulate the churches' approach on alcohol and drug use and support present practical responses and encourage their expansion.

Medical Council on Alcoholism
1 St Andrew Place
London NW1 4LB
Tel: 01 487 4445
This is a voluntary organisation which is concerned with the education of the medical profession on all aspects of alcoholism and problem drinking.

Turning Point
CAP House
9–12 Long Lane
London EC1A 9HA
Tel: 01 606 3947
This organisation aims to help rehabilitate drug addicts and alcoholics.

Standing Conference on Drug Abuse (SCODA)
1 Hatton Place
London EC1
Tel: 01 430 2341
SCODA was established in 1971 to coordinate the work of the voluntary agencies in the drugs field.

Release
1 Elgin Avenue
London W9 3PR
Tel: 01 289 1123
24 hour emergency number: 01 603 8654
Release offers an advice and information service for people charged with drug offences.

Gamblers Anonymous
17/23 Blantyre Street
Cheyne Walk
London SW10
Tel: 01 352 3060
Helps compulsive gamblers stop gambling and return to a normal way of life.

Society of St Dismas
30 Cranbury Avenue
Southampton SO2 0LT
Tel: 0703 23443
Hon. Secretary:
K. J. Ovey
Caring for men with social and personal needs associated with alcoholism.

Pastoral care of drug addicts

Addicts must decide for themselves to give up drugs. This decision must not be for the sake of others, but for themselves. In St Luke's Gospel, it was only when the prodigal son was hungry and friendless that he made a decision to return to the father. Healing then began.

Lying, cheating and manipulation become part of the addict's everyday behaviour. They try to cover up their own low self-esteem and there is much self-hatred. About fifteen per cent try suicide and many others threaten to take their own lives.

If you suspect drug abuse, don't panic. Handle the situation calmly and do not challenge the person if they are under the influence of drugs. Wait until they are able to communicate; most abusers have trouble with communication, particularly with their families. They may be emotionally insecure, feel inadequate or cannot express themselves. Try and get the facts which you know to be true, facts that cannot be denied. For example, why the young person has new friends and why they are staying out late at night.

A young person's drug abuse can tear a family apart. But an attempt by parents and family members to rescue a child from drugs can strengthen and reunite a family. There is always hope. When you have your facts, whether the user admits or denies drug abuse, seek help from a professional agency.

It can take up to four years before symptoms of drug abuse are recognised. Behavioural changes include increased irritability, aggressiveness, an inability to concentrate and loss of interest in work or school, sports or hobbies.

Other signs of drug-taking are:

Selling possessions or stealing from home, to raise money;
Receiving threatening telephone calls (demands for money);
Lying about friends and activities;
Unfamiliar tablets or substances in the house;
Physical changes caused by hard drugs, including loss of appetite, slurred speech, pinpoint pupils, as well as constant examining of the arms;
Fidgeting, perspiring, flushed face, irrational laughter (usually just after taking drugs).

Remember that some changes in behaviour may be due to the normal process of growing up.

The following hospitals and clinics can offer immediate help and referrals to other drug addiction centres.

London
Charing Cross Hospital
Drug Dependency Unit
Aspenlea Road
London W6

Birmingham
All Saints Hospital
Lodge Road
Birmingham B18 5SD

Manchester
Prestwich Hospital
Prestwich
Manchester M25 7BL

Liverpool
Sefton General Hospital
Smithdown Road
Liverpool L15 2HE

Leeds
St James University Hospital
Beckett Street
Leeds LS9 9TF

Newcastle
Parkwood House Alcohol and Drug
Dependence Unit
St Nicholas Hospital
Gosforth
Newcastle NE3 3XT

Glasgow
Duke Street Hospital
255 Duke Street
Glasgow G31 1HY

Edinburgh
Royal Edinburgh Hospital
Morningside Terrace
Edinburgh EH10

Cardiff
University Hospital of Wales
Heath Park
Cardiff CF4 4XW

Belfast
Shaftesbury Square Hospital
116–118 Great Victoria Street
Belfast BT2 7BG

Dublin
National Drug Advisory and
Treatment Centre
Jervis Street
Dublin 1

Pastoral care of vagrants

There is hardly a priest up and down the country who, at times, doesn't question his approach to the caller at the presbytery door. He either feels that he cannot cope or that he has been fooled too often, and dismisses all without a hearing. Sometimes he errs in the name of charity and causes further problems. Experience teaches that those most in need hesitate to approach the presbytery or, for that matter, any charity. But there must be a Christian approach.

I believe that our first response must be one of welcome and openness. The caller is in need, whether it be of food or friendship, and the greater is his need when he seeks to extract money through false pretences. It is best to chat in the privacy of the waiting-room and write up a case history, if necessary. The information gathered will be of enormous help if another agency is to be approached. Discernment, too, is the key, for the approach to the 'regular' who seeks no more than a cup of tea and a sandwich, will differ from that to the person who claims that his Welfare benefit has not come through and he needs overnight accommodation. Records are important, and having an up-to-date index of local community services and agencies to hand is essential. A good working relationship with the officers of these agencies is vital. Some basic information on

Welfare and Unemployment benefits, and on the statutory obligations of the local council, will also be very useful.

How, then, can we help? As a rule of thumb, money should not
be given without a serious investigation of the circumstances. Giving money may lead to the person having to sleep rough because the
night shelters are barred to those under the influence of drink. The
money, too, could be used to buy a 'fix', punt on the horses and
dogs, play the gambling machine, or pay the rent of a fictitious flat.
Giving money at the presbytery door is often a quick way of getting
rid of the caller, and tantamount to saying that we are not interested. It may even be a conscience solver, but does it help the
individual?

The presbytery door is a school for learning. Behind that simple
request for a train fare to Dover or a loan until the Social Welfare
benefits come through is, perhaps, a life of loneliness and rejection,
a failed marriage, a mental breakdown or a long history of alcoholism or the like. Probe a little deeper and the revelation is even more
startling, for we find an ordinary human being – our brother or sister
– with a sense of humour and a spirit still alive, and with many gifts.
What a staggering experience it is to find oneself face to face with
the poor and on the receiving end! This chance meeting, which
should never be underestimated, may prove to be a moment of
conversion for the person seeking help and the helper – a moment
when the 'do-gooder' attitude is found wanting, and the Beatitude
'Blessed are the poor in spirit' explodes into meaning. I believe,
too, that we must work for the full restoration of this person into our
society. It is a two-way process in which the 'caller' must also be free
to make his/her personal contribution.

The interview over, what will it mean? For some, referral to the
Emergency Social Security Office, the nearest drug or detoxifica-
tion unit; for others, a meal by arrangement with a local café or a
night in a Salvation Army hostel or a Reception Centre. Some can
be helped through the local Conference of St Vincent de Paul or
other welfare groups. There will be very many who cannot be
helped because they do not wish to be helped – the sole reason for
their visit was the extraction of money. In all cases, we will have
tried and that is important.

The demands made at the presbytery door today are such that the
task of responding is often quite beyond the priest. The situation is
aggravated by high unemployment, poor housing, and the plight of
so many in our communities who are under stress. Care of the poor
is the joint responsibility of the Church, the government, and the

community at large. It is essential that each parish community with its priest has an established approach to the poor, whereby the caring mission of the Church is seen in action. In most cases, this will mean not only working with the voluntary and statutory bodies and other caring groups, but also becoming initiators where new needs are identified.

Handouts, either in money, clothing or food, are not the answer. Poverty is evil, and the Church must be careful not to perpetuate it through ill-advised, though well-intentioned, actions. Solutions don't come easily and often come from the poor themselves, with our help. The work is fraught with all sorts of difficulties but, strangely enough, many of these arise within ourselves – in our attitudes and motives, our inhibitions and hang-ups. We must be careful not to unload our problems on people already overburdened.

Giving ourselves to the poor is the most marvellous work on earth, for there we can be truly ourselves – rid of pretensions and notions of superiority, helpless in the face of the immensity of the problem but alive to new possibilities. To know and accept them as brothers and sisters is to have a solidarity with them and with Christ, our brother. To give to them is to give to Christ; to receive from them is to receive from Christ. This is what it is to be poor among the poor.

With insights such as these, the poor claim a new place in our lives, at the presbytery door and elsewhere, and the defeat of poverty takes on a new urgency and our motivation demands a daily scrutiny.

P.O'D.

Accommodation for the Homeless: Useful Addresses

Catholic Housing Aid Society (CHAS)
189A Old Brompton Road
London SW5 0AN
Tel: 01 373 4961
Housing advice to anyone in need, regardless of race or religion. CHAS urges individuals and groups to 'Invest in Social Justice' by making loans at low rates of interest to support work with the homeless.

Church Housing Association
Welford House
112A Shirland Road
London W9 2BT
Tel: 01 289 2241
Director:
Peter Naish
National housing association linked to the Church of England. Housing families, the elderly and single people.

The Catholic Fund for Homeless and Destitute Men
St Martin of Tours House
162 New North Road
London N1 7BH
Tel: 01 226 7516
Director:
Martin Curran
Caring for homeless and destitute men who suffer from mental and/or emotional disorders.

The Housing Campaign for Single People (CHAR)
5–15 Cromer Street
London WC1H 8LS
Tel: 01 833 2071
This service has been set up in various cities to provide overnight accommodation for those unable to find it elsewhere.

The National Association of Voluntary Hostels
33 Long Acre
London WC2
Tel: 01 836 0193
This association is concerned with the residential care of the homeless and offers a placement service to social workers, probation officers, etc., who are seeking accommodation for homeless single clients.

Shelter
157 Waterloo Road
London SE1 8UU
Tel: 01 633 9377
Advisory Service for Squatters:
2 St Paul's Road
London N1
Tel: 01 359 8814
The above addresses will lead to further information connected with squatting.

Simon Community
St Joseph's House
129 Malden Road
London NW5 4HS
Tel: 01 485 6639
Secretary:
Oonagh H. Gaye
Ecumenical, but Catholic inspired, grass-roots community working with homeless and rootless people from the streets of London.

Pastoral care of prisoners and their families

'Remember those in prison', urges the author of Hebrews, 'as if you were their fellow prisoners' (13:2). This 'remembering' – a truly Christian remembering always leads to action – takes many forms.

First of all there is *Prayer* – for prisoners, for their families, for prison officers and staff. This way of 'visiting him in prison' is within the scope of everyone. Wherever there is a penal establishment, the Christians of the locality ought regularly to hold up in prayer before the Lord that institution and those who live and work there. The Guild of St Leonard (enquiries to Mrs A. Raymond, Hound Street, Sherborne, Dorset DT9 3AA) has as its purpose 'to pray for all prisoners, those on licence, or probation and all who care for them'. Many prison chaplains have their own prayer lists which they circulate to interested people and most of the Carmelite convents in the country are actively engaged in prayer for the imprisoned.

Next to prayer comes the *formation of public opinion*. In a society where many voices are raised to foster a punitive and vengeful attitude towards wrong-doers, Christians have an important contribution to make, which while sensitive to the sufferings of the victims of crime is also inspired by the Gospel ideals of compassion and forgiveness, and based upon the intrinsic dignity of every human being. It needs to be a well-informed contribution, and publications like *Prisons and Prisoners in England Today* by the Church of England Board of Social Responsibilty and *A Time for Justice* by the Catholic Social Service Welfare Commission may prove very helpful in this respect. An ecumenical 'Prisoners' Week' is now held each year in November with the aim of sensitising Christians and all people of good will to their duties towards the imprisoned.

'Remembering those in prison' leads some Christians to more *direct action* in three particular areas:

Helping Prisoners Themselves

In the forefront are the *Chaplains*. A Church of England, Roman Catholic and Methodist Chaplain is appointed to every penal establishment. This book does not offer advice to a clergyman who undertakes this work because, happily, his needs will be adequately met: first, by the support he will receive from a senior chaplain; second, by the *Prison Service Chaplaincy Handbook*, drawn up with the needs of new chaplains specially in mind; and third, by an Induction Course, available to new recruits within the first eighteen months of their service.

The ministry of chaplains can often be enriched by at least occasional *Pastoral Visits* made by parochial clergy to their parishioners in prison. Such visits, arranged through the appropriate chaplain, take place whenever possible in the privacy of the chaplain's office and do not count against the number of official visits an inmate is allowed.

Many chaplains are assisted in their work by lay people and/or religious Sisters:

1. as *Voluntary helpers* who undertake a wide variety of services, from running religious discussion groups to pastoral cell visiting.
2. as *Prison Visitors* who befriend prisoners by visiting them in their cells on a regular basis.

3. as *Organists* providing music for services and often helping to run a choir.

4. as *members of organisations*, such as the Church of England Men's Society or the St Vincent de Paul Society, who have traditionally been involved in the prison ministry. Another interdenominational organisation which has recently appeared is Prison Fellowship, whose members meet together for prayer and are available to help the chaplains in any ways that are deemed appropriate. Their address is:

Prison Fellowship
PO Box 263
London SW1
Tel: 01 582 6221

(It is vital to stress that not everyone is suitable for work in prison. That is why it is recommended that prospective volunteers should in the first place seek the advice of a local prison chaplain.)

Helping Prisoners' Families

When a man or woman goes to prison, they are seldom alone in paying for their crimes: their families suffer also. Indeed, prisoners are usually the first to admit that the suffering of their families – left, for example, without a bread-winner and/or parent – is even greater than their own.

There are organisations like the St Vincent de Paul Society and the Catholic Social Service for Prisoners who have considerable experience and expertise in visiting and helping such families in a variety of ways: e.g. counselling, assisting the family to visit, etc. Individuals also may be able to offer support, provided always that they do so with prudence and sensitivity. Not all families wish to be visited or to be helped, though at the same time it is tragic to hear of cases where families have been ignored and even deliberately shunned, sometimes by fellow-parishioners, because one of their members is 'inside'.

Helping Prisoners on Release

The period following upon release is sometimes experienced as more painful than imprisonment itself. The ex-prisoner needs work, he may need accommodation. If he has a home to go to, he has to reinstate himself with his family and be accepted by society. In all these areas the Christian community may have a useful contribution to make, though once again it must do so discreetly and with respect for the individuals concerned.

Information about the many agencies which are involved in aftercare for prisoners can be found in diocesan directories or other handbooks, such as the *Directory of Projects* (obtainable from PO Box 156, Chersley, Aylesbury, Bucks HP18) and the *UK Christian Handbook* (obtainable from the Bible Society, 146 Queen Victoria Street, London EC4V 4BX).

Clergy especially have to deal with ex-prisoners who arrive unexpectedly looking for help, usually of the financial kind. The following information may prove relevant in such cases:

1. A *discharge grant* is made to virtually all adult prisoners and young offenders who have served a sentence of over 14 days. The standard rate for adults is £27.75; the homeless rate is £64.90 (though this is reduced if the prisoner has considerable personal resources). (1986 rates.)
2. A *travel warrant* (or the payment of fares) to their home or destination within the British Isles, and also a *subsistence allowance*, intended to cover their immediate needs until they can reach an office of the DHSS, are available to all prisoners, even those who do not qualify for a discharge grant. (NB This information is not meant to suggest that grants are always adequate or that ex-prisoners never have legitimate financial needs, e.g. the money to pursue a job by buying local newspapers, making phone calls, etc., but simply to provide a clergyman with some basic background information.)

The Catholic Social Service for Prisoners (CSSP) have designed a card – they would not object to clergy following their example – which has spaces for the phone numbers of 'local points of help', such as Unemployment Benefit Office, nearest night shelter/hostel, Probation Office, Citizens' Advice Bureau, Social Security Office. Such a card, strategically placed by the phone in a clergy house, should prove an invaluable ally, especially in dealing with the casual caller.

The CSSP card ends with a pastoral message which is simple but of profound significance: 'your time, a friendly ear, and your prayers are no less valuable than a cup of tea and a sandwich'. In the spirit of Vincent de Paul, a pioneer in the pastoral care of prisoners, one might say that prisoners, ex-prisoners and their families who are on the receiving end of our 'remembering activities' will find it hard to forgive us unless they are convinced that what we give, we give out of genuine loving concern for them as our brothers and sisters.

R.A.

Prisoners and their Families

Apex Trust
31 Clapham Road
London SW9 0JE
Tel: 01 582 3171
The Trust helps find employment for certain offenders and runs a general information service for ex-offenders.

Catholic Social Service for Prisoners
189a Old Brompton Road
London SW5 0AR
Tel: 01 370 6612
Helping prisoners whilst serving sentences and ex-prisoners, both men and women. Also working with all kinds of people, alcoholics, drug addicts, etc.

The Circle Trust (A Trust for the Care and Support of Prisoners and their Families)
25 Camberwell Grove
London SE5
Tel: 01 703 6545
Runs a club for the homeless, most of whom are ex-offenders.

NACRO (National Association for the Care and Resettlement of Offenders)
169 Clapham Road
London SW9 0PU
Tel: 01 582 6500
NACRO's work is devoted to developing more humane and effective ways of dealing with crime.

Prisoners' Sunday Committee
c/o The Lodge
Pope John House
Hale Street
London E14 0BT
Tel: 01 987 4663
The Committee is an ecumenical group which aims to raise the level of awareness and public consciousness about prisoners and their families.

Prisoners' Wives and Families Society
254 Caledonian Road
Islington
London N1
Tel: 01 278 3981
Aims to alleviate the distress and poverty of prisoners' wives and dependents.

PROP (The National Prisoners' Movement)
BM-PROP
London WC1N 3XX
Tel: 01 542 3744
A pressure group run by ex-prisoners concerned with the welfare of those who are in prison.

Pastoral care of widows and the bereaved

There are many more widows (3 million in Britain) than widowers, and many of the most serious consequences of losing a marriage partner apply more to women than to men. The widow is more likely to suffer a severe drop in income and to have less experience and knowledge in running the finances of the family. She will need help to cope with taxes, mortgages, insurance, etc. Indeed it has been said that the time a woman most needs the help and support of her husband is on the day he dies.

Apart from the emotional shock, which can obviously affect either sex with equal intensity, the widow is less socially 'acceptable', less able to remarry or to make a new and independent life. Men can more easily find women happy to give practical help with housekeeping or children. A widowed mother's needs are less easily supplied, but more urgent.

Whether the death is foreseen or unexpected, there is always shock and grief. This takes a predictable course, and the responses required of those concerned to help and comfort are clear. The first two or three days can produce combinations of numbed shock and uncontrollable weeping. There is need for close contact, physical and moral: holding hands, hugging, a shoulder to weep on. Encourage her to weep, not to hold it in and feel guilty about it. A widow needs ready cash; drink and food; children fed and looked after; someone sleeping in the house; paperwork for death and funeral; relatives contacted; food for mourners after the funeral.

Intense grief can last a year or more. At times she will feel paralysed and unable to do or decide anything: remorse at failures in her relationship with her husband, resentment at being left alone, and at those still enjoying marriage when *her* husband is dead, and then guilt at these resentments. Teenage children can increase guilt by somehow (rarely explicitly) blaming the surviving parent for surviving, or even for being responsible for the death. She can feel that nobody understands her state, and will be unpredictable, unable to control weeping, but frightened of driving away would-be support. She feels only half a person, for even in an unhappy marriage life is bound up in the other. There is the sudden withdrawal of physical and sexual comfort.

Help involves visiting, especially at weekends (when the husband would be home), recalling the life and death of the partner, praying together – prayer for the dead is to help them respond to God's call to glory. This is outside time, so there is no 'before' or 'after': we remain in contact, through the mystical body of Christ and the dead also support us from heaven. Apply Christ's words to the dead partner: 'I go now to prepare a place for you . . . that where I am you may also be' (John 24). Use Psalms such as 68, 129 and 138, which can answer something deep within the mourner. Avoid attempts at contact through spiritualists which are unchristian, frustrating and dangerous.

Grief's intensity will lessen, but the widow will often feel vulnerable and overpowered by waves of emotion: sorrow, remorse, fear, anger, loneliness and pointlessness. Those who supported her will drift away, but help is still essential: help her to go through her husband's clothes; do not avoid mentioning him, even if she weeps; have someone with her on the anniversaries of his death, the wedding day, his birthday. Help her to pray on these days, get her to go to Mass and to be in touch through Communion. Encourage some work or interest which takes her out of the house and among other people: gardening, evening classes, charity work, a paid job if she needs money. Often a widow 'blossoms' some time after her husband's death into a much more positive character and finds skills she was unaware of. She can be a listener and supporter of the newly bereaved. Invite her out to parties. Do not be put off by moods and reactions of one particular day: later she will regret a bitter word, a failure to respond. She should be given many chances to come alive again. If she has teenage children she can need male support for both sons and daughters. Godfathers, uncles, priests can, by showing interest and concern, help them through what is a difficult time even when both parents are alive and loving.

Finally, encourage prayer and growth in the Spirit. This must provide the pathway to sublimation of all that has been lost, as they look to their homecoming in heaven, 'where all we loved is always dear'.

P.J.

Useful Books

Widowed by Dom Philip Jebb. Out of print in the UK but the US edition available from Downside Abbey Bookshop, Stratton-on-the-Fosse, Bath BA3 4RJ. Written by a Catholic priest, it combines plenty of practical advice with a lot of spiritual content. Relevant both for the bereaved and those who want to help them.
Grief and how to live with it, Sarah Morris, Allen and Unwin. A very clear analysis of the whole process of grieving by a widow. Provides a useful bibliography.
Bereavement, Colin Murray Parkes, Pelican. A scientific study of the subject, including a long chapter of practical help for the bereaved and a wide-ranging bibliography.

A Grief Observed, C. S. Lewis, Faber. A very literary diary recording a widower's reactions. Not essentially *practical*, like the other
three, but very perceptive and giving a masculine viewpoint.

The national organisation to help widows is CRUSE (below).

Some useful addresses

Catholic Association of Widows
84 Baldwins Lane
Croxley Green
Rickmansworth
Herts. WD3 3LP
Tel: 0293 21532
President:
Mrs K. Cusack
Secretary:
Mrs M. Chadwick
9 Lawrence Road
London W5
To make better known the 'Greatness
of Christian Widowhood' and to
encourage the members to use their
state of life to the best advantage for
themselves and the Church.

CRUSE
Charter House
126 Sheen Road
Richmond
Surrey TW9 1UR
Tel: 01 940 4818/9047
A national organisation for the
widowed and their children, which
offers a comprehensive service of
counselling by trained and selected
people.

Pastoral care of bereaved parents

There is no death so sad as that of a child. And, perhaps, no death so
hard to come to terms with. In the kind of society we have today,
parents do not expect their children to die before them. Yet, every
year, more than 15,000 children and young people die in Great
Britain. So every year thousands of parents face the loss of their
beloved children; every year they have to try to rebuild their
shattered lives. It is far from easy. The friends and relatives who
offered help and support immediately after the tragedy drift
away, and the grieving parents may be left feeling isolated and
depressed.

Bereavement grieving is not an illness, but a process that must be
allowed to run its course. This takes time. Our society today has lost
the mourning rituals once routinely accepted, that helped families
in their sadness. We do not give time to grieve, so those involved
must create emotional space and help the family when a child dies.
Grieving parents need to be able to share their deep inner feeling of
heartache and desolation. They need to talk constantly about their
child, his life and his death. The times of sadness are recalled many

times, as well as the precious moments of happiness and laughter. In our Western culture children are not expected to die, so their loss throws the whole purpose and meaning of life into sharp focus. Many parents find themselves grappling with the 'why' of such suffering. Some find comfort through their religious or philosophical beliefs and even though there seem to be no answers, if their restless searching can be patiently understood, general benefit often results.

The 'if only' comments frequently made by parents should not be met with trite responses or false reassurance, but with the recognition that parents may have an overwhelming sense of impotence and a wish that they had done more for their child. Guilt and anger are parts of the grieving process and may add to the stress of the family.

Sometimes parents experience zany thoughts that can be very frightening. They fear mental disturbance, though their reactions are probably perfectly normal in the circumstances. If there were preceding difficulties in the marriage, such a tragedy may put added strain on the relationship. Some partners cannot easily talk to each other and share their grief. There is an understandable wish to run away from it all. At a time of such devastating upheaval it is hard to think about the needs of surviving brothers and sisters, let alone to understand how the sibling's death may be affecting them. They can be confused and bewildered by parental response to them.

The sharing of some of these concerns with people who have trodden the same path can be of enormous benefit, for they too have known the sense of inner loneliness and social isolation. This is the core of the work of the Compassionate Friends – an international organisation of bereaved parents offering friendship and understanding to others who are newly bereaved.

To help people who know bereaved parents, the Compassionate Friends have drawn up a list of Do's and Dont's:

DO
let your concern and caring show;
be available – to listen, run errands, help with the children or whatever else seems needed at the time;
say you are sorry about what happened to their child and about their pain;
allow them to express as much grief as they are feeling at the moment and are willing to share;

encourage them to be patient with themselves and not to expect too much;

allow them to talk about the child they have lost as much and as often as they want to;

talk about the special qualities of that child;

give extra attention to brothers or sisters (they too are hurt and confused and in need of attention which their parents may not be able to give at this time);

reassure them they did everything they could and tell them of everything true and positive about the care given to their child.

DON'T

avoid them because *you* are uncomfortable (being avoided by friends adds pain to an already intolerably painful experience);

say you know how they feel (have you lost a child?);

tell them what they should feel or do – like saying 'You ought to be feeling better now' or 'You must pull yourself together';

change the subject when they mention their dead child;

avoid mentioning their child's name because you are scared to remind them of their pain (they won't have forgotten it);

try to find something positive about the death (e.g. closer ties with the rest of the family, a moral lesson);

suggest they can have another child (it wouldn't replace the one they've lost);

say it's good they've still got other children (children are not interchangeable);

make any comments which in any way suggest that the care given to their child at home, in hospital or wherever was inadequate (parents are plagued by feelings of doubt and guilt without any help from their family and friends);

let your own sense of helplessness keep you from reaching out a hand to a bereaved parent.

The Compassionate Friends

National Secretary:
Gill Hodder
6 Denmark Street
Bristol BS1 5DQ
Tel: 0272 292778

National Adviser:
Margaret Atkin
Principal Social Worker
Hospital for Sick Children
Great Ormond Street
London WC1N 3JH
Tel: 01 405 9200, ext. 105

Social Services:
Ena Mirren
35 Assisi Road
Salisbury ST1 3QZ
Tel: 0722 27774

Librarian:
Miriam Blake
Tiny Cottage
Hornes Green
Cudham Lane South
Sevenoaks
Tel: 0959 32252

(For pastoral care of homosexual people, one parent families, and separated and divorced Catholics, see pages 257–77.)

The Pastoral Care of Mental Pain

Mental illness and emotional disturbance are so widespread that priests and other pastoral workers will inevitably come across them in the course of their work. They will also have many opportunities to foster mental health. Some will find it congenial to work with the demands of psychological crisis or chronic mental illness. Others will prefer, on recognising a problem, to call in professional help. At times, it may be safer for all concerned to do that.

There is no one simple prescription for meeting these different eventualities. In many instances all the personal resources of a pastor will be challenged and patience and kindness called for as well as the suspension of pre-judgement about adherence to the practice of the faith.

Acceptance, availability, understanding and flexibility are necessary attributes for the ministry to the mentally ill. It also needs an attitude of search in faith and prayer and a readiness to give oneself to the unexpected.

Further reading

The pastoral care of people suffering from mental illness, The Catholic Bishops' Conference of England and Wales, 1984.
Christian ministry to the sick, ed. Tom Coyle, Geoffrey Chapman, 1986.
Meaning in madness: the pastor and the mentally ill, John Foslett, SPCK, 1984.

Useful addresses

The Dympna Centre
24 Blandford Street
London W1
Offers psychotherapy and counselling
for priests and religious.

MIND
22 Harley Street
London W1N 2ED
The National Association for Mental
Health.

See also page 412 for further addresses.

CHAPTER SEVEN

The School

The Role and Responsibilities of a School Governor

A Foundation Governor of a Catholic school is appointed on the authority of the bishop of the diocese. The responsibilities of such a governor are fivefold. First, to see that the school is conducted in accordance with the Trust Deed under which the school was set up. A second responsibility is to the local community to see that the school provides for and fulfils all the functions and expectations of a Catholic school. Thirdly, there is a responsibility, through the governing body, to all those employed in the school (the only exception being the school meals staff). The governing body is the employer of all these people and as such must be a fair and just employer. The fourth responsibility is to see that meetings are conducted properly, in accordance with the Instruments and Articles of Government. Lastly, there is the responsibility for the care and maintenance of the property and the supervision necessary to see that all is provided to enable the school to function efficiently.

Conduct in accordance with the Trust Deed

It is essential for every governor, once he or she is appointed, to have a copy of the Instruments and Articles of Government. In addition to this it is important to have a list which gives the names, addresses and telephone numbers of each of the other governors, which should also indicate their status. For example, are they fellow Foundation Governors or are they local authority nominees or elected representatives?

A governor needs to be acquainted with all the necessary information about the school, i.e. the size of the school, number on roll and an outline of the school's organisation. A list of members of the school staff should be at hand and this should indicate a precise statement of the position held.

A Foundation Governor should know the composition of the Diocesan Schools Commission and whom to contact immediately for help or information. Similarly, one should know how the name of the Local Education Officer and his office address and telephone number.

Functions and expectations of a Catholic school

The governors are responsible for the admissions policy of the school and its implementation. Each year an information booklet on the school should be prepared and made available. The minimum content of this is set out in the 1980 Act. The Act of 1981 makes it quite clear that governors must see that the school caters for the needs of all pupils and there is a specific responsibility to handicapped children and those with special educational needs. Governors' meetings need to consider the school curriculum, taking a special interest in the provision for Religious Education. Any Religious Education programmes or events should receive the interest, encouragement and cooperation of the governors.

Responsibility to those employed in the school

Through their visits to the school the governors should seek to build a relationship with the staff and develop an awareness and appreciation of their roles and responsibilities within the school. Each governor should be aware of the contracts of employment of each of the employees and the grievance procedure available to employees. Some knowledge of the staff union representatives together with the name of the staff health and safety representative would be an advantage. Any disciplinary procedure must be in accord with the Employment Terms and Acts. If the need arises, advice should be sought from the Schools' Commission and the Local Authority, and one should proceed with care.

Meetings conducted according to the Instruments and Articles of Government

The clerk to the governors should send out a prepared agenda, together with copies of reports (all reports and requests to governors should be in writing) so that they are received seven clear days before the next meeting. A governor must at all times respect the confidentiality of the meetings and never act from purely personal motives. Copies of the agenda should be sent to the Schools' Commission and the Local Authority. Any representative of another body only attends at the invitation of the governors and may only offer advice.

Minutes of the meeting should be sent as soon as possible to the Schools' Commission and the Local Authority. Signed minutes must also be available for inspection by the public on request, although confidential matters may be omitted from this copy.

Care and maintenance of the school property

Someone from the governing body should regularly inspect the premises. It is important that governors are aware of the financial restrictions on repairs and maintenance and on the procedure to be followed both within the diocese and within the Local Authority. They must also know the procedures to be followed to claim money due or to be paid by the Department of Education and Science. Forms are usually available from the Education Office.

As a body, the governors should never forget their duty to the parents of children attending the school: keeping them informed of the school's aims and performance and, where possible, working with them for the development of a sense of community in the school.

Some useful books

Guidelines for Governors, published by the Archdiocese of Cardiff and available from the Catholic Truth Society, Welsh Province, 27–31 High Street Arcade, Cardiff. This is the best available commentary on the Acts.

The Educational System of England and Wales, published by Department of Education and Science and available from HMSO but this is detailed and not specifically for Voluntary Aided Schools.

The Open University Community Education Programme provides a very good course on *Governing Schools* but this again is meant more for the government of County Schools.

The Catholic Education Council pamphlets on the various Acts or aspects of them are detailed and informative as well as being authoritative.

G.C.

Some Useful Addresses

Adult Literacy and Basic Skills Unit
Kingsbourne House
229/231 High Holborn
London WC1V 7DA
Tel: 01 405 4017
Information from the above address
can be obtained to help adults who
have serious difficulties in reading and
writing.

Association of Religious in Education
41 Cromwell Road
London SW7 2DH
Tel: 01 584 7494
Secretary: Sister Hilda Mitchell SHC
To assist and support religious involved
in the work of education by
communication and cooperation with
church bodies.

Catholic Teachers' Federation
'Edenvale'
Stone Road
Tittensor
Stoke-on-Trent ST12 9HR
Secretary:

To promote welfare of Catholic
teachers.

*Christian Association for Adult and
Continuing Education*
Archdeacon's House
Dodderhill
Droitwich
Worcs. WR9 8LW
Secretary:
Ven. Robin Bennett, Archdeacon of
Dudley
Christian Adult Education giving
assistance by publications, support,
special workshops.

*National Association of School
Chaplains*
Holy Family Convent
Lowerhouse Lane
Liverpool L11 2SF
Hon. Secretary:
Sister Margaret Doherty
To further the spiritual and pastoral
welfare of chaplains in schools.

National Christian Education Council
Robert Denholm House
Nutfield
Redhill
Surrey RH1 4HW
Tel: 073782 2411
Secretary:
Rev. Simon Oxley
Promotion and development of
Christian education, particularly in the
parish, through Sunday School type
activities.

*National Association of Development
Education Centre*
6 Endsleigh Street
London WC1H 0DX
Tel: 01 388 2670
NADEC seeks to further development
education by promoting development
education centres and coordinating
information to government bodies and
the general public.

*The National Council for Voluntary
Youth Services*
Wellington House
29 Albion Street
Leicester LE1 6GD
Tel: 0553 554910
Information may be obtained from the
above relating to all types of youth and
community services.

National Youth Bureau
17/23 Albion Street
Leicester LE1 6GD
Tel: 0533 554775
Detailed information about local
schemes in youth work can be obtained
from the above.

Our Lady's Catechists
36 Meadowfield
Sleaford
Lincs. NG34 7AZ
Secretary: Mrs D. M. Bristow
To teach the Catholic faith by: training
catechists by correspondence courses,
for work in the parishes; or by means of
the Children's Postal Course which
provides lessons under a qualified
catechist for children who either do not
attend Catholic schools or cannot
attend parish classes for Religious
Instruction.

The Future of Chaplains in Catholic Schools

When the Hierarchy, following the 1944 Education Act, resolved to
appoint chaplains to the new secondary schools, they were remind-
ing the faithful of the very important fact that Catholic education, to
be true to its mission, must keep firmly in its sights the spiritual
development of our children. Since many of these schools were
parish schools, the presence of the priest, continuing his ministry
within the school, served not only the spiritual life of the school but
reinforced the pastoral structures within the parish. From a pastoral
point of view this was an ideal situation, but it proved short-lived
with the advent in the sixties and seventies of the comprehensive
school whose sizeable population engulfed the smaller schools into
one large unit. It was against this background that new problems
arose, as was evident when chaplains began to meet in 1974 to share
problems and experience.

By virtue of their size the new schools, to be effective, required a
full-time chaplain. Unfortunately, the decline in vocations during
this period militated against such appointments. The majority of
dioceses could provide only part-time chaplains who seemed unsure
of the nature of their duties. The problem of limited access to a
school, which was often the size of a healthy parish, was added to
the conflicting demands of various parish-priest governors. Problems with Headteachers demanded a reappraisal of priorities and an
examination of those traditional roles associated with the duties of
chaplaincy. It proved relatively straightforward at conferences to
see the chaplain as leader in liturgies, counsellor, bridge-builder,
home and hospital visitor, animator and alter-Christus but how
could one realise these roles in the course of restricted visits to

school? Furthermore, how could one innovate liturgically in the teeth of opposition from fellow priests who were governors? How could a chaplain cope should a conflict of pastoral roles create tension between him and the Head or senior school staff?

The demands of the job prove dispiriting to some and perplexing to others. This is not to undervalue the excellent work of the priest chaplains who, whatever their problems, are, in the main, a group whose virtue and dedication are inspirational among a teaching profession who can no longer be assumed to support Catholic values.

In stating this one is not so much referring to the considerable numbers of non-Christians in our schools as to those Catholics who are lukewarm, uncommitted or quite simply lapsed – colleagues in need of spiritual healing and of the chaplain's ministry.

It seems unlikely, even to the most optimistic, that the supply of priests will increase sufficiently to provide all our schools with full-time priest-chaplains – barring such unlikely events as the intro-duction of married priests which in any case would take years to have an effect after approval. Does this mean then that the original vision of the Hierarchy to reinforce this unique spiritual dimension in the life of our schools must perish? Clearly it must not, since that would destroy something too precious to lose.

The problem facing the Church will increasingly centre on how best to use the priestly manpower available if we wish to maintain the sacramental life of our schools. More and more schools are benefiting from the ministries of sister-chaplains whose work is having such a beneficial effect on their pastoral life – but how long can this source be tapped? Not long perhaps, but at least it gives a respite and has proved that much of the traditional work of the chaplain does not need a priest. It does also show, however, that the way forward will still demand a solution involving the priest as partner in a team ministry where the sacraments he brings will sanctify and inspire the pastoral life of our schools, now increasingly tended by others.

As we value our Catholic schools, we cannot afford to sit back ignoring the problem in the hope that a solution will come of its own accord.

P.E.

RE Diocesan Directors in England and Wales

Arundel and Brighton
Very Rev. Mgr Patrick Oliver
Christian Education Centre
4 Southgate Drive
Crawley
W. Sussex RH10 6RP
Tel: Crawley (0293) 515666/7

Birmingham
Rev. J. D. McHugh
Maryvale Centre
Old Oscott Hill
Birmingham B44 9AG
Tel: 021 360 8118

Brentwood
Rev. G. Stokes
Cathedral House
Ingrave Road
Brentwood
Essex CM15 8AT
Tel: 0277 215689

Cardiff
Very Rev. Canon Edwin Regan
Archbishop's House
43 Cathedral Road
Cardiff CF1 9HD
Tel: 0222 33838

Clifton
Rev. B. McEvoy
CREC
Emmaus House
Clifton Hill
Bristol BS8 4PD
Tel: Bristol (0272) 735276

East Anglia
Rev. A. Philpot
Catholic Rectory
Hills Road
Cambridge CB2 1JR
Tel: 0223 350787

Hallam
Miss C. Dodd
Quarters
Carsick Hill Way
Sheffield S10 3LT
Tel: 0742 309101

Hexham and Newcastle
Rev. P. Carroll
Catechetical Centre
St Vincent's
The Roman Way
West Denton
Newcastle upon Tyne NE15 7LT
Tel: 091 264 3676

Lancaster
Rev. F. Flynn
Christ the King
Gateside Drive
Blackpool
Lancs FY3 7PL
Tel: 0253 31002

Leeds
Mgr F. Robinson
RE Centre
College of the BVM
62 Headingley Lane
Leeds LS6 2BO
Tel: 0532 740344

Liverpool
Rev. F. A. Mooney
Christian Education Centre
152 Brownlow Hill
Liverpool L3 5RQ
Tel: 051 709 2197

Menevia
Rev. P. J. Breen
Brigidine Convent
Plas yn Green
Denbigh
Clwyd LL16 4BH
Tel: 074 571 4895

Middlesbrough
Mgr S. Kilbane
St George's Rectory
Peel Street
York YO1 1PZ
Tel: 0904 23728

Northampton
Rev. J. Glen
St Mary's RE Centre
118 Bromham Road
Bedford MK40 2QR
Tel: 0234 50093

Nottingham
Rev. K. O'Riordan
Highfields Centre
Highfields
Broadway
Derby DE3 1AU
Tel: 0332 557294

Plymouth
Rev. B. Jaffa
4 Church Street
Paignton
S. Devon
Tel: 0803 521850

Portsmouth
Mgr P. Murphy-O'Connor
RE Council
La Sainte Union College of Hr. Ed.
The Avenue
Southampton SO9 5HB
Tel: 0703 31194

Salford
Rev. W. Byrne
RE Centre
5 Gerald Road
Pendleton
Salford M6 6DL
Tel: 061 737 9617

Shrewsbury
Rev. P. Morgan
RE Centre
2 Park Road South
Birkenhead
Merseyside
Tel: 051 652 9855

Southwark
Rev. J. Redford
Catechetical Centre
Institute for Christian Ed.
21 Tooting Bec Road
London SW17 8BS
Tel: 01 672 7684
and 01 672 2422

Westminster
Mrs K. O'Gorman
WDES
33 Wilfred St
London SW1E 6PS
Tel: 01 834 7987

RE Diocesan Centres in Scotland

*Archdiocese of St Andrews and
Edinburgh*
Religious Education Office
26 George Square
Edinburgh EH8 9LD
Tel: 031 667 9015

Diocese of Aberdeen
Pastoral and Catechetical Centre
16 Huntly Street
Aberdeen
Tel: 0224 645401

Diocese of Dunkeld
Religious Education Office
Cathedral House
150 Nethergate
Dundee DD1 4EA
Tel: 0382 27343

Diocese of Galloway
Religious Education Centre
c/o 8 Corsehill Rd
Ayr KA7 2ST
Tel: 0292 266750

Archdiocese of Glasgow
Religious Education Centre
69a Carlton Place
Glasgow G5 9TD
Tel: 041 429 0463

Diocese of Motherwell
Religious Education Centre
Coursington Rd
Motherwell ML1 1PW
Tel: 0698 52447

Diocese of Paisley
Diocesan Centre
13 Newark Street
Greenock
Renfrewshire PA16 7UH
Tel: 0475 25161/2

The School Liturgy

Easter stands not only as the astonishing fact of the Christian life, the resounding achievement of God in the world, but the supreme gift of God to humanity for all time. Not surprisingly, therefore, and more so since Vatican II, Catholic schools have begun to emphasise the need not only of educating pupils into *understanding* Easter but also into *celebrating* Easter. All schools are expected to fashion the personal, social and cultural development of pupils via the school curriculum, ethos and variety of social exchange. A Catholic school roots this work of building up pupils' sense of identity, *ex professo*, in the event of Easter. Celebrating the paschal mystery of redemption, day by day, week by week, term by term, is not something optional in the life of a Catholic school. Rather, it is of the very essence to the professed aim of every Catholic school.

Infant and Junior Schools

The principal expression of Easter in infant and junior schools is the *School Assembly*. Simply assembling together in obedience to the Word of God in order to listen to the voice of the Risen Lord is a constant reminder to children of the permanence and power of the resurrection. For this reason school assembly, in a Catholic school, articulates a spiritual vision. Notices, sports results, disciplinary matters, important and necessary though they be to the school, ought never to obscure that simple fact.

The liturgy itself suggests a work-a-day model for school assemblies in the format of the liturgy of the Word. So one begins with a moment of Christian welcome to all present, an invitation to prayer, followed by a time to listen and respond to the Word of God. The scriptures require interpretation and reflection and so a short explanation and word of encouragement by the one who presides is always necessary. Finally, the celebration can be concluded with a joyful but prayerful dismissal. In infant and junior schools there is much to be recommended in head teachers and staff members leading the school assemblies. The practice now, however, is widely established of different classes leading the school assembly once a week. Experience has shown that both the classes and the rest of the school profit from these occasions immensely. The success of these school assemblies, however, should be gauged by the degree to which the class has involved the whole assembly actively and consciously in the celebration. Children learn their liturgy best of all through celebrating it.

It is also possible, however, for infant and junior school classes to celebrate their Easter faith in their own class assemblies. Within the classroom setting it becomes possible to gather up all the mistakes, quarrels, joys and sorrows into the mystery of Easter, the cross and the resurrection. Normally, the class teacher is the most obvious person to preside; a priest, when present, might prefer to sit with the children during such moments and perhaps conclude the celebration with a blessing.

During the year, in addition, there will be times when both teacher and priest judge the class ready to celebrate Easter in its full sacramental expression, especially in a class mass or in the sacrament of reconciliation. The fullness of celebration should reflect the fullness of work and life which comes together to be offered to the Father through the risen Christ. The frequency of such sacramental celebrations, therefore, is always a careful decision. Their rhythm depends much upon the nascent faith of the children, the relationship between priest and class, the demands of the curriculum and the availability of parents.

The express purpose of all sacramental and non-sacramental celebrations of Easter, nonetheless, is not to replace those of the local parish community; rather, the school is but attempting to educate children into the awareness of the need for a life-long context, enduring long after the school years, in which to celebrate the mystery of Easter in their lives. For this reason, the liturgical life of the infant and junior school should be intimately associated with that of the feeder parishes' weekly Sunday eucharist. Some schools have already begun to link in their work of preparing children for the first reception of the eucharist and penance with the life of the parish. The various stages of development are celebrated, at regular intervals, within the Sunday eucharist. Other schools assist with the singing at Mass on a Sunday; some hand out the hymn-books; others again bring some of the children's work in school to decorate the walls of the church for particular times and seasons. Such liturgical resources and skills have undoubtedly begun to enrich the liturgical life of the parishes. This new relationship, however, is very much still in its infancy and depends for its success upon the wider sense of confidence and trust between school and parish. The signs in this direction are, in general, most hopeful.

Secondary and Comprehensive Schools

Most Catholic secondary and comprehensive schools are still in the process of *creating* an appropriate liturgical tradition and not of *inheriting* one. This makes special demands on all members of the school staff, pupils, parents and governors. The task is clearly beyond the capacities of the Religious Education department of any large school, even though such a department will play a crucial part in the formation of a school liturgical tradition.

Pupils do expect, rightly or wrongly, real leadership from their teachers in the prayer life of the school: so too do parents, governors and clergy. The expectation, in many cases, is born out of the earlier tradition in infant and junior school, and, while pupils normally expect the liturgical life of the secondary or comprehensive school to be different, they do not expect it to be entirely abandoned.

This pupil and parental assumption is an initial point of departure upon which to build Easter into the life of a Catholic secondary or comprehensive school. It will not always be easy for teachers to fashion a pattern of Christian celebration within secondary and comprehensive schools but already some schools are beginning to inch forward. The first way has emerged through the use of the pastoral care system of the school. Most Catholic secondary and comprehensive schools have introduced, with Local Authority encouragement, a pastoral care system to cope with the manifold problems associated with large pupil populations. These systems vary from school to school reflecting local preferences for vertical or horizontal groupings, House or Year identity. Some schools have already begun to build up a tradition of celebrating the beginning and end of the school year, Christmas and Easter, days of importance in the Christian life, on the basis of House or Year groups. The advantages of grafting the liturgical life of the school on to the pastoral care framework are clear. Teachers and pupils identify easily with these structures. Furthermore, over the course of the years, where whole families continue to be associated with the same House, the same teachers, the same Head of House, bonds of real friendship are forged. Likewise, the priest associated with the particular House or Year Group, has, at his disposal, a specialist team of teachers ready and willing to cooperate in the planning and preparation of the liturgy.

The key to the long-term success of the liturgical life of secondary and comprehensive schools lies precisely here, in the planning and preparation of the celebrations. Non-Catholic members of staff are usually only too delighted, if asked in the proper way, to play their part in the preparations. Nor should they be excluded, by accident or design, from priest and staff deliberations. Often their counsels can help in deciding whether a sacramental or non-sacramental celebration in a particular instance is the more appropriate. For this reason, all priests should be familiar with the pastoral care responsibilities of subject teachers, and, of course, liaise most carefully with the Head of Year or the Head of House teachers.

Large secondary and comprehensive schools attempt to combat the sense of anonymity among pupils and staff by creating form or tutorial periods. Often, these small but permanent gatherings can provide the focus for a more intimate and personal celebration of the mystery of Easter. Some schools use the form or tutorial periods not only to begin the school day with a formal prayer, but in the short fifteen or twenty-five minute period, have a scripture reading with a slide background (see section on *Visual Images*, pages 56–60) or a music background – such as that by Fr Ernest Sands or the St Louis Jesuits. Experience, again, shows that such celebrations become an accepted and welcome manner of reinforcing the presence of the Easter Christ in the consciousness of pupils.

A number of Catholic secondary and comprehensive schools are developing ways of sacramentally expressing the mystery of Easter in the life of the school outside of the administrative structures.

During Advent and Lent many schools have midday prayer groups centred on the prayer of the Church or charismatic prayer. Some schools also have a weekly midday Mass, or an early morning Mass before school; others provide opportunities for a chaplain-priest or sister-chaplain to counsel pupils and eventually encourage pupils to seek sacramental reconciliation. The importance of such celebrations is obvious. First, they provide a liturgical setting which is at once intimate and personal. In large schools, where anonymity is a real danger to pupils' sense of worth, the small group liturgy is an important counterbalance. Secondly, since liturgy is of its nature the supreme expression of Christian freedom, the maximum of effort and imagination must be deployed to ensure that Christian freedom within a framework, which is of necessity a compulsory environment.

Finally, Easter is to be found not only on *occasions* in Catholic secondary and comprehensive schools; it is found most potently in *persons*, and none more so than in the teachers and in the school chaplain. No Catholic secondary or comprehensive school should be without a school chaplain or senior school chaplain coordinator. The presence of a school chaplain is a constant reminder to pupils, teachers, governors, Catholic community, of the deep and underlying purpose of the school community, namely, the figuring of the Risen Christ in and out of the lives of everyone in the school. The chaplain, like the Risen Christ, is a person available to everyone. A school has a right to expect someone of quality and dedication, with the time and resources requisite for the task. Here again, the whole Catholic community has to examine its conscience. A school without a chaplain loses one of the images of Easter in its life and cannot but be the poorer for it.

What we have been insisting upon, both in infant/junior and secondary Catholic schools, is that liturgy is possible only where there is a real school life. The pressures upon teachers, pupils, governors and parents to reduce school to a workplace are enormous. To the degree, however, that parents, teachers, pupils and governors genuinely share each other's lives, hopes, fears, struggles, successes and failures, feel a sense of mutual solidarity and responsibility for each other's lives, then, and only then, does true liturgy become possible in a school. For liturgy springs out of a school that is more tuned into giving than exploiting; a school where the ethos of giving is expressly recognised as the presence of the Holy Spirit, the Easter gift of Father and Son.

J.G.

Some Useful Assembly Books

Listen, A. J. McCallen, Collins.
Praise, A. J. McCallen, Collins.
Doing Dance and Drama, Wrigley and Murphy, Ave Maria.
Children's Liturgies, Bernadette Kenny, Paulist Press.
Assemblies (Junior/Middle), Harry Smith, Heinemann.
Assemble Together, Tony Castle, Geoffrey Chapman.
Assembly, Redvers Brandling, Macmillan.
Words for Worship, Campling and Davis, Arnold.
Poems for Assemblies, T. G. Daffern, Blackwell.
More Words for Worship, Michael Davis, Arnold.
Sharing God's Life, Source Book, St Paul's.
Day by Day, Rowland Purton, Blackwell.
Quotes and Anecdotes for Preachers and Teachers, Tony Castle, Kevin Mayhew.
See *Music*, pages 54–6, for music for the school assembly, and *Visual Images*, pages 58–60.

CHAPTER EIGHT

Youth Work

Young People in the Parish

The Task

Parish youth work used to be a thing of clubs, Cubs and Brownies. These organisations still have their importance but only in the context of a broader concern for the Christian formation, personal development and social education of young people. At the heart of our work with those who have left school should be a twofold preoccupation:

that our Catholic young men and women should be active participants in the worshipping and serving church which is our parish

that the members of our parish should offer to all the young people of the neighbourhood a care derived from the ideals and standards of the Gospel.

Training

Youth work is about how a community (family, parish, deanery, borough) responds to the needs of its young people and about how young men and women respond to the needs of their community. It is about sensitive listening and creating space for the exercise of responsibility.

Native wit requires sharpening up by training. We have to look into and understand each other's worlds, pick up tips on technique and know what materials, schemes, programmes and people are available. Nowadays, you can go away for training, for evenings, weekends or years. Or it can come to you and the people of your parish either through the diocesan youth officer, the borough youth officer or on video packages from religious and secular associations and the Open University.

Management

Once you have decided what you want to do, you have to decide whether it can be knitted into the ordinary fabric of parish life (like a mini-retreat, prayer-group, pilgrimage or young peoples' Mass) or whether you need to create or recruit an organisation to do it. If you need the latter, be clear about its purpose (to provide recreation in decent surroundings, to train young catechetists, to promote community service by the unemployed) and who it is for (young Catholics, all the local youngsters). Who is going to do it, how will they divide responsibilities, where will they meet and how often? How much will it cost and who pays? Write it down when it is understood and agreed and then, if the borough or the tax-man asks for it, you can turn it into a Constitution.

Money and Premises

Young people are no different from the rest of the parish. The parish should support them according to their needs and they should support the parish according to their capabilities. They may need subsidy by way of the use of parish premises or help with the rent of a school-room or hall. But they will invest money, time and energy in worthwhile and well-organised ventures for themselves or within the wider context of parish community life. They are entitled to know what responsibilities they have undertaken and how they have been discharged. Agree a budget, stick to it and make any new venture self-financing.

Unworthy premises are an affliction to the spirit and invitation to vandalism. The first project, for the initial enthusiasts, is to make the room or hall dry, warm, bright, modestly attractive and easily maintained. If there are no suitable parish rooms have a look at the facilities of the local schools.

Programmes

Use whatever premises you have as a place for social encounter, for small group study and discussions and for planning a programme which uses the more elaborate and diverse facilities in your district which it would be foolhardy to duplicate (schools, sport and leisure centres, playing fields, residential centres, fields, woods, mountains and railway trains). The nub of the thing is to live and grow together by doing together what interests you.

A Wider Span

The people of your parish should be encouraged to make an effort to understand the needs of the young people of the district. There is nothing particularly Catholic about being unhappy at home or at work, or falling in or out of love, or not having a job, or drinking and glue-sniffing. But there is something very Christian in listening and in starting and supporting schemes which do something to restore confidence and self-respect.

Local Resources

The Diocesan Youth Chaplain or Officer (address in your diocesan directory) has training programmes for young and old, is in touch with the local authorities and the youth groups of other Churches and associations with access to their training materials and re- sources.

The Local Authority Youth Officer (at the Town Hall in either the Education Department or Directorate of Leisure and Recreation). The Youth Officer will call if invited with advice and information about local youth work, use of premises, sports and recreation facilities, competitions, grants for equipment and training and news about your neighbours in the borough.

C.A.J.

Further Afield

Catholic Youth Services is an agency of the Bishops' Conference, established to provide a service of professional information and advice to all engaged in work among young people.

Contact Catholic Youth Services

for information and advice on formation and development pro- grammes suitable for the young adult
to get in touch with any of the national Catholic youth associations or your diocesan youth officer
for information on programmes for young people sponsored by government departments, especially the Departments of Education and Science, Environment, Health and Social Security and the Manpower Services Commission
for advice on professional training and information on conditions of service

for liaison with youth work abroad, the international Catholic associations and young peoples' exchanges
for contact with the youth departments of other Churches and the major secular youth associations
for information on grants from government departments, trusts and foundations
for advice and information on legal, insurance and financial obligations in youth work.

Catholic Youth Services (England and Wales):
41 Cromwell Road
London SW7 2DH
Tel: 01 589 7550

Catholic Youth Council (Scotland):
14a Newton Place
Glasgow G3 7PY
Tel: 041 332 6103

A reading list

Resources for Youth Ministry, Michael Warren, ed., Paulist Press, New York, 1978.
Youth and the Future of the Church, Michael Warren, Seabury Press, N. York, 1982, Geoffrey Chapman.
Religious Education and Young Adults, Donal O'Leary, St Paul Publications, 1983.
Teenagers and the Church, A profile of Church-going youth, Collins, 1984.
Experience and Participation. Report on the Youth Service, HMSO, Cmnd 8686, 1982.

The Young Christian Workers

The Young Christian Worker Movement is for ordinary young people aged 16–25, who leave school to go to work, to unemployment or short-term further education. It offers a means through which their potential, confidence and sense of responsibility can be developed.

Aims
The YCW aims to help young people enquire into and be aware of the situations and issues that affect their lives, to discover their God-given dignity and the message of Jesus Christ, and to take responsible action for change.

Method
The YCW works on the experience that the best apostle to a young person is another young person. It carries out its aims by calling together and training young leaders from among the young people themselves who will contact and involve other young people in their meetings and actions.

The YCW Group
The basis of the YCW Movement is the local group which consists of about 8–10 young people. These meet regularly (usually once a week) and follow the YCW method of enquiry, SEE, JUDGE and ACT. The young people run this meeting themselves and all other activities which they decide on. They are assisted by a chaplain whose role it is to animate and guide them but never to take over their proper responsibility (the chaplain can be a priest/minister, a religious brother or sister, or a lay person).

The Movement
The YCW hold regional and national representative training and social events for both young leaders and chaplains. It is also an international movement present in 70 countries around the world, offering opportunity for international education and exchange.

The Action of the YCW

YCWs take action as a result of their weekly enquiry; this action depends greatly on the situations they discover to be important in their area, in their places of work or leisure, and in their homes. It ranges from small personal action to improve things in their own life to the organisation of events and activities involving other young people.

Review
The YCW method of education is one of discovery through reflection on life and action. An important part of this is the review in which the young leaders look back on events and actions of the past week and draw out their significance in the light of the Gospel.

Starting a YCW group

In starting a YCW group in your area the first important step is to contact the YCW Movement at either the local or national office. It is most important to establish who will be the chaplain, since the chaplain has a vital role in the early stages of the group.

Advice, literature and personal support is available from local YCW workers in certain areas, and more distant help can be obtained from:

YCW National HQ
120A West Heath Road
London NW3 7TY
Tel: 01 458 8416

J.M.

Baden-Powell Units

The Scout Movement

A third of all sponsored Scout Groups, with a total membership of 627,000, are sponsored by the Anglican Church. There is no separate Anglican Scout Association for the same reason that there is no Catholic Association. (The Movement has a policy, which has the approval of the heads of the leading religious bodies in the UK. The Association encourages the different religions to apply their own programme in implementing that part of the Scout Promise which deals with duty to God.)

Founded in 1908 to encourage the physical, mental and spiritual development of young people, the Scout Movement remains the most widely supported single youth movement in Britain.

It is divided into four sections:
Beavers: Colonies may have up to twenty-four boys, aged 6 to 8 years.
Cub Scouts: Packs may consist of up to thirty-six boys, aged 8 to 10½ years.
Scouts: Troops can be of any size for boys up to 10½ to 15½.
Venture Scouts: Units can consist of boys and girls from 15½ to 21.

Many Scout Groups (consisting of one or more of the above sections) are sponsored by the Catholic Church. In the majority of cases the sponsoring authority is the parish priest of the parish to which the group is attached. It may, however, be any approved body, such as the Parish or Deanery Council, the St Vincent de Paul Society, or a school.

The Girl Guides Association

Founded in 1910, wth the same intentions as the Scout Movement, the Association is open to all girls – as Brownies or Guides – who are prepared to make the three-fold Promise of duty to God, to the Queen and other people and accept the Guide Law.

Brownies: Packs
Guides: Companies

The President of the Girl Guides Association is HRH the Princess Margaret and the Chief Commissioner is the Lady Baden-Powell.

Catholic Scout/Guide Advisory Councils

These councils are the official advisory bodies which represent the bishops of England and Wales, and all Catholics in the Baden-Powell units.

Correspondence for the Catholic Scout Advisory Council (England and Wales) should be addressed to:

The National Chaplain
Rev. Roger Barralet OFM
The Scout Association
Gilwell Park
Chingford
London E4 7HT

or

Catholic Scout Advisory Council
(Scotland)
118 Stanley Street
Glasgow G41 1JH
Tel: 041 332 9473

Any parish wishing to start a section should contact the local District Commissioner whose telephone number and address can be obtained by contacting:

The Scout Association
Records Office
Churchill Industrial Estate
Lancing
West Sussex BN15 8UG
Tel: 0903 755353

Correspondence for the Catholic Guide Advisory Council should be addressed to:

The National Chaplain
Rev. P. J. Rogers
17–19 Buckingham Palace Road
London SW1W 0PT

Scottish Guide Headquarters
16 Coates Crescent
Edinburgh EH3 7AH
Tel: 031 226 4511

For the Guide Association contact the National Chaplain at the address given above.

Youth Work: Some Useful Addresses

Anglican Young Peoples Association
Chi Rho House
53 Cedar Drive
Keynsham
Bristol BS18 2TX
Tel: 0275 61306
Secretary:
Miss Denise Atkinson
Provides for pre- and post-confirmation training for members of the Church of England in their teens and early twenties, membership being largely through branches in individual parishes.

The Boys' Brigade
Brigade House
Parsons Green
London SW6 4TH
Tel: 01 222 8661
Secretary:
Aldred Hudson CBE
Interdenominational organisation.

The Campaigners
Campaigner House
St Mark's Close
Colney Heath
Nr St Albans
Herts AL4 0NQ
Secretary:
Rev. K. G. Argent
Uniformed Evangelical youth organisation.

Catholic International Students' Chaplaincy
8 Portland Rise
London N4
Tel: 01 802 9673
National Chaplain:
Rev. Vincent Maguire MA (Ed.), Dip.Ed.
The pastoral care of overseas students in this country, accommodation facilities in London, counselling.

Catholic Students' Council of England and Wales
c/o Young Christian Students
Plunkett House
Shadwell Street
Birmingham B4 6EY
Tel: 021 236 8458
Chaplain:
Dom Raphael Appleby OSB
An organisation run by and for students in higher education, seeking to encourage Catholic students to explore and express their faith and to relate that faith to their experience and to society.

The Church Lads' and Church Girls' Brigade
Claude Hardy House
15 Etchingham Park Road
Finchley
London N3 2DU
Secretary:
Rev. Charles Grice MBE
To extend the Kingdom of Christ among boys and girls and to make them faithful members of the Church of England.

Church Pastoral Aid Society
Falcon Court
32 Fleet Street
London EC4Y 1DB
Tel: 01 353 0751
Secretary:
Rev. David Bubbers
Producing Christian education materials; an Anglican society organising ventures, camps and houseparties for 9,000 young people.

Crusaders
2 Romeland Hill
St Albans
Herts. AL3 4ET
Director:
E. W. Addicott MA
Youth evangelism and Bible teaching for 8–18 years old, open to all, but Evangelical Church of England directed.

Frontier Youth Trust
Scripture Union House
130 City Road
London EC1V 2NJ
Secretary:
Michael Eastman
The Trust links together Christian
adults working with disadvantaged
young and provides services of training,
information and resources.

The Girls' Brigade
Brigade House
Parsons Green
London SW6 4TH
National Secretary:
Miss Daphne Cosser
Tel: 01 222 8661
An interdenominational Christian
uniformed organisation for girls.

Min-y-Don Christian Adventure Centre
Arthog
Gwynedd LL39 1BZ
Tel: 0341 250433
Interdenominational but emphasis is
upon youth evangelism.

Northorpe Hall Trust
Northorpe Lane
Mirfield
W. Yorks WF14 0QL
Director:
Mr M. Harrison
Work with youngsters (aged 12–16) in
difficulties in Leeds and Kirklees,
directed by Church of England
leadership.

*St Dominic Savio Apostolate for the
Young*
49 Surrey Lane
London SW11 3PN
President:
Rev. Terence O'Brien SDB
Guidance and counselling for young
Catholics. Help through leaflets,
publications. One to one counselling.

Young Christian Students
Plunkett House
Shadwell St
Birmingham B4 6EY
Tel: 021 236 8458
President:
Miss Sarah Bull
Secretary:
Ms Christine Allen
Ecumenical in aim and direction.

Residential Centres for Young People

If the name and address of a centre to take young people to for a
residential weekend, week or course is required, first refer to the
selection here then to the retreat houses/conference centres list on
pages 319–35.

SE England

Allington Castle
Maidstone
Kent ME16 0NB
Tel: 0622 54080
A Catholic centre

Herne Bay Court
Canterbury Rd
Herne Bay
Kent CT6 5TD
Tel: 022 73 3254
Interdenominational but under
evangelical direction

Hildenborough Hall
Otford Hills
Sevenoaks
Kent TN15 6XL
Tel: 0732 61030
(as Herne Bay Court)

The Rock Youth Centre
Bradwell Rd
St Lawrence
Southminster
Essex CM0 7LW
Tel: 0621 87308
Anglican/Methodist

Central Southern

The Grafham Centre
Bramley
Surrey
Bookings to Diocesan House
Quarry St
Guildford GU1 3XG
Tel: 0483 571826
An Anglican centre

SW England

Sheldon Centre
Dunsford
Exeter
Devon EX6 7LE
Tel: 0647 52203
An Anglican centre

St Rita's Youth and Pastoral Centre
Ottery Moor
Honiton
Devon EX14 8AP
Tel: 0404 2601
A Catholic centre

East Anglia

Horstead Centre
Horstead
Norwich
Norfolk NR12 7EP
Tel: 0603 737215
An Anglican centre

The Pickenham Centre
North Pickenham
Swaffham
Norfolk PE37 8LG
Tel: 0760 440427
A Low Church centre

Midlands

The Briars
Crich Common
Crich
Matlock
Derbyshire DE4 5BW
Tel: 077 385 2044
A Catholic centre

Eton/Dorney Project
Dorney Vicarage
Windsor
Berks. SL4 6QS
Tel: 06286 62823
An Anglican centre

Far Forest Centre
c/o Far Forest Vicarage
Kidderminster
Worcs. DY14 9TT
Tel: 0299 266580
An Anglican centre

John F. Kennedy House
Coventry Cathedral
7 Priory Row
Coventry CV1 5ES
Tel: 0203 20933
An ecumenical venture

NE England

The Elsdon Centre
Elsdon Old School
Northumberland NE19 1AA
Tel: 0830 20389
An Anglican centre

Seahouses Hostel
North Sunderland Vicarage
Seahouses
Northumberland NE68 7TU
Tel: 0665 720202
An Anglican centre

Postgate House
Lartington
Barnard Castle
Co. Durham DL12 9DA
Tel: 0833 50262
A Catholic centre

NW England

Coniston Youth Centre
c/o Mrs M. Stephens
1 The Forge
Coniston
Cumbria LA21 8DB
Tel: 09664 41326
An Anglican centre

St John in the Vale
The Vicarage
Naddle
Keswick
Cumbria CA12 4TF
Tel: 0596 72542
An Anglican centre

Rydal House
Youth Centre
Rydal
Ambleside
Cumbria LA22 9LX
Tel: 0966 32050
An Anglican centre

Wales

Plas yr Antur
Fairbourn
Gwynedd LL38 2BQ
Tel: 0341 250282
An Anglican centre

Lawrence House
Port Dinorwic
Gwynedd
Bookings to Church House (Diocesan
Board of Education)
1 Hanover Street
Liverpool L1 3DW
Tel: 051 709 9722

Scotland

Laetare
Catholic Youth International Holiday
Hostel
53 Blackness Road
Linlithgow
West Lothian EH49 7JA
Tel: 0506 842145
and 0506 842214

Most of the centres listed are happy to receive enquiries and bookings from any Christian youth group. The denominational identification refers only to the sponsoring or organising authority.

CHAPTER NINE

The Family

The Family Today – A Changing Scene

Married couples, I speak to you of the hopes and ideals that sustain the Christian vision of marriage and family life. You will find the strength to be faithful to your marriage vows in your love for God and your love for each other in the face of every storm and temptation.

Pope John Paul II, York

The social climate into which marriage fitted fifty years ago was supportive of marriage, even though, in some circles, established attitudes to marriage and family were being questioned. It was maintained – socially – that marriage was an institution which state and people should foster and guard. Because of this socially protective view of marriage, the concept of family was much stronger. It is a matter of interest that in many places there remained something of this old-style approach of society to marriage as late as after the Second World War. To a large extent this supportive background has been replaced within living memory. Unhappily for marriage as an institution, the society which once actively supported marriage is now unconsciously, to put it no higher, inimical to marriage and the family.

Marriage and the family are now subject to a host of external pressures. To mention a few examples: many families feel isolated, especially in high-rise flats and on some new housing estates. The growth of consumerism and the development of the credit card system tend to put economic pressures on families. This, combined with the cost and difficulty of finding a house, is making the two-wage family the norm. Frequently families find themselves spending less and less time together. Television too easily becomes the substitute for a listening presence.

Unemployment and inflation have now placed added strains and tensions on family life. Often without realising it, many families live

above their means. Frequently spouses have to find extra employment just to meet expenses, to the neglect of one another and their
children. In an age of consumerism human life itself is considered
disposable and expendable. Children are often seen as a bother, an
expense. Mobility of families can mean increased rootlessness. In
the past, many marriages were supported by the 'extended family'
where children, parents, grandparents and relatives lived in close
proximity. But the small isolated family is a fact of modern life.
Without the benefit of lasting friendships and support systems it has
to cope alone with the frustrations of daily life.

Today we are not so much preoccupied with survival as with the
quality of life. As the standards of living and social expectations
have risen, so have the psychological expectations. The more economic and material needs are satisfied, the more important does
personal growth become. There is a greater emphasis in marriage
on the need for individual fulfilment, as well as generally higher
expectations of the marriage. Much of this is to be welcomed and is
reflected in the theological thinking of the Church. But a proper
understanding of these ideas is important; they are too easily exaggerated and distorted.

It is, perhaps, inevitable that we focus on the problem areas, but
we must properly recognise that the vast majority of marriages are
successful and enriching. Despite the negative thrusts, marriage
today has probably a greater potential for Christian fulfilment.
Many factors exist and serve to sustain and enrich marriage and
family life. Despite the erosion of recent times, living standards
have seen a general improvement, so also have medical care and
education. We see a greater awareness of the radical equality of
men and women and of the emotional needs of all the members of
the family.

The Christian family naturally does not live its life detached from
the evolution of the family in modern society. Those who minister
to marriage and family are in the front-line of the Church's loving
concern. They must confirm and support couples in seeing their
marriage as a vocation leading to holiness, as a way of life that
affords opportunity for spiritual growth. 'The gift of Jesus Christ is
not exhausted in the actual celebration of the sacrament of marriage, but accompanies the married couple throughout their lives'
(*Familiaris Consortio* n.56). Because married couples are influ-
enced by the character and customs of modern society, priests must
be alert to the changing circumstances in which marriages now
take place and in which families have to live. More significantly,

they should be aware of the developments that have taken place in the Church's understanding of the sacramental vocation of marriage.

At this time, when the family is subject to so many pressures 'the Church perceives in a more urgent and compelling way her mission of proclaiming to all people the plan of God for marriage and the family, ensuring their full vitality and human and Christian development, and thus contributing to the renewal of society and of the People of God'. (*Familiaris Consortio* n.3.)

M.Q.

(*Familiaris Consortio* is available from the Catholic Truth Society, pamphlet no. S357.)

A Charter of Family Rights

Springing from the 1980 Synod of Bishops' meeting on Family Life, the following 12 articles of the 'Charter of the Rights of the Family' were published by the Vatican in 1983.

The Holy See, having consulted the Bishops' Conferences, now presents this 'Charter of the Rights of the Family' and urges all states, international organisations and all interested institutions and persons to promote respect for these rights and to secure their effective recognition and observance.

Article 1 All persons have the right to the free choice of their state of life and thus to marry and establish a family or to remain single.
Article 2 Marriage cannot be contracted except by the free and full consent of the spouses duly expressed.
Article 3 The spouses have the inalienable right to found a family and to decide on the spacing of births and the number of children to be born, taking into full consideration their duties towards themselves, their children already born, the family and society, in a just hierarchy of values and in accordance with the objective moral order which excludes recourse to contraception, sterilisation and abortion.
Article 4 Human life must be respected and protected, absolutely, from the moment of conception.
Article 5 Since they have conferred life on their children, parents have the original, primary and inalienable right to educate them; hence, they must be acknowledged as the first and foremost educators of their children.

Article 6 The family has the right to exist and to progress as a family.

Article 7 Every family has the right to live freely its own domestic religious life under the guidance of the parents, as well as the right to profess publicly and to propagate the faith, to take part in public worship and in freely chosen programmes of religious instruction, without suffering discrimination.

Article 8 The family has the right to exercise its social and political functions in the construction of society.

Article 9 Families have the right to be able to rely on an adequate family policy on the part of public authorities in the juridical, economic, social and fiscal domains, without any discrimination whatsoever.

Article 10 Families have a right to a social and economic order in which the organisation of work permits the members to live together and does not hinder the unity, well-being, health and the stability of the family, while offering also the possibility of wholesome recreation.

Article 11 The family has the right to decent housing, adequate for family life and commensurate to the number of the members, in a physical environment that provides the basic services for the life of the family and the community.

Article 12 The families of migrants have the right to the same protection as that accorded other families.

(The above is reproduced, with permission, from CTS pamphlet number S371.)

Family Liturgy

During his historic visit to Britain, Pope John Paul II spoke several times of the family and of the sanctity of family life. Echoing the Second Vatican Council, which spoke of the family as 'the domestic sanctuary of the Church' (*Decree on the Laity* 11), he said, 'may your homes become schools of prayer for both parents and children' (Wembley Stadium). And at York, 'I urge that your homes be centres of prayer; homes where families are at ease in the presence of God.'

Are these just beautiful papal ideals or exhortations that can be translated into practical everyday action? Using the Church's Year, with a little courage and a lot of perseverance, a family can become 'at ease in the presence of God'. The pastor has the serious responsibility of placing the ideal before the families in his pastoral care, encouraging them and making available to them (through the parish library, see pages 113–14, or the parish bookstall, see pages 114–15) the resources they will need.

The Church's Year provides the structure for a renewal of family life; a renewal that needs to be constantly worked at. Advent or Lent are perfect opportunities for making a start. The 'expectation' of these seasons allows, for example, for the commencement of grace before and after meals (this assumes that the family is eating together) and the development of that opportunity into real family prayer. (This is more fully worked out in the book, *Let's Celebrate*, referred to below.)

Every year *The Universe* newspaper provides its readers with a liturgical calendar. Many families pin this up on the family notice board, or sellotape it to the inside of a kitchen cupboard. On it should be added the dates of all the family birthdays, all the feast days of the members of the family (if not shown already, the local parish priest may assist with the correct date) and the baptismal day of each member of the family. In this way every member of the family has three days to celebrate in the course of the year: birthday, baptismal day and feast day.

The very best time to introduce such new ideas is when the family is in its infancy, so that children grow up from their highchair days considering it natural to hold hands round the table for grace before meals, and as natural to have a candle on the meal table to celebrate a baptismal day as to have candles on a birthday cake.

Advent is the easiest season to celebrate in the home. With an Advent wreath as a centrepiece for the dining table and an Advent calendar in the kitchen, parents only have to link these prayerfully, at the time for grace before meals and night prayers, to the 'coming' of the Messiah.

Lent must be celebrated as a preparation for Easter and not just as a time for 'giving up'; it is better considered in the family as a time for 'taking on'. Parents can see it as an opportunity to develop a little what they have already begun during Advent, or to recommence what, through family pressures, has been dropped.

Most parents lack 'know-how' and confidence, and both of these can be supplied by their priest. He may personally have little experience of teaching young children to pray, or of making an Advent wreath, etc., but he does have it in his power to make simple, attractive books available and bring into the parish, to meet with the

Union of Catholic Mothers or the Women's Guild, those who do have the experience and expertise.

Further reading

Let's Celebrate: Through the Church's Year in the family, Tony Castle, Hodder and Stoughton, 1983.
How to bring up children today, Chuck Gallagher and Cathy Davis, Veritas Family Resources.
How to pray with your children, Mickey and Terri Quinn, Veritas Family Resources.
How to interest your children in the Mass, Mickey and Terri Quinn, Veritas Family Resources.
How to hand on the Faith to your children, Mickey and Terri Quinn, Veritas Family Resources.

What is Christian Marriage?

A human reality and a saving mystery

Marriage is an eminently human institution (*Gaudium et Spes*, n.49) established by the Author of life (Genesis 2:24) and restored by Christ to become 'the pathway to holiness for all the members of a family' (Pope John Paul II, York). It develops from the process of the communication of self and the attraction to and acceptance of another (*Gaudium et Spes*, n.48). This process, indeed, is seen as reflecting the communication between Christ and his Church (*Gaudium et Spes*, n.48), or between God and Man, which is consummated in the total giving of Jesus himself, as a life-giving sacrifice. The two people involved in the self-communication which leads to and sustains marriage gradually discover and come to delight in the mystery of each other (Isaiah 62:4–5). Indeed, through the same process, they actually enable each other (and their children) to discover and be themselves.

In Catholic tradition, marriage is identified as a sacrament, that is, one of seven unique channels of redemptive grace brought forth in the Church by Christ himself. When we speak of marriage as a sacrament, we are saying more than that marriage is a sacred covenant and an enriching sanctifying bond. It includes these realities and at the same time transcends them. For sacramental marriage is an instruction from Christ himself to enrich the life of the Church in a unique way, and 'sacrament' designates the lifelong relationship of husband and wife.

Matrimonial Consent

The mutual self-communication in all the stages of the relationship, whilst aided by affection, is an act of the will and not only emotion. As the relationship between a couple reaches the stage when both parties decide to share the whole of their lives together it is through an act of the will, expressed in a personal consent, that they communicate themselves to each other in such a way as to constitute marriage. It is a symbolic and juridical act which has certain implications for the participants. Since 'persons cannot be turned into objects to be handed over and received' (*Summa Theol.* 1, q.30, a.4, ad sec.), the spouses give themselves to each other in those acts which embody and communicate the totality of their being. These include not only acts of sexual intercourse but all the acts, both ordinary and extraordinary, which symbolise a true communication of self and effect a communion of life. Because the gift of self is a total one, reflecting the total giving of Jesus for his Church, it is directed towards one partner (*Familiaris Consortio*, n.19) and it effects a union which is indissoluble (*Familiaris Consortio*, n.20). As the total giving of Jesus gives life and draws others into the family of the Church (in this context 'the Church' refers only secondarily to an institution; primarily it refers to people – all the baptised, including the hierarchy, in their common body of unity in the Lord), so the self-communication in marriage is ordered towards the procreation and education of children (can. 1055).

Marriage as parenthood

It is important that we should have a vision of parenthood as a sharing in the creativity of God. Parents – in the fullest sense – bring their child to life; they give birth but then they help their child progressively realise all its potential, awaking its sensitivities, gently bringing it to God (*Marriage and the Family*, 1979, Catholic Bishops of England and Wales).

Just as the parents through love enable each other to discover and be themselves, so also, through love, they enable their children to take the first steps on a similar road to discovery, a road that will lead them eventually to an awareness and a love of God and to the fulfilment of their own particular vocation in life. Parenthood, therefore, necessarily includes the education of children born of the union and this responsibility does not cease when the child reaches school age for then, too, the parents, and not the schoolteachers, are the principal educators.

Marriage and the Christian Community

Marriage is not only a pathway to holiness for the members of a particular family, it is also a sacrament of love to others. It is not only a *consortium vitae* where true love is fostered and protected; it is also a revelation and proclamation of God's love to the world. Marriage is not so much something a couple receives as something that a couple becomes.

The family is the primary cell of society where human development takes place. It is there that we are educated in the social and Christian virtues and are given the security which will enable us to play a constructive and worthy role in the Christian community and in society as a whole. As such, marriage is a sacrament to be celebrated and supported by the whole Christian community and not merely the family and friends of the spouses.

M.Q.

Preparation for Marriage

The Role of the Priest

When a couple have decided to get married, they have 101 things on their minds; buying or decorating a house, possibly choosing the date, booking the place of the reception, compiling a list of guests and many more things. It is at this juncture that every couple getting married in the Church must come into contact with the priest. This contact presents a unique pastoral opportunity to help the couple prepare adequately for the sacrament of marriage.

The manner of receiving and dealing with them is very important. The priest should take the time to welcome and to hear them out. For this reason, it is important that the place of interview should be comfortable and congenial – a spartan waiting-room does not provide a friendly atmosphere.

At this first meeting, there should be no question of filling in the customary canonical forms for the pre-nuptial enquiry nor should the priest ask the couple to obtain the required legal documents. Such a procedure might lead them to believe that the priest accepts the celebration of their marriage as a simple matter of course. Many couples feel at this stage that their relationship is already sufficiently established to enable them to enter marriage without any formal preparation. This may well be true in some cases but the occasion is the opportunity to show that the Church – and, on the personal level, the priest – is most concerned about the quality of their marriage.

The purpose of the initial meeting or meetings is to assess whether the couple are capable and willing to enter into marriage. This demands of the priest that he make a positive assessment of their situation. It also obviously demands that in each case he sees the parties separately at least once. Otherwise it is difficult to see how he can assess that each is free from any unwarranted pressure. It is for this reason that before a wedding is booked, the priest should meet the couple and be satisfied that they are capable and free from any pressures.

Once a couple actually decide to get married a more specialised preparation is called for. For this reason it is now required in some dioceses that couples give six months notice to their priest of their intention to marry.

Pre-Marriage Courses

To ensure adequate preparation in the period before marriage, all couples should attend a pre-marriage or other similar course. Whatever form the course may take couples should be encouraged to attend in good time, at least six months before their marriage.

In many deaneries, pre-marriage courses are already organised and it is recommended that each deanery should organise such courses. Catholic Marriage Advisory Council and Engaged Encounter are also involved in this apostolate and provide sterling service in this ministry.

In some cases a priest may feel confident that he can provide adequate preparation himself. In such cases it is most helpful to involve married couples who can give the benefit of their own lived experience. With help and encouragement, many such couples will be willing to share in this work at the parish level.

Attendance at a pre-marriage course never removes the responsibility from the priest to assure himself that the couple are in fact adequately prepared for marriage.

The benefits of a pre-marriage course

The course is primarily designed to help the couple to get to know each other better and to be in a better position to understand some of the problems that may arise and to cope with them. Sometimes couples enter marriage with only a superficial knowledge of each other. Because they have enjoyed their period of courtship they have assumed that the relationship is sufficiently established to enable them to live together in marriage for the rest of their lives.

Experience has shown that courtship and marriage are different and the courtship is wasted unless they have used the time to develop those qualities necessary to live together in harmony as man and wife.

There are many things to be discussed and faced by the couple about to enter marriage. There are agreements to be made – on housing, work, finance, household bills and the sharing of household duties and, of course, children. It makes little sense to leave all these matters until the marriage has taken place. A pre-marriage course brings such matters out into the open and the voice of experience is readily available with advice on how to cope with them.

It occasionally happens that the priest does not feel the couple are ready for marriage and also the couple themselves may discover that they do not know each other as well as they thought. This can result in the proposed marriage being delayed or even abandoned. When this happens, there is, of course, pain and disappointment, but it is better to pause at this stage than to find themselves living out their lives in an unhappy marriage or facing the pain of a failed marriage.

Each couple is unique. They are at different stages of maturity and preparedness and the meetings with them must be adjusted accordingly. Even the vocabulary used must suit the various levels of education and articulateness. It would be a mistake to assume that a well-educated and articulate couple are less in need of help and preparation. Intelligence or education do not in themselves bring insight and maturity. On the other hand, couples who have had limited education may be better endowed with sensitivity to one another and the ability to communicate feelings rather than ideas, which is so important to a successful marriage.

As we have mentioned already, marriage is a sacrament. In the marriage of Christians, the natural marriage contract is raised to a new level. By means of the sacrament the married couple share in a most special way the love Christ has for his Church. Their union is a sign of that love and a means of sharing it with each other. The pre-marriage course is intended to help them to realise this and to learn that the ordinary activities of married life are ways of sanctifying themselves, of sanctifying each other through the grace of the sacrament. By sharing in pre-marriage courses, more mature couples will make the courses a much richer experience for all who take part.

M.Q.

An Outline Course

First Session: Looking at the Relationship
1. Start where the couple are now. They are in love, and they hope to marry. Help them to assess how well they know one another, and how well they get on together. Are there areas of common interest? Are there areas of difference? Or are there areas of conflict? How do they cope with these, and how do they think these will affect their future marriage?
2. Get them to compare their ideas of marriage as related to their different family backgrounds. Have they got to know one another's parents and future in-laws? If so, has this helped them to understand one another better – their respective attitudes and values?
3. Evaluate their practical plans for the future. Now that they have decided to marry, what plans do they have? Handling money – do they know what the other is earning and are they saving jointly? Sharing household chores?

Second Session: The Sacrament of Married Love
1. To help the couple to see the sacrament of marriage in the context of their faith in Christ. Preparation for any sacrament means preparation in faith. What the sacrament of marriage will mean to the couple. Will it be an equal partnership before God?
2. The exchange of marital consent will initiate a lifelong covenant of love. Emphasise that the sacrament is not merely a ceremony which takes place in church, but a living out of their married life in all its aspects. Emphasise their part in God's providence – two unique people in a unique marriage. Because they have been baptised, their total commitment to each other in marriage will make present to them and witness to the community the love of Christ for his Church.
3. Explore the riches of the Church's understanding of marriage. Have a look at the Rite of Marriage – give them copies and explain how to choose the form which is most meaningful to them. In this context discuss the Church's understanding of marriage – love, fidelity, unity, indissolubility, children and the grace of partnership. In discussing the form of consent, the priest will be aware that many young people are fearful of the implication of a permanent lifelong commitment. They will be encouraged by an assurance of God's abiding help and his loving presence in their marriage.
4. How their prayer, alone and together, will keep alive their love for God and for each other.

Third Session: Building a Home

1. Where to live – if they are buying a house, will it be in their joint names? Advice regarding mortgage, etc.
2. Marriage and money – budgeting; advice on handling of their money. Their attitudes to money now are a good indicator of how they will handle money as husband and wife.
3. A home of their own; if either party is unable or unwilling to make a break from home, it will involve the other party in a marriage relationship which is somehow diminished.
4. Will both partners continue to work after marriage? Is this a joint decision?

Fourth Session: The Joys of Married Love and Communication

1. Focus on the sexual relationship in marriage and the practical consequences of fertility. What do they think makes marriage unique – the exclusive, total, loving sexual relationship? How do married couples express their love for each other? There are many ways – friendship, kindness, generosity, thoughtfulness. The expression which is special to marriage is the sexual relationship.

Marriage is the commitment of the total person to another person. Because the commitment is total, the giving must be total. The giving of one person to another demands sacrifice. Sacrifice without love is difficult and irksome, but love can make sacrifice easy and love can make it a joy. We give in proportion as we love. Love is not measured by what we receive but by what we give and then, the giving is complete – love is perfect.

2. Necessity of communication; many couples have problems in understanding one another's different needs and feelings in this area. Stress the importance of communicating their needs and feelings to one another in the intimacy of their relationship. Without good communication between husband and wife, the marriage relationship begins to suffer from great pressures and tensions. Ways to avoid turning discussion into argument: the time for such discussion is important (evening – after dinner); the invitation to talk things over should be friendly and not belligerent; young children or other persons should not be present; productive discussion demands consideration of the other person's point of view; if the discussion becomes bitter, it should be set for another definite time; never forget the words 'I'm sorry'.

3. Praying together to God is a very important part of communication.

Fifth Session: Parenthood: The Fruits of Married Love
1. The act of love, in God's design, is also the act by which children can be conceived. Have they thought about the possibility of having children, or the fact that some couples cannot have children?
2. Responsible parenthood means combining the two aspects of marriage, unitive and procreative; the Church's teaching as set out in *Humanae Vitae* points out that both aspects must be respected.
3. Outline the principles behind natural family planning and the availability of approved methods of family planning which are both reliable and morally acceptable. Opportunity of talking about the meaning of sexual morality in marriage and the role of conscience.
4. The home should be the redolent of faith, hope and charity and of all the virtues which foster the three. In sanctifying their children, their supreme task and privilege, parents sanctify themselves. The family is the domestic church and the school of love for the couple and their children. Prayer and the sacraments will sustain them in their married love. (See pages 232–4.)

M.Q.

Catholic Marriage Advisory Council

Since its foundation in 1946 many thousands of families have made use of the Council's services. There are today over 1,000 counsellors, auxiliary members, lawyers, doctors and priests working for CMAC. The marriage counsellors who offer their services, supported by consultants who are experts in their own fields, seek to provide remedial, educational, medical/sexual and legal support to married couples, or those contemplating marriage.

Remedial Helping people to repair damaged marriage relationships is what the CMAC understands by remedial counselling. Naturally the success in remedial counselling depends to a large extent upon the quality of the counsellors. This is strictly controlled by long-established and tried procedures of selection and training. All counsellors are married people with some years experience of married life.

Educational The most important aspect of educational counselling is the provision of pre-marriage courses for which the tutors are specially trained. The second important aspect of educational work is the help made available to teachers. A core curriculum with a range of options to fit different age levels is available. Speakers are also available for any conference concerning marriage and the family.

Medical/Sexual Some cases of disharmony in marriage arise from medical/sexual causes. Access is then needed to skilled medical personnel, who are grounded in Christian moral principles. Medical advisers help with the whole spectrum of such problems. Family planning is the largest category where help is sought and the Natural Family Planning Service provides help in an area of ever-growing demand.

Legal Each local centre has access to the services of a qualified lawyer who is often also a trained remedial counsellor.

For further information contact:

The Catholic Marriage Advisory
Council
15 Lansdowne Rd
London W11 3AJ
Tel: 01 727 0141
or
18 Park Circus
Glasgow G3 6BE
Tel: 041 332 4914

A List of Centres

London

Blackheath
5 Cresswell Park
London SE3 9RD
Tel: 01 852 5420

Croydon
Southwark Catholic Children's Society
49 Russell Hill Road
Purley CR2 2XB
Tel: 01 668 2181

Enfield
The Community Centre
Our Lady of Mount Carmel & St
George
Enfield
Middx EN2 6DR
Tel: 01 937 3781

Havering & Brentwood
Tel: Upminster 26244

Ilford
Kenwood Clinic
Kenwood Gardens
Barkingside
Essex
Tel: 01 554 4680

Wimbledon
Guild House
30/32 Worple Road
London SW19
Tel: 01 947 8285

SE England

Canterbury
Tel: Canterbury 52582

Medway Towns
1 Hills Terrace
Chatham
Kent ME4 6PU
Tel: Medway 724083

East Anglia

Chelmsford
122/128 New London Road
Chelmsford
Essex CM2 0RG
Tel: Chelmsford 59715

Colchester
33 Walsingham Road
Colchester CO2 7BP
Tel: Colchester (0206) 574186

Harlow
Holy Ghost Church
Tracey's Road
Harlow
Essex
Tel: Harlow 442320

Ipswich
Room 38
19 Tower Street
Ipswich IP1 3BE
Tel: 0473 75913

Norwich
Catholic Education Centre
Surrey Street
Norwich
Tel: Norwich 58107

Southend
7 Carnarvon Road
Southend on Sea
Essex
Tel: Southend 67394

Central Southern England

Brighton
63 Church Road
Hove BN3 2BD
Tel: Worthing 505338

Eastbourne
St Agnes' Parish Centre
Whitley Road
Eastbourne
BN22 8NJ
Tel: Eastbourne (0323) 32637

Southampton
100 Wilton Avenue
Southampton
Tel: Southampton 770212

West Surrey
Marist Convent
58 Old Woking Road
West Byfleet
Surrey KT14 6HS
Tel: Weybridge (0932) 42328

SW England

Bristol
58 Alma Road
Clifton
Bristol BS8 2DQ
Tel: Bristol (0272) 64805

Exeter
Tel: Topsham 3217

Gloucester & Cheltenham
1 Vernon Place
Cheltenham GL53 7HB
Tel: 0242 34882

Plymouth
Christ the King Presbytery
Armada Way
Plymouth
Tel: Plymouth 773651 and 772530

Portsmouth
Social Bureau
Edinburgh Road
Portsmouth PO1 3HG
Tel: Portsmouth 732382

Torbay
Tel: Paignton (0803) 551739

Midlands

Birmingham
30 All Saints Road
King's Heath
Birmingham B14 7LL
Tel: 021 444 2293

Coventry
16 Stoney Road
Coventry CV1 2NP
Tel: Coventry 415430

Derby
Queen's Hall
London Road
Derby
Tel: Derby 673745

Leicester
65 London Road
Leicester
Tel: Leicester 553607
for Market Harborough, Tel: Leicester
737434
for Loughborough and Coalville, Tel:
Loughborough 261021

Luton and South Beds.
52 Castle Street
Luton LU1 3AG
Tel: Luton (0582) 23865

Mid-Herts.
Our Lady's Family Centre
141 Woodhall Lane
Welwyn Garden City
Herts. AL7 3TP
Tel: 0707 323957/328066

Northampton
20a Park Avenue North
Northampton NN3 2HS
Tel: Northampton 39697

North Staffs.
4 Broad Street
Hanley
Stoke-on-Trent ST1 4EB
Tel: 0782 23018

Nottingham
4 Oxford Street
Nottingham NG1 5BH
Tel: Nottingham 201343

Oxford
Littlemore Hall
82a St Aldate's
Oxford OX1 1RA
Tel: 0865 245214

Reading
The Community Centre
64 Liebenrood Road
Tilehurst
Reading RG3 2DU
Tel: Reading 53127

South Bucks
Tel: High Wycombe 35450

Swindon
2 Groundswell Road
Swindon
Wilts.
Tel: Marlborough 40784

Watford
Tel: Watford 55236

Worcestershire
49 Spetchley Road
Worcester WR5 2LR
Tel: 0905 352967

NE England

Cleveland
John Paul II Centre
55 Grange Road
Middlesbrough TS1 5AW
Tel: 0642 812212

Darlington
Tel: Darlington 50896

Leeds
Cathedral House
Gt George Street
Leeds LS2 8BE
Tel: Leeds 654499

Sheffield
22 Norfolk Row
Sheffield S1 2PA
Tel: 0742 51329

South Humberside
Tel: Grimsby 58280
or Scunthorpe 732829
or Grimsby 9240473

Sunderland & South Tyneside
28/29 Bridge Street
Sunderland
Tyne and Wear
Tel: Sunderland 283584

Tyneside
Mea House
Ellison Place
Newcastle-upon-Tyne NE1 8XS
Tel: Newcastle-upon-Tyne 320342

York
Tel: 0904 794571

NW England

Blackburn & Burnley
87 Preston New Road
Blackburn BB2 6AY
Tel: Blackburn 47275

Blackpool & Fylde
Salvation Army HQ
Raikes Parade
off Church Street
Blackpool
Lancs.
Tel: Blackpool 43038

Bolton
Deansgate Health Centre
Deansgate
Bolton BL1 1JE
Tel: Bolton 73304

Bradford
Sedgefield Terrace
Bradford 1
Tel: 0274 21160

Chester
Tel: Chester 45511

Halton
c/o Dunsdale West
Carriage Drive
Frodsham
Cheshire
Tel: Frodsham 69098

Lancaster & Morecambe
Tel: Carnforth 824209

Liverpool
150 Brownlow Hill
Liverpool 3
Tel: 051 709 9238

Manchester
Clitherow House
Lower Chatham Street
All Saints
Manchester M15 6BY
Tel: 061 236 5426/7

Preston
58 Pole Street
Preston PR1 1DX
Tel: Preston 612921

Rochdale
Champness Hall
Drake Street
Rochdale OL16 1PB
Tel: Rochdale 49706

St Helens
50 Claughton Street
St Helens
Lancs.
Tel: 051 426 6762

Salford
Clitherow House
Lower Chatham Street
Manchester M15 6BY
Tel: 061 236 5426

South and Mid Cheshire
73 Swallow Lane
Winsford
Cheshire CW7 1JD
Tel: Crewe 55359
or Winsford 4443

Southport
25 Weld Road
Birkdale
Merseyside
Tel: 69650

Stockport
Tel: 061 439 3632

Warrington
Ashton Hall
Buttermarket Street
Warrington
Cheshire
Tel: Warrington 35448

West Cumbria
The Priory
Banklands
Workington
W. Cumbria CA14 3EP
Tel: Whitehaven 2458

Wigan
1 Parson's Walk
Wigan
Lancs.
Tel: Wigan 41294

Wirral
St Joseph's Centre
Greenbank Road
Birkenhead L42 7JS
Tel: 051 342 1030

Wales

Cardiff
St Vincent's House
13 Westbourne Crescent
Whitchurch
Cardiff
Tel: Cardiff 753912

Newport
8 Corn Street
Newport
Gwent
Tel: Newport (0633) 276156

Swansea
115 Walter Road
Swansea SA1 5RE
Tel: Port Talbot 882835

Scotland

Aberdeen
132 Huntly Street
Aberdeen AB1 1SU
Tel: 0224 643174

Ayrshire
2 Woodlands Grove
Kilmarnock
Ayrshire
Tel: Alloway (0292) 41142
or Saltcoats (0294) 67161

Dundee
Our Lady of Sorrows
Finlarig Terrace
Fintry
Dundee DD4 9JF
Tel: 0382 502068

Edinburgh
Bonnington Bank House
205 Ferry Road
Edinburgh EH6 4NN
Tel: 031 553 5150

Falkirk
SCMAC
Hope Street
Falkirk
Tel: 0324 485194

Glasgow
18 Park Circus
Glasgow G3 6BE
Tel: 041 332 4914

Motherwell
Diocesan Centre
Coursington Road
Motherwell ML1 1PW
Tel: Wishaw (0698) 376816

Paisley
50 Greenock Road
Paisley PA3 2LB
Tel: 041 644 2640

Human Sexuality

General Reading
The Art of Loving, Eric Fromm, Allen and Unwin, 1972; a classic study of growth in the ability to love and care.
The Mystery of Sexuality, Rosemary Haughton, Darton, Longman and Todd, 1975.
Humanity and Sexuality, Basil and Rachel Moss, Church Information Office; a preliminary study of 'the theology of sexuality in the light of present theological and psychiatric understanding', prepared for the General Synod of the Church of England.
A Christian Understanding of Human Sexuality; reports presented to the Methodist Conference in 1980 and 1982.
God's Yes to Sexuality, ed. Rachel Moss, Fount; prepared by a working group of the British Council of Churches.
Flesh of my Flesh, Una Kroll, Darton, Longman and Todd, 1973; a discussion of sexism in contemporary society.
Love and Will, Rollo May, Fount, 1972; a study of the spiritual and emotional values in sex.
Embodiment: An Approach to Sexuality and Christian Theology, James Nelson, SPCK, 1979; a consideration of specific questions, e.g. pre-marital sex, homosexuality, the handicapped and the elderly, etc.
Sex and Christian Freedom, Leonard Hodgson, SCM.
Freedom in Love, A.E. Dyson, SPCK.

Recognition of our Sexuality; Personal Growth and Wholeness
Cycles of Affirmation, Jack Dominian, Darton, Longman and Todd.
Man as Male and Female, Paul Jewett, Grand Rapids, Wm B. Eerdmans; a study in sexual relationships from a theological point of view.
The Spirit and the Forms of Love, Daniel Day Williams, New York: Harper and Row, 1968.
Sex and Love: New Thoughts on Old Contradictions, Rosalind Coward, Women's Press.
Christianity and Eros, Philip Sherrard, SPCK.

Sexual Orientation
Homosexual Relationships – A Contribution to Discussion 1979, Church Information Office; Report of Church of England Working Party.

The Twisting Lane, Tony Parker, Panther, 1970.
Time for Consent, Norman Pittenger, SCM.
Homosexuality: A New Christian Ethic, Elizabeth Moberly, James Clarke, 1983.
Psychogenesis: The Early Development of Gender Identity, Elizabeth Moberly, Routledge and Kegan Paul, 1983.
The Church and the Homosexual, J. McNeil S.J., Darton, Longman and Todd.
Catholics, Homosexuality and Human Rights, ed. M. Mitlehener.
Rediscovering Gay History, J. Boswell, G.C.M., 1982.
The Making of the Modern Homosexual, ed. K. Plummer, Hutchinson, 1981.
Homosexual People in Society, Catholic Council for Church and Society (The Netherlands).
An Introduction to the Pastoral Care of Homosexual People, Catholic Social Welfare Commission, 1979 (see pages 271–6 for extract).

Expressing our Sexuality; Marriage Today
Marriage, Faith and Love, Jack Dominian, Darton, Longman and Todd.
Christian Marriage, Jack Dominian, Darton, Longman and Todd; an historical survey and a practical examination.
How goes Christian Marriage?, Richard Jones, Epworth.
Families and how to survive them, Robin Skinner and John Cleese, Methuen.

Sexuality and the Single Person
The Mystery of Sexuality, Rosemary Haughton, Darton, Longman and Todd.
Who Walk Alone, Margaret Evening, Hodder and Stoughton. A Christian consideration of the possibilities open to those who live a single life.
God's Yes to Sexuality, ed. Rachel Moss, Fount, 1981.

Sexuality and the Disabled Person
Entitled to Love, Wendy Greengross, Malaby Press, London.
Sexuality and the Physically Disabled – An Introduction for Counsellors, SPOD. A comprehensive outline of material and advice is available from SPOD (The Association for the Sexual and Personal Relationships of the Disabled): 286 Camden Road, London N7 0BJ, Tel: 01 607 8851/2.

Partners in Life – Handicapped People and the Church. Published by World Council of Churches for the International Year.
Invisible Barriers: Pastoral Care with physically handicapped people – Jessie Van Dongen-Garrad. New Library of Pastoral Care (Society for Propagation of Christian Knowledge).

Wider Issues; Women and Men in Society
Circles of Community, a study booklet, BCC.
A Map of the New Country, Sara Maitland, Routledge.
Mary, the Feminine Face of the Church, SCM.
The Liberating Word, Letty Russell, Phil.
Walking on the Water – women talking about spirituality, Virago, 1983.
Where are the Women?, Pauline Webb, Epworth.
Women in the Christian Tradition, G. H. Tavard.

The Basis of Decision Making
Proposals for a New Sexual Ethic, Jack Dominian, Darton, Longman and Todd.
A Dictionary of Christian Ethics, John Macquarrie, SCM.
Sex and Christian Freedom, Leonard Hodgson, SCM.
The Ethics of Sex, H. Thielicke, J. Clarke.

Family Care Societies

Association of Parents and Friends of Spastics
7 Queen's Crescent
St George's Cross
Glasgow G4 9BW
Tel: 041 332 4616
A self-help group running day centres and clubs for spastics, their relatives and friends.

Association of Parents of Vaccine-Damaged Children
2 Church Street
Shipton-on-Stour
Warwickshire CV36 4AP
A pressure group which campaigns for a compensation scheme for vaccine-damaged children.

Catholic Child Welfare Council
1A Stert Street
Abingdon
Oxon. OX14 3JF
Secretary:
Rt Rev. Mgr Michael F. Connelly
The CCWC is a federation of the Diocesan Children's Societies engaged in child care in England and Wales.

The Church of England Children's Society
Old Town Hall
Kennington Road
London SE11 4QD
Director:
Miss C.W. Stone
To help children and families in need through preventive work and a network of social work support.

The Couple to Couple League
Centrepoint
13 Roe Green Lane
Hatfield
Herts.
Tel: 07072 69036
Contact Couple:
James and Netta Windle
Promotes teaching of Natural Family Planning (Sympto-Thermal method) within the context of Christian marriage.

Family Rights Group
6–9 Manor Gardens
Holloway Road
London N7 6AL
Tel: 01 272 4231 or 01 272 7308
FRG has a list of agencies and solicitors who are willing to act in care proceedings.

Family Service Units
207 Old Marylebone Road
London NW1 5QP
Tel: 01 402 51575/6
Provides a comprehensive family welfare service for families under strain.

Family Welfare Association
501–5 Kingsland Road
London E8 4AU
Tel: 01 254 6251
Provides a professional family social work service. Other groups served include the elderly, adolescents and the recently bereaved.

The Institute of Marital Studies
The Tavistock Centre
120 Belsize Lane
London NW3 5BA
Tel: 01 435 7111
This unit undertakes to help with marital problems, offers training and consultation to allied professional groups.

The National Association for the Childless
318 Summer Lane
Birmingham B19 3RL
Tel: 021 359 4887
Provides self-help groups to assist childless people to come to terms with their situation.

National Children's Home
85 Highbury Park
London N5 1UD
Tel: 01 226 2033
A comprehensive service for children and young people is provided in various forms of residential and community care.

National Marriage Guidance Council
Herbert Gray College
Little Church Street
Rugby
Warwickshire CV21 3AP
Chief Officer:
Nicholas Tyndall
Through 160 local councils providing counselling service for people with relationship problems and education to family life.

National Society for the Prevention of Cruelty to Children (NSPCC)
1 Riding House Street
London W1P 8AA
Tel: 01 580 8812
Aims to prevent the public and private wrongs of children and the corruption of their morals.

The National Stepfamily Association
Room 3
Ross Street Community Centre
Ross Street
Cambridge
Tel: 0223 215370
Secretary:
Mrs. Elizabeth Hodder
The organisation helps the problems of stepfamilies (parents and children), dealing with legal problems, financial and social problems.

Natural Family Planning, Scottish Association For
69a Carlton Place
Glasgow G5 9TD
Tel: 041 959 1935
Office tel: 041 429 3197
Secretary:
Mrs Eileen Grieg

The Pre-School Playgroups Association (PPA)
Alford House
Aveline Street
London SE11 5DH
Tel: 01 582 8871
Catering for the needs of children between the ages of 2½ and 5 years.

Organisation for Parents Under Stress
29 Newmarket Way
Hornchurch
Essex
Tel: Hornchurch (04024) 51538

Society for the Protection of the Unborn Child (SPUC)
7 Tufton Street
London SW1P 3QN
Tel: 01 222 5845
SPUC runs campaigns in Parliament and throughout the country against legalised abortion.

Approved Adoption Societies

England – Non Metropolitan Counties

Avon
Clifton Catholic Children's Society
58 Alma Road
Clifton
Bristol BS8 2DQ

Bedfordshire
St Francis Children's Society
15 High Street
Shefford
Beds. SG17 5DD

Berkshire
Oxford Diocesan Council For Social Work
48 Bath Rd
Reading RG1 6PQ

Cambridgeshire
The East Anglia Adoption and Family Care Association (formerly Cambridge Association for Social Welfare)
9 Petersfield
Cambridge CB1 1BB

Cheshire
Chester Diocesan Board for Social Responsibility
Diocesan House
Raymond Street
Chester CH1 4PN

Devon
Council for Christian Care
Glenn House
96 Old Tiverton Rd
Exeter
Devon EX4 6LD

Plymouth Diocesan Catholic Children's Society
25 Lyndhurst Road
Wonford
Exeter EX2 4PA

Durham
Durham Diocesan Family Welfare Council
Agriculture House
Stonebridge
Durham DH1 3RY

Lancashire
Blackburn Diocesan Board for Social Responsibility Ltd
Diocesan Offices
Cathedral Close
Blackburn BB1 5AA

Lancaster Diocesan Catholic Children's Society Ltd
(formerly Lancaster Catholic Child Welfare Society)
218 Tulketh Road
Preston PR2 1ES

North Yorkshire
Catholic Child Welfare Society (Diocese of Middlesbrough)
(formerly Middlesbrough Diocesan Rescue Society)
110A Lawrence Street
York YO1 3EB

Nottinghamshire
Catholic Children's Society (R.C. Diocese of Nottingham)
(formerly Nottingham Catholic Children's Society)
7 Colwick Road
West Bridgford
Nottingham NG2 5FR

Southwell Diocesan Council for Family Care
Warren House
1 Plantagenet Street
Nottingham NG3 1HL

Sussex East
Chichester Diocesan Association for Family Social Work
Diocesan Church House
9 Brunswick Square
Hove BN3 1EN

England – Metropolitan Districts

Birmingham
Father Hudson's Society
Coventry Road
Coleshill
Birmingham B46 3ED

Church of Jesus Christ of Latter Day Saints (LDS Social Services)
399 Garretts Green Lane
Sheldon
Birmingham B33 0UH

Doncaster
Doncaster Adoption and Family Welfare Society Ltd
25 Highfield Road
Doncaster DN1 2LA

Leeds
Catholic Child Welfare Society (Dioceses of Leeds and Hallam)
(formerly Leeds Diocesan Rescue Protection and Child Welfare Society)
22 Norfolk Road
Sheffield S1 2PA

Liverpool
Catholic Social Services (Archdiocese of Liverpool)
(formerly Liverpool Catholic Social Services)
150 Brownlow Hill
Liverpool L3 5RF

Manchester
Catholic Children's Rescue Society. (Diocese of Salford) Incorporated
(formerly Salford Catholic Children's Rescue Society)
390 Parrs Wood Road
Didsbury
Manchester M20 0NA

Newcastle upon Tyne
Hexham and Newcastle Diocesan Rescue Society
St John Bosco
Dene Brow
9 Jesmond Park West
Newcastle upon Tyne NE7 7DL

Salford
The Manchester Adoption Society
(formerly Manchester Diocesan Adoption Society)
27 Blackfriars Road
Salford M3 7AQ

Wirral
Shrewsbury Diocesan Catholic Children's Society and Family Advice Service (Incorporated)
(formerly Shrewsbury Diocesan Children's Rescue Society)
111 Shrewsbury Road
Birkenhead L43 8SS

London Boroughs

Brent
National Adoption Society
Hooper Cottage
Kimberley Road
Off Willesden Lane
London NW6

Camden
Thomas Coram Foundation for Children
40 Brunswick Square
WC1N 1AZ

Parents For Children
222 Camden High Street
NW1 8QR

Croydon
The Catholic Children's Society (Arundel and Brighton, Portsmouth and Southwark)
49 Russell Hill Road
Purley
Surrey CR2 2XB

Mission of Hope for Children's Aid and Adoption
14 South Park Hill Road
South Croydon
Surrey CR2 7YB

Islington
National Children's Home
85 Highbury Park
N5 1UD

Kensington and Chelsea
The Catholic Children's Society (Westminster)
73 St Charles Square
Ladbroke Grove
W10 6EJ

Lambeth
Church of England Children's Society
Old Town Hall
Kennington Road
SE11 4QD

International Social Service of Great Britain
Cranmer House
39 Brixton Road
SW9 6DD

Redbridge
Dr Barnardo's
Head Office
Tanners Lane
Barkingside
Ilford
Essex IG6 1QG

Southwark
British Agencies for Adoption and Fostering
11 Southwark Street
London SE1 1RQ
Tel: 01 407 8000
Source of further information on member agencies.

Independent Adoption Service
(formerly Independent Adoption Society)
121–123 Camberwell Road
SE5 0HB

Wandsworth
The Phyllis Holman Richards Adoption Society
88 West Hill
SW15 2UJ

Westminster
Church Adoption Society
282 Vauxhall Bridge Road
London SW1V 1AJ

Soldiers', Sailors' and Airmen's Families
Association
16–18 Old Queen Street
London SW1H 9HP

Wales

Gwynedd
Bangor Diocesan Adoption Society
The Vicarage
Llandegai
Bangor LL57 4LG

South Glamorgan
Catholic Children's Society (Wales)
St Vincent's House
13 Westbourne Crescent
Whitchurch
Cardiff CF4 2XN

Scotland

Aberdeen
Voluntary Service
38 Castle Street
Aberdeen AB9 1AU

Family Care
21 Castle Street
Edinburgh EH2 3DN

Edinburgh
Scottish Adoption Association
69 Dublin Street
Edinburgh EH3 6NS

Glasgow
St Margaret of Scotland Adoption
Society
274 Bath Street
Glasgow G2 4JR

St Andrews Children's Society
Bonnington Bank House
205 Ferry Road
Edinburgh EH6 4NW

Worldwide Marriage Encounter

Worldwide Marriage Encounter is a movement within both the Catholic Church and the Anglican Communion devoted to the renewal of the Church through a renewal of the sacrament of matrimony. Central to this renewal is the experience by couples and priests of a Marriage Encounter Weekend.

God's plan for every married couple is that they should live an open, intimate, responsive, communicating relationship. Priests too are called to build this kind of relationship with others. The process of developing such relationships is often hampered by our lack of awareness of what helps and what hinders good communication. For married people, behaviour patterns, a poor self-image, the difficulties we have in listening, the conflict we experience between the world's understanding of marriage and God's plan of marriage, the failure to distinguish marriage from the sacrament of matrimony and above all the difficulties we have sharing feelings, not just thoughts and ideas; all these result in couples settling for an 'ordinary' marriage, instead of the continual enrichment that comes from striving together to live out the vocation of matrimony.

We can sometimes discourage ourselves from further effort by saying 'We are getting along all right'; 'There's no such thing as a perfect marriage'; 'We don't want to rock the boat'. None of these attitudes excuse us from our responsibility to make our relationship as good as it can be. We are all pilgrims on a journey to the Promised Land. We are all teachers and learners in the business of developing our relationships.

The Marriage Encounter Weekend offers couples an opportunity to experience the benefits of examining what they want for their relationship, and of sharing their deepest feelings. The three couples and the priest who form the team do not teach couples how to live their lives, nor do they offer any counselling. They give a series of presentations in which they share their own experience of striving to improve their relationship in order to be a better sign of Christ's love for his Church. They then invite the couples and priests undertaking the weekend to reflect on their own lives and relationships in the light of what they have heard. They write down this reflection and then share it with their partner in the privacy of their own room. There is no group sharing.

Fear is the greatest obstacle we have to overcome in our efforts to build more intimate and communicating relationships. We have a tremendous need to be loved and accepted by others, but we fear we will be rejected if we share our deepest self. We have a great need to see that we have worth in ourselves. We need to 'belong'; we fear loneliness and isolation. We all have a need to be 'ourselves', and fear being taken over by others, even those we love. We have to overcome our fears, be ready to confront and to risk rejection if we are to grow in love.

The weekend offers a series of choices, as does life itself. These choices affect ourselves, others, our children, the Church and the world. We have the responsibility to look at the choices we are making, and to use every means known to us to grow in our love. Our love will then flow out from us on to our children and those around us. They will experience Christ's love, alive in us!

The weekends are held at retreat centres and are intended for Catholic or Anglican couples with good or average marriages but many couples of 'mixed' religion and non-Christian religions choose to come. At the end of the weekend couples and priests are handed a blank envelope and asked to make a donation.

It would be sad if the benefits gained from their weekend experience were not further explored. Opportunities exist to do this. Monthly meetings are held in which couples and priests continue to reflect on their relationships in an effort to become a better sign to their fellow Christians of what it means to 'love one another as I have loved you'.

Marriage Encounter offers couples and priests the opportunity to share the experience of hundreds of thousands of couples and priests who have built on the insights of Fr Gabriel Calvo and the group of couples who started Marriage Encounter in Spain over twenty years ago. All over the world they are inviting others to share with them their own experience as they too strive to live out in their lives Christ's command to 'love one another as I have loved you'.

F.O'S.

More information can be obtained from:

Catholic Marriage Encounter	*Anglican*
Executives:	Clive and Sue Hewitt
David and Pauline Perkins	5 Castle Grove
75 Station Road	Callender
West Horndon	Perthshire
Brentwood	
Essex CM13 3TW	
Tel: 0277 810158	

The Civil Law of Marriage

According to English Law, marriage is deemed to be a contractual relationship between a man and a woman whereby they enter into a certain legal relationship with each other. This creates and imposes mutual rights and duties. It is therefore a form of contract and presents like problems, for example, of form and capacity, and it may be void or voidable.

The term 'marriage' has two separate meanings. The first refers to the ceremony itself by which a man and woman become husband and wife and the second, the relationship which subsequently exists between the two or the state of being married.

There is another aspect of marriage which is much more important. This is the aspect whereby a status is created between a man and a woman to which the law has assigned certain legal capacities or incapacities. A marriage may also affect the rights and duties of third persons, quite unlike a commercial contract which cannot affect the legal position of anyone who is not a party to it. Lord Penzance, in a leading case, defined marriage in English Law thus: 'I conceive that marriage as understood in Christendom may ... be defined as a voluntary union for the life of one man and one woman to the exclusion of all others.' The definition refers to three conditions, namely:

1. The marriage must be of a voluntary nature.
2. The marriage must be for life.
3. The marriage must be monogamous, i.e. neither spouse may contract another marriage so long as the original union subsists.

There are two conditions which have to be satisfied in order that a man and woman may become husband and wife namely:

1. They must both possess the capacity to contract a marriage.
2. They must observe the necessary formalities.

To have capacity to contract a valid marriage in England the following must be satisfied:

1. One party must be male and the other female.
2. Neither party must be already married.
3. Both parties must be over the age of 16.
4. The parties must not be related within the prohibited degrees of consanguinity or affinity.

M.Q.

Pastoral Care of One-Parent Families

There are today many households with a single parent as sole instrument of both material and psychological-spiritual support. Each parish needs to consider how it can minister to its one-parent families and help them to play an active and responsible part in the church and the community.

So many parents in this situation feel a sense of rejection even from the parish. The effect on self-confidence is sometimes devastating. Experience teaches that families in this situation often feel they are outsiders and either fall away from the church or if they go to church, tend to creep in and stay at the back. There is a great need for education in this field. People are becoming more aware of the problems facing one-parent families, especially where this has resulted from separation or divorce. Although death brings great pain and separation to the surviving marriage partner, there is a natural feeling of sympathy from the parish community, but separated and divorced people, especially Catholics, feel a great sense of stigma. People, sometimes from shyness and embarrassment, don't know how to react to them. We must be caring and attentive in our approach and avoid any appearance of condescension.

Some useful addresses

Clasp
Linden
Shorter Avenue
Shenfield CM15 8RE
Secretary:
Mrs C. Tuffnel
The Christian Link Association of Single Parents.

Gingerbread
35 Wellington Street
London WC2
Tel: 01 240 0953
Mutual support, practical help and social activities for single-parent families.

Gingerbread Holidays
Lloyds Bank Chambers
Camborne
Cornwall
Tel: 0209 715901
Low-cost holidays for single-parent families, bereaved families of those serving in the Armed Forces or serving prison sentences. Exchanges arranged.

Families Need Fathers
Elfrida Hall
Campshill Road
London SE13
Tel: 01 852 7123
Self-help organisation maintaining contact and relationship for children during and following parents' divorce or separation. Gives advice on custody, care and control for fathers.

Messenger House Trust
8 Malcolm Road
Wimbledon
London SW19 4AS
Tel: 01 947 8903
A national organisation which houses both unmarried mothers and their children and illegitimate young men who have been brought up in care and need support once they have been discharged.

National Council for One-Parent Families
255 Kentish Town Road
London NW5 2LX
Tel: 01 267 1361
Help and advice but no counselling for one-parent families and single pregnant women and girls.

National Federation of Solo Clubs
7–8 Ruskin Chambers
191 Corporation Street
Birmingham B4
Tel: 021 236 2879
Provides social activities and welfare facilities for widowed, divorced and separated people and their children.

One-Parent Family Holidays
25 Fore Street
Praze
Camborne
Cornwall TR14 0JX
Tel: 0209 831274
Offering one-parent families a
continental holiday with other people
in a similar position.

The Scottish Council for Single Parents
13 Gayfield Square
Edinburgh EH1 3NX
This is a referral agency and will ensure
that all applicants are referred to an
agency most suited to their needs.

Singlehanded Limited
Thorne House
Hankham Place
Stone Cross
Pevensey
East Sussex BN24 5ER
Tel: 0323 767507
Nationwide service for single parents to
widen social contact and provide a
number of services including individual
and group counselling, short breaks.

Annulment of Marriage

The Catholic Church understands the marriage covenant to be an exclusive and enduring partnership for the giving and receiving of love and the procreation and upbringing of children. And for those who have been baptised a valid marriage is at the same time the sacrament of matrimony.

The Church teaches that marriage comes into existence through the consent of the husband and wife, whether or not either or both are Catholic or non-Catholic. Further she insists that this consent must be given freely, fully and properly given, by persons who are able to do so. Where consent has been exchanged then every marriage 'enjoys the favour of the law' and is presumed valid.

In every presumption the opposite may be true. If sufficient evidence can be shown that a particular marriage is invalid, the original presumption no longer holds.

Nullity of marriage (annulment) has always been accepted as a possibility in the Church. Furthermore, the Church lays down the specific ways and means whereby nullity is to be established. Nullity then is not something new, indeed it follows logically from the teaching of the Church on marriage and matrimonial consent.

There is a real difference between a divorce and an annulment. Divorce is the breaking of a genuine marriage bond. A Church annulment is a declaration from the Catholic Church that a particular union, presumably begun in good faith and thought by all to be a marriage, was in fact an invalid union as the Church defines marriage.

There is no attempt in the annulment procedure to impute guilt or to punish persons. On the contrary the purpose of the annulment procedure is to serve one's conscience and spirit and to reconcile persons to full sacramental participation in the community of the People of God. Despite the use of legal terms, there are absolutely no civil effects to a Church annulment in Great Britain. It does not affect in any manner the legitimacy of children, property rights, inheritance rights, names etc. Nor does it affect the duty of both parents to care for their children, if any.

Grounds for Annulment

There are three broad headings under which an annulment can be granted

   (i)   because of an undispensed impediment;
   (ii) because of lack of due canonical form viz. the proper formalities were not observed
   (iii) because the consent was defective.

Undispensed impediments
The impediments to marriage, which render a person or persons unable to marry, include such factors as:

non-age (being under the canonical age for marriage)
impotence (perpetual and antecedent to marriage)
previous valid marriage
relationship (consanguinity/affinity)
holy orders
solemn religious vows

Lack of due Canonical Form
The invalidity of such marriages depends upon the rule that a *baptised Catholic is bound to the form of marriage.* The formalities require that the marriage takes place before a properly authorised priest and two witnesses unless a dispensation is granted releasing certain persons from the law. Where a marriage takes place, without such a dispensation, in a church of another denomination or in a register office, it is regarded as not being a marriage conforming to the rules of the Catholic Church. It is the role of the Tribunal or Chancery Office to deal with such.

Defective consent

Much of the development in the canon law of annulment has concerned defective matrimonial consent. The consent of the parties is
what brings about a true valid marriage and no one, except the
couple, can supply this.

> For matrimonial consent to exist, it is necessary that the contract-
> ing parties be at least not ignorant of the fact that marriage is a
> permanent partnership between a man and woman, ordered to
> the procreation of children through some form of sexual coopera-
> tion. (Can. 1096 S.1.)

It follows, therefore, that if there was something lacking in the
nature, the quality or the object of that consent no true marriage
came into being – the marriage would be invalid from the outset. An
example of this would be the case of a couple who entered marriage
with the intention of seeking a divorce and remarriage if their
marriage turned out to be unhappy. So quite independently of
whether the relationship is successful or not, the fact of nullity exists
– the marriage was invalid from the outset. The point is not whether
the couple's life together proved to be happy but their position at
the time they married.

It follows then that if a declaration of nullity is granted, the cause
of that nullity must be rooted in the nature, quality and object of the
consent which was given by one or both parties at the time of the
wedding itself.

At the practical level this means: Did they have a fully Christian
understanding of marriage? Did they undertake the partnership of
their whole life which Christians see in marriage? Or was there
something lacking? Were they able to take on such a partnership?

The terms of the marriage contract are already fixed and are not
negotiable. So matrimonial consent will be defective if either partner, by a positive act of the will, excludes some essential element of
Christian marriage. If one or both partners intend something other
than what marriage involves, there is no true marriage. Likewise if
one or both partners exclude or intend to exclude, or limit or intend
to limit the rights and obligations involved in permanence, faithfulness (exclusiveness) and openness to children they destroy the
consent because they are consenting to something other than true
Christian marriage.

Capacity/incapacity for marriage

It is in this area that we have seen developments in the canon law of
the Church relating to nullity of marriage. It arose in answer to the

question 'Who are incapable of contracting marriage?' or to put it another way 'When would a person lack the mental ability to give true matrimonial consent?' A distinction is made between knowledge and discretion. The knowledge about marriage may arrive early in life but the ability to appreciate and carry out what marriage involves may not arrive until much later in life. The marriage courts recognise that a person may be extremely competent in his professional life but, at the same time, lack maturity of judgement when it comes to marriage. And it is the ability to appreciate the nature of the obligations involved and to make a reasonable practical judgement about personally undertaking them that is known as due discretion. Canon 1095 of the Code of Canon Law outlines the three forms that psychological incapacity may take:

(i)   Total incapacity for consent
(ii) Lack of Due Discretion
(iii) Inability to assume the essential obligations of marriage.

(i)   *Total incapacity.* If a person lacks sufficient use of reason so as not to know what he/she is doing at the time of the marriage (when the consent is exchanged) then there is no true consent. This use of reason can be impeded by a mental illness or disorder such as severe mental retardation, paranoia and schizophrenia. The presence of such, at the time of the wedding would give rise to this incapacity. (cf. Canon 1095 S.1.)
(ii) *Lack of Due Discretion* Canon 1095 S.2 states:

> They are incapable of contracting marriage – who labour under a serious defect of judgemental discretion concerning the essential matrimonial rights and duties which are to be mutually handed over and received.

Due Discretion is perhaps best understood in conjunction with the previous paragraph (total incapacity) and means the capacity to evaluate sufficiently the nature of marriage viz. to realise and appreciate that in marriage one is committing oneself to a partnership of life and love with another person, that this partnership is permanent and that it must be open to the procreation and upbringing of children. And that having evaluated it, he/she freely chooses this state. If a person so lacks the ability to judge maturely what is understood of marriage, the marriage would be invalid. The situation arises in people suffering from serious psychological disturbances – perhaps only temporary – which make them incapable of appreciating sufficiently what Christian marriage is all about.

(iii) *Inability to assume the essential obligations of marriage:* Canon 1095 S.3 states:

> They are incapable of contracting marriage – who, because of psychological reasons, are not strong enough to assume the essential obligations of marriage.

In addition to the capacity of being able to understand what Christian marriage is, spouses must be psychologically capable of assuming and fulfilling the essential obligations of marriage. So, in a given situation, a person may clearly understand what marriage is but be quite unable to sustain a lifelong stable man–woman relationship. If that is so, he/she is incapable of marriage. We are speaking here of a disability. Further it is a disability to *assume*. One may well question: how does one decide whether a person is unable to assume obligations? In practice we look at the matter indirectly. The direct object of the Tribunal's investigation is the ability/inability of the person to *fulfil* the obligations of marriage. If in the examination of the performance of the person before and after the marriage, the conclusion is reached that the person did not fulfil essential duties and responsibilities and indeed could not, the Tribunal will conclude that the person was unable to assume the same duties and responsibilities. No one is bound to the impossible and it is axiomatic that one cannot assume what one cannot fulfil.

A marriage cannot be declared null and void simply because everything is not or did not turn out perfect. It is not the non-fulfilment of the responsibilities or subsequent failure that invalidates a marriage but the simple fact that the non-fulfilment is due to one or other of the parties being incapable of undertaking the marriage relationship.

Sometimes this inability to *assume* is absolute, viz. a person is incapable of marrying anyone. But there are people who are incapable of establishing a stable relationship with one another although they may be quite capable of entering a true marriage with another party. The inability is said to be relative and the invalidity is alleged to arise from the interaction of their characters and not just from personality disorder(s) – the personality structures can be such that the parties are radically incapable of fulfilling one or other of the essential obligations of marriage even though they may sincerely try to make a success of the marriage. It is important therefore, that a person's capacity be always judged relative to the marriage in question and not just to marriage in general. And since every marriage is a relationship, if there is not capacity for the relationship there is no marriage.

Procedure

At the beginning we said that in every presumption the opposite may be true. The presumption of validity given to marriages duly celebrated according to the canon law yields to proof of the opposite. The fact that a marriage has broken down, whatever the circumstances of that unhappy event, is not in itself a reason for granting an annulment. Neither is the fact that a decree of civil divorce has been obtained. Nor is a desire, however genuine and well-intentioned, to enter marriage with someone else. An annulment can only be granted when it is clearly proved, to the satisfaction of the Tribunal, that the marriage was null and void from the very beginning. The onus of proof lies with the person who asserts that no real marriage came into being. The degree of certainty required is what is called moral certainty, viz. certainty that excludes reasonable doubt.

The whole procedure for nullity is aimed at arriving at moral certainty. It involves the collection of written evidence from the parties as well as from other persons (witnesses) who would be in a position to support the plea. The evidence/testimonies collected is then studied by advocates representing the parties as well as by the official of the Tribunal called the 'Defender of the Marriage Bond'. The duty of the latter is to point out any flaws in the arguments presented in favour of nullity as well as to give reasons, if these are present, for upholding the validity of the marriage. The evidence of the case, together with the submissions of the advocates and Defender of the Marriage Bond, are then studied by three judges who have already been appointed to consider the case. They decide the issue, giving their reasons, in law and in fact, for saying that the marriage is null and void or that the nullity of the marriage is not proven. Their reasons are outlined in what is called the 'Sentence'. The Sentence is then communicated to the representatives of the parties and to the Defender of the Marriage Bond. If the decision of the judges is that nullity has not been proven, the petitioner may appeal against that decision. If the decision is for the nullity of the marriage, the Defender of the Marriage Bond must, by law, appeal against the decision. If the Appeal Court upholds the Decision a Decree of Nullity is issued. However, where two consecutive courts give different decisions the case is referred to the Sacred Roman

Rota, or with permission to a third court in the local area. For a Declaration of Nullity to be granted there must be two conforming decisions in favour of the nullity of the marriage.

M.Q.

Pastoral Care of Separated and Divorced Catholics

Divorce is affecting, directly or indirectly, more and more Catholics. Ministry to the separated and divorced must become a significant part of our total ministry to marriage and family. Separated and divorced Catholics are now engaging in a like-to-like ministry; for example in the Association for Separated and Divorced Catholics. The mutual support which is given helps to counteract the sense of stigma which many feel. 'The ecclesial community must support such people more than ever. It must give them much respect, solidarity, understanding and practical help, so that they can preserve their fidelity even in their difficult situation' (*Familiaris Consortio* n.83). *Familiaris Consortio* enjoins a very strict obligation on all – priests and people – to regard with special compassion those who are separated and divorced. It is not our duty to judge, but to 'pray and encourage', in other words, to recognise their special need, acknowledge that need and show by our public concern and practice that they are equally important members of the community.

From exchanges with separated and divorced Catholics, we know that many of them, far from taking the easy way out, tried to maintain their marital relationship for years under increasing hardship. We also know that they are often among the strongest defenders of the indissolubility of marriage while striving to maintain their place within the Church and reaching out to others to help them do the same. We must also be attentive to their needs. The following needs emerged from recent pastoral exchanges:

the need for moral acceptance
the need to be taken out of isolation
the need for contact with understanding adults
the need for better financial provision
the need to be welcomed by the local community of the parish
the need for emotional support when coping with marriage breakdown.

By remaining true to their marriage vows even though separated or divorced, people can still speak to us of God's faithful love and be a powerful witness in the Christian community (cf. *Fam. Con.* n.83).

There are some areas of special concern. The simple fact of divorce does not bar a person from the sacraments. As we become more aware of the nature of Christian marriage and the psychological conditions needed for true matrimonial consent, the grounds have been broadened on which an annulment may be granted. In such matters no one should be the judge in his or her own case but should approach the diocesan tribunal for expert advice on the marital situation. There is a need for positive pastoral help and support, at the parish level, for the person who approaches the matrimonial tribunal and more especially if the process for nullity has been introduced. The cooperation of parish and tribunal is important if this process is to help the person engaged in it to come to grips with what he or she has experienced in marital breakdown, and to point the way to a fuller life.

Divorced and Remarried

Those who have been divorced and are remarried outside the Church should also approach the tribunal to explore the possibility of regularising their present marital status so that they may be permitted to take part in the sacramental life of the Church. We know that deprivation of the sacraments can involve tremendous pain for those who are invalidly married. Nevertheless it would be wrong for the Church simply to accept the seeming nullity of one marriage-covenant and entry into another without seeking to discern the truth of the matter.

There is, of course, the painful situation of the couple whose marriage cannot be regularised because in the eyes of the Church and perhaps in their own eyes there exists a previous bond of marriage which survives the application of all the tests relevant to the case. Unless a couple in this situation choose to live a life of absolute continence, they cannot be readmitted to the sacraments.

It is important that couples in this situation should realise that the Church feels their pain and shares it. The words of Pope John Paul II emphasise this point:

Together with the Synod, I earnestly call upon pastors and the whole community of the faithful to help the divorced, and with solicitous care, to make sure that they do not consider themselves as separated from the Church, for as baptised persons, they can and indeed must, share in her life. They should be encouraged to listen to the word of God, to attend the

Sacrifice of the Mass, to persevere in prayer, to contribute to works of charity and to community efforts in favour of justice, to bring up their children in the Christian faith, to cultivate the spirit and practice of penance and thus implore, day by day, God's grace. Let the Church pray for them, encourage them and show herself a merciful mother, and thus sustain them in faith and hope.

(*Familiaris Consortio* n.84)

It is important to understand that the sacraments, especially the eucharist, are not merely rewards for good behaviour. They are the signs of our faith and the unity of the Church – the sacrament of matrimony as surely as the other sacraments. When a marriage does not seem to be that experience of faith and unity because of a prior bond, the reception of the eucharist by a couple would be contradictory to the sacrament's meaning since the Church is unable to discern in their union the sign of (covenant) love between Christ and his Church.

As the Holy Father said in *Familiaris Consortio*, when a couple is in a situation in which they cannot receive the sacraments, the community – priests and people – must show special care and concern. No one should presume to judge the consciences of such couples or their personal responsibility. Only God sees and judges the depths of the heart. Instead we must encourage such couples to take their place in the community, to pray, to attend the Sacrifice of the Mass and give their children an education in the faith.

When an invalidly married couple cannot obtain an annulment because of lack of evidence or any other reason, it may be possible to readmit them to the sacraments through a process sometimes called the 'internal forum' solution. We must emphasise that married couples must never bypass the annulment procedure in favour of this solution. They should always come to the tribunal first. The 'internal forum' solution can be used only when there is moral certainty of the invalidity of the previous marriage in the light of the teaching and the canon law of the Church and when it is morally or physically impossible for that invalidity to be declared in the external forum (viz. the tribunal). We recommend that the priest counselling the couple consult with the chancery or tribunal to clarify their situation. Although this matter remains within the internal forum, it should not be dealt with in the confessional. The people involved should be invited to the presbytery where the case can be discussed in depth. 'Similarly, the respect due to the sacrament of Matrimony, to the couples themselves and their families, and also the community of the faithful, forbids any pastor, for whatever reason or pretext, even of a pastoral nature, to perform ceremonies of any kind for divorced or people who remarry.' (*Familiaris Consortio* n.84.) Such action would confuse and disturb the faithful and derogate from the sacrament of marriage.

M.Q.

Useful addresses

Association for Separated and Divorced Catholics
c/o The Holy Name Presbytery
8 Portsmouth Street
Manchester M13 9GB
Secretary:
Marie McIlroy
Self-help group for the divorced and separated. Assistance is given by names being passed on to those who need help, especially with the children, and pastoral or financial/legal problems.

The National Council for the Divorced and Separated
13 High Street
Little Shelford
Cambridge CB2 5ES
Tel: 0923 22181
Promotes the needs of all divorced and separated people giving free legal, welfare and social advice.

The pre-school child

Pre-school playgroups

Many churches, and other voluntary associations and organisations, have organised and provided playgroups to cater for the needs of children between 2½ and 5. Children attend the group for an average of two and a half hours a day, between two and five times a week. Parents pay a fee towards the cost of wages, rent, heating, equipment and so on.

Social Services departments are responsible, under the Nurseries and Child-Minders Regulation Act 1948, for registering and supervising the groups. Further information, including how to set up and run a group, can be obtained from:

The Pre-School Playgroups Association
Alford House
Aveline Street
London SE11 5DH
Tel: 01 582 8871

Child-minding

The definition of a child-minder is someone who cares for one or more children under the age of 5 to whom they are not related, in their own home for a period of two hours or more in a day, and for a reward. Under the Nurseries and Child-Minders Regulation Act 1948 (amended 1968), child-minders have to be registered with the local authority. Recognition may not be given by the authority if the premises are considered unsuitable for the care of young children. A limit may also be placed on the number of children cared for and other conditions may be imposed regarding safety.

State Benefits – a summary

The range of benefits available to provide income support to individuals and families is wide and complex. Space here merely permits of passing reference; fuller information and advice can be obtained from the agencies listed at the end of this section.

The Department of Health and Social Security is the central authority responsible for the national system of social security. The forms of income support administered by DHSS fall into three categories. *Benefits paid in cash*: a good example of this is the retirement pension. *Benefits in kind*: for example, free dental treatment for expectant mothers. *Subsidising benefits*: for example, the free school dinners available to the children of certain parents. The first two kinds of benefit are usually referred to as Social Security Benefits.

Contributory and non-contributory benefits

Those who have paid, as members of the National Insurance Scheme, have a right to certain benefits. But the amount of the benefit paid is generally related to the number of contributions made, over the years, to the scheme. The principal contributory benefits are the retirement and widow's pensions, and sickness, unemployment, invalidity and maternity benefits. *Non-contributory benefits* do not depend upon contributions, but are paid to all who meet the conditions of the benefit. Principally these are Supplementary Benefit, Family Income Supplement, benefits to help the severely disabled and Child Benefit.

Means-tested Benefits

Some non-contributory benefits are subject to a means test and some are not. A statement of income of the family or individual has to be made to the agency supervising the benefit. Entitlement to the benefit and the amount to be paid depends upon the income currently being received by the family. The two principal means-tested benefits (there are others) are the Supplementary Benefit, for those not in full-time work, and Family Income Supplement, for those on low incomes.

Taxable Benefits

Some benefits are taxable when added to a family's income. Where tax is being paid by a family on earned income, the tax will increase when a taxable benefit is added.

Further details and advice about benefits available and how to claim them can be obtained from the following statutory and voluntary agencies.

Statutory
The local Department of Health and Social Security office can be traced through the telephone directory or at the local Post Office.

Voluntary
Most towns have a Citizens Advice Bureau (see below for further information) and the address can be traced through the telephone directory or the local Post Office. Child Poverty Action Group has many branches throughout the country but centrally can be contacted at:

1 Macklin Street
Drury Lane
London WC2B 5NH
Tel: 01 242 3223/9149

Citizens' Advice Bureaux

Most of Britain's cities and larger towns have at least one Citizens' Advice Bureau. Most people should now have easy access to their services because there are over 900, including a number of mobile bureaux. The two principal assets of the CAB system are that the information available is all-embracing and all enquiries are dealt with in the strictest confidence.

The organisation's work is coordinated by The National Association of Citizens' Advice Bureaux. It disseminates information about legislation, social services and other matters of interest and importance. Central government gives grant-aid to the National Association and shows great appreciation of the role played by the bureaux in the life of the country.

Bureaux are able to assist with a large range of problems, including those of a personal nature, matrimonial disputes, unfair dismissal, consumer problems, etc. Where the CAB worker, specially trained, is unable to help the client, referral will be made, with the client's approval, to an appropriate professional body.

The service provided is not only confidential but also free. The address of a local bureau can be found in the telephone directory, library or direct from the National Association.

The National Association of Citizens' Advice Bureaux
110 Drury Lane
London WC2B 5SW
Tel: 01 836 9231

Pastoral Care of Homosexual People

Pastoral Guidelines

In general terms the pastoral task might be considered as helping homosexual persons, or those who consider themselves to be homosexual persons, to understand and examine the meaning of their behaviour, sexual or otherwise, in the light of the love of God and the love of neighbour, together with the moral and pastoral teaching of Christianity. There are still many unanswered questions regarding the proper pastoral care of homosexuals. In the wake of research in the theological and social sciences and the experience of those already involved in pastoral care of homosexuals, the following guidelines could be offered.

The Church in her pastoral effort is concerned first of all with people. How people are classified is secondary and is intended merely to be a help towards understanding people. Unfortunately, many classifications tend to have judgemental connotations. It is unfortunate that the term 'homosexual' tends to classify people principally by their sexuality. The pastor and counsellor must see all people, irrespective of their sexuality, as children of God and destined for eternal life.

Before attempting to provide spiritual guidance or moral counselling to a homosexual person, pastors need to be aware of the homosexual condition itself. Homosexuality is commonly understood to imply only an erotic, sexual attraction of a person towards members of the same sex. It sometimes also means the absence of attraction to members of the opposite sex, even to the extent of positive disgust for sexual relationships with the opposite sex.

It is difficult to categorise people as simply heterosexual or homosexual. Empirical evidence suggests that sexual orientation in a limited number of individuals is totally exclusive. In those individuals in whom heterosexual disposition is dominant, there seems to exist a latent potentiality for homosexual interest of which the person may not be aware.

Before attempting to provide spiritual guidance or counselling for a homosexual person the pastor must be aware of his own limitations. Unconscious prejudice resulting from a biased social tradition does injustice to the homosexual and renders effective counselling impossible. No real benefit can be expected unless the pastor clears away all traces of the misunderstandings that make real communication impossible.

One of the most important aspects of homosexuality is the awareness of being 'different' from the majority of people. This consciousness of being 'different', of belonging to a minority, leaves the homosexual person suffering from the same problems as all minority groups with the added factor that their 'difference' is secret. This leads to a deeper alienation. In a society that can see them as objects of cruel jokes and contempt, homosexuals commonly suffer from lack of self-esteem and a loneliness that heterosexuals find difficult, if not impossible, to comprehend. In ordinary mixed society, homosexuals feel like strangers. They are shunned and despised by people who may have an inaccurate or distorted knowledge of the homosexual person. Many homosexuals are reserved and even withdrawn, not anxious to draw attention to their difficulties. However, among both heterosexuals and homosexuals there are people who are exhibitionists – explicit and vulgar. In both categories these are a minority and the attention they attract is out of proportion to their numbers. Before 1967 the constant fear associated with homosexual acts was that of blackmail, but since the law has withdrawn the penalty for homosexual acts between consenting adults there have been explicit portrayals of the homosexual as ridiculous and bizarre. This means that the judgement of many people, including Christians, is based on a limited knowledge which is unaware of the deeper, distressing tensions which beset the person who is homosexual.

It is the role of the pastor to offer encouragement and support. Many good people who are homosexual are constantly struggling against the demands of their condition, and they must not be allowed to despair. It is unworthy of a pastor to offer only superficial advice for such an intractable problem.

Pastors can be especially helpful in the 'coming out' process. This is the point at which the homosexual person admits openly to his or her homosexuality and it is frequently the first stage of being able to cope. The pastor seems to be an obvious person with whom to share these confidences and his own response must be sensitive and sympathetic. A clear re-affirmation of moral standards may be required but this must not be a blunt rejection based on prejudice and ignorance. Rejection can force homosexuals to rely exclusively on the companionship of fellow homosexuals where at least they will be met with the understanding which has been denied by the pastor.

Some would argue that societies specifically for homosexuals are the ideal setting for allowing people with the same tendencies to understand and cope with shared anxieties. It is difficult to assess the value of such associations. The pastor must advise against the homosexual society which has as its main purpose the introduction of, or a meeting with, people with at least the implied, if not explicit, purpose of encouraging homosexual activities. This form of group is quite unacceptable.

On the other hand, the existence of societies for homosexuals who are also Christians means that certain moral standards must be recognised. There are Christian groups explicitly formed for the encouragement of homosexuals to cope with their difficulties. The goodwill of these societies must not be automatically questioned, especially because their very existence may be due to the insensitivity of the general public. On the other hand, there are obvious dangers. Moral support may easily be turned to moral danger and the pastor must encourage the person who seeks his advice to face up to this real possibility. In addition, a society formed originally for the moral support of the homosexual might, even unwittingly, deepen an already existing problem. It might tend to relax standards rather than support efforts to cope with difficulties and homosexual activity may be nurtured rather than avoided.

However, the situation must be kept in proportion. A comparison with accepted social occasions might help to avoid exaggerated or prejudiced decisions. To condemn a social gathering simply because of possible moral dangers could lead to ridiculous restrictions. It could condemn a parish dance or a youth club. It would forbid the sharing of a flat. In fact, such an extreme attitude of mind would be so unreasonable that all social friendships could be under suspicion. This is an unhealthy attitude which destroys human relationships and frustrates that unity within the society which the pastor is supposed to be promoting.

Marriage has not proved to be a successful answer for most homosexuals. Marriage in these circumstances can be unfair to the partner and even extend the distress of the homosexual to the whole family. It may be marriage for the wrong reasons and, in any case, marriage must not be thought of as the only gateway to God and the only way to fulfillment.

Professional psychiatric treatment or psychological counselling is by no means the proven remedy for the homosexual condition. Very often it proves to be a frustrating experience that only heightens anxiety. Pastors and counsellors may suggest psychological testing to determine whether a person is exclusively or predominantly homosexual, as opposed to a 'transition' homosexual, who is passing through a temporary phase of psychological development. In the case of true homosexuals or 'inverts', professional therapy may be helpful to assist them in accepting their condition positively, but therapy should never be suggested in a way that raises false expectations of a reverse or modification of the homosexual condition.

A positive help to the homosexual is the channelling of his energy into a variety of interests, but this sublimation must be positive and genuine. An artificial diversion is unconvincing.

However much is uncertain about the subject of homosexuality, it seems that the generic term does include three more specific and important categories:

1. those who are well adjusted, stable people who have come to terms with their homosexuality, who never seek help and who are never in trouble with the law. These people are psychologically adjusted, sometimes even better than the average heterosexual;
2. those homosexuals who have psychological problems, e.g. neurosis and alcoholism. This group has more in common with other neurotics than with other homosexuals;
3. those homosexuals who have personality disorders which lead to deviant behaviour, e.g. criminal offences. This group have more in common with other social deviants than with other homosexuals.

The Church has a serious responsibility to work towards the elimination of any injustices perpetrated on homosexuals by society. As a group that has suffered more than its share of oppression and contempt, the homosexual community has particular claim upon the concern of the Church. Homosexuals have a right to enlightened and effective pastoral care with pastoral ministers who are properly trained to meet their pastoral needs.

Homosexuals have the same need for the sacraments as the heterosexual. They also have the same right to receive the sacraments. In determining whether or not to administer Absolution or give Communion to a homosexual, a pastor must be guided by the general principles of fundamental theology that only a certain moral obligation may be imposed. An invincible doubt, whether of law or fact, permits one to follow a true and solidly 'probable opinion' in favour of a more liberal interpretation.

Homosexuals may feel that nature in some way cheated them and produced tensions which are undeserved. The homosexual can be shattered on discovering that he or she has, through no personal fault, permanent tendencies which arouse antagonism, ridicule and rejection in society. The Christian task is to understand homosexuals and restore respect for them as persons. They may well feel that the Church is demanding impossible standards. This challenge may lead to an abandonment of faith, but it also offers an added opportunity and resource. Truth is never reached by turning down the clear directives of God and the Gospel. Such a course could only complicate the already existing confusion. God sets certain standards, but his power of sustaining is comprehensive. Christ emphasised his concern for those whom society has rejected. The many difficulties which the homosexual encounters ensures that the strength of God will be at hand. Christ asks that we take up our Cross and follow him, and this may mean that the homosexual person is very near to true Christianity if he responds to this invitation.

The problem of the homosexual is part of a greater problem of the human incompleteness of a people who are on the way to God. Maturity comes when problems are acknowledged and faced. Only confusion arises when the problems are allowed to dictate or there is a pretence that they do not exist.

The pastor will help souls if he introduces them to an understanding of that love which is more comprehensive than sexuality. His role is to introduce people to Christian life in all its fullness. This does not mean instant serenity. There must be gradual purification and real growth in holiness. Every person with spiritual ambitions must cope with his personal limitations. These vary from person to person and are frequently complex and discouraging, but all people who, in spite of limitations and even failure, continue to struggle and grow in holiness of life deserve encouragement. Such people are very near to God.

(Reproduced with permission from the Catholic Social Welfare Commission's *Introduction to the Pastoral Care of Homosexual People.*)

Further Reading

Declaration on Certain Questions concerning Sexual Ethics, CTS, Vatican City, 1975.

The following bibliography has been compiled from many sources. Some of the books listed take a moral stance unacceptable to the Christian tradition but they give sociological and pastoral comment which might be helpful in the understanding of the homosexual condition.

The Invert and his Social Adjustment, 'Anomaly', Baillière, Tindall & Cox, London.

We speak for Ourselves: Experiences in Homosexual Counselling, J. Babuscio, London, SPCK.

Homosexuality: Time to tell the Truth, L. Barnett, Gollancz, London.

We're Here: Conversations with Lesbian Women, J. Cassidy and A. Stewart-Park.

The Homosexual Way – A Christian Option?, D. Field, Grove Booklet on Ethics, No. 9.

The Other Love, H. M. Hyde, Mayflower Books Ltd.

Sexuality and Homosexuality, A. Karlen.

Homosexuality, F. E. Kenyon, BMA Booklet.

Human Sexuality, A. Kosnik, ed., Search Press, 1977.

The Church and the Homosexual, J. J. McNeill, Darton, Longman and Todd

The Christian and Homosexuality, R. Moss.

The Truth in Love, Nationwide Festival of Light.

Counselling Homosexuals, National Council of Social Service.

Time for Consent, N. Pittenger, SCM, London.

Sociological Aspects of Homosexuality, M. G. Scholfield, Boston, Little, Brown.

Sexual Deviation, A. Storr, Penguin, Baltimore.

In Defence of Purity, D. von Hildebrand, Sheed and Ward.

Coming Out: Homosexual Politics in Britain from the 19th Century to the Present, J. Weeks, Quartet Books, London.

Society and the Healthy Homosexual, G. H. Weinberg, Colin Smythe, Gerrards Cross.
Homosexuality, D. West, Penguin.
The Same Sex: An Appraisal of Homosexuality, R. W. Weltge, ed., Pilgrim Press.

PART TWO

The Churches in Britain

National Church Structures

The Catholic Church

England and Wales

The Province of Westminster consists of the Archiepiscopal See of Westminster, with the four Suffragan Sees of Brentwood, East Anglia, Northampton and Nottingham and the Ukrainian Exarchate.

The Province of Birmingham consists of the Archiepiscopal See of Birmingham, with the two Suffragan Sees of Clifton and Shrewsbury.

The Province of Liverpool consists of the Archiepiscopal See of Liverpool with the six Suffragan Sees of Hallam, Hexham and Newcastle, Lancaster, Leeds, Middlesbrough and Salford.

The Province of Cardiff consists of the Archiepiscopal See of Cardiff with the Suffragan See of Menevia.

The Province of Southwark consists of the Archiepiscopal See of Southwark with the three Suffragan Sees of Arundel and Brighton, Plymouth and Portsmouth.

The present order of precedence of the Archbishops and Bishops according to priority of election is: Westminster, Liverpool, Southwark, Birmingham, Cardiff; the Exarch for the Ukrainians; Nottingham, Hexham and Newcastle, Clifton, East Anglia, Portsmouth, Arundel and Brighton, Middlesbrough, the Bishop-in-Ordinary to HM Forces, Hallam, Brentwood, Northampton, Menevia, Salford, Lancaster, Leeds, Plymouth.

Province of Westminster

His Eminence Cardinal G. Basil Hume
OSB, Archbishop of Westminster
Archbishop's House
Ambrosden Avenue
London SW1P 1QJ
Tel: 01 834 4717

Auxiliaries

Right Rev. B. Christopher Butler OSB
St Edmund's College
Old Hall Green
Ware
Herts
Tel: Ware 821723

Right Rev. Victor Guazzelli
The Lodge
Pope John House
Hale St
London E14 0BT
Tel: 01 987 4663

Right Rev. Gerald Mahon MHM
34 Whitehall Gardens
Acton
London W3 9RD
Tel: 01 993 0270

Right Rev. Philip Harvey
4 Egerton Gardens
Hendon
London NW4 4BA
Tel: 01 202 5211

Right Rev. James J. O'Brien
The Farm Cottage
All Saints Pastoral Centre
London Colney
Herts. AL2 1AQ
Tel: 0727 24664

Suffragans

Right Rev. Francis Thomas,
Bishop of Northampton
Bishop's House
Marriott Street
Northampton NN2 6AW
Tel: 0604 715635

Right Rev. Thomas McMahon,
Bishop of Brentwood
Bishop's House
Stock
Ingatestone
Essex CM4 9BU
Tel: 0277 232266

Right Rev. James J. McGuinness,
Bishop of Nottingham
Bishop's House
27 Cavendish Road East
The Park
Nottingham NG7 1BB
Tel: 0602 474786

Right Rev. Alan C. Clark,
Bishop of East Anglia
The White House
21 Upgate
Poringland
Norwich NR14 7SH
Tel: 050 86 2202

Right Rev. Augustine Eugene
Hornyak OSBM, Apostolic Exarch for
Ukrainians in Great Britain
22 Binney Street
London W1Y 1YN
Tel: 01 629 1073

Province of Birmingham

Most Rev. Maurice Couve de Murville,
Archbishop of Birmingham
57 Mearse Lane
Barnt Green
Birmingham B45 5HJ
Tel: 021 445 1467

Auxiliaries

Right Rev. Joseph Francis Cleary
SS Mary & John
Snow Hill
Wolverhampton WV2 4AD
Tel: 0902 21676

Right Rev. Patrick Leo McCartie
84 St Bernard's Road
Olton
Solihull
W. Midlands
Tel: 021 706 9721

Suffragans

Right Rev. Joseph Gray,
Bishop of Shrewsbury
Bishop's House
Eleanor Road
Birkenhead LA3 7QW
Tel: 051 653 3600

Right Rev. Mervyn A. Alexander,
Bishop of Clifton
St Ambrose
North Road
Leigh Woods
Bristol BS8 3PW
Tel: 0272 733072

Province of Liverpool

Most Rev. Derek Worlock,
Archbishop of Liverpool
Archbishop's House
87 Green Lane
Mossley Hill
Liverpool L18 2EP
Tel: 051 722 2379

Auxiliaries

Right Rev. Kevin O'Connor
12 Richmond Close
Ecclestone
St Helens WA10 5JE
Tel: 0744 23535

Right Rev. Anthony Hitchen
55 Victoria Road
Freshfield
Liverpool L37 1LN
Tel: 07048 79901

Right Rev. John Rawsthorne
St Joseph's College
Upholland
Lancs. WN8 0PZ
Tel: 0695 625525

Suffragans

Right Rev. John Brewer,
Bishop of Lancaster
Bishop's House
Cannon Hill
Lancaster LA1 5HG
Tel: 0524 32231

Right Rev. Patrick Altham Kelly,
Bishop of Salford
Wardley Hall
Worsley
Manchester M28 5ND
Tel: 061 794 2825

Auxiliary

Right Rev. Geoffrey Burke
Cathedral House
250 Chapel Street
Salford M3 5LL
Tel: 061 834 0333

Right Rev. David Konstant,
Bishop of Leeds
Bishop's House
Eltofts
Carr Lane
Thorner
Leeds LS14 3HF
Tel: 0532 892687

Right Rev. Augustine Harris,
Bishop of Middlesbrough
Bishop's House
16 Cambridge Road
Middlesbrough
Cleveland TS5 5NN
Tel: 0642 818253

Province of Cardiff

Most Rev. John Aloysius Ward
OFM Cap, Archbishop of Cardiff
Archbishop's House
43 Cathedral Road
Cardiff CF1 9HD
Tel: 0222 20411

Auxiliary

Right Rev. Daniel Mullins
'Maes-Gwyn'
63 Margam Road
Port Talbot
W. Glam SA13 2HR
Tel: 0639 883323

Auxiliary

Right Rev. Kevin O'Brien
St Charles' Rectory
12 Jarratt Street
Hull
N. Humberside HU1 3HB
Tel: 0482 29100

Right Rev. Hugh Lindsay,
Bishop of Hexham and Newcastle
Bishop's House
East Denton Hall
800 West Road
Newcastle upon Tyne NE5 2BJ
Tel: 091 2742007

Auxiliary

Right Rev. Owen Swindlehurst
Oaklea
Tunstall Road
Sunderland
Tyne & Wear SR2 7JR
Tel: 0783 41158

Right Rev. Gerald Moverley,
Bishop of Hallam
'Quarters'
Carsick Hill Way
Sheffield S10 3LT
Tel: 0742 309101

Suffragan

Right Rev. James Hannigan,
Bishop of Menevia
Bishop's House
Sontley Road
Wrexham
Clwyd LL13 7EW
Tel: 0978 262726

Province of Southwark

Most Rev. Michael Bowen,
Archbishop of Southwark
Archbishop's House
St George's Road
Southwark
London SE1 6HX
Tel: 01 928 2495

Auxiliaries

Right Rev. Charles Henderson
Park House
6A Cresswell Park
Blackheath
London SE3 9RD
Tel: 01 318 1094

Right Rev. Howard Tripp
8 Arterberry Road
London SW20 8AJ
Tel: 01 946 4609

Right Rev. John Jukes OFM Conv.
The Hermitage
More Park
West Malling
Kent ME19 6HN
Tel: 0732 845486

Suffragans

Right Rev. Hugh Christopher Budd,
Bishop of Plymouth
Vescourt
Hartley Road
Plymouth PL3 5LR
Tel: 0752 772950

Right Rev. Anthony J. Emery,
Bishop of Portsmouth
Bishop's House
Edinburgh Road
Portsmouth
Hants. PO1 3HG
Tel: 0705 820894

Right Rev. Cormac
Murphy-O'Connor,
Bishop of Arundel and Brighton
St Joseph's Hall
Greyfriars Lane
Storrington
Pulborough
W. Sussex RH20 4HE
Tel: 09066 2172

Military Vicariate

Ordinary

Right Rev. Francis J. Walmsley
Bishop's Oak
26 The Crescent
Farnborough Park
Farnborough
Hants. GU14 7AS
Tel: 0252 543649

Bishops' Conference of England and Wales

President:
Cardinal Hume
Vice-President:
Archbishop Worlock
Membership:
The Diocesan Bishops, the Apostolic Exarch for Ukrainians, the Bishop-in-Ordinary to HM Forces, the Auxiliary Bishops.
Standing Committee:
The Archbishops and the Chairmen of the Departments.
General Secretariat:
39 Eccleston Square
London SW1V 1PD

General Secretary:
Mgr Vincent Nichols
Tel: 01 630 8220

Asst. General Secretaries:
Mr Nicholas Coote
Tel: 01 630 8221
Rev. Peter Verity
Tel: 01 821 5411

Administrative Officer:
Mr Aldwyn Dias
Tel: 01 630 8279

Asst. to the General Secretary:
Miss Jenny Bond
Tel: 01 630 8220

Unless otherwise stated, the following Committees may be contacted at 39 Eccleston Square, London SW1V 1PD (Liturgy Office postcode is SW1V 1PL).

Department for Christian Life and Worship

Chairman:
Archbishop M. Bowen

Committee for Pastoral Liturgy
Chairman:
Bishop T. McMahon

Committee for Church Music
Chairman:
Bishop T. McMahon

Committee for Church Art and Architecture
Chairman:
Bishop M. Alexander

These three Committees are served by the Liturgy Office:
Tel: 01 821 0553
Secretary:
Rev. E. Matthews
Assistant Secretary:
Mrs. J. Demolder

Committee for Family Life
Chairman:
Bishop C. Budd

Committee for Consecrated Life
Chairman
Bishop J. Gray

Department for Mission and Unity

Chairman:
Bishop A. Clark

Committee for Christian Unity
Chairman:
Bishop C. Murphy-O'Connor
Secretary:
Canon D. Corbishley
Tel: 01 834 5612

Committee for Catholic/Jewish Relations
Chairman:
Bishop G. Burke

Committee for Other Faiths
Chairman:
Bishop C. Henderson
Secretary:
Miss C. Blackden
Park House
6A Cresswell Park
Blackheath
London SE3 9RD
Tel: 01 318 1094

Committee for Non-Believers
Chairman:
Bishop V. Guazzelli
Secretary:
Rev. J. Gaine
St Teresa's
27 Everton Road
Birkdale
Southport
Merseyside PR8 4BT
Tel: 0704 66865

Committee for Home Mission
Chairman:
Bishop K. O'Brien

Committee for Overseas Mission
Chairman:
Bishop G. Mahon
Secretary:
Rev. J. Brankin
Holcombe House
The Ridgeway
London NW7 4HY
Tel: 01 906 1642

Department for Christian Doctrine and Formation

Chairman:
Bishop D. Konstant

Committee for Christian Formation
Chairman:
Bishop D. Konstant
Secretary:
Rev. P. Purnell SJ
Tel: 01 630 5101

Theology Committee
Chairman:
Bishop F. Thomas
Secretary:
Rev. P. Wilkinson
Upholland Northern Institute
College Road
Skelmersdale
Lancs WN8 0PZ
Tel: 0695 625255

Committee for Family and School Education
Chairman:
Bishop A. Emery
Secretary:
Rev. J. O'Shea
Diocesan RE Centre
La Sainte Union College
The Avenue
Southampton SO9 5HB
Tel: 0703 31194

Committee for Young People
Chairman:
Bishop J. McGuinness
Secretary:
Sr Margaret Foley SND
Tel: 01 630 5101

Committee for People in Higher Education
Chairman:
Bishop D. Mullins
Secretary:
Sr Margaret Foley SND
Tel: 01 630 5101

Committee for Adult Christian Education
Chairman:
Bishop J. Rawsthorne
Secretary:
Rev. P. Purnell SJ
Tel: 01 630 5101

Committee for Ministerial Formation
Chairman:
Bishop J. Brewer
Secretary:
Rev. J. Danson
Our Lady Star of the Sea
2 St Annes Road East
St Annes-on-Sea
Lancs FY8 1UL
Tel: 0253 723661

Department for Social Responsibility

Chairman:
Bishop A. Harris

Committee for Social Welfare
Chairman:
Bishop P. Harvey
Secretary:
Mgr M. Connelly
1A Stert Street
Abingdon
Oxon OX14 3JF
Tel: 0235 21812

Committee for Bio-Ethical Issues
Chairman:
Bishop A. Harris
Secretary:
Mgr M. Connelly
1A Stert Street
Abingdon
Oxon OX14 3JF
Tel: 0235 21812

Department for Christian Citizenship

Chairman:
Bishop L. McCartie

Committee for Public Life
Chairman:
Bishop H. Tripp
Secretary:
Mr K. Muir
Tel: 01 834 5442

Committee for the World of Work
Chairman:
Bishop J. Jukes
Secretary:
Mr K. Muir
Tel: 01 834 5442

Committee for Community Relations
Chairman:
Bishop L. McCartie
Secretary:
Mr R. Zipfel
Tel: 01 834 8692

*Committee for Communications –
Development and Policy*
Chairman:
Bishop A. Andrew

Department for International Affairs

Chairman:
Bishop J. O'Brien

*Committee for International Justice and
Peace*
Chairman:
Bishop J. O'Brien
Secretary:
Rev. Mr R. Beresford
Tel: 01 834 6138

Committee for European Affairs
Chairman:
Archbishop M. Couve de Murville
Secretary:
Sr Benedict Davies
St Angela's Convent
St George's Road
London E7 8HX
Tel: 01 472 6022

Committee for Migrants
Chairman:
Bishop K. O'Connor

The Consultative Bodies

National Conference of Priests
Chairman:
Rev. P. Crowe
Secretary:
Rev. B. O'Sullivan
91 Harvest Road
Englefield Green
Surrey TW20 0QR
Tel: 0784 34280
Episcopal Liaison:
Archbishop D. Worlock

*Conference of Major Religious
Superiors*
President:
Sr Gabriel Robin CSA
Secretary:
Sr Louis Marie Lyons
114 Mount Street
London W1Y 6AH
Tel: 01 493 1817
Episcopal Liaison:
Archbishop Ward, Bishop Gray,
Bishop Moverley

National Council for the Lay Apostolate
President:
Mr U. Russell
Hon. Sec:
Mr S. Gilvin
59 Penbroke Road
Leicester LE5 0SA
Episcopal Liaison:
Bishop J. Cleary

National Board of Catholic Women
President:
Mrs A. McMurray
Hon. Sec:
Miss Y. Nulty
Delves
London Road
Forest Row
Sussex RH18 5EF
Ecclesiastical Liaison:
Bishop H. Lindsay

Catholic Union of Great Britain
President:
Major-General Duke of Norfolk
Vice-President:
Mr K. McDonnell
Secretary:
Mrs J. Stuyt
1 Bolton Garden Mews
London SW10 9LW
Tel: 01 373 3515
Ecclesiastical Adviser:
Mgr V. Nichols

Canon Law Society
President:
Mgr R. Brown VG, JCD
Secretary:
Mgr J. Joyce LLB
c/o Archbishop's House
Ambrosden Avenue
London SW1P 1QJ

Conference Agencies

Catholic Education Council
Chairman:
Bishop J. Hannigan
Secretary:
Mr R. Cunningham
41 Cromwell Road
London SW7 2DJ
Tel: 01 584 7491

Catholic Youth Service Council
Chairman:
Bishop J. McGuinness
Secretary:
Mr C. A. James
41 Cromwell Road
London SW7 2DH
Tel: 01 589 7550

Catholic Fund for Overseas Development (CAFOD)
Chairman:
Bishop A. Hitchen
Director:
Mr J. Filochowski
2 Garden Close
Stockwell Road
London SW9 9TY
Tel: 01 733 7900

National Missionary Council
President:
Bishop G. Mahon
Secretary:
Rev. J. Brankin
Holcombe House
The Ridgeway
London NW7 4HY
Tel: 01 906 1642

National Catholic Fund
Finance Advisory Committee:
Chairman:
Archbishop D. Worlock
Secretary:
Mgr V. Nichols
39 Eccleston Square
London SW1V 1PD
Tel: 01 630 8220

Catholic Media Office
Coordinator, Catholic Media Services:
Mgr G. Leonard
Tel: 01 828 6548
Director:
Mgr J. Hook
23 Kensington Square
London W8 5HN
Tel: 01 938 2583/4/5

Catholic Child Welfare Council
President:
Bishop P. Harvey
Secretary:
Mgr M. Connelly
1A Stert Street
Abingdon
Oxon. OX14 3JF
Tel: 0235 21812

Apostleship of the Sea
Chairman:
Bishop K. O'Connor
Secretary:
Rev. A. Stringfellow
Stella Maris
New Strand
Bootle
Merseyside L20 4TQ
Tel: 051 922 6161

Scotland

The Province of St Andrews and Edinburgh consists of the Archiepiscopal See of St Andrews and Edinburgh; and the Suffragan Sees of Aberdeen, Argyll and the Isles, Dunkeld and Galloway. *The Province of Glasgow* consists of the Archiepiscopal See of Glasgow; and the Suffragan Sees of Motherwell and Paisley.

Provinces of St Andrews and Edinburgh

Most Rev. Keith Patrick O'Brien,
Archbishop of St Andrews and
Edinburgh
St Bennet's
42 Greenhill Gardens
Edinburgh EH10 4BJ
Tel: 031 447 3337

Auxiliary

Right Rev. James Monaghan
Holy Cross Presbytery
252 Ferry Road
Edinburgh EH5 3AN
Tel: 031 552 3957

Suffragans

Right Rev. Maurice Taylor, Bishop of
Galloway
Candida Casa
8 Corsehill Road
Ayr KA7 2ST
Tel: 0292 266750

Right Rev. Vincent Logan, Bishop of
Dunkeld
Bishop's House
29 Roseangle
Dundee DD1 4LX
Tel: 0382 24327

Right Rev. Mario Conti, Bishop of
Aberdeen
Bishop's House
156 King's Gate
Aberdeen AB2 6BR
Tel: 0224 319154

Right Rev. Colin MacPherson, Bishop
of Argyll and the Isles
Bishop's House
Esplanade
Oban
Argyll PA34 5AB
Tel: 0631 62010

Province of Glasgow

Most Rev. Thomas Winning,
Archbishop of Glasgow
40 Newlands Road
Glasgow G43 2JD

Auxiliaries

Right Rev. Charles Renfrew
St Joseph's
38 Mansionhouse Road
Glasgow G41 3DW
Tel: 041 649 2228

Right Rev. John Mone
89 Muiryfauld Drive
Glasgow G31 5RU
Tel: 041 556 5533

Suffragans

Right Rev. Stephen McGill, Bishop of
Paisley
Bishop's House
Porterfield Road
Kilmacolm
Renfrewshire PA13 4PD
Tel: Kilmacolm (050 587) 2494

Right Rev. Joseph Devine, Bishop of
Motherwell
17 Viewpark Road
Motherwell
Lanarkshire ML1 3ER
Tel: 0698 63715

Bishops' Conference of Scotland

President:
The Archbishop of Glasgow
Secretary:
The Bishop of Galloway
Candida Casa
8 Corsehill Road
Ayr KA7 2ST
Press and Media Relations Officer to
the Hierarchy:
The Reverend Thomas Connelly
Press Officer:
5 St Vincent Place
Glasgow G1 2DH
Tel: 041 221 1168/69
Home tel: 041 641 2244

Vocations Commission
President:
The Bishop of Dunkeld
Secretary:
The Reverend John Kelly
Offices of the Commission:
33 Briar Road
Glasgow G43 2TU
Tel: 041 633 0484

Commission on Priestly Formation
President:
The Bishop of Dunkeld

Liturgy and Art Commission
President:
The Bishop of Galloway
Church Music Secretary:
The Reverend David Trainer
Immaculate Conception
2049 Maryhill Road
Glasgow G20 0AA
Tel: 041 946 2071
Art and Christian Heritage Secretary:
The Reverend John McIntyre STL,
MA
Blairs College
Aberdeen AB9 2LA
Tel: 0224 861177/861517

Catholic Education Commission
President:
The Archbishop of Glasgow
Education Officer and Secretary:
Mr James McGrath MA
Offices of the Commission:
43 Greenhill Road
Rutherglen
Glasgow G73 2SW
Tel: 041 647 2986

Commission for Christian Doctrine and Unity
President:
The Bishop of Aberdeen
Secretary (Christian Doctrine):
The Reverend James Cunningham STD
St Francis'
Auchenbothie Road
Port Glasgow
Renfrewshire PA14 6JD
Tel: 0475 43222

Secretary (Christian Unity):
The Rev. James Quinn SJ
28 Lauriston Street
Edinburgh EH3 9DJ
Tel: 031 229 9821

Communications Commission
President:
The Bishop of Motherwell
General Secretary:
Press and Media Relations Officer to the Hierarchy Offices of the Commission:
Catholic Press and Media Office
5 St Vincent Place
Glasgow G1 2DH
Tel: 041 221 1168/69
For UNDA Scotland:
Catholic Broadcasting Centre
4 Easterhill Street
Tollcross
Glasgow G32 8LZ
Tel: 041 763 1757

Commission for Pastoral and Social Care
President:
The Right Rev. Charles Renfrew,
Auxiliary Bishop of Glasgow
National Coordinator:
Mr David McCann
Offices of the Commission:
33 Briar Road
Glasgow G43 2TU

Secretariat for the Pastoral Care of Migrant Workers and Tourists
Apostleship of the Sea
National Director:
The Rev. Andrew Hosie
St Paul's
1213 Dumbarton Road
Glasgow G14 9UP

Apostolate to Oil Workers
Director (Diocese of Aberdeen):
The Rev. Myles Lovell SJ
Sacred Heart
15 Grampian Road
Torry
Aberdeen AB1 3ED

Justice and Peace Commission
President:
The Right Rev. James Monaghan,
Auxiliary Bishop of St Andrews and Edinburgh
Secretary:
Sr Mary Kilpatrick SND
Offices of the Commission:
28 Rose Street
Glasgow G3 6RE
Tel: 041 333 0238

Council of European Bishops' Conferences
Member for Scotland:
The Bishop of Argyll and the Isles

*Joint Commission of Bishops and
Council of Major Religious Superiors*
Secretary:
Sister Veronica Blount RSCJ
Convent of the Sacred Heart
8 Nile Grove
Edinburgh EH10 4RF
Official address:
CMRS Secretariate
28 Rose Street
Glasgow G3 4RE

*Bodies Assisting or Advising the
Bishops' Conference*
President:
The Right Rev. James Monaghan,
Auxiliary Bishop of St Andrews and
Edinburgh

1. Pontifical Society for the
Propagation of the Faith
Secretary:
The Rev. Joseph Coyle STD
Immaculate Heart of Mary
162 Broomfield Road
Glasgow G21 3UE

2. Native Priest Fund
Secretary:
The Rev. Daniel Foley
St Columba's
9 Upper Gray Street
Edinburgh EH9 1SN

3. Missionary Children
Secretary:
Right Rev. Mgr Benjamin Canon
Donachie MA, Dip.Ed., VG
St James'
5 High Street
Kinross KY13 7AN

*Scottish Catholic International Aid
Fund*
President & Treasurer:
The Right Rev. John Mone, Auxiliary
Bishop of Glasgow
Offices of the Fund:
43 Greenhill Road
Rutherglen
Glasgow G73 2SW
Tel: 041 647 2986

Secretariat for the Laity
President:
The Bishop of Motherwell
Secretary:
Mr John Coultas
72 Etive Crescent
Bishopbriggs
Glasgow G64 1EY

The Scottish Catholic Tribunal
President:
The Rev. John Cunningham JCD
Tribunal Offices:
22 Woodrow Road
Glasgow G41 5PN
Tel: 041 427 4212

The Scottish Catholic Archives
The Reverend Gerard Mark Dilworth,
OSB
Columba House
16 Drummond Place
Edinburgh EH3 6PL
Tel: 031 556 3661

The Church of England

Diocese of Bath and Wells
Bishop
Rt Rev. John Monier Bickersteth
The Palace
Wells
Somerset BA5 2PD
Tel: 0749 72341
Suffragan Bishop
Rt Rev. N. McCuldoch (Taunton)

Diocese of Birmingham
Bishop
Rt Rev. Hugh William Montefiore DD
Bishop's Croft
Harborne
Birmingham
West Midlands B17 0BG
Tel: 021 427 1163
Suffragan Bishop
Rt Rev. Colin Ogilvie Buchanan
(Aston)

Diocese of Blackburn
Bishop
Rt Rev. David Stewart Cross
Bishop's House
Ribchester Road
Blackburn
Lancs. BB1 9EF
Tel: 0254 48234
Suffragan Bishops
Rt Rev. Ian Harland (Lancaster)
Rt Rev. Richard Charles Challinor
Watson (Burnley)

Diocese of Bradford
Bishop
Rt Rev. Robert Kerr Williamson
Bishopscroft
Ashwell Road
Bradford
West Yorkshire BD9 4AU
Tel: 0274 745414

Diocese of Bristol
Bishop
Rt Rev. Barry Rogerson
Bishop's House
Clifton Hill
Bristol
Avon BS8 1BW
Tel: 0272 730222
Suffragan Bishop
Rt Rev. Peter James Firth
(Malmesbury)

Diocese of Canterbury
Archbishop
Most Rev. and Rt Hon. Robert
Alexander Kennedy Runcie MC, DD
Primate of All England and
Metropolitan
Lambeth Palace
London SE1 7JU
Tel: 01 928 8282

and

Old Palace
Canterbury
Kent CT1 2EE
Matters relating to the Diocese of
Canterbury should be in the first
instance referred to the Bishop of
Dover (see below).
Suffragan Bishops
Rt Rev. Richard Henry McPhail Third
(Dover)
Upway
St Martin's Hill
Canterbury
Kent CT1 1PR
Tel: 0227 464537
Office:
1 Lady Wootton's Green
Canterbury CT1 1TL
Tel: 0227 459382
Rt Rev. Robert Maynard Hardy
(Maidstone)
Assistant Bishops
Rt Rev. Frederick Donald Coggan OC,
DD

Rt Rev. John Taylor Hughes CBE
Rt Rev. Harold Isherwood MVO,
OBE
Rt Rev. Ross Hook MC, DLitt.

Diocese of Carlisle
Bishop
Rt Rev. Henry David Halsey
Rose Castle
Dalston
Carlisle
Cumbria CA5 7BZ
Tel: 069 96 274
Suffragan Bishop
Rt Rev. George Lanyon Hacker
(Penrith)

Diocese of Chelmsford
Bishop
Rt Rev. John Waine
Bishopscourt
Main Road
Margaretting
Ingatestone
Essex CM4 0HD
Tel: 0277 352001
Suffragan Bishops
Rt Rev. James William Roxburgh
(Barking)
Rt Rev. Roderic Norman Coote DD
(Colchester)
Rt Rev. Charles Derek Bond
(Bradwell)

Diocese of Chester
Bishop
Rt Rev. Michael Alfred Baughen
Bishop's House
Chester CH1 2JD
Tel: 0244 20864
Suffragan Bishops
Rt Rev. Frank Pilkington Sargeant
(Stockport)
Rt Rev. Ronald Brown (Birkenhead)

Diocese of Chichester
Bishop
Rt Rev. Eric Waldram Kemp DD
The Palace
Chichester
West Sussex PO19 1PY
Tel: 0243 782161
Suffragan Bishops
Rt Rev. Ivor Colin Docker (Horsham)
Rt Rev. Peter John Ball CGA (Lewes)
Assistant Bishops
Rt Rev. William Warren Hunt
Rt Rev. Mark Green MC MA

Diocese of Coventry
Bishop
Rt Rev. Simon Barrington-Ward
Bishop's House
23 Davenport Road
Coventry
West Midlands CV5 6PW
Tel: 0203 72244
Suffragan Bishop
Rt Rev. Keith Appleby Arnold
(Warwick)

Diocese of Derby
Bishop
Rt Rev. Cyril William Johnston Bowles
The Bishop's House
6 King Street
Duffield
Derby DE6 4EU
Tel: 0332 46744 (Office); 0332 840132
(Home)
Suffragan Bishop
Rt Rev. Francis Henry Arthur
Richmond (Repton)
Assistant Bishop
Rt Rev. Cecil Allen Warren

Diocese of Durham
Bishop
Rt Rev. David Jenkins
Auckland Castle
Bishop Auckland
Co. Durham DL14 7NR
Tel: 0388 602576
Suffragan Bishop
Rt Rev. M. T. Ball
(Jarrow)

Diocese of Ely
Bishop
Rt Rev. Peter Knight Walker DD
The Bishop's House
Ely
Cambs. CB7 4DW
Tel: 0353 2749
Suffragan Bishop
Rt Rev. William Gordon Roe
(Huntingdon)
Assistant Bishop
Rt Rev. Michael Fisher SSF

Diocese in Europe
Bishop
Rt Rev. John Richard Satterthwaite
The Bishop's House
19 Brunswick Gardens
Kensington
London W8 4NG
Tel: 01 727 0329

Correspondence to:
Diocesan Office
5A Gregory Place
Kensington
London W8 4NG
Tel: 01 937 2796
Suffragan Bishop
Rt Rev. E. Holland (In Europe)

Diocese of Exeter
Bishop
Rt Rev. Hewlett Thompson
The Palace
Exeter
Devon EX1 1HY
Tel: 0392 72362
Suffragan Bishops
Rt Rev. Peter Coleman (Crediton)
Rt Rev. Kenneth Albert Newing
(Plymouth)
Assistant Bishops
Rt Rev. John Armstrong CB OBE
Rt Rev. Charles Robert Claxton DD
Rt Rev. Ronald Cedric Osbourne
Goodchild
Rt Rev. Philip John Pasterfield

Diocese of Gloucester
Bishop
Rt Rev. John Yates
Bishopscourt
Pitt Street
Gloucester GL1 2BQ
Tel: 0452 24598
Suffragan Bishop
Rt Rev. G. D. J. Walsh (Tewkesbury)

Diocese of Guildford
Bishop
Rt Rev. Michael Edgar Adie
Willow Grange
Woking Road
Guildford
Surrey GU4 7QS
Tel: 0483 573922
Suffragan Bishop
Rt Rev. D. P. Wilcox
(Dorking)
Assistant Bishop
Rt Rev. Kenneth Dawson Evans

Diocese of Hereford
Bishop
Rt Rev. John Richard Gordon
Eastaugh
The Bishop's House
The Palace
Hereford HR4 9BN
Tel: 0432 271355
Suffragan Bishop
Rt Rev. Stanley Mark Wood (Ludlow)

Diocese of Leicester
Bishop
Rt Rev. Cecil Richard Rutt CBE,
D.Litt, OCM
Bishop's Lodge
10 Springfield Road
Leicester LE2 3BD
Tel: 0533 708985
Assistant Bishop
Rt Rev. John Ernest Llewelyn Mort
CBE, LLD

Diocese of Lichfield
Bishop
Rt Rev. Keith Norman Sutton
Bishop's House
22 The Close
Lichfield
Staffs WS13 7LG
Tel: 0543 262251
Suffragan Bishops
Rt Rev. John Stevens Waller (Stafford)
Rt Rev. C. J. Mayfield
(Wolverhampton)
Rt Rev. Leslie Lloyd Rees
(Shrewsbury)

Diocese of Lincoln
Bishop
Rt Rev. Simon Wilton Phipps
Bishop's House
Eastgate
Lincoln LN2 1QQ
Tel: 0522 34701
Suffragan Bishops
Rt Rev. Dennis Gascoyne Hawker
(Grantham)
Rt Rev. David Tustin (Grimsby)
Assistant Bishops
Rt Rev. Anthony Otter
Rt Rev. Gerald Fitzmaurice Colin

Diocese of Liverpool
Bishop
Rt Rev. David Stuart Sheppard
Bishop's Lodge
Woolton Park
Woolton
Liverpool L25 6DT
Tel: 051 708 9480
Suffragan Bishop
Rt Rev. Michael Henshall
(Warrington)
Assistant Bishops
Rt Rev. William Scott Baker
Rt Rev. John William Hawkins Flagg

Diocese of London
Bishop
Rt Rev. and Rt Hon. Graham Douglas
Leonard DD, DCL
London House
8 Barton Street
London SW1P 3NE
Tel: 01 222 8661
Area Bishops
Rt Rev. Tom F. Butler PhD
(Willesden)
173 Willesden Lane
London NW6 7YN
Tel: 01 451 0189
Rt Rev. Brian John Masters
(Edmonton)
13 North Audley Street
London W1Y 1FW
Tel: 01 629 3891
Rt Rev. James Lawton Thompson
FCA (Stepney)
23 Tredegar Square
Bow
London E3 5AG
Tel: 01 981 2323
Rt Rev. Mark Santer (Kensington)
19 Campden Hill Square
London W8 7JY
Tel: 01 727 9818
Suffragan Bishop
Rt Rev. John Klyberg (Fulham)
Assistant Bishops
Rt Rev. Edward George Knapp-Fisher
Rt Rev. George Edmund Reindorp
Rt Rev. Maurice Wood
Rt Rev. Michael Marshall
Rt Rev. D. S. Arden (in Willesden)

Diocese of Manchester
Bishop
Rt Rev. Stanley Eric Francis Booth-
Clibborn
Bishopscourt
Bury New Road
Manchester M7 0LE
Tel: 061 792 2096
Suffragan Bishops
Rt Rev. David George Galliford
(Bolton)
Rt Rev. Donald Alexander Tytler
(Middleton)
Rt Rev. C. J. F. Scott (Hulme)
Assistant Bishops
Rt Rev. Kenneth Venner Ramsey
Rt Rev. Edward Ralph Wickham

Diocese of Newcastle
Bishop
Rt Rev. Andrew Alexander Kenny
Graham
Bishop's House
29 Moor Road South
Gosforth
Newcastle upon Tyne NE3 1PA
Tel: 091 285 2220
Assistant Bishop
Rt Rev. Kenneth Gill

Diocese of Norwich
Bishop
Rt Rev. Peter Nott
Bishop's House
Norwich
Norfolk NR3 1SB
Tel: 0603 629001
Suffragan Bishops
Rt Rev. Timothy Dudley-Smith
(Thetford)
Rt Rev. D. E. Bentley (Lynn)

Diocese of Oxford
Bishop
Rt Rev. Patrick Campbell Rodger
Diocesan Church House
North Hinksey
Oxford OX2 0NB
Tel: 0865 244566/245114 (Office)
Suffragan Bishops
Rt Rev. Ronald Graham Gregory
Foley (Reading)
Rt Rev. Simon Hedley Burrows
(Buckingham)
Rt Rev. Conrad John Eustace Meyer
(Dorchester)
Assistant Bishops
Rt Rev. Sydney Cyril Bulley
Rt Rev. Albert Kenneth Cragg
Rt Rev. Eric Wild
Rt Rev. Leonard Ashton

Diocese of Peterborough
Bishop
Rt Rev. William John Westwood
The Palace
Peterborough
Cambs PE1 1YA
Tel: 0733 62492
Assistant Bishop
Rt Rev. William Alfred Franklin OBE

Diocese of Portsmouth
Bishop
Rt Rev. Timothy John Bavin
Bishopswood
Fareham
Hants PO14 1NT
Tel: 0329 20247
Hon. Assistant Bishops
Rt Rev. Ernest Edwin Curtis CBE
Rt Rev. Cyril Easthaugh MC
Rt Rev. William Warren Hunt
Rt Rev. Edward James Keymer
Roberts DD

Diocese of Ripon
Bishop
Rt Rev. David Nigel de Lorentz Young
Bishop Mount
Ripon
North Yorkshire HG4 5DP
Tel: 0765 2045
Suffragan Bishop
Rt Rev.   (Knaresborough)

Diocese of Rochester
Bishop
Rt Rev. Richard David Say DD
Bishopscourt
Rochester
Kent ME1 1TS
Tel: 0634 42721
Suffragan Bishop
Rt Rev. David Henry Bartleet
(Tonbridge)
Hon. Assistant Bishop
Rt Rev. Ambrose Weekes

Diocese of St Albans
Bishop
Rt Rev. John Bernard Taylor
Abbey Gate House
St Albans
Herts AL3 4HD
Tel: 0727 53305
Suffragan Bishops
Rt Rev. Kenneth Harold Pillar
(Hertford)
Rt Rev. David John Farmbrough
(Bedford)

*Diocese of St Edmundsbury and
Ipswich*
Bishop
Rt Rev. John Dennis
Bishop's House
4 Park Road
Ipswich
Suffolk IP1 3ST
Tel: 0473 52829
Suffragan Bishop
Rt Rev. Eric Devenport (Dunwich)

Diocese of Salisbury
Bishop
Rt Rev. John Austin Baker
South Canonry
71 The Close
Salisbury
Wilts SP1 2ER
Tel: 0722 334031
Area Bishops
Rt Rev. John Dudley Galtrey Kirkham
(Sherborne)
Rt Rev. John Robert Geoffrey Neale
AKC (Ramsbury)

Diocese of Sheffield
Bishop
Rt Rev. David Ramsay Lunn
Bishopscroft
Snaithing Lane
Sheffield
South Yorkshire S10 2LG
Tel: 0742 302170
Suffragan Bishop
Rt Rev. William Michael Dermot
Persson (Doncaster)

Diocese of Sodor and Man
Bishop
Rt Rev. Arthur Henry Attwell
The Bishop's House
Quarterbridge Road
Douglas
Isle of Man
Tel: 0624 22108

Diocese of Southwark
Bishop
Rt Rev. Ronald Oliver Bowlby
Bishop's House
38 Tooting Bec Gardens
London SW16 1QZ
Tel: 01 769 3256
Suffragan Bishops
Rt Rev. Peter Stephen Maurice Selby
(Kingston-Upon-Thames)
Rt Rev. Albert Peter Hall (Woolwich)
Rt Rev. Wilfred Deniston Wood
(Croydon)
Assistant Bishops
Rt Rev. Edward George Knapp-Fisher
Rt Rev. Edmund Michael Hubert
Capper OBE
Rt Rev. A. R. McDonald Gordon

Diocese of Southwell
Bishop
Rt Rev. Michael Humphrey Dickens
Whinney
Bishop's Manor
Southwell
Notts NG25 0JP
Tel: 0636 812112
Suffragan Bishop
Rt Rev. Harold Richard Darby
(Sherwood)

Diocese of Truro
Bishop
Rt Rev. Peter Mumford
Lis Escop
Truro
Cornwall TR3 6QQ
Tel: 0872 862657
Suffragan Bishop
Rt Rev. John Richard Allen Llewellin
(St Germans)

Diocese of Wakefield
Bishop
Rt Rev. Dr David Hope
Bishop's Lodge
Woodthorpe Lane
Wakefield WF2 6JJ
Tel: 0924 255349
Suffragan Bishop
Rt Rev. Thomas Richard Hare
(Pontefract)
Assistant Bishops
Rt Rev. Philip William Wheeldon OBE
Rt Rev. Ralph Emmerson
Rt Rev. Anselm Genders CR

Diocese of Winchester
Bishop
Rt Rev. Colin James
Wolvesey
Winchester
Hants SO23 9ND
Tel: 0962 54050
Suffragan Bishops
Rt Rev. E. D. Cartwright
(Southampton)
Rt Rev. Michael Richard John
Manktelow (Basingstoke)

Assistant Bishop
Rt Rev. Hassan Dehqani-Tafti
President-Bishop of the Episcopal
Church of Jerusalem and the Middle
East and Bishop in Iran

Diocese of Worcester
Bishop
Rt Rev. Philip Harold Ernest Goodrich
The Bishop's House
Hartlebury Castle
Kidderminster
Worcs. DY11 7XX
Tel: 0299 250214
Suffragan Bishop
Rt Rev. Anthony Charles Dumper
(Dudley)
Hon. Assistant Bishops
Rt Rev. David Howard Nicholas
Allenby SSM
Rt Rev. Oliver Stratford Tomkins DD

Diocese of York
Archbishop
Most Rev. and Rt Hon. John Stapylton
Habgood, Primate of England and
Metropolitan
Bishopthorpe
York
North Yorkshire YO2 1QE
Tel: 0904 707021/2
Suffragan Bishops
Rt Rev. Donald George Snelgrove
(Hull)
Rt Rev. Gordon Bates (Whitby)
Rt Rev. Clifford Conder Barker
(Selby)
Assistant Bishops
Rt Rev. George Eyles Irwin Cockin
Rt Rev. Richard Knyvet Wimbush
Rt Rev. George Edward Holderness

Other Christian Churches

During the Week of Prayer for Christian Unity (see page 370), in order to encourage knowledge and appreciation of other ecclesial communities, a speaker may be required. If a local speaker is not available, an enquiry directed to the principal address will receive interested attention.

The Apostolic Church
Off Bryncwar Road
Penygroes
Llanelli
Dyfed SA14 7PA
Tel: 0269 842349
President:
Rev. M. J. Seaborne

Assemblies of God in Great Britain and Ireland
106–14 Talbot Street
Nottingham NG1 5GH
Tel: 0602 474525
General Secretary:
Rev. Keith W. Munday

Baptist Union of Great Britain and Ireland
4 Southampton Row
London WC1B 4AB
Tel: 01 405 9803
General Secretary:
Rev. Bernard Green

Baptist Union of Ireland
3 Fitzwilliam Street
Belfast
Northern Ireland BT9 6AW
Tel: 0232 22303

Baptist Union of Scotland
14 Aytoun Road
Glasgow G41 5RT
Tel: 041 423 6169
General Secretary:
Rev. Peter H. Barber

Baptist Union of Wales
Ty Ilston
94 Mansel Street
Swansea
West Glamorgan SA1 5TU
Tel: 0792 55468
General Secretary:
Rev. D. Islwyn Davies

Catholic Episcopal Church
100A Avenue Road
Beckenham
Kent BR3 4SA
Tel: 01 659 1838
Bishop:
Rt Rev. Francis E. Glenn

Chinese Church in London
Chinese Church Centre
81 Chiltern Street
London W1M 1HT
Tel: 01 486 0592
Pastor:
Mr K. T. Tan

Christian Brethren
Christian Brethren Research Fellowship
13 The Meads
Northchurch
Berkhamstead
Herts HP4 3QX
Tel: 044 27 2654
Executive Director:
Dr John Boyes

Church in Wales
39 Cathedral Road
Cardiff
South Glamorgan CF1 9XF
Tel: 0222 31638

Church of Ireland
Church of Ireland House
Church Avenue
Rathmines
Dublin 6
Irish Republic
Tel: 0001 978422
Chief Officer:
Mr H. R. Roberts

Church of Scotland
121 George Street
Edinburgh EH2 4YN
Tel: 031 225 5722
Principal Clerk:
Rev. Donald F. M. Macdonald CBE

Congregational Federation
4 Castle Gate
Nottingham NG1 7AS
Tel: 0602 413801
General Secretary:
Mr John B. Wilcox

Congregational Union of Ireland
38 Edgecambe Gardens
Belfast
Northern Ireland BT4 2EH
Tel: 0232 653140
Secretary:
Rev. Malcolm Coles

Congregational Union of Scotland
PO Box 189
Glasgow G1 2BQ
Tel: 041 332 7667
General Secretary:
Rev. Robert Waters

Cornerstone Ministries
King's House
316 Shirley Road
Southampton
Hampshire SO1 3HL
Tel: 0703 776357
Team Leader:
Mr Tony Morton

Countess of Huntingdon's Connexion
8 Woodlands Avenue
Rayleigh
Essex SS6 7RD
Tel: 0268 743017
Secretary:
Mr Douglas Staplehurst

Danish Church of St Katharine
4 St Katharine's Precinct
Regents Park
London NW1 4HH
Tel: 01 935 1723
Pastor:
Paul-Erik Fabricius

Elim Pentecostal Churches
PO Box 38
Cheltenham
Gloucester GL50 3HN
Tel: 0242 519904
Secretary-General:
Rev. T. W. Walker

Emmanuel Holiness Church
1 Palm Grove
Birkenhead
Merseyside L43 1TE
Tel: 051 652 2342
Chairman:
Rev. R. J. Newton

Evangelical Fellowship of Congregational Churches
8 Northfield
Braughing
Ware
Herts SG11 2QQ
Tel: 0920 821479
Secretary:
Rev. Edward S. Guest

Evangelical Lutheran Church of England
110 Warwick Way
London SW1V 1SD
Tel: 01 834 3033
Chairman:
Rev. Arnold E. Rakow

Evangelical Mennonites
London Mennonite Centre
14 Shepherds Hill
Highgate
London N6 5AQ
Tel: 01 340 8775
Secretary:
Dr A. F. Kreider

Evangelical Presbyterian Church
15 College Square East
Belfast
Northern Ireland BT1 6DD
Tel: 0232 20529
Clerk:
Rev. S. Watson

Fellowship of Churches of Christ
65 Hurst Street
Birmingham
West Midlands B5 4TE
Tel: 021 622 2351
General Secretary:
Rev. Martin Robinson

Fellowship of Independent Evangelical Churches
136 Rosendale Road
London SE21 8LG
Tel: 01 670 5815
General Secretary:
Rev. David Mingard

The Free Church of England
28 Sedgebrook
Liden
Swindon
Wilts SN3 6EY
Tel: 0793 695838
General Secretary:
Rt Rev. Dr Arthur Ward

Free Church of Scotland
The Mound
Edinburgh EH1 2LS
Tel: 031 226 5286
Principal Clerk:
Rev. Prof. C. Graham

Free Methodist Church in the United Kingdom
14 Southlands Road
Goostrey
Crewe
Cheshire CW4 8JF
Tel: 0477 35216
Conference Superintendent:
Rev. Victor Trinder

Free Presbyterian Church of Scotland
13 Kingsborough Gardens
Glasgow G12 9NH
Tel: 041 339 0553
Clerk of Synod:
Rev. Donald MacLean

Free Presbyterian Church of Ulster
Church House
356 Ravenhill Road
Belfast BT6 8GL
Tel: 0232 57106
Clerk of Presbytery:
Rev. John Douglas

Independent Methodist Church
Old Police House
Croxton
Stafford ST21 6PE
Tel: 063 082 671
General Secretary:
Rev. John M. Day

Lutheran Council of Great Britain
8 Collingham Gardens
London SW5 0HW
Tel: 01 373 1141/5566
Chairman:
Very Rev. Robert J. Patkai

Methodist Church (The Wesleyan, Primitive and United Methodist Churches)
1 Central Buildings
Westminster
London SW1H 9NH
Tel: 01 222 8010
Secretary:
Rev. Brian Beck

Methodist Church in Ireland
3 Upper Malone Road
Belfast
Northern Ireland BT9 6TD
Tel: 0232 668458
Secretary:
Rev. Charles G. Eyre

Moravian Church in Great Britain and Ireland
Moravian Church House
5 Muswell Hill
London N10 3TJ
Tel: 01 883 3409
Secretary:
Rev. F. Linyard

New Apostolic Church (UK)
30 Abingdon Close
Hillingdon
Middlesex UB10 0BU
Tel: 0895 53204

New Testament Assembly (Pentecostal)
7 Beechcroft Road
Tooting, London SW17 7BU
Tel: 01 672 9416/5415
General Secretary:
Rev. I. M. Smith

New Testament Church of God
Main House
Overstone Park
Overstone
Northampton NN6 0AD
Tel: 0604 43311/45944
National Overseer:
Rev. J. McIntyre

Old Baptist Union
32 Wessex Gardens
Totley Brook
Sheffield S17 3PQ
Tel: 0742 352739
General Secretary:
Rev. Arthur H. Sommers

Old Roman Catholic Church
Priory of Our Lady of Port-Royal
10 Barnmead Road
Beckenham
Kent BR3 1JE
Tel: 01 778 3317
Archbishop:
Monsignor Frederick G. Linale

The Orthodox Church of the British Isles
Church Secretariat
10 Heathwood Gardens
Charlton
London SE7 8EP
Tel: 01 854 3090
Metropolitan of Glastonbury:
His Beatitude Mar Seraphim

Presbyterian Church in Ireland
Church House
Fisherwick Place
Belfast
Northern Ireland BT1 6DW
Tel: 0232 222284
General Secretary:
The Very Rev. Dr A. J. Weir

Presbyterian Church of Wales
53 Richmond Road
Cardiff CF2 3UP
Tel: 0222 494913
General Secretary:
Rev. D. H. Owen

The Protestant Evangelical Church of England
1022 Leeds Road
Woodkirk
Dewsbury
West Yorkshire WF12 7QR
Tel: 0924 441787
Primus:
Rt Rev. C. Leslie Saul

Religious Society of Friends
Friends House
Euston Road
London NW1 2BJ
Tel: 01 387 3601
Recording Clerk:
Mr Geoffrey Bowes

Salvation Army
PO Box 249
101 Queen Victoria Street
London EC4P 4EP
Tel: 01 236 5222
British Commissioner:
Commissioner Francy Cachelin

Scottish Episcopal Church
21 Grosvenor Crescent
Edinburgh EH12 5EE
Tel: 031 225 6537
General Secretary:
Mr Ian D. Stuart

Union of Evangelical Churches
44 Wharf Road
Stanford-le-Hope
Essex SS17 0DY
Tel: 0375 672826
General Secretary:
Pastor P. F. Outen

Union of Welsh Independents
Ty John Penry
11 St Helens Road
Swansea
West Glamorgan SA1 4AL
Tel: 0792 52092 or 52542
General Secretary:
Rev. Derwyn Morris Jones

United Free Church of Scotland
11 Newton Place
Glasgow G3 7PR
Tel: 041 332 3435
General Secretary:
Mrs I. D. Baird

United Pentecostal Church of Great Britain and Ireland
c/o Life Tabernacle
32 Battersea Park Road
London SW11 4HY
Tel: 01 622 6289
Superintendent:
Rev. James Dallas

United Reformed Church in the United Kingdom
86 Tavistock Place
London WC1H 9RT
Tel: 01 837 7661
General Secretary:
Rev. Bernard G. Thorogood

Wesleyan Holiness Church
Holyhead Road
Handsworth
Birmingham
West Midlands B21 0LA
Tel: 021 523 7849
District Superintendent:
Rev. Desmond V. Pemberton

Wesleyan Reform Union
123 Queen Street
Sheffield
South Yorks S1 2DU
Tel: 0742 21938
General Secretary:
Rev. D. A. Morris

For Eastern Orthodox Churches, see pages 373–4.

CHAPTER TWO

National Associations, Organisations and Societies

Catholic Centres for Foreign Nationals

All Catholics, whatever their country of origin, belong to the parish in which they live and have an equal claim on the parochial clergy. However, the Church does recognise special pastoral needs and provides for them as best she can, and among these are the needs of people of overseas races and cultures.

In the case of Catholics with their own ancestral language and culture, for example the Poles and the Italians, special churches have been set aside and social and cultural centres established. The situation of Catholics from the new Commonwealth, especially those of Afro-Caribbean and Asian origin, is somewhat different. These Catholics can be cared for by the parishes in which they live but not always with ease. Accordingly, some dioceses with large Afro-Caribbean or Asian communities have set up special chaplaincies to supplement the work of the parishes and to be at their service. There is an Asian Catholic Chaplaincy in the Westminster Diocese and chaplaincies to the Caribbean community exist in Westminster, Southwark, Birmingham and Salford Dioceses.

Asian Catholics including Goans, and also Africans, are usually very faithful worshippers but do not always take part in parish activities. Catholics of Caribbean origin generally need a great deal of personal interest and encouragement, but their responses can be most generous. It is a great help with both the Afro-Caribbean and Asian communities if the clergy can show some interest and understanding of their homeland and culture. If this interest can be expressed in the life of the parish by such observances as St Francis Xavier's Day for Asian Catholics and St Lucy's Day and other commemorations beloved of the Caribbean and African peoples, so much the better. These can also be occasions when such ethnic communities can be host to the parish at a social event. It is excellent if the whole parish can learn to share in these cultural heritages, including their liturgical idioms. The quest is for a fully multi-cultural Church witnessing for a fully multi-cultural society.

Diocesan Chaplaincies

Westminster
Rev. Arthur Moraes (Asian)
Flat C
22 Melbury Road
London W14 8BU
Tel: 01 602 3215

Rev. Brian Creak (Caribbean)
7 Henry Road
London N4 2LH
Tel: 01 809 3253

Southwark
Very Rev. Canon Charles Walker
(Caribbean)
John Archer House
135 Nightingale Lane
London SW12 8NE
Tel: 01 673 1071

Birmingham
Rev. Kevin Dunn (Caribbean)
46 Little Oaks Road
Birmingham B6 6JX
Tel: 021 326 6964

Salford
Rev. Gerard Rimmer (Caribbean)
4 Palfrey Place
Ardwick
Manchester M12 6BY
Tel: 061 273 3421

In other dioceses there are generally particular parishes which have special experience of ethnic minority needs.

National Chaplaincies and Centres

Asian Chaplaincy
48 Gt Peter Street
London SW1P 2HA
Tel: 01 222 2895
Chaplain:
Rev. A. Moraes

Austrian Catholic Centre
29 Brook Green
London W6 7EP
Tel: 01 603 2697

Byelorussian Catholic Mission
Marian House
Holden Avenue
London N12 8HY
Tel: 01 445 1938

Catholic Council for Polish Welfare
26 Pont Street
London SW1X 0AB
Tel: 01 589 7656 (01 460 7008 after
8 p.m.)

Chinese Catholic Centre
21A Soho Square
London W1V 5FL
Tel: 01 437 0892
Director:
Rev. Louis Tchang

Croatian Chaplaincy
17 Boutflower Road
London SW11 1RE
Tel: 01 223 3530
Director:
Rev. D. Berisć

Czech Catholic Centre
22 Ladbroke Square
London W11 3NA
Tel: 01 727 7849
Director:
Very Rev. Guy Wernet

French Church
Notre Dame de France
5 Leicester Place
London WC2H 7BP
Tel: 01 437 9363

German Church
St Boniface
47 Adler Street
London E1 1EE
Tel: 01 247 9529
Director:
Rev. Felix Leushacke
German Social Centre:
St Lioba's House
40 Exeter Road
London NW2 4SB
Tel: 01 452 8566

German-Speaking Catholic Centre
Ardmory
30 Langside Drive
Glasgow G43 2QQ
Tel: 041 637 3316

Hungarian Chaplaincy
56 Randall Avenue
London NW2 7ST
Tel: 01 452 7953
Director:
Very Rev. Mgr Bela Ispanki

Irish Centre
52 Camden Square
London NW1 9XB
Tel: 01 485 0512
Director:
Rev. C. Malone
Men's Hostel:
Conway House
20 Quex Street
London NW6
Tel: 01 624 2918
Women's Hostel:
33 Medway Street
London SW1
Tel: 01 222 2071

Italian Church
St Peter
Clerkenwell Road
London EC1
Tel: 01 837 1528
Parish Priest:
Rev. R. Russo

Missione Cattolica per gli Italiani in Scozia
c/o St Anthony's
62 Langlands Road
Glasgow G51 3BD
Tel: 041 440 1534
Chaplain:
Rev. Pietro Zorza

Latvian Centre
84 Craven Street
Coventry CV5 8DW
Tel: 0203 70981

Lithuanian Church
St Casimir
21 The Oval
Hackney Road
London E2 9DT
Tel: 01 739 8735
Director:
Rev. John Sakevicius

Maltese Centre
22 St George's Drive
London SW1V 4BN
Tel: 01 834 4020
Director:
Rev. Hugh Attard

Polish Church
Our Lady of Czestochowa and St
Casimir
2 Devonia Road
Islington
London N1 8JJ
Tel: 01 226 3439
Vicar Delegate for Poles in England
and Wales:
Rt. Rev. Mgr Karol Zielinski

*Office of the Polish Catholic Mission in
Scotland*
11 Drummond Place
Edinburgh EH3 6PJ
Tel: 031 556 1011

Portuguese Church
165 Arlington Road
London NW1 7EX
Tel: 01 267 9612
Director:
Rev. Manuel Soares

Slovak Centre
41 Holden Road
London N12 8HS
Tel: 01 445 7774
Director:
Rev. Joseph Babik

Slovene Centre
62 Offley Road
London SW9 0LS
Tel: 01 735 6655
Director:
Rev. Ludwig Roth

Spanish Centre
47 Palace Court
London W2 4LS
Tel: 01 229 8815
Director:
Rev. E. Atanes

Ukrainian Centre
22 Binney Street
London W1Y 1YN
Tel: 01 629 1534

Vietnamese Centre
12 Wye Cliff Road
Handsworth
Birmingham
Tel: 021 554 8082
Director:
Rev. Peter Dao Duc Diem

West Indian Centre
46 Little Oaks Road
Aston
Birmingham B6 6JX
Tel: 021 326 6964
Director:
Rev. Kevin J. Dunn

8 Montpelier Avenue
London W5 2XP
Tel: 01 997 8850
Director:
Rev. Paul Foster
St Aloysius

4 Palfrey Place
Ardwick
Manchester M12 6BY
Tel: 061 273 3421
Director:
Rev. Gerard Rimmer

Evangelisation

The Association for Christian Communication (AFCC)
Robertson House
Leas Road
Guildford
Surrey GU1 4QW
Director:
Rev. Alec Gilmore MA, BD
AFCC was founded in 1983 by 19 British Churches and missionary bodies to coordinate the work of Christian communication at home and overseas.

Evangelical Coalition for Urban Mission
130 City Road
London EC1V 2NJ
Secretary:
Michael Eastman
The Coalition provides training, resources, publications and means of association for those engaged in urban mission and ministry in inner city and new housing areas.

Feed the Minds
Robertson House
Leas Road
Guildford
Surrey GU1 4QW
Director:
Rev. Alec Gilmore MA, BD
Christian charity set up by the Churches to raise funds for Christian literature and communication programmes in the Third World and in Eastern Europe.

'Message'
The Christian Telephone Service
47 The Drive
Sevenoaks
Kent
Secretary:
Mr F. J. Ainsworth
To put out 2-minute Christian messages, new each day, prepared by local Christians in each area and supply call-back where callers need it.

Partners
17 Edward Road
Dorchester DT1 2HL
Secretary:
Rev. J. Hamilton-Brown
To help the local church in mission and evangelism.

United Society for Christian Literature (USCL)
Robertson House
Leas Road
Guildford
Surrey GU1 4QW
Secretary:
Rev. Alec Gilmore MA, BD
USCL channels all its donated income through Feed the Minds which includes Eurolit.

Urban Theology Unit
210 Abbeyfield Road
Sheffield S4 7AZ
Tel: 0742 383438
Director:
Rev. Dr John J. Vincent
Ministry and laity training for urban work. Contextual theology. Developing a personal theology. Working with small inner-city congregations.

WEC International
Bulstrode
Oxford Road
Gerrards Cross
Bucks. SL9 8SZ
Tel: 0753 884631
WEC is a multi-racial, interdenominational missionary organisation working in more than 30 countries.

World Association for Christian Communication
122 Kings Road
London SW3 4TR
Tel: 01 589 1484
Secretary:
Dr Hans W. Florin
Involved in grassroots media, particularly with an emphasis on Christian communication in order to help less advantaged people to learn and to express themselves.

Catholic Societies

Catholic Missionary Education Centre
Holcombe House
The Ridgeway
London NW7 4HY
Tel: 01 906 1642
General Secretary:
Rev. J. Brankin WF
Resource centre for audio visual materials describing the pastoral aspects of the Church throughout the world.

Catholic Missionary Society
114 West Heath Road
London NW3 7TX
Tel: 01 458 3316
Director:
Rev. Thomas McHugh
To promote and foster evangelisation in England and Wales. Work proceeds through parish missions, the Catholic Enquiry Centre and the Office for Evangelisation.

Legion of Mary
Senatus of London
1 Warwick Rd
Earls Court
London SW5 9UL
Tel: 01 373 4194

Legion of Mary
Senatus of Scotland
Montfort House
38 Lansdowne Crescent
Glasgow G20 6NH
Tel: 041 339 3902
For the sanctification of its members and outreach to others.

Mission Secretariat
Holcombe House
The Ridgeway
London NW7 4HY
Tel: 01 906 1642
General Secretary:
Rev. J. Brankin
Secretariat services the National Missionary Council which is the forum of all those organisations and societies engaged in missionary work overseas.

Movement for a Better World
The Lodge
Harborne Hall
Birmingham B17 0BE
Tel: 021 426 5340
Director:
Rev. Adrian B. Smith WF
To cooperate with all those who strive for a better world. To be co-creators with God of the Kingdom he desires for us.

Office for Evangelisation
120 West Heath Road
London NW3 7TY
Secretary:
Dermot Walshe
Making available to parishes literature and information concerning evangelisation in the community.

Pastoral Care and Support

Christians Abroad
Livingstone House
11 Carteret Street
London SW1H 9DL
Tel: 01 222 2165
and 121 George Street
Edinburgh EH2 4YN
Tel: 031 225 5722
Secretary:
Miss Rachel E. Stephens
Information and advice about overseas work and vacancies. Introduction to the Church overseas for those going to live abroad.

Catholic Societies

Apostleship of the Sea
New Strand
Bootle
Liverpool L20 4QT
Tel: 051 922 6161
National Director:
Rev. A. Stringfellow
Cares for the spiritual and social welfare of seafarers.

Association of Nursing Religious
St Joseph's Room
56 Anne's Settlement
46 Harleyford Road
London SE11 5AY
Tel: 01 735 9672
To support nursing religious in their healing ministry.

Pontifical Mission Aid Societies
23 Eccleston Square
London SW1V 1NU
National Director:
Canon M.R. Swaby
Mission information and funding.

Young Christian Workers, see page 220.

Intercontinental Church Society
175 Tower Bridge Road
London SE1 2AQ
Secretary:
Canon Donald R. Irving
Ministry to English-speaking people overseas, mainly in Europe but also parts of North Africa, South America and Falkland Islands. ICS is an Anglican Society.

The Missions to Seamen
St Michael
Paternoster Royal
College Hill
London EC4R 2RL
General Secretary:
Rev. Bill Down
Promotes the well-being of seafarers of all nationalities and their families.

Catholic Nurses Guild of England and Wales
Hon. Secretary:
Miss M. Baird
26 Southend Parade
Hebburn
Tyne and Wear
To promote the spiritual well-being of its members.

Catholic Nurses Guild of Scotland
The Whinnocks
11 Grieve Rd
Greenock
Scotland

Converts' Aid Society
Secretary
20 Holmes Road
Twickenham
Middlesex TW1 4RE
To assist convert clergymen and
convert Anglican sisters.

Converts' Aid Society
Scottish representative
Rev. Ronald Walls
St Anne's
Sweyn Road
Thurso
Caithness KW14 7NW
Tel: 0847 63196

Sanctuary Association (Glasgow) Ltd
Sanctuary House
8 Staneley Rd
Paisley
Renfrewshire PA2 6MA
Tel: 041 889 4624
For the rehabilitation of alcoholics,
drug addicts, discharged prisoners and
other destitute men.

Society of St Vincent de Paul
24 George Street
Marylebone
London W1H 5RB
Tel: 01 935 7625
A lay society to help the needy by
active works of charity.

Society of St Vincent de Paul (Scotland)
546 Sauchiehall St
Glasgow G2 3NG
Tel: 041 332 7752

*Travelling Mission to the Travelling
People*
St Joseph's House
18 Leopold Street
Oxford OX4 1PS
Tel: 0865 240325
National Director:
Rev. E. Daly.
The Travelling Mission is pastorally
responsible for gypsies and travelling
people in England and Wales.

United Services Catholic Association
c/o Duke of York Headquarters
Kings Road
London SW3
Secretary:
Major (Rtd) A. W. E. Gracie
Assistance to service chaplains in their
pastoral care of members of HM Forces
and their dependents.

Men's Organisations

Catholic

Archconfraternity of St Stephen
For altar servers. See page 76.

Catenian Association
Secretary
8 Chesham Place
London SW1X 8HP
Tel: 01 235 6671
For professional and business men.
Scotland:
4 Anderson Drive
Aberdeen AB1 6TY
Tel: 0224 37223

Catholic Men's Society of Great Britain
Cathedral Buildings
152 Brownlow Hill
Liverpool L3 5RQ
Tel: 051 709 5078
To help and encourage men to fulfil
their full and proper role as laymen as
outlined by the Second Vatican
Council.
Scotland:
7 Coltpark Avenue
Bishopbriggs
Glasgow G64 2AT
Tel: 041 772 1020

Knights of St Columba
Secretary
75 Hillington Road South
Glasgow G52 2AE
A fraternal order for Catholic men.

Pueri Cantores
c/o The Presbytery
Rant Meadow
Hemel Hempstead
Herts. HP3 8PG
An international organisation of choirs
to foster peace among nations by
singing.

Serra International See page 10.

Interdenominational

Young Men's Christian Association
National Council of YMCA
640 Forest Rd
London E17 3DZ
Tel: 01 520 5599

To promote the physical, intellectual,
and spiritual well-being of young men.

Women's Organisations

The Anglican Group Educational Trust
St Hilary's House
Reculver Walk
Senacre
Maidstone
Kent ME15 8SW
Hon. Secretary:
Deaconess Anthea Williams
Making grants to individuals and
bodies engaged in education in
women's ministry.

Life Care and Housing Trust
c/o 29 Devonshire Road
Bolton
Secretary:
Mrs Sheila Hogg
Counselling and practical help for
women under pressure to have an
abortion or homeless unsupported
mothers.

Men, Women and God
c/o LICC
St Peter's Church
Vere Street
London W1M 9HP
Contact:
Kathy Keay
Feminism from a biblical perspective.

The Mothers' Union
Mary Sumner House
24 Tufton Street
London SW1P 3RB
Tel: 01 222 5533
Secretary:
Mrs M. Chapman MA
The strengthening and preservation of
marriage and Christian family life.

Movement for the Ordination of Women
Napier Hall
Hide Place
Vincent Street
London SW1P 4NJ
Secretary:
Mrs Margaret Webster
To promote the ordination of women in the Anglican Churches of the British Isles.

Society for the Ministry of Women in the Church
Applecroft
8 Samian Way
Dorchester-on-Thames
Oxon OX9 8JS
Tel: 0865 340224
Promotion of women's ministry in Churches of all denominations.

Women in Theology
Holy Trinity Church
Orsett Terrace
London W2 6AH
Tel: 01 723 9735
Contact:
Hannah CSF
Advances the theological education of women.

Women's World Day of Prayer
Strawberry Lodge
Strawberry Lane
Carshalton
Surrey SM5 2NQ
Tel: 01 647 0604
An annual day of prayer – first Friday in March – bringing together women of various races, cultures and traditions.

Catholic Societies

Christian Women's Information and Resource Centre
Blackfriars
St Giles
Oxford OX1 3LY
Main contacts:
Kate Mertes & Patricia Marsh
Collection and dissemination of particularly feminist literature in the Christian Church.

Catholic Women's League
48 Great Peter Street
London SW1P 2HA
Scotland:
22 Laverock Drive
Largs
Ayrshire
KA30 9DJ
President:
Mrs M. van den Bosch
Founded in 1906 by Margaret Fletcher, to train and encourage women to use their talents and skills in the service of the Church and community at local,

national and international level. The work was to develop freely and as need arose, but always on distinctively Catholic lines, under the patronage of the Hierarchy. Today the same general principles guide their work.

The League is established in every Diocese in England and Wales, in Scotland and there are Branches all round the world, as far afield as Fiji. The main work of the League in England and Wales is carried out through a number of standing committees:

1. *International Committee*. The League is a founder member of the World Union of Catholic Women's Organisations, now numbering 30 million members from 120 Catholic women's organisations.

2. *Our Lady's Catechists*. Founded in 1923 to help with the religious education of children unable to attend Catholic schools. Men and women are trained as catechists, and when

qualified teach in parishes or instruct children through postal courses. Work is carried out in cooperation with Diocesan Catechetical Centres.

3. *Relief & Refugee Committee.* Founded in 1943 to provide relief for refugees from Europe, and since then has extended its work to the Middle East, welcomed Vietnamese to this country, and assisted many individuals in difficulties.

Much of the disaster aid this committee used to give has now been taken over by the Catholic Fund for Overseas Development, which organisation grew from the Family Fast Days initiated by the League and the Union of Catholic Mothers.

4. *Children's Catechetical Camps.* Started in 1952 in Plymouth Diocese, for children who had no access to Catholic education, and now extended to many other Dioceses. 'Camps' are run in a holiday atmosphere, centred round the daily Mass, for which children prepare the liturgy. Popularity of the 'camps' is demonstrated by the eagerness with which many children ask to return each summer. Some of these children eventually join the team of helpers which is composed of a chaplain, teachers, housemothers, cooks, seminarians and sixth formers. Accommodation varies from spartan to the ideal in schools and other youth centres.

5. *Social Welfare.* This committee assists members working in all fields of welfare and coordinates their work with other organisations. Care of the elderly is its prime concern and members are involved in the running of housing associations and day centres, hospital visiting, etc. Other work includes support for one parent families, battered wives and children, the handicapped and their carers, and so on.

6. *Services Committee.* Considers cases of hardship among members of the armed forces and their dependents. Assistance is given from funds which derive from the sale of huts and canteens which were run by the League during the world wars.

C.W.L. News, published quarterly, provides a forum for members, and is noted for its book reviews.

The Catholic Women's League is represented on a number of national organisations. Mass is offered daily on a rota basis, and is attended by members throughout the country. Days of recollection and pilgrimages are arranged on a local, Diocesan and National level.

Catholic Women's Network
2 Umbria Street
London SW15 5DP
Tel: 01 788 3333

or

42 Priory Road
Hampton
Middx.
Tel: 01 979 5902

Christian Women's Resource Centre
36 Court Lane
Dulwich
London SE21 7DR
Tel: 01 693 1438
Secretary:
Mrs I. Pratt
To act as a centre of advice implementing 'The Easter People's' call to women to take fuller and more positive part in the life of the Church.

Dorcas Group: Roman Catholic Feminists
21 Chatsworth Gardens
New Malden
Surrey KT3 6DW
Coordinator:
Dora Turbin
To work for real equality of the sexes within the Latin Church.

International Catholic Society for Girls
St Patrick's International Youth Centre
24 Great Chapel Street
London W1V 3AF
Tel: 01 734 2156
and 01 439 0116
Secretary:
Sister Sheelah Clarke
To help girls travelling or living
temporarily in UK.

National Board of Catholic Women
Arley
Glebe Road
Merstham
Redhill
Surrey RH1 3AB
Tel: 07375 52823
Secretary:
Y. Nulty
The official Catholic coordinating body
of women in Catholic organisations.

Roman Catholic Feminists
c/o 33 Arlow Road
London N21 3JS
Coordinator:
Jackie Field
To provide a network of contacts/
groups for women seeking to integrate
feminism and Catholicism.

St Joan's International Alliance
117 Bow Common Lane
London E3
Tel: 01 987 1706
Contact:
Kathie Walsh
An international Catholic women's
organisation dedicated to the
advancement of women in all fields. It
works for political rights of women the
world over, their equal access to
education, vocational training, equal
opportunities, elimination of all
discrimination.

*Union of Catholic Mothers (England
and Wales)*
'Tralee'
Aughton Street
Ormskirk
Lancs. L39 3LQ
To help Catholic married women to
appreciate the sacramental character,
responsibilities and permanence of
marriage, and to live in unselfish love
observing the laws of God and his
Church. To assist them to bring up
their children as practising Catholics
and public-spirited citizens. To teach
and defend Christian values in family
life and to ensure their Catholic
education. To offer love, sympathy and
practical help to the family in difficulty.

Special Interests

Catholic

Catholic Archives Society
St Peter's Grange
Prinknash Abbey
Cranham
Gloucester GL4 8EX
Hon. Secretary:
Sr Marguerite-Andree
The care and presentation of the
records and archives of the dioceses,
religious foundations, institutions and
societies in the UK and Eire.

Catholic Police Guild
42 Francis Street
London SW1P 1QW
Secretary:
J.P. Anthony
The Guild is interested in
communication with, and bringing
together, serving and retired police
officers and cadets and special
constables.

Catholic Record Society
c/o 114 Mount St
London W1Y 6AH
To promote the study of post-Reformation Catholic history in England and Wales.

Civil Service Catholic Guild
512 London Road
Mitcham
Surrey CR4 4BA
Tel: 01 646 5459
Secretary:
Mrs M.I. Flament
To help members to develop their spiritual life, greater awareness of moral responsibilities attached to work in public administration and to meet each other socially.

Catholic Stage Guild
1 Maiden Lane
London WC2E 7NA
Tel: 01 836 4240
Secretary:
Alan Foss
To serve Catholics in all branches of the entertainment world spiritually and socially.

Catholic Study Circle for Animal Welfare
39 Onslow Gardens
South Woodford
London E18 1ND
Tel: 01 989 0478
Secretary:
Mrs M. Bocking
To study and propagate Catholic teaching on animal questions to combat abuse and to promote better treatment for animals.

The Newman Association
22 Cortayne Road
London SW6 3QA
Scotland:
4 Gillespie Terrace
The Scores
St Andrews
Fife KY 16
Secretary:
J.T. Davey
The Association is open to any Roman Catholic but its work attracts graduates and professional people. Its programmes are designed to fit in with current Church priorities; it discusses problems affecting the Church and promotes the study of theology, liturgy, ecumenical activity and other relevant issues.

Anglican

Anglican Society for the Welfare of Animals
10 Chester Avenue
Hawkenbury
Tunbridge Wells TN2 4TZ
Tel: 0892 25594
Secretary:
Miss E.V. Elliott
To cooperate with other religious or secular organisations on behalf of animals.

Church Society
Whitfield House
186 Kennington Park Road
London SE11 4BT
Tel: 01 582 0132
Director:
Rev. Dr David N. Samuel
The Church Society helps to meet educational needs in the parishes, theological needs in the Church and scriptural needs in the nation.

Ecclesia
St Stephen's Presbytery
29 Westbourne Avenue
Hull HU5 3HN
Tel: 0482 46075
Chairperson:
Francis Bown
The Society seeks to guide and support
Anglicans (both priests and laity) who
hold to traditional Catholic faith and
practice.

Lord's Day Observance Society
47 Parish Lane
London SE20 7LU
Tel: 01 659 1117
Secretary:
Mr John G. Roberts
Promotion and preservation of the
Lord's Day.

Modern Churchman's Union
4 Cathedral Close
Guildford GU2 5TL
Tel: 0483 575140
Secretary:
Rev. Canon Peter Croft
To advance liberal Christian thought.

Order of Christian Unity
Christian Unity House
58 Hanover Gardens
London SW11 5TN
Director:
Mr Philip Vickers
Protection of the family and sanctity of
human life especially through Christian
education, medical ethics, family
welfare and the mass media.

The Prayer Book Society
40 Great Smith Street
London SW1P 3BU
Joint Hon. Secretaries:
Miss E. M. Gwyer & Dr Roger Homan
To encourage the use of the Book of
Common Prayer for the training of
ordinands and confirmands and to
spread knowledge of the Book of
Common Prayer.

The Society of Mary
St Luke's Vicarage
4 Burton Road
Kingston-upon-Thames
Surrey KT2 5TE
Secretary:
Rev. C.W. Bryan Vickery
To promote devotion of Our Blessed
Lady by parish groups working
together in a pastoral situation
following the rules of the Society.

Retreat Houses and Conference Centres

South-East England

Aylesford, Kent
The Friars
Aylesford
Maidstone
Kent ME20 7BX
Tel: Maidstone 77272
Pilgrimage centre, conference centre,
retreat house (private); RC Carmelite
Order.
Apply the Secretary; 30 doubles, 20
singles, dormitory; conference
facilities.

Bletchingley, Redhill, Surrey
Wychcroft
Bletchingley
Redhill
Surrey RH1 4NE
Tel: Godstone 843041
Anglican Diocesan Training Centre,
conducted retreats only.
Apply the Secretary; 14 doubles, 17
singles; conference facilities.

Bramley, Guildford, Surrey
Maryvale
Snowdenham Hall
Bramley
Guildford
Surrey GU5 0BD
Tel: Bramley (0483) 892765
RC Pastoral Centre for Diocese of
Arundel and Brighton; outside groups
occasionally catered for.
Apply the Secretary; 3 doubles, 30
singles.

Chislehurst, Kent
Graham Chiesman House
St Paul's Cray Road
Chislehurst
Kent BR7 6QA
Tel: 01 467 6087
Anglican conference house with
emphasis on youth activities.
Apply the Warden; 22 double rooms, 6
singles.

Coolham, Horsham, West Sussex
St Julian's
Coolham
Horsham
West Sussex RH13 8QL
Tel: Coolham 220
Ecumenical, non-retreatants, no one
over 65 years old.
Apply the Warden; 7 doubles, 9
singles.

Crawley Down, West Sussex
The Monastery of the Holy Trinity
Crawley Down
Nr Crawley
West Sussex RH10 4LH
Tel: Copthorne 712074
Anglican, men only.
Apply to Guestmaster; 6 singles.

Crockham Hill, Kent
Centre Space
Coakham Farm
Crockham Hill
Kent
Tel: Crockham Hill 338
Ecumenical study centre and
consultancy.
Apply to Mark and Catherine Collier; 3
double rooms, 4 singles.

East Grinstead, West Sussex
St Margaret's Convent
Moat Road
East Grinstead
West Sussex RH19 3LE
Tel: East Grinstead 23497
Anglican, non-retreatants.
Apply to Mother Superior; 2 doubles, 7
singles.

Farncombe, Godalming, Surrey
The Farncombe Community
5 Wolseley Road
Farncombe
Godalming
Surrey GU7 3DX
Tel: Godalming (04868) 7253 or 28265
Ecumenical, private retreats.
Apply to Head of Community;
1 double, 4 singles.

Godalming, Surrey
Ladywell Retreat and Conference
Centre
Ashtead Lane
Godalming
Surrey GU7 1ST
Tel: Godalming 23764
RC, non-retreatants. Part convent,
part retreat and conference centre.
Apply to Retreat Secretary; 33
conference residents, 150 conference
day, 2 doubles, 31 singles.

Heathfield, East Sussex
St Mary's Retreat
Tilsmore Road
Heathfield
East Sussex TN21 0XT
Anglican Retreat House.
Apply to Sister in Charge; 12
conference, 2 doubles, 7 singles.

Hindhead, Surrey
Cenacle Retreat and Conference
Centre
Headley Road
Grayshott
Hindhead
Surrey GU26 6DN
Tel: Hindhead 4412
Retreat and conference centre.
Apply to Sister in Charge; 12 doubles,
17 singles.

*Lindfield, Haywards Heath, West
Sussex*
Convent of the Holy Rood
Lindfield
Haywards Heath
West Sussex RH16 2RA
Tel: Lindfield 2345
Anglican Conference Centre.
Apply to Rev. Mother; 50 conference
day, 1 double, 1 small flat.

Maidstone, Kent
Allington Castle
Maidstone
Kent ME16 0NB
Tel: Maidstone 54080
Retreat and Conference Centre. RC
Carmelite Order.
Apply to Secretary; 40 conference, 10
doubles, 10 singles.

Minster, Nr Ramsgate, Kent
Minster Abbey
Minster
Nr Ramsgate
Kent CT12 4HF
Tel: Minster 254
Retreat Centre; RC Benedictine nuns.
Apply to Mother Prioress; 1 double, 11
singles.

Ramsgate, Kent
St Augustine's Abbey
Ramsgate
Kent CT11 9PA
Tel: Thanet 53045
Retreat Centre; RC (Benedictine),
men only in monastery, men and
women in guest house.
Apply to Rev. Fr Guestmaster, OSB; 6
doubles, 15 singles, 30 dormitory, self-
catering (groups and families).

*Sayers Common, Hassocks, West
Sussex*
Priory of Our Lady
Sayers Common
Hassocks
West Sussex BN6 9HT
Tel: Hurstpierpoint 832901
Retreat Centre; RC (Augustinian),
non-retreatants.
Apply to Retreat Secretary; 17
doubles, 7 singles, some rooms
downstairs for disabled.

Westgate-on-Sea, Kent
St Gabriel's Retreat and Conference
House
Elm Grove
Westgate-on-Sea
Kent CT8 8LB
Tel: Thanet 32033 or 31228
Retreat and Conference House;
Anglican.
Apply to Warden; 32 conference, 9
doubles, 13 singles.

West Kingsdown, Nr Sevenoaks, Kent
Stacklands Retreat House
West Kingsdown
Nr Sevenoaks
Kent TN15 6AN
Tel: West Kingsdown 2247
Retreat Centre and Training Centre for
priests wishing to become professional
retreat conductors; Anglican.
Apply to Administrator; 18 singles.

Central Southern

Alton, Hants
Alton Abbey
Alton
Hants. GU34 4AP
Tel: Alton 62145
Anglican (Order of St Benedict); men
only.
Apply to Guestmaster; 13 singles, self-
catering flat.

Arundel, Sussex
Convent of Poor Clares
Cross Bush
Arundel
Sussex BN18 9PJ
Tel: Arundel 882536
RC; women only.
Apply to Mother Abbess; 6 single
rooms.

Ascot, Berks
Ascot Priory
Ascot
Berks. SL5 8RT
Tel: 0344 885813
Anglican Retreat Centre.
Apply to Encounter Sister; 2 doubles, 8
singles.

Binfield, Nr Bracknell, Berks
The Priory
Binfield
Nr Bracknell
Berks.
Tel: Bracknell (0344) 483417
Retreat Centre, ecumenical.
Apply to Mrs G. Stanley; 2 doubles, 15
day seminars.

Burnham, Slough
The Cenacle Retreat and Conference
Centre
Parliament Lane
Burnham
Slough SL1 8NU
Tel: Burnham 2761
RC Retreat and Conference Centre.
Apply to Retreat Secretary; 10
doubles, 22 singles, 3 rooms for
disabled.

Burnham, Slough
Nashdom Abbey
Burnham
Slough SL1 8NL
Tel: Burnham (062 86) 3176
Anglican Retreat Centre (men only)
but women day visitors.
Apply to Guestmaster; 10 singles.

Cold Ash, Berks
Cold Ash Centre
The Ridge
Cold Ash
Berks. RG16 9HU
Tel: Newbury (0635) 65353
RC Conference and Retreat Centre.
Apply to Secretary; 1 double, 31 singles.

Horndean, Nr Portsmouth, Hants
Catherington House
Horndean
Nr Portsmouth
Hants. PO8 0TD
Tel: Horndean 593251
Anglican Retreat and Conference
Centre.
Apply to Warden; 7 doubles, 11 singles.

Kintbury, Newbury, Berks
St Cassian's Centre
Wallington's Road
Kintbury
Newbury
Berks. RG15 0SR
Tel: Kintbury 267
RC residential Retreat Centre for
groups of young people.
Apply to Director; 28 doubles, 12
singles.

Maidenhead, Berks
Burnham Abbey
Lake End Road
Maidenhead
Berks. SL6 0PW
Tel: Burnham 4080
Anglican (enclosed community).
Apply to Guest Sister; 2 bed-sitting
rooms.

Old Alresford, Hants
Old Alresford Place
Old Alresford
Hants. SO24 9DH
Tel: Alresford 2518
Anglican Retreat House.
Apply to Domestic Warden; 8 doubles, 14 singles.

Ryde, Isle of Wight
Quarr Abbey
Ryde
Isle of Wight PO33 4ES
Tel: Wooton Bridge 882420
RC (Benedictine) men only for private retreats.
Apply to Fr Guestmaster; 16 singles.

Ventnor, Isle of Wight
St Mary's House
Kemming Road
Whitwell
Ventnor
Isle of Wight PO38 2QT
Tel: Niton (0983) 730446
Anglican.
Apply to Warden; 2 doubles, 2 singles.

Wickham, Fareham, Hants
Park Place Pastoral Centre
Wickham
Fareham
Hants. PO17 5HA
Tel: Wickham 833043
RC Pastoral Centre run by a community of Franciscan sisters.
Apply to Secretary; 15 doubles, 31 singles.

Windsor, Berks
Convent of St John Baptist
Hatch Lane
Clewer
Windsor
Berks. SL4 3QR
Tel: Windsor (0753) 866100
Anglican Retreat House.
Apply to Sister in Charge of retreats; 20 single rooms, 20 conference.

Woking, Surrey
St Columba's House
Maybury Hill
Woking
Surrey GU22 8AB
Tel: Woking 66498
Anglican Retreat and Conference Centre.
Apply to Lady Warden; 25 conference, 25 singles, 1 room for disabled.

South-West

Almondsbury, Bristol
Almondsbury Conference House
Almondsbury
Bristol
Avon
Tel: Almondsbury 613041
Anglican Diocesan Centre for conferences, retreats, etc.
Apply to Warden; 35 conference, 4 doubles, 27 singles.

Bristol
Emmaus House
Clifton Hill
Bristol
Avon BS8 4PD
Tel: Bristol 38056
Mainly geared to Clifton RC diocese but all denominations are welcome.
Apply to Director; 30 conference resident, 150 conference day, 9 doubles, 1 single, 2 multiple rooms.

Knowle, Bristol
St Agnes Retreat and Conference
House
St Agnes Avenue
Knowle
Bristol
Avon BS4 2HH
Tel: Bristol 776806
Anglican Retreat and Conference
Centre.
Apply to Sister in Charge; 30
conference, 9 doubles, 15 singles.

Buckfastleigh, Devon
Buckfast Abbey
Buckfastleigh
Devon TQ11 0EE
Tel: Buckfastleigh 3301
RC (Benedictine), men only.
Apply to Guestmaster; 12 singles.

Castle Cary, Somerset
St John's Priory
Castle Cary
Somerset BA7 7DF
Tel: Castle Cary 50429
RC (Sister of Jesus Crucified), offers
group and individuals a suitable place
for quiet holidays, retreats, prayer and
reflection.
Apply to Guestmistress; 10 conference,
2 doubles, 6 singles.

Compton Durville, Somerset
The Community of St Francis
Compton Durville
South Petherton
Somerset TA13 5ES
Tel: South Petherton 40473
Anglican.
Apply to Guestmistress; 12 conference,
2 doubles, 8 singles.

Dunsford, Exeter, Devon
The Sheldon Centre
Dunsford
Exeter
Devon EX6 7LE
Tel: Christow (0647) 52203
Anglican (Church Army); mainly a
self-catering centre where church and
school groups of up to 50 do their own
thing.
Apply to Capt. Carl A. Lee, CA; 7
doubles, 8 singles, 2 multiple rooms.

Glastonbury, Somerset
The Abbey House
Glastonbury
Somerset BA6 8DH
Tel: Glastonbury 31112
Anglican Retreat House which can be
used for refresher courses, parish
holiday groups, summer schools, house
parties, etc.
Apply to Sister in Charge; 32
conference, 7 doubles, 18 singles.

Hilfield, Dorchester, Dorset
The Society of St Francis
The Friary
Hilfield
Dorchester
Dorset DT2 7BE
Tel: Cerne Abbas 345/6
Anglican Retreat House.
Apply to Guestmaster; 13 singles.

Lynton, Devon
Lee Abbey Fellowship
Lee Abbey
Lynton
Devon EX35 6JJ
Tel: Lynton 2621/2
Ecumenical holiday centre.
Apply to The Secretary; 120
conference, 24 doubles, 21 singles,
shared rooms.

Radstock, Bath
Ammerdown Study Centre
Ammerdown
Radstock
Bath
Avon BA3 5SW
Tel: Radstock (0761) 33709
Ecumenical centre.
Apply to Warden; 40 conference
(resident), 60 conference (day), 4
doubles, 32 singles, rooms for disabled.

Truro, Cornwall
Convent of the Epiphany
Tregolls Road
Truro
Cornwall TR1 1JG
Tel: Truro 2249
Anglican Convent.
Apply to Rev. Mother; 20 conference,
3 doubles, 14 singles, self-catering flat.

Greater London

Barking
Anchor House
81 Barking Road
London E16 4HB
Tel: 01 476 6062
Conference Centre (Apostleship of the
Sea).
Apply to The Manager; 13 doubles, 98
singles.

Butcher Row, London
Royal Foundation of St Katharine
Butcher Row
London E14 8DS
Tel: 01 790 3540 and 1003
Anglican Retreat, Conference and
many other activities.
Apply to Receptionist; 29 conference,
5 doubles, 19 singles.

Mill Hill, London
Damascus House
The Ridgeway
Mill Hill
London NW7 1HH
Tel: 01 959 8971
RC Retreat Centre; school retreats of
one day or longer are often held.
Apply to Director; 12 doubles, 50
singles.

Oakleigh Park South, London
St Peter's Bourne
40 Oakleigh Park South
London N20 9JN
Tel: 01 445 5535
Anglican.
Apply to Sister in Charge; 11
conference, 3 doubles, 5 singles.

Pinner, Middlesex
The Grail
Waxwell Farm House
125 Waxwell Lane
Pinner
Middlesex HA5 3ER
Tel: 01 866 2195/0505
RC Lay Community. The Grail offers a
place for renewal where individuals and
groups can come to discuss, pray, relax
and find peace within themselves.
Apply to Secretary of Conference
Centre; 35 conference resident, 100
conference day, 16 doubles, 4 singles.

Teddington, Middlesex
St Paul's Convent
252 Kingston Road
Teddington
Middlesex TW11 9JQ
Tel: 01 977 4034
Retreat House.
Apply to Retreat Secretary; 15 singles.

West Wickham, Kent
Emmaus Retreat and Conference
Centre
Layhams Road
West Wickham
Kent BR4 9HH
Tel: 01 777 2000
RC Retreat and Conference Centre.
Apply to Secretary; 78 conference, 26
doubles, 25 singles.

Westbourne Park, London
St Andrew's House
2 Tavistock Road
Westbourne Park
London W11 1BA
Tel: 01 229 2662
Anglican.
Apply to Reverend Mother; quiet days,
20 conference (day only), 3 singles.

Wimbledon, London
Convent of Marie Reparatrice
115 The Ridgeway
Wimbledon
London SW19 4RB
Tel: 01 946 1088
RC Retreat and Study Centre.
Apply to Sister in charge of Retreats;
30 conference, 30 singles.

East Midlands and East Anglia

Bedford
Clapham Park Conference Centre
Clapham
Bedford MK41 6EY
Tel: Bedford 50609
RC Conference Centre.
Apply to Warden; 40 conference, 6
doubles, 34 singles.

Bury St Edmunds, Suffolk
Hengrave Hall
Bury St Edmunds
Suffolk IP28 6LZ
Tel: 0284 701561
Ecumenical Retreat and Conference
Centre; also a youth annexe nearby.
Apply to Warden; 33 conference (or 75
conference sharing rooms), 15 doubles,
18 singles, 3 rooms for disabled. Youth
annexe has dormitory-type
accommodation for 30 to 40 people.

Ditchingham, Suffolk
Holy Cross House
All Hallows House and St Michaels
House
Ditchingham
Bungay
Suffolk NR35 2DT
Tel: Bungay 2749
Anglican Conference and Retreat
house.
Apply to Rev. Mother; 2 doubles, 18
singles (Holy Cross House); 35
conference day, 20 singles, self-catering
or full board (St Michael's House).

East Hanningfield, Essex
The Convent
Moon Hall Lane
East Hanningfield
Chelmsford
Essex CM3 5AS
Tel: Danbury (024 541) 3136
Anglican Guest House.
Apply to Guestmistress; 4 singles in
guest house, 2 singles in garden hut.

East Norton, Leicester
Launde Abbey
East Norton
Leics.
Tel: Belton 254
Anglican Retreat House, Conference
Centre and training establishment for
ordinands.
Apply to Warden; 9 doubles, 11
singles.

Ecton, Northampton
Ecton House
Ecton
Northampton NN6 0QE
Tel: Northampton 406442
Anglican Conference and Retreat
Centre.
Apply to Warden; 25 conference, 25
singles.

Ely, Cambs.
Bishop Woodford House
Barton Road
Ely
Cambs. CB7 4DB
Tel: Ely 3039
Anglican Retreat and Conference
Centre.
Apply to Warden; 33 conference, 33
single rooms.

Hemingford Grey, Cambs.
St Francis' House
Hemingford Grey
Huntingdon
Cambs. PE18 9BJ
Tel: St Ives 62185
Anglican Retreat House.
Apply to Warden; 30 conference, 24
singles (or 5 doubles and 20 singles).

Little Massingham, Norfolk
Massingham St Mary
Little Massingham
Nr King's Lynn
Norfolk PE32 2JU
Tel: Great Massingham 245
RC Retreat House.
Apply to Retreat Secretary; 30
conference, 5 doubles, 18 singles, 7
rooms in bungalow (self-catering).

Lincoln
Edward King House
The Old Palace
Lincoln LN2 1PU
Tel: Lincoln 28778
Anglican Retreat House.
Apply to Bursar; 30 conference, 12
doubles, 6 singles.

London Colney, Herts.
All Saints Pastoral Centre
London Colney
Herts. AL2 1AF
Tel: Bowmansgreen 22010
RC; a residential training centre for the
Roman Catholic diocese of
Westminster. School parties and youth
groups are particularly well catered for.
Apply to Conference Secretary; 100
conference, 21 doubles, 70 singles.

Lowestoft, Suffolk
St Mary's Convent
Rectory Road
Lowestoft
Suffolk NR33 0DA
Tel: 0502 65828
RC Retreat House.
Apply to Retreat Secretary; 1 double,
14 singles.

Pleshey, Chelmsford, Essex
House of Retreat
Pleshey
Chelmsford
Essex CM3 1HA
Tel: Pleshey 251
Anglican Retreat House.
Apply to Warden; 2 doubles, 21
singles.

St Albans, Herts.
Verulam House
Verulam Road
St Albans
Herts. AL3 4DH
Tel: St Albans 53991
Anglican Conference and Retreat
House.
Apply to Secretary; 32 conference, 8
doubles, 16 singles.

Turvey, Bedfordshire
Turvey Abbey Retreat and Conference
Centre
Turvey
Bedfordshire MK43 8DE
Tel: 023 064 432
Retreat and Conference Centre.
Apply to Retreat Secretary; 4 doubles,
10 singles.

Theddingworth, Leics.
Hothorpe Hall
Theddingworth
Lutterworth
Leics. LE17 6QX
Tel: Market Harborough 880257
Lutheran. Hothorpe is run by an
international group of volunteer
workers who offer hospitality to guests.
Facilities are extensive and holidays
may be spent here.
Apply to Director; 130 conference, 20
multiple rooms, 3 singles.

Walsingham, Norfolk
National Shrine of Our Lady
Walsingham
Norfolk
Tel: Walsingham 217/8
RC holiday centre.
Apply to Pilgrim Bureau, Friday
Market, Walsingham, Norfolk; double
and single rooms for 120, dormitory.

West Midlands

Belper, Derby
Convent of St Lawrence
Belper
Derby DE5 1DD
Tel: Belper 2585
Anglican. The sisters run a home for
elderly women and provide a house
where people of all ages can come and
experience a few days rest and renewal.
Apply to Rev. Mother Superior;
Conference (15 women or 11 men), 10
singles.

Birmingham
Harborne Hall
Old Church Road
Harborne
Birmingham B17 0BD
Tel: 021 427 1044 or 4374
RC Retreat House, women only.
Apply to Directress of Retreats; 40
conference, 5 doubles, 35 singles.

Callow End, Worcester
Stanbrook Abbey
Private Guesthouse
The Hermitage
Callow End
Worcester WR2 4TD
Tel: Worcester 830307
RC Retreat House.
Apply to Secretary; 5 doubles, 2
singles.

Charney Bassett, Oxon.
Charney Manor
Charney Bassett
Wantage
Oxon. OX12 0EJ
Tel: West Hanney (023 587) 206
Society of Friends Retreat House.
Apply to Warden; 35 conference
(groups only), 10 doubles, 9 singles,
dormitory.

Cropthorne, Worcs.
Holland House
Cropthorne
Nr Pershore
Worcs.
Tel: Evesham 860330
Interdenominational Retreat House.
Apply to Warden; 3 doubles, 19
singles.

Freeland, Oxford
St Mary's Convent and The Old
Parsonage
Freeland
Oxford OX7 2AJ
Tel: Freeland 881225
Anglican Retreat House.
Apply to Rev. Mother; 10 conference,
3 doubles, 4 singles.

Gloucester
Prinknash Abbey
Gloucester GL4 8EX
Tel: Painswick 812455
RC.
Apply to Rev. Fr Leo Roud; self-
catering if desired.

Malmesbury, Wilts.
The Abbey House
Malmesbury
Wilts. SN16 9AS
Tel: Malmesbury (06662) 2212
Anglican Retreat House.
Apply to Sister in Charge; 2 singles.

Morley, Derby
Morley Retreat and Conference Centre
Morley Rectory
Morley
Derby DE7 6DE
Tel: Derby 831293
Anglican Retreat and Conference
Centre.
Apply to Warden; 28 conference, 2
doubles, 28 singles.

Norton Bridge, Staffs.
Shallowford House
Norton Bridge
Stone
Staffs. ST15 0NZ
Tel: Stafford 760233
Anglican Retreat and Conference
Centre.
Apply to Warden; 37 conference, 11
doubles, 15 singles.

Offchurch, Warwicks.
Coventry Diocesan Retreat House
Offchurch
Nr Leamington Spa
Warwicks CV33 9AS
Tel: Leamington Spa 23309
Anglican Retreat House.
Apply to Warden; 26 conference, 3
doubles, 20 singles.

Shrawley, Worcs.
St Mary at the Cross
Glasshampton
Shrawley
Worcs. WR6 6TQ
Tel: Gt Witley 345
Anglican (Society of St Francis) men
only.
Apply to Guestmaster (letter only); 5
singles.

Shrewsbury
Hawkstone Hall
Weston
Shrewsbury SY4 5LG
Tel: Hodnet (063 084) 242
RC Pastoral and Study Centre, which
shares its community life with other
men and women.
Apply to Rev. Director; 60 conference,
2 doubles, 60 singles.

Stone, Staffs.
Oulton Abbey
Stone
Staffs. ST15 8UP
Tel: Stone (0785) 812049
RC Retreat House.
Apply to Rt Rev. Lady Abbess; 25
conference, 25 singles (or 4 doubles, 21
singles).

Swanwick, Derbyshire
Hayes Conference Centre
Swanwick
Derbyshire BE55 10AU
Tel: 077 360 2482/3
Conference Centre.
Apply to The Conference Secretary;
accommodates 300.

Wales

Bwlch, Powys
Llangasty Retreat House
Bwlch
Powys LD3 7PJ
Tel: Llangorse 250
Anglican Retreat House.
Apply to Sister in Charge; 17
conference, 3 doubles, 11 singles.

Isle of Caldey
Caldey Abbey
Isle of Caldey
Tenby
Dyfed
Tel: Tenby 2632
RC, men only; Retreat House.
Apply to Rev. Fr Abbot; 1 double, 19
singles.

Llandudno, Gwynedd
Ty'r Brodyr
Vicarage Road
Llandudno
Gwynedd LL30 1PT
Tel: Llandudno 78833
Anglican, men only. Franciscan Friary.
Apply to Guardian; 3 singles.

Penmaenmawr, Gwynedd
Convent of the Sacred Heart of Mary
Noddfa Retreat Centre
Conway Old Road
Penmaenmawr
Gwynedd
Tel: Penmaenmawr 623473
RC Retreat Centre.
Apply to Sister in Charge; 34
conference, 34 singles.

Tremeirchion, Clwyd
St Beuno's
Tremeirchion
St Asaph
Clwyd LL17 0AS
Tel: St Asaph 583444
RC Retreat House.
Apply to Retreat Secretary; 35
conference, 35 singles, 4 rooms for
disabled.

St David's, Dyfed
St Non's Retreat
St David's
Haverfordwest
Dyfed
Tel: St David's 224
RC Retreat Centre.
Apply to Fr Superior; 11 doubles or
singles; also camping.

St David's, Haverfordwest
The Priory
St David's
Haverfordwest
Dyfed SA62 6PG
Tel: St David's 359
Anglican Guest house.
Apply to Rev. Mother Superior; 13
conference, 2 doubles, 9 singles.

North-East

Alnwick, Northumberland
Alnmouth Friary
Alnwick
Northumberland NE66 3NJ
Tel: 0665 830213
Anglican Retreat House.
Apply to Guardian; 12 conference, 1
double, 10 singles.

Holy Island, Berwick-on-Tweed,
Northumberland
Marygate House
Holy Island
Berwick-on-Tweed
Northumberland TD15 2SD
Tel: Berwick (0289) 89246
Interdenominational Retreat House.
Apply to Warden; 20 conference, 1
single, 4 rooms with 4 beds, 1 room 3
beds, youth weeks.

Consett, Co. Durham
Passionist Retreat Centre
Minsteracres
Consett
Co. Durham DA6 9RT
Tel: Slaley 248
RC Retreat House.
Apply to Retreat Director; 19 doubles,
12 singles, rooms for disabled.

Newcastle-upon-Tyne
Convent of Marie Reparatrice
12 Osborne Road
Newcastle-upon-Tyne NE2 2AD
Tel: Newcastle-upon-Tyne 811605
RC Retreat Centre.
Apply to Retreat Secretary; 35
conference, 35 singles.

Riding Mill, Northumberland
Shepherds Dene
Riding Mill
Northumberland NE44 6AF
Tel: Riding Mill 212
Anglican Retreat Centre; conducted
retreat only.
Apply to Warden; 10 doubles, 7 singles.

Yorkshire

Ampleforth, York
The Grange
Ampleforth Abbey
Ampleforth
York YO6 4HD
Tel: Ampleforth 440
RC Conference and Retreat Centre
within a monastic setting.
Apply to Warden; 20 conference, 4
doubles, 16 singles.

Brompton-by-Sawdon, Scarborough,
North Yorkshire
Wydale Hall
Brompton-by-Sawdon
Scarborough
North Yorkshire YO13 9DG
Tel: Scarborough (0723) 85270
Anglican Retreat House.
Apply to Warden; 46 conference, 13
doubles, 9 singles, 1 room for
handicapped, 4 dormitories.

Horbury, West Yorkshire
St Hilda's Retreat House
St Peter's Convent
Dovecote Lane
Horbury
West Yorkshire WF4 6BB
Tel: Wakefield 272181
Anglican Convent; Retreat house, and
the sisters also run a school for children
aged 4–11.
Apply to Guestmistress; 1 double, 18
singles.

Ilkley, West Yorkshire
The Briery Retreat House
38 Victoria Avenue
Ilkley
West Yorkshire LS29 9BW
Tel: Ilkley 607287
RC Retreat House.
Apply to Sister in Charge; 12 doubles,
24 singles.

Ilkley, West Yorkshire
St Paul's Retreat House
Myddelton Lodge
Ilkley
West Yorkshire LS29 0EB
Tel: Ilkley 607887 and 607144
RC Retreat House and Monastery.
Men or mixed groups.
Apply to Rev. Fr Rector; 50
conference, 5 doubles, 35 singles, 2
trebles.

Kettlewell, Yorkshire
Scargill House
Kettlewell
Skipton
N. Yorkshire BD23 5HU
Tel: Kettlewell (075 676) 234
Anglican Retreat House. Many visitors
come for holiday houseparties, some
privately.
Apply to Bookings Secretary; 89
conference, 22 doubles, 13 singles, 13
double cabins, 6 single cabins, 2 family
rooms.

*Kirkbyoverblow, Nr Harrogate, North
Yorkshire*
Ripon Diocesan House
'Barrowby'
Kirkbyoverblow
Nr Harrogate
North Yorkshire HG3 1HY
Tel: Harewood 886240
Anglican Retreat House, with 8½ acres
of landscaped garden making a safe
place for children to play.
Apply to Warden; 36 conference, 12
doubles, 8 singles.

Sheffield
Whirlow Grange
Ecclesall Road South
Sheffield S11 9PZ
Tel: Sheffield 363173
Anglican Conference Centre.
Apply to Warden; 34 conference, 5
doubles, 15 singles, 2 family rooms.

Skyreholme, Skipton, North Yorkshire
Parcevall Hall
Skyreholme
Skipton
North Yorkshire BD23 6DG
Tel: Burnsall 213
Anglican Retreat House, Conference
Centre and holidays.
Apply to Warden; 10 doubles, 4
singles.

Tadcaster, Yorkshire
Hazlewood Castle
Tadcaster
Yorkshire LS24 9NJ
Tel: Tadcaster 832738
RC Retreat House.
Apply to Fr Director; 38 conference, 14
doubles, 9 singles.

Thwing, Driffield, Humberside
Lamplugh House Conference Centre
Thwing
Driffield
N. Humberside YO25 0DY
Tel: Thwing (026 287) 282
Anglican teaching and pastoral centre.
Apply to Warden; 45 conference, 3
doubles, 22 singles, 1 room for
disabled, multiple rooms.

Wetherby, West Yorkshire
Wood Hall Centre
Linton
Nr Wetherby
West Yorkshire LS22 4JA
Tel: Wetherby 62033
RC Pastoral and Ecumenical Centre.
Apply to Warden; limited
accommodation is possible with
catering, but young people are always
welcome to bring a sleeping bag and
cater for themselves.

North-West

Ambleside, Cumbria
Rydal Hall
Ambleside
Cumbria LA22 9LX
Tel: Ambleside (0966) 32050
Anglican. More suited to conferences
and houseparties than retreats.
Apply to Warden; 58 conference, 16
doubles, 5 singles, 4 triples, 1 four-
bedded dormitory (53 beds).

Blackpool, Lancs.
Marie Reparatrice Retreat Centre
183 Newton Drive
Blackpool
Lancs. FY3 8NU
Tel: 0253 31549
RC Retreat Centre run by Sisters of
Marie Reparatrice.
Apply to Retreat Secretary; 5 singles,
day groups 25.

Carnforth, Lancs.
The Monastery of Our Lady of Hyning
Warton
Carnforth
Lancs. LA5 9SE
Tel: Carnforth (0524) 732684
RC Retreat Centre. Particularly
suitable for private retreats.
Apply to Sister in Charge; 36
conference, 12 doubles, 18 singles.

Chester
The Retreat House
11 Abbey Square
Chester CH1 2HU
Tel: Chester 21801
Anglican Retreat House.
Apply to Warden; 2 doubles, 25
singles.

Crawshawbooth, Lancs.
Crawshawbooth Conference Centre
(Manchester Diocesan Conference
House)
Burnley Road
Crawshawbooth
Rossendale
Lancs. BB4 8LZ
Tel: Rossendale (0706) 215120;
guest tel: 213698
Anglican Conference House.
Apply to Warden; 42 conference, 3
doubles, 26 singles, 3 trebles.

Crewe
St Therese
Wistaston Hall
89 Broughton Lane
Crewe CW2 8JS
Tel: 0270 68653
RC Retreat Centre.
Apply to Retreat Secretary; 15
doubles.

Greystoke, Cumbria
Lattendales
Greystoke
Penrith
Cumbria CA11 0UE
Tel: Greystoke (085 33) 229
Society of Friends. The aim of the house for all guests is to provide a holiday with a friendly, relaxed family atmosphere.
Apply to Warden; 25 conference (winter only), 4 doubles, 4 singles.

Lancaster
St Paul's Priory
Quernmore Park
Lancaster LA2 9HN
Tel: Caton 770567
Anglican. The work of this community lies in various branches of study and teaching.
Apply to Prior; 19 conference, 5 doubles, 9 singles.

Liverpool
Cenacle Retreat and Conference Centre
7 Lance Lane
Liverpool L15 6TW
Tel: 041 722 2271/2
RC Retreat and Conference Centre.
Apply to Retreat Secretary; 42 conference, 16 doubles, 11 singles.

Malpas, Cheshire
St Joseph's Retreat and Conference Centre
Malpas
Cheshire SY14 7DD
Tel: Malpas 416
RC Retreat and Conference Centre.
Apply to Warden; 30 conference, 30 singles.

Manchester
Cenacle Retreat and Conference Centre
28 Alexander Road South
Manchester M16 8HU
Tel: 061 226 1241
RC Retreat and Conference Centre.
Apply to Retreat Secretary; 16 conference, 5 doubles, 6 singles.

Rainhall, Merseyside
Loyola Hall
Warrington Road
Rainhill
Prescot
Merseyside L35 6NZ
Tel: 041 426 4137
RC Retreat House. Youth and student groups on retreat welcomed.
Apply to Rev. Superior; 50 singles, 4 × 6 beds.

Whalley, Lancs.
Whalley Abbey
Whalley
Nr Blackburn
Lancs. BB6 9SS
Tel: Whalley 2268
Anglican Retreat and Conference Centre.
Apply to Warden; 21 doubles, 3 singles.

Scotland

Barrhead, Glasgow
Montfort House
Retreat Centre
Darnley Road
Barrhead
Glasgow
RC Retreat Centre.
Apply to the Secretary.

Bothwell, Glasgow
Craighead Retreat House
Bothwell
Glasgow G71 8AU
Tel: Hamilton 285300
RC Retreat Centre.
Apply to Rev. Fr Superior; 32 conference, 32 singles.

Coodham, Kilmarnock
Fatima House
Coodham
Kilmarnock KA1 5PJ
Tel: Symington 830296
RC Retreat House.
Apply to Guestmaster; 85 conference, 40 doubles, 5 singles.

Crieff, Tayside
St Ninian's Centre
Comrie Road
Crieff
Tayside PH7 4BG
Tel: Crieff (0764) 3766
Church of Scotland Conference and Retreat House. Popular centre for youth groups.
Apply to Warden; 36 conference (plus 44 in youth annexe), 8 doubles, 20 singles (44 dormitory in annexe).

Dunblane, Perth
Scottish Churches' House
Kirk Street
Dunblane
Perthshire FK15 0AJ
Tel: Dunblane (0786) 823588
Ecumenical Retreat Centre. This Centre is run jointly by 7 Scottish churches, Salvation Army, Society of Friends and inter-church organisations.
Apply to House Secretary; 50 conference, 20 doubles, 9 singles.

Elgin, Grampian
Pluscarden Abbey
Elgin
Grampian LV30 3UA
Tel: Dallas 257
RC (Benedictine monastery). During the winter men only.
Apply to Guestmaster; 12 to 15 conference, 8 singles for women, 12 singles for men.

Glenshee, Tayside
Glenshee Lodge
Glenshee
By Blairgowrie
Tayside PH10 7QD
Tel: Glenshee (025 085) 209
Interdenominational Retreat House.
Apply to Warden; 46 conference, 46 dormitory (bring sleeping bags).

Iona, Strathclyde
The Iona Community
Iona
Strathclyde PA76 6SN
Not a retreat house, but people are welcome to visit.
Bishop's House
Iona
Strathclyde PA76 6SJ
Tel: Iona 306
Scottish Episcopal Church Retreat Centre. Closed October to Easter.
Apply to Warden; 14 conference, 5 doubles, 4 singles.

Musselburgh, Lothian
Carberry Tower
Musselburgh
Lothian EH21 8PY
Tel: 031 665 3135 and 3488
Church of Scotland Education Residential Centre.
Apply to Warden; 87 conference, 19 doubles, 11 singles.

Newmains, Lanarks.
Helpers of the Holy Souls Convent
50 Bonkle Road
Newmains
Wishaw
Lanarks. ML2 9AP
Tel: Wishaw 73397
RC Retreat House.
Apply to Guest Sister; 6 doubles, 11 singles, 4 trebles, 1 room for 4.

Nunraw, East Lothian
Sancta Maria Abbey
Nunraw
Haddington
East Lothian EH41 4LW
Tel: Garvald 228
RC Retreat House.
Apply to Guestmaster; 4 singles for
men, 3 doubles and 1 single for women.

PART THREE

The Church Worldwide

CHAPTER ONE

The Catholic Church

Principal Dates and Events in Church History

First Century

42	Persecution of Christians in Palestine under rule of Herod Agrippa.
c. 49	Council of Jerusalem.
51–7	Missionary journeys of St Paul.
64/65	Martyrdom of St Peter at Rome.
64	Persecutions under Nero.
70	Destruction of Jerusalem.
c. 100	Death of St John and the end of the Apostolic Age.

Second Century

117–38	Persecution under Hadrian.
c. 115	St Polycarp martyred.
196	Easter controversy.

Third Century

202	Persecution under Septimius Severus.
249–51	The Decian persecution.
257	Persecution under Valerian.
258	St Cyprian martyred.
292	Emperor Diocletian divided the Roman Empire into East and West.

Fourth Century

303	Persecution under Diocletian.
313	The Edict of Milan and the conversion of Constantine.
325	Council of Nicaea; condemned Arianism.
361–3	Julian the Apostate waged campaign against the Church.
379	Death of St Basil.
381	Council of Constantinople.
382	Canon of Sacred Scripture listed.
396	Augustine became bishop of Hippo.

Fifth Century

410	Alaric and the Visigoths sack Rome.
430	Death of St Augustine of Hippo.
431	Council of Ephesus.
432	St Patrick arrived in Ireland.
451	Council of Chalcedon.
455	Vandals sacked Rome.
496	Clovis, King of the Franks, was converted.

Sixth Century

525	Foundation of Monte Cassino by St Benedict.
553–5	Council of Constantinople.
590–604	Pontificate of Pope St Gregory the Great.
596	Gregory sent St Augustine of Canterbury to England.
597	St Columba died on Iona.

Seventh Century

622	The flight of Mohammed from Mecca and the birth of Islam.
649	Lateran Synod condemns Monothelitism.
664	Synod of Whitby advances the adoption of Roman usages and the adoption of the Roman date of Easter in England.
680–1	Council of Constantinople.

Eighth Century

711	Moslems began the conquest of Spain.
731	Venerable Bede wrote his *History of the English People.*
732	Moslem advance through France halted by Charles Martel.
c. 755	St Boniface, Apostle of Germany, was martyred.
787	Council of Nicaea. The Famous *Book of Kells* dates from this period.

Ninth Century

800	Charlemagne crowned Emperor by Pope Leo III Egbert became king of West Saxons; he strengthened the See of Canterbury.
846	Moslems attacked Rome.
868	Cyril and Methodius consecrated bishops.
869	Council of Constantinople.
c. 871–900	Reign of Alfred the Great.

Tenth Century

989	Vladimir, ruler of Russia, baptised.
997	St Stephen became ruler of Hungary.
996	Otto III crowned Emperor.

Eleventh Century

1009	Beginning of lasting East–West schism.
1054	East–West break definitive.
1066	Death of St Edward the Confessor, restorer of Westminster Abbey.
1073–85	Pontificate of the reforming St Gregory VII (Hildebrand).
1084	St Bruno founded the Carthusians.
1096	Beginning of the First Crusade.

Twelfth Century

1115	St Bernard founded the Abbey of Clairvaux.
1122	The Concordat of Worms.

1123	First Council of the Lateran.
1139	Second Lateran Council.
1170	St Thomas Becket was murdered at Canterbury.
1179	Third Lateran Council.
1181	Crusade against the Albigenses.
1189	Beginning of the Third Crusade.

Thirteenth Century

1209	Verbal approval given by Pope Innocent III to Franciscan Rule.
1212	Poor Clares founded.
1215	Fourth Lateran Council.
1216	Dominican Rule approved.
1226	Death of St Francis of Assisi.
1245	Council of Lyons.
1247	Preliminary approval of Carmelite Rule.
1270	Eighth and last Crusade.
1274	Death of St Thomas Aquinas.

Fourteenth Century

1302	Pope Boniface VIII issued *Unam Sanctam*.
1308–78	Popes reside at Avignon.
1377	Beginning of the Hundred Years War.
1378	Beginning of the Great Schism.

Fifteenth Century

1409	Council of Pisa attempted unsuccessfully to end the Great Schism.
1414–18	Council of Constance ended the Schism.
1431–99	Council of Basle.
1453	Fall of Constantinople to the Turks.
1493	Council of Florence.

Sixteenth Century

1512–17	Fifth Council of the Lateran.
1517	Publication of Luther's ninety-five theses.
1533	Excommunication of Henry VIII.
1535	Execution of Sts John Fisher and Thomas More.

1540	Constitutions of the Society of Jesus approved.
1545–63	Council of Trent.
1563	First text of 39 articles of Church of England issued.
1570	Queen Elizabeth I excommunicated.

Seventeenth Century

1605	The Gunpowder plot.
1611	Foundation of the Oratorians.
1625	Foundation of the Vincentians.
1648	Peace of Westphalia.
1653	Jansenism condemned by Innocent X.
1685	Revocation of Edict of Nantes.

Eighteenth Century

1720	Passionists founded by St Paul of the Cross.
1732	Redemptorists founded by St Alphonsus Liguori.
1738	Freemasonry condemned and Catholics forbidden to join.
	Beginning of the Methodist revival.
1764	Febronianism condemned.
1773	Suppression of the Jesuits (restored in 1814).
1786	Synod of Pistoia.
1789	Beginning of the French Revolution.

Nineteenth Century

1801	Concordat with Napoleon.
1809	Pius VII made captive of Napoleon.
1820	Long persecution in China ended.
1829	The Catholic Emancipation Act.
1832	Publication of the encyclical *Mirari Vos*.
1833	Start of the Oxford Movement.
1850	Hierarchy reestablished in England.
1854	Definition of the dogma of the Immaculate Conception.
1858	The Blessed Virgin Mary appeared at Lourdes.
1864	Publication of the *Syllabus of Errors*.
1869–70	The First Vatican Council.
1879	Publication of *Aeterni Patris*.
1891	Publication of *Rerum Novarum*.

Twentieth Century

1905	Separation of Church and State in France.
1917	Apparitions at Fatima.
1918	Code of Canon Law enacted.
1922	Papal mission to Russia.
1926	Catholic Relief Act in England.
1929	Lateran Treaty.
1936–9	Spanish Civil War.
1950	Proclamation of the dogma of the Assumption.
1962	Opening of the Second Vatican Council.
1978	The thirty-four-day pontificate of John Paul I.
1983	The revised *Code of Canon Law* promulgated.

List of Popes and Their Reigns

St Peter	29–64 or 67
St Linus	67–76
St Anacletus or Cletus	76–88
St Clement	88–97
St Evaristus	97–105
St Alexander I	105–15
St Sixtus I	115–25
St Telesphorus	125–36
St Hyginus	136–40
St Pius I	140–55
St Anicetus	155–66
St Soter	166–75
St Eleutherius	175–89
St Victor I	189–98
St Zephyrinus	199–217
St Callistus I	217–22
St Urban I	222–30
St Pontian	230–5
St Anterus	235–6
St Fabian	236–50
St Cornelius	251–3
St Lucius I	253–4
St Stephen I	254–7
St Sixtus II	257–8
St Dionysius	259–68
St Felix I	269–74

St Eutychian	275–83
St Caius	283–96
St Marcellinus	296–304
St Marcellus I	308–9
St Eusebius	309–10
St Melchiades	311–14
St Silvester I	314–35
St Mark	336
St Julius I	337–52
Liberius	352–66
St Damasus I	366–84
St Siricius	384–99
St Anastasius I	399–401
St Innocent I	401–17
St Zosimus	417–18
St Boniface I	418–22
St Celestine I	422–32
St Sixtus III	432–40
St Leo I (the Great)	440–61
St Hilary	461–8
St Simplicius	468–83
St Felix III	483–92
St Gelasius I	492–6
St Anastasius II	496–8
St Symmachus	498–514
St Hormisdas	514–23
St John I	523–6
St Felix IV	526–30
Boniface II	530–2
John II	533–5
St Agapitus I	535–6
St Silverius	536–7
Vigilius	537–55
Pelagius I	556–61
John III	561–74
Benedict I	575–9
Pelagius II	579–90
St Gregory I (the Great)	590–604
Sabinian	604–6
Boniface III	607
St Boniface IV	608–15
St Deusdedit I	615–19

Boniface V	619–25
Honorius I	625–38
Severinus	640
John IV	640–2
Theodore I	642–9
St Martin I	649–55
St Eugene I	654–7
St Vitalian	657–72
Deusdedit II	672–6
Donus	676–8
St Agatho	678–81
St Leo II	682–3
St Benedict II	684–5
John V	685–6
Conon	686–7
St Sergius I	687–701
John VI	701–5
John VII	705–7
Sisinnius	708
Constantine	708–15
St Gregory II	715–31
St Gregory III	731–41
St Zachary	741–52
St Stephen II (III)	752–7
St Paul I	757–67
Stephen III (IV)	768–72
Hadrian (or Adrian) I	772–95
St Leo III	795–816
Stephen IV (V)	816–17
St Paschal I	817–24
Eugene II	824–7
Valentine	827
Gregory IV	827–44
Sergius II	844–7
St Leo IV	847–55
Benedict III	855–8
St Nicholas I (the Great)	858–67
Adrian II	867–72
John VIII	872–82
Marinus I	882–4
St Adrian III	884–5
Stephen V (VI)	885–91

Formosus	891–6
Boniface VI	896
Stephen VI (VII)	896–7
Romanus	897
Theodore II	897
John IX	898–900
Benedict IV	900–3
Leo V	903
(Christopher	903–4)
Sergius III	904–11
Anastasius III	911–13
Landon	913–14
John X	914–28
Leo VI	928
Stephen VII (VIII)	928–31
John XI	931–5
Leo VII	936–9
Stephen VIII (IX)	939–42
Marinus II	942–6
Agapitus II	946–55
John XII	955–63
Leo VIII	963–5
Benedict V	964–5
John XIII	965–72
Benedict VI	973–4
Benedict VII	974–83
John XIV	983–4
John XV	985–96
Gregory V	996–9
Silvester II	999–1003
John XVII	1003
John XVIII	1004–9
Sergius IV	1009–12
Benedict VIII	1012–24
John XIX	1024–32
Benedict IX (1st and 2nd terms)	1032–45
Gregory VI	1045–6
Clement II	1046–7
Benedict IX (3rd term)	1047–8
Damasus II	1048
St Leo IX	1049–54
Victor II	1055–7

Stephen IX (X)	1057–8
Nicholas II	1059–61
Alexander II	1061–73
St Gregory VII	1073–85
B. Victor III	1086–7
B. Urban II	1088–99
Paschal II	1099–1118
Gelasius II	1118–19
Callistus II	1119–24
Honorius II	1124–30
Innocent II	1130–43
Celestine II	1143–4
Lucius II	1144–5
B. Eugene III	1145–53
Anastasius IV	1153–4
Adrian IV (N. Breakspear)	1154–9
Alexander III	1159–81
Lucius III	1181–5
Urban III	1185–7
Gregory VIII	1187
Clement III	1187–91
Celestine III	1191–8
Innocent III	1198–1216
Honorius III	1216–27
Gregory IX	1227–41
Celestine IV	1241
Innocent IV	1243–54
Alexander IV	1254–61
Urban IV	1261–4
Clement IV	1265–8
B. Gregory X	1271–6
B. Innocent V	1276
Adrian V	1276
John XXI	1276–7
Nicholas III	1277–80
Martin IV	1281–5
Honorius IV	1285–7
Nicholas IV	1288–92
St Celestine V	1294
Boniface VIII	1294–1303
B. Benedict XI	1303–4
Clement V	1305–14

John XXII	1316–34
Benedict XII	1334–42
Clement VI	1342–52
Innocent VI	1352–62
B. Urban V	1362–70
Gregory XI	1370–8
Urban VI	1378–89
Boniface IX	1389–1404
Innocent VII	1404–6
Gregory XII	1406–15
(Clement VII	1378–94)
(Benedict XIII	1394–1409)
(Alexander V } (Great Schism)	1409–10)
(John XXIII	1410–15)
Martin V (Colonna)	1417–31
Eugene IV (Condulmer)	1431–47
Nicholas V (Parentucelli)	1447–55
Callistus III (Borgia)	1455–8
Pius II (Piccolomini)	1458–64
Paul II (Barbo)	1464–71
Sixtus IV (della Rovere)	1471–84
Innocent VIII (Cibo)	1484–92
Alexander VI (Borgia)	1492–1503
Pius III (Piccolomini)	1503
Julius II (della Rovere)	1503–13
Leo X (Medici)	1513–21
Adrian VI (Florensz)	1522–3
Clement VII (Medici)	1523–34
Paul III (Farnese)	1534–49
Julius III (del Monte)	1550–5
Marcellus II (Cervini)	1555
Paul IV (Carafa)	1555–9
Pius IV (Medici)	1559–65
St Pius V (Ghislieri)	1566–72
Gregory XIII (Buoncompagni)	1572–85
Sixtus V (Peretti)	1585–90
Urban VII (Castagna)	1590
Gregory XIV (Sfondrati)	1590–1
Innocent IX (Facchinetti)	1591
Clement VIII (Aldobrandini)	1592–1605
Leo XI (Medici)	1605
Paul V (Borghese)	1605–21

Gregory XV (Ludovisi)	1621–3
Urban VIII (Barberini)	1623–44
Innocent X (Pamfili)	1644–55
Alexander VII (Chigi)	1655–67
Clement IX (Rospigliosi)	1667–9
Clement X (Altieri)	1670–6
B. Innocent XI (Odescalchi)	1676–89
Alexander VIII (Ottoboni)	1689–91
Innocent XII (Pignatelli)	1691–1700
Clement XI (Albani)	1700–21
Innocent XIII (Conti)	1721–4
Benedict XIII (Orsini)	1724–30
Clement XII (Corsini)	1730–40
Benedict XIV (Lambertini)	1740–58
Clement XIII (Rezzonico)	1758–69
Clement XIV (Ganganelli)	1769–74
Pius VI (Braschi)	1775–99
Pius VII (Chiaramonti)	1800–23
Leo XII (della Genga)	1823–9
Pius VIII (Castiglioni)	1829–30
Gregory XVI (Cappellari)	1831–46
Pius IX (Mastai-Ferretti)	1846–78
Leo XIII (Pecci)	1878–1903
St Pius X (Sarto)	1903–14
Benedict XV (della Chiesa)	1914–22
Pius XI (Ratti)	1922–39
Pius XII (Pacelli)	1939–58
John XXIII (Roncalli)	1958–63
Paul VI (Montini)	1963–78
John Paul I (Luciani)	1978
John Paul II (Wojtyla)	1978–

Structure of the Curia

The Roman Curia consists of the Secretariat of State, the Sacred Council for the Public Affairs of the Church, ten congregations, three tribunals, three secretariats and a complex of commissions, councils and offices which administer church affairs at the highest level.

Pope Paul VI gave the following short account of the background of the Curia in the apostolic constitution, *Regimini Ecclesiae Uni-*

versae ('For the Government of the Universal Church'), dated August 15 1967:

The Roman Pontiffs, successors to Blessed Peter, have striven to provide for the government of the Universal Church by making use of experts to advise and assist them.

In this connection, we should remember both the Presbyterium of the City of Rome and the College of Cardinals of the Holy Roman Church which in the course of centuries evolved from it. Then, little by little, as we know, out of that office (Apostolic Chancery) which was set up in the fourth century to transmit papal documents, many offices developed; to these was added the Auditorium, which was a well-developed tribunal in the 13th century and which was more thoroughly organised by John XXII (1316–1334).

With an increase in the volume of things to be dealt with, bodies or commissions of cardinals selected to treat of specific questions began to be more efficiently organised in the 16th century, from which eventually arose the congregation of the Roman Curia. It is to the credit of our predecessor Sixtus V that, in the constitution *Immensa Aeterni Dei* of Jan. 22, 1588, he arranged the sacred councils in an orderly manner and wisely described the structure of the Roman Curia.

With the progress of time, however, it happened that some of them became obsolete, others had to be added, and others had to be restructured. This is the work our predecessor St Pius X set out to do with the constitution *Sapienti Consilio* of June 29, 1908. Its provisions, a lasting testimony to that wise and ingenious pastor of the Church, were with a few changes incorporated into the Code of Canon Law.

Departments

Secretariat of State
Provides the pope with the closest possible assistance in the care of the universal Church and in dealings with all departments of the Curia.

The cardinal secretary is the key coordinator of curial operations. He has authority to call meetings of the prefects of all departments for expediting the conduct of business, for consultations and inter-communications. He handles: any and all matters entrusted to him by the pope, and ordinary matters which are not within the competence of other departments; some relations with bishops; relations with representatives of the Holy See, civil governments and their representatives, without prejudice to the competence of the Council for the Public Affairs of the Church.

The cardinal secretary has been likened to a prime minister or head of government because of the significant role he plays in coordinating curial operations at the highest level.

Officials: Cardinal Agostino Casaroli, secretary of state; Most Rev. Eduardo Martínez Somalo, undersecretary.

Council for the Public Affairs of the Church

Handles diplomatic and other relations with civil governments. With the Secretariat of State, it supervises matters concerning nunciatures and apostolic delegations. It also has supervision of the Pontifical Commission for Russia.

Officials: Cardinal Agostino Casaroli, prefect, secretary of state; Most Rev. Achille Silvestrini, secretary.

Congregations

Sacred Congregation for the Doctrine of the Faith

Has responsibility to safeguard the doctrine of faith and morals.

Accordingly it examines doctrinal questions; promotes studies thereon; evaluates theological opinions and, when necessary and after prior consultation with concerned bishops, reproves those regarded as opposed to principles of the faith; examines books on doctrinal matters and can reprove such works, if the contents so warrant, after giving authors the opportunity to defend themselves.

Officials: Cardinal Joseph Ratzinger, prefect; Most Rev. Alberto Bovone, secretary.

Sacred Congregation for the Oriental Churches

Has competence in matters concerning the persons and discipline of Eastern Rite Churches. To assure adequate and equal representations, it has as many offices as there are rites of Oriental Churches in communion with the Holy See.

Officials: Cardinal Simon Lourdusamy, prefect; Most Rev. Miroslav Stefan Marusyn, secretary. Members include all Eastern Rite patriarchs and the president of the Secretariat for Promoting Christian Unity. Consultors include the secretary of the same secretariat.

Sacred Congregation for Bishops

Formerly called the Sacred Consistorial Congregation; has functions related in one way or another to bishops and the jurisdictions in which they serve.

Officials: Cardinal Bernardin Gantin, prefect; Most Rev. Lucas Moreira Neves, OP, secretary.

Sacred Congregation for the Sacraments
Supervises the discipline of the sacraments without prejudice to the
competencies of the Congregation for the Doctrine of the Faith and
other curial departments.
Officials: Cardinal Augustin Mayer, OSB, prefect; Most Rev.
Lajos Kada, secretary.

Sacred Congregation for Divine Worship
Has general competence over the ritual and pastoral aspects of
divine worship in the Roman and other Western rites.
Officials: Cardinal Augustin Mayer, OSB, prefect; Most Rev. Vir-
gilio Noè, secretary.

Sacred Congregation for the Causes of Saints
Handles matters connected with beatification and canonisation
causes (in accordance with revised procedures decreed in 1983),
and the preservation of relics.
Officials: Cardinal Pietro Palazzini, prefect; Most Rev. Traian Cri-
san, secretary.

Sacred Congregation for the Clergy
Formerly called the Sacred Congregation of the Council; handles
matters concerning the persons, work and pastoral ministry of
clerics who exercise their apostolate in a diocese. Such clerics are
diocesan deacons and priests, and religious who are engaged in
ordinary parochial ministry in a diocese.
Officials: Cardinal Antonio Innocenti, prefect; Most Rev. Maximino
Romero de Lema, secretary.

Sacred Congregation for Religious and Secular Institutes
Formerly known as the Sacred Congregation of Religious or for the
Affairs of Religious; has dual competence over institutes of religious, together with societies of the common life without vows, and
secular institutes.
Officials: Cardinal Jérôme Hamer, OP, prefect; Most Rev. Vin-
cenzo Fagiolo, secretary.

Sacred Congregation for Catholic Education
Formerly known as the Sacred Congregation of Seminaries and
Universities; has supervisory competence over institutions and
works of Catholic education.
Officials: Cardinal William Wakefield Baum, prefect; Most Rev.
Antonio M. Javierre Ortas, SDB, secretary.

Sacred Congregation for the Evangelization of Peoples (for the Propagation of the Faith)
Directs and coordinates missionary work throughout the world.
Officials: Cardinal Jozef Tomko, prefect; Most Rev. José Sanchez, secretary.

Tribunals

Sacred Apostolic Penitentiary
Has jurisdiction for the internal forum only (sacramental and non-sacramental). It issues decisions on questions of conscience; grants absolutions, dispensations, commutations, sanations and condonations; has charge of non-doctrinal matters pertaining to indulgences.
Officials: Cardinal Luigi Dadaglio, major penitentiary; Msgr Luigi de Magistris, regent.

Apostolic Segnatura
The principal concerns of this supreme court of the Church are to resolve questions concerning juridical procedure and to supervise the observance of laws and rights at the highest level. It decides the jurisdictional competence of lower courts and has jurisdiction in cases involving personnel and decisions of the Rota. It is the supreme court of the State of Vatican City.
Officials: Cardinal Aurelio Sabattani, prefect; Most Rev. Zenon Grocholewski, secretary.

Sacred Roman Rota
The ordinary court of appeal for cases appealed to the Holy See. It is best known for its competence and decisions in cases concerning the validity of marriage.
Official: Msgr Arturo De Jorio, dean.

Secretariats

Secretariat for Promoting Christian Unity
Handles relations with members of other Christian ecclesial communities; deals with the correct interpretation and execution of the principles of ecumenism; initiates or promotes Catholic ecumenical groups and coordinates on national and international levels the efforts of those promoting Christian unity; undertakes dialogue regarding ecumenical questions and activities with churches and ecclesial communities separated from the Apostolic See; sends

Catholic observer-representatives to Christian gatherings, and invites to Catholic gatherings observers of other churches; orders into execution concilliar decrees dealing with ecumenical affairs.

The Commission for Catholic-Jewish Relations is attached to the secretariat.

Official: Cardinal Johannes Willebrands, president.

Secretariat for Non-Christians

Is concerned with persons who are not Christians but profess some kind of religious faith. Its function is to promote studies and dialogue for the purpose of increasing mutual understanding and respect between Christians and non-Christians.

Officials: Cardinal Francis Arinze, president; Very Rev. Marcello Zago, OMI, secretary.

Secretariat for Non-Believers

Studies the background and philosophy of atheism, and initiates and carries on dialogue with non-believers.

Officials: Cardinal Paul Poupard, president; Very Rev. Jordan P. Gallego, secretary.

Councils and Commissions

Laity, Pontifical Council for.
Justice and Peace, Pontifical Commission.
Authentic Interpretation of the Code of Canon Law, Pontifical Commission.
Revision of the Code of Oriental Canon Law.
Social Communications.
Latin America, Commission.
Migration and Tourism, Commission.
Cor Unum, Council.
Family, Pontifical Council.
Theological Commission.
Biblical Commission.
Revision and Emendation of the Vulgate, Pontifical Commission.
Sacred Archaeology, Commission.
Historical Sciences, Committee.
Ecclesiastical Archives of Italy, Commission.
Sacred Art in Italy, Commission.
Sanctuaries of Pompei, Loreto and Bari, Cardinalatial Commission.
Russia, Commission.

Catholic-Jewish Relations, Commission.
Catholic-Moslem Relations, Commission.
State of Vatican City, Commission.
Protection of the Historical and Artistic Monuments of the Holy
See, Commission.
Preservation of the Faith, Erection of New Churches in Rome.
Roman Curia, Commission for Discipline.
Works of Religion, Commission.
Council of Cardinals for Study of Organisational and Economic
Problems of the Holy See.
Culture, Pontifical Council.

Offices

Prefecture for the Economic Affairs of the Holy See
A financial office which coordinates and supervises administration
of the temporalities of the Holy See.
Officials: Cardinal Giuseppe Caprio, president; Msgr Luigi Spo-
sito, secretary.

Apostolic Chamber
Administers the temporal goods and rights of the Holy See between
the death of one pope and the election of another, in accordance
with special laws.
Officials: Cardinal Sebastiano Baggio, chamberlain of the Holy
Roman Church; Most Rev. Ettore Cunial, vice-chamberlain.

Administration of the Patrimony of the Apostolic See
Handles the estate of the Apostolic See under the direction of papal
delegates acting with ordinary or extraordinary authorisation.
Officials: Cardinal Agnelo Rossi, president; Most Rev. Lorenzo
Antonetti, secretary.

Prefecture of the Pontifical Household
Oversees the papal chapel – which is at the service of the pope in his
capacity as spiritual head of the Church – and the pontifical family –
which is at the service of the pope as a sovereign. It arranges papal
audiences, has charge of preparing non-liturgical elements of papal
ceremonies, makes all necessary arrangements for papal visits and
trips outside the Vatican, and settles questions of protocol connected with papal audiences and other formalities.
Officials: Most Rev. Jacques Martin, prefect; Msgr Dino Mond-
uzzi, regent.

Central Statistics Office
Compiles, systematises and analyses information of the status and condition of the Church and the needs of its pastoral ministry, from parish to top levels. The office is one of the organs of the Secretariat of State.

Aid Office
Distributes alms and aid to the aged, sick, handicapped and other persons in need.
Official: Most Rev. Antonio M. Travia, director.

Vatican II Archives
Preserves the acts and other documents of the Second Vatican Council.
Official: Msgr Michele Buro.

Theological Commission

The purpose of the Commission is to provide the Doctrinal Congregation with the consultative and advisory services of theologians and scriptural and liturgical experts representative of various schools of thought. The international membership is restricted to 30 and the ordinary term of membership is five years (renewable).

Biblical Commission

This Commission receives questions and studies topics referred to it by a variety of sources, from the pope to Catholic universities and biblical associations.

It is required to meet in plenary session at least once a year and to submit conclusions reached in such meetings to the pope and the Congregation for the Doctrine of the Faith. The Commission must also promote relationships with non-Catholic as well as Catholic institutes of biblical studies and expects to be consulted before any new norms on biblical matters are issued.

Principal Encyclicals of the Twentieth Century

Saint Pius X 1903–14

1903: *E Supremi* (Restoration of All Things in Christ), 4 Oct.
1905: *Acerbo Nimis* (Teaching of Christian Doctrine), 15 Apr.
1907: *Pascendi Dominici Gregis* (Modernism), 8 Sept.

Benedict XV 1914–22

1914: *Ad Beatissimi Apostolorum* (Appeal for Peace), 1 Nov.
1917: *Humani Generis Redemptionem* (Preaching), 15 June.
1920: *Pacem, Dei Munus Pulcherrimum* (Peace and Christian Reconciliation), 23 May.
1920: *Spiritus Paraclitus* (Holy Scripture), 15 Sept.

Pius XI 1922–39

1922: *Ubi Arcano Dei Consilio* (Peace of Christ in the Kingdom of Christ), 23 Dec.
1925: *Quas Primas* (Feast of Christ the King), 11 Dec.
1926: *Rerum Ecclesiae* (Catholic Missions), 28 Feb.
1928: *Miserentissimus Redemptor* (Reparation due the Sacred Heart), 8 May.
1928: *Rerum Orientalium* (Reunion with the Eastern Churches), 8 Sept.
1930: *Casti Connubii* (Christian Marriage), 31 Dec.
1931: *Quadragesimo Anno* (Social Reconstuction), 15 May.
1932: *Caritate Christi Compulsi* (Sacred Heart and World Distress), 3 May.
1935: *Ad Catholici Sacerdotii* (Catholic Priesthood), 20 Dec.
1936: *Vigilanti Cura* (Clean Motion Pictures), 29 June.
1937: *Divini Redemptoris* (Atheistic Communism), 19 Mar.

Pius XII 1939–58

1939: *Summi Pontificatus* (Function of the State in Modern World), 20 Oct.
1943: *Mystici Corporis Christi* (Mystical Body), 29 June.
1943: *Divino Afflante Spiritu* (Biblical Studies), 30 Sept.
1947: *Mediator Dei* (Sacred Liturgy), 20 Nov.
1950: *Humani Generis* (Warnings against Attempts to Distort Catholic Truths), 12 Aug.
1954: *Sacra Virginitas* (Pre-eminence of Evangelical Chastity), 25 Mar.
1955: *Musicae Sacrae* (Sacred Music), 25 Dec.
1956: *Haurietis Aquas* (The Sacred Heart), 15 May.
1957: *Fidei Donum* (Missionary Effort, especially in Africa), 21 Apr.
1957: *Miranda Prorsus* (Radio, TV and Motion Pictures), 8 Sept.

John XXIII 1958–63

1961: *Mater et Magistra* (Christianity and Social Progress), 15 May.
1962: *Paenitentiam Agere* (Appeal for Works of Penance for Success of the Second Vatican Council), 1 July.
1963: *Pacem in Terris* (Peace on Earth), 11 Apr.

Paul VI 1963–78

1965: *Mysterium Fidel* (The Eucharist), 3 Sept.
1966: *Christi Matri* (The Rosary), 15 Sept.
1967: *Populorum Progressio* (Development of peoples), 26 Mar.
1967: *Sacerdotalis Caelibatus* (Priestly celibacy), 24 June.
1968: *Humanae Vitae* (on the regulation of birth), 25 July.

John Paul II 1978–

1979: *Redemptor Hominis* (Redemption and dignity of the human race), 4 Mar.
1980: *Dives in Misericordia* (On the mercy of God), 30 Nov.
1981: *Laborem Exercens* (On human work), 14 Sept.

Pontifical Orders of Knighthood and Awards of Merit

Pontifical Orders

Supreme Order of Christ (Militia of Our Lord Jesus Christ)
This is the highest of the five pontifical orders of knighthood; it was approved on 14 March 1319 by Pope John XXII as a continuation in Portugal of the suppressed Order of Templars. Paul VI in 1966 restricted conferment of the order to Roman Catholic heads of state.

Order of the Golden Spur (Golden Militia)
One of the oldest of the knighthoods, Gregory XVI replaced it with the Order of St Sylvester. In 1905 St Pius X restored the Order of the Golden Spur in its own right. Paul VI in 1966 restricted conferment of the order to Christian heads of state.

Order of Pius IX
Founded by Pius IX, on 17 June 1847, the order may be given to non-Catholics as well as Catholics, and is today conferred mainly on diplomats accredited to the Holy See and members of visiting official delegations.

On 25 December 1957, Pius XII created the highest class, the Golden Collar. In 1966, Paul VI restricted this award to visiting heads of state 'in solemn circumstances'.

Order of St Gregory the Great
This Order was first established by Gregory XVI in 1831 to honour citizens of the Papal States; it is conferred strictly on merit, for services to the Holy See.

Order of Pope St Sylvester
Instituted in 1841 by Gregory XVI to absorb the Order of the Golden Spur, this order is conferred on laymen active in the apostolate, particularly professional men, or masters of the arts.

Papal Awards

Golden Rose
An award of the highest distinction, dating from 1049. Now conferred on Catholic female sovereigns, as the equivalent of the Supreme Order of Christ.

Pro Ecclesia et Pontifice ('For the Church and the Pontiff')
Instituted in 1888 by Leo XIII, and changed by Paul VI from a medal to a gilt bronze cross. It is awarded in recognition of service to the Church and the Pope.

Benemerenti ('To a well-deserving person')
Founded 1798, made permanent by Leo XIII, and changed by Paul VI to a gilt bronze cross. Conferred for exceptional services.
  Both these awards may be given by the Pope to men or women.

Pontifical *medals* are also sometimes struck, for presentation on special occasions.

Religious Orders of Knighthood

Order of the Holy Sepulchre
This Order has had a long and complex history. Though under the patronage of the Holy See, with a Cardinal as its Grand Master, it is not a papal order. It now has five classes: 12 Knights of the Collar and four degrees, with separate divisions of each for men and women – Grand Cross, Commanders with Plaque, Commanders

and Knights. Three honorary decorations are awarded: the Cross of Merit (which may be bestowed on non-Catholics), the Holy Land Pilgrim's Cross and the Palm of the Order; the last two are conferred on pilgrims by the Latin Patriarch of Jerusalem.

Investiture ceremonies combine a profession of faith with the ancient ritual of a knighthood dubbing. Candidates do not take monastic vows but pledge an upright Christian life and loyalty to the Pope.

Order of Malta

The Sovereign Military Hospitaller Order of St John of Jerusalem of Rhodes and of Malta traces its origins to a group of men who maintained a Christian hospital in the Holy Land in the eleventh century. The group was approved as a religious order – the Hospitallers of St John – by Paschal II in 1113.

Traditionally the order is restricted to nobles, though in some places the rules have been relaxed. By the 1961 charter, members must be Roman Catholics. The Prince and Grand Master is elected by the Council of the order, but his election must be confirmed by the Pope.

The sovereignty of the order, which is based on international law, is recognised by the Holy See and by 40 countries with which full diplomatic relations are maintained. The five main classifications of members are: Knights and Dames of Justice; Knights of Obedience; Knights and Dames of Honour and Devotion; Knights and Dames of Grace and Devotion, of noble lineage; and Knights of Magistral Grace. There are also chaplains and Donats of the order.

The order also awards an Order and Medals of Merit which do not imply membership of the order as such.

The order has grand priories, sub-priories and national associations, and is devoted to hospital and charitable work of all kinds in many countries.

Further information: *Orders of Knighthood, Awards and the Holy See*, Hyginus Eugene Cardinale, ed. and rev. Peter Bander van Duren; Gerrards Cross, 1985.

P.B. van D.

Eastern Catholic Churches

The Second Vatican Council, in its *Decree on Eastern Catholic Churches*, stated the following:

The Catholic Church holds in high esteem the institutions of the Eastern Churches, their liturgical rites, ecclesiastical traditions, and Christian way of life. For, distinguished as they are by their venerable antiquity, they are bright with that tradition which was handed down from the apostles through the Fathers, and which forms part of the divinely revealed and undivided heritage of the universal Church (No. 1).

Origin

As the Church spread out from its roots in the Holy Land, certain cities or jurisdictions became key centres of Christian life and missionary endeavour. Notable among these were Jerusalem, Alexandria, Antioch and Constantinople in the East, and Rome in the West; the result was that their practices became diffused throughout their spheres of influence. Various rites originated from these practices which, although rooted in the essentials of Christian faith, were different in significant respects because of their relationships to particular cultural patterns.

Patriarchal Jurisdictions

The main lines of Eastern Church organisation and liturgy were drawn before the Roman Empire was separated into Eastern and Western divisions in 292. It was originally coextensive with the boundaries of the Eastern Empire. Its jurisdictions were those of the patriarchates of Alexandria and Antioch (recognised as such by the Council of Nicaea in 325), and of Jerusalem and Constantinople (given similar recognition by the Council of Chalcedon in 451). These were the major parent bodies of the Eastern Rite Churches which for centuries were identifiable only with limited numbers of nationality and language groups in Eastern Europe, the Middle East and parts of Asia and Africa. However their members are now scattered throughout the world.

Rites and Faithful of Eastern Churches

The Byzantine, Alexandrian, Antiochene, Armenian and Chaldean are the five principal rites used in their entirety or in modified form by the various Eastern Churches. The number of Eastern Catholics throughout the world is more than 12 million.

Alexandrian Rite

Called the Liturgy of St Mark, the Alexandrian Rite was modified by the Copts and Melkites and contains elements of the Byzantine Rite of St Basil and the liturgies of Sts Mark, Cyril and Gregory Nazianzen. The liturgy is substantially that of the Coptic Church, which is divided into two branches – the Coptic or Egyptian, and the Ethiopian or Abyssinian.

The faithful of this rite are:

Copts: Returned to Catholic unity about 1741; situated in Egypt, the Near East; liturgical languages are Coptic, Arabic.

Ethiopians: Returned to Catholic unity in 1846; situated in Ethiopia, Eritrea, Jerusalem, Somalia; liturgical language is Geez.

Antiochene Rite

This is the source of more derived rites than any of the other parent rites. Its origin can be traced to the Eighth Book of the *Apostolic Constitutions* and to the Liturgy of St James of Jerusalem, which ultimately spread throughout the whole patriarchate and displaced older forms based on the *Apostolic Constitutions*.

The faithful of this rite are:

Malankarese: Returned to Catholic unity in 1930; situated in India; liturgical languages are Syriac, Malayalam.

Maronites: United to the Holy See since the time of their founder, St Maron; have no counterparts among the separated Eastern Christians; situated throughout the world; liturgical languages are Syriac, Arabic.

Syrians: Returned to Catholic unity in 1781; situated in Asia, Africa, the Americas, Australia; liturgical languages are Syriac, Arabic.

Armenian Rite

Substantially, although using a different language, this is the Greek Liturgy of St Basil; it is considered an older form of the Byzantine Rite, and incorporates some modifications from the Antiochene Rite.

The faithful of this rite are:

Armenians, exclusively: Returned to Catholic unity during the time of the Crusades; situated in the Near East, Europe, Africa, the Americas, Australasia; liturgical language is Classical Armenian.

Byzantine Rite

Based on the Rite of St James of Jerusalem and the Churches of Antioch, and reformed by Sts Basil and John Chrysostom, the

Byzantine Rite is proper to the Church of Constantinople. (The city was called Byzantium before Constantine changed its name; the modern name is Istanbul.) It is now used by the majority of Eastern Catholics and by the Eastern Orthodox Church (which is not in union with Rome). It is, after the Roman, the most widely used rite.

The faithful of this rite:

Albanians: Returned to Catholic unity about 1628; situated in Albania; liturgical language is Albanian.

Bulgarians: Returned to Catholic unity about 1861; situated in Bulgaria; liturgical language is Old Slavonic.

Byelorussians, also known as *White Russians:* Returned to Catholic unity in the seventeenth century; situated in Europe, the Americas, Australia; liturgical language is Old Slavonic.

Georgians: Returned to Catholic unity in 1829; situated in Georgia (Southern Russia), France; liturgical language is Georgian.

Greeks: Returned to Catholic unity in 1829; situated in Greece, Asia Minor, Europe; liturgical language is Greek.

Hungarians: Descendants of Ruthenians who returned to Catholic unity in 1646; situated in Hungary, the rest of Europe, the Americas; liturgical languages are Greek, Hungarian, English.

Italo-Albanians: Have never been separated from Rome; situated in Italy, Sicily, the Americas; liturgical languages are Greek, Italo-Albanian.

Melkites (Greek Catholic Melkites): Returned to Catholic unity during the time of the Crusades, but definitive reunion did not take place until early in the eighteenth century; situated in the Middle East, Asia, Africa, Europe, the Americas, Australia; liturgical languages are Greek, Arabic, English, Portuguese, Spanish.

Romanians: Returned to Catholic unity in 1697; situated in Rumania, the rest of Europe, the Americas; liturgical language is Modern Romanian.

Russians: Returned to Catholic unity about 1905; situated in Europe, the Americas, Australia, China; liturgical language is Old Slavonic.

Ruthenians, or Carpatho-Russians (Rusins): Returned to Catholic unity in the Union of Brest-Litovsk, 1596, and the Union of Uzhorod, 24 April 1646; situated in Hungary, Czechoslovakia, elsewhere in Europe, the Americas, Australia; liturgical languages are Old Slavonic, English.

Slovaks: Jurisdiction (located in Czechoslovakia): one diocese (also has jurisdiction over Byzantine-rite Catholics in Czechoslovakia).

Ukrainians or Galician Ruthenians: Returned to Catholic unity about 1595; situated in Europe, the Americas, Australasia; liturgical languages are Old Slavonic and Ukrainian.

Yugoslavs, Serbs and Croatians: Returned to Catholic unity in 1611; situated in Yugoslavia, the Americas; liturgical language is Old Slavonic.

Chaldean Rite

This rite, listed as separate and distinct by the Sacred Congregation for the Oriental Churches, was derived from the Antiochene Rite.

The faithful of this rite are:

Chaldeans: Descendants of the Nestorians, returned to Catholic unity in 1692; situated throughout the Middle East, in Europe, Africa, the Americas; liturgical languages are Syriac, Arabic.

Syro-Malabarese: Descended from the St Thomas Christians of India; situated mostly in the Malabar region of India; they use a Westernised and Latinised form of the Chaldean Rite in Syriac and Malayalam.

(*Source:* adapted with permission from *1985 Catholic Almanac*, published by Our Sunday Visitor, Inc., Huntingdon, Indiana.)

Ecumenism and Interchurch Bodies

For many Christians, Church unity is a distant and apparently irrelevant issue; it does not impinge upon their daily life. But there are others for whom it is a very immediate, relevant and personal concern. They are the partners and parents in mixed marriages.

Mixed Marriages and Interchurch Families

Prior to the Second Vatican Council, 'mixed marriage' was a term applied by Roman Catholics to any marriage in which one partner was a Catholic and the other not. Such marriages were forbidden by Canon Law, but bishops could dispense from the obligation to marry a fellow Catholic, and in countries like England did so very freely. The condition (in force since 1917) was that both partners should sign a promise that all children of the marriage would be baptised and brought up as Catholics.

A change of perspective developed following the new insights of the Second Vatican Council. Roman Catholics came to have a more positive regard for other Christians. Where marriages of Catholics with other Christians were concerned, it was acknowledged that the non-Catholic could make a positive contribution to building up a truly Christian marriage, and indeed could contribute positively to the Christian upbringing of the children. Moreover the right of non-Catholics to share their faith with their children was acknowledged.

Roman Catholic legislation on mixed marriages changed in line with these new insights (cf. the *motu proprio* of 31 March 1970, as presented in the *Revised Directory by the Episcopal Conference of England and Wales*, 1977). To obtain a dispensation from the bishop to marry, a Catholic had to undertake to do all he or she could to have the children of the marriage baptised and brought up as Catholics; this was not an absolute promise, and the non-Catholic partner was not asked for any undertaking. More recently the parish priest has been able to give the dispensation (though not to refuse it); every case no longer has to go to the bishop. It is also possible to obtain from the bishop a dispensation from form, so that the wedding can take place in a non-Catholic church; and such dispensations are given with increasing frequency, especially where the bride is a practising Christian but not a Roman Catholic.

Gradually it has become possible to see marriages between Roman Catholics and other Christians not just as a pastoral problem, but as a pastoral opportunity. It is a field where the clergy of different churches can work together. A joint RC–British Council of Churches Working Group has produced some guidelines for *The Joint Pastoral Care of Interchurch Marriages in England, Wales and Scotland* (BCC, 1971).

'Interchurch marriages' was a term which had been coined by a group of married couples, one of whom was a practising Roman Catholic and the other a practising Christian of another tradition. By this term they distinguished their marriages from the 'mixed marriages' in which only one or neither partner practised his Christian faith. In England couples of this kind formed an Association of Interchurch Families in 1969. Interchurch marriages have come to be seen as having a positive value in the context of the ecumenical movement. The bishops of England and Wales in *The Easter People* (1980) 'recognise the potential ecumenical significance of marriages between committed Christians'. Pope John Paul II, addressing interchurch couples in York at Pentecost 1982, said: 'You live in your marriage the hopes and difficulties of the path to Christian unity.'

Some interchurch couples have responded to this ecumenical vocation, and have grown into a sense of the 'double loyalty' which they owe as a couple to the two church traditions represented within their one family unit in Christ, their 'domestic church'. There will always be tensions for them so long as the churches are divided, and as they pray and work for unity in their marriage and their family they become conscious of an ecumenical urgency unknown to most Christians. They are therefore a potential asset to the churches as they grow together into unity.

Mixed marriages celebrated in Roman Catholic churches in England and Wales are very common; 65 per cent of all marriages involve a partner who is not a Catholic. The Catholic bishops have estimated that not more than 10 per cent of these might properly be called interchurch marriages.

So there are a very large number of mixed marriages in which only one partner, or neither, practises his or her faith, for included in this number are those where a Catholic marries in another church or register office without informing the authorities of his own church (in this case the marriage is not recognised as such by the Roman Catholic Church).

As in the case of interchurch families, there is a wide field here for joint pastoral care by the clergy of both churches. It is often more likely that a 'nominal' Christian will become a 'practising' Christian in the tradition in which he or she was brought up than if an attempt is made to 'convert' him or her to another tradition. A two-church approach may be valid even in the case of a mixed marriage where only one partner regularly attends worship; the road to becoming a more fully Christian family is not simply by one partner changing allegiance to the church of the other (although in some cases this succeeds). The first step may well be for the more practising partner to help the other towards becoming a better Christian in his or her own tradition, and the role of the clergy may be to support and encourage this approach, in the conviction that two-church families *can* work.

R.R.

A reading list

Two-Church Families, Association of Interchurch Families.
Sharing Communion, Ruth Reardon and Melanie Finch, Collins.
Mixed Marriages between Christians, John Coventry, CTS.
Interchurch Families, biannual newsletter of the Association of Interchurch Families and leaflets on *Getting Married, Baptism, First Communion, Confirmation, Prayer*, etc.

Addresses

Association of Interchurch Families
The Old Bakery
Danehill
Sussex RH17 7ET

Scottish AIF
3 Buckstone Hill
Edinburgh EH10 6TJ

AIF (Dublin)
8 Sycamore Road
Dublin 16

Nimma (N. Ireland Mixed Marriage Association)
8 Upper Crescent
Belfast BT7 1NT

Some pastoral-ecumenical principles

Local Covenants

In 1976 the Churches' Unity Commission published *Ten Propositions* for Christian Unity, to which all the principal Christian Churches in England made their official responses over the next year or so. Those which felt able to do so formed the Churches' Council for Covenanting, to discuss a possible national covenant between them. The Roman Catholic bishops were unable to take this step but they expressed forcibly their commitment to local ecumenical work. A booklet with the title *Local Covenants* was published by the then RC Ecumenical Commission of England and Wales early in 1979, with practical suggestions for putting that commitment into effect (now available from Committee for Christian Unity, 39 Eccleston Square, London SW1V 1PD).

By the autumn of 1982 the situation had changed. It had become clear that no national covenant, or indeed any scheme for unity, was in prospect for the foreseeable future. The way ahead was seen to lie through local development. So in the spring of 1983 a new booklet, *Local Churches in Covenant* was published with the approval of the Roman Catholic bishops of England and Wales (available as above). It is worth making a few points about it.

First, although a Roman Catholic publication, it is for everyone. It must be emphasised that a local convenant is a form of local ecumenical project, a form that is particularly useful in places where for good reasons there is not likely to be any sharing of buildings.

Second, because the word 'covenant' is a biblical one it is not to be used lightly – and it is not used lightly in this booklet. A covenant is made before God in a solemn act of worship after a time of prayerful reflection and planning and with the written approval of the authorities of each denomination taking part.

Third, it has been well said that the verb is more important than the noun in this context. In other words, the stress is on the act of covenant*ing* rather than on the subject-matter of the covenant that is being made. The latter will vary from place to place (there are examples in the booklet), and even in the same place at different times, but the commitment to one's fellow Christians ought to be constant.

Fourth, local covenants are not schemes for unity, nor are they a pretence that the churches involved are fully united. They exist so that Christians may express the degree of unity that, by the Lord's gift, they already enjoy, and that they may more effectively pray and work for full unity and minister to the neighbourhood in which they live.

Fifth, a local covenant should not be undertaken unless it has sufficient support from the congregations as well as the clergy concerned. At the same time it would be unrealistic to forget that most church activities are supported only by a minority of our people, and we cannot expect more for ecumenical activities than for domestic ones.

Sixth, Christians involved in local covenants ought to be more, not less, concerned with what is happening in the wider church. Recently, many congregations have been assessing BEM and ARCIC; they have also been involved in discussion on the nature and mission of the church. Where there are already relationships of trust between congregations these discussions will happen more easily; where people come together on an *ad hoc* basis for the discussions, one may hope that a local covenant will emerge.

Week of Prayer for Christian Unity

The character of the Octave of Prayer has changed. The emphasis in many places is not so much on big events in city-centre churches as on smaller local groupings. (There is an interesting parallel here with councils of churches, which have tended to become smaller, more local and more numerous.)

There are still two basic types of united services; the local Christians may agree to join together in a form of worship that is ecumenical in character; or they may decide to have a service in one church building, using the form of worship (eucharistic or otherwise) of the denomination concerned. There is a place for both forms of service, and there should not be too much of either on its own.

Where there is a denominational service, much of the liturgy may be allowed to speak for itself, and visitors often remark on the convergences that are now taking place. But there is a place for a few words of introduction and explanation for the benefit of newcomers to a particular church's worship.

The golden rule for planning an ecumenical service (i.e., one that does not follow the rites of any particular tradition) is that it should be ecumenically planned. A small working party which includes lay people of different traditions should choose prayers, hymns and readings and make sure that the preacher is informed of these in good time. It is fashionable mildly to disparage the 'hymn sandwich', but like other sandwiches it can be excellent with the right ingredients.

D.C.

Church of England: Relations with Other Churches

The year 1982 was a watershed for the Church of England's relations with other Churches in England. On the one hand the talks about unity with the Free Churches which had lasted for decades came to an abrupt and divisive end, when the Proposals of the Churches' Council for Covenanting failed to get sufficient backing in the General Synod of the Church of England.

On the other hand, the same year brought an event of a totally different nature. Pope John Paul II's visit, and especially the united service in Canterbury Cathedral, changed the scene and made ecumenism a truly 'catholic' word applying to all Churches.

Since 1982 progress is being made at three related levels:

The International Scene

As part of the world-wide Anglican Communion, the Church of England has been engaged in five dialogues with other world communions. In common with the major Protestant Churches, the Orthodox Churches and the Roman Catholic Church, it has been studying the World Council of Churches' Report *Baptism, Eucharist and Ministry* (WCC, 1982).

Anglicans are also studying *The Final Report* (CTS, SPCK, 1982, £1.95) of the Anglican–Roman Catholic International Commission (ARCIC), which has been meeting since 1970. The Report has covered the main points of disagreement between the two Communions and has come to a remarkable degree of consensus on Eucharist and Ministry, and of convergence on Authority. There is, however, further work to be done on infallibility and the actual practice of authority in the Church before complete agreement is reached on these issues.

Two Anglican–Lutheran reports have appeared (*Anglican–Lutheran Dialogue*, SPCK, 1983, £1.95; and *Anglican–Lutheran Relations*, Anglican Consultative Council, 1983, 70p) which propose closer pastoral relations between Lutherans and Anglicans, including some eucharistic and ministerial sharing.

The Anglican–Reformed Report, *God's Reign and Our Unity* (SPCK, 1984, £2.95), attempts to discover why so many unity schemes between Anglican and Reformed Churches have foundered. It proposes that the search for the unity of the Church should be more closely related to the mission of the Church, the unity of humanity and the coming of God's Kingdom.

The Anglican–Orthodox Joint Doctrinal Discussions have published *Anglican–Orthodox Dialogue* (SPCK, 1985, £2.50). This is the second report of a dialogue which has been continuing for twelve years, and which is turning its attention to the pastoral and practical dimension of doctrinal discussions. However, barriers to union between Orthodox and Anglicans still remain, including the understanding of the nature of the Church and the ordination of women to the priesthood in other provinces of the Anglican Communion.

In all these discussions a process of reception is now underway and a most encouraging degree of convergence in all of them can be noted.

The National Scene

The Papal visit started off a series of debates between the Roman Catholic Church and those in membership of the British Council of Churches and this has led to a three-year programme of discussions on the nature and purpose of the Church which involves a uniquely wide range of British Churches. Following widespread local discussions there is expected to be a final conference in the summer of 1987. From this it is hoped that there will be both a more effective instrument for Church cooperation in Britain, and also a deeper understanding of each Church's concept of Christian unity and commitment to it.

The Local Scene

Some ecumenical observers feel that the particular English contribution in all this has been the growth of local ecumenical projects, where the ideas being debated by theologians and Church leaders are being lived out in practical and pastoral terms. In 1985, 450 such projects existed, involving Anglicans, Methodists, United Reformed, Baptists and a growing number of Roman Catholic Churches. In these projects, which exist under the authority of a regional sponsoring body, on which the Church leaders of all the main traditions are represented, many different patterns of local ecumenism are being developed in new and old areas.

A further considerable growth in local ecumenism is anticipated, first because of the 1983 Roman Catholic document *Local Churches in Covenant* (CIS), and secondly because of Church of England work on local ecumenical development. It seems very likely that by the end of 1987 the Church of England will have new Ecumenical Canons that will give encouragement to local ecumenism, especially in those places where a deep commitment to each other has become the accepted way of life and mission.

M.R. and D.P.

Churches of Orthodox Origin

There are a number of Churches of the Eastern tradition, not in union with the Roman Catholic Church, in the United Kingdom (see pages 360–5 for Eastern Churches in Union with the Catholic Church). They are of particular interest for their liturgical customs and traditions. Visits can be organised by prior arrangement by direct contact with the individual church.

Armenian Apostolic Church
Iverna Gardens
Kensington
London W8 6TN
Tel: 01 937 0152
Prelate:
Rt Rev. Bishop Yegishe Gizirian

Assyrian Church of the East
89 Leighton Road
Ealing
London W13 9DR
Tel: 01 579 7259
Archdeacon:
Rev. Yonan Yowel Yonan

Byelorussian Autocephalic Orthodox Church
Holy Mother of God of Zyrovicy Church
Chapel Road
Rainsough
Manchester M22 4JW
Tel: 061 740 8230
Administrator:
Very Rev. Father John Ababurko
Also:
7 Haycroft Road
Stevenage
Hertfordshire SG1 3JL
Tel: 0438 58916
Administrator:
Rev. Father John Piekarski

Coptic Orthodox Church
19 Falkland House
Manloes Road
London W8 6LQ
Tel: 01 937 6508
Head of the Church:
Rev. Fr Bishoy Boushra

Ethiopian Orthodox
253B Ladbroke Grove
London W10 6HF
Tel: 01 960 3848
Head Priest:
Very Rev. Aragawi Wolde Gabriel

Greek Orthodox Archdiocese
Thyateira House
5 Craven Hill
London W2 3EN
Tel: 01 723 4787
Archbishop:
Dr Methodios Fouyas

Latvian Orthodox Church Abroad
c/o St Thomas' Presbytery
194 Drayton Park
Highbury
London N5 1LU
Tel: 01 226 3115
Representative:
Very Rev. Dean Alexander Cherney

Orthodox Syrian Church
154 Bramley Road
London N14 4HU
Tel: 01 449 2915
Resident Priest:
Rev. Father K. A. George

Polish Orthodox Church Abroad
95 Finborough Road
London SW10 9DU
Tel: 01 373 9394
Head of the Church Abroad:
Rt Rev. Bishop Matthew of Aspendos

*Romanian Orthodox Church in
London*
St Dunstan's-in-the-West
184A Fleet Street
London EC4A 2HD
Tel: 01 242 6027
Priest-in-Charge:
Rev. S. P. Pufulete

Russian Orthodox Church
All Saints
Ennismore Gardens
London SW7 1NH
Tel: 01 584 0096
Metropolitan:
Metropolitan Anthony Bloom

Russian Orthodox Church in Exile
Church House
14 St Dunstan's Road
London W6 8RB
Tel: 01 748 4232
Ruling Bishop:
His Excellence the Most Reverend
Bishop Constantine

Serbian Orthodox Church
89 Lancaster Road
London W11 1QQ
Tel: 01 727 8367
Rector:
Rev. Milun Kostic

*Ukrainian Autocephalous Orthodox
Church*
1A Newton Avenue
Acton
London W3 8AJ
Tel: 01 992 4689
Chairman of Diocesan Council:
Very Rev. Protopresbyter Sylvester
Bohateretz

A useful address

Society of St John Chrysostom
Marian House
Holden Avenue
London N12 8HY
Chairperson:
Father Alexander Hadson.

A Catholic ecumenical society
concerned with promoting unity with
Churches of Eastern tradition,
especially Orthodox, and working for
closer friendship and understanding.
The Society has a small journal which is
published twice a year.

The British Council of Churches

During the Second World War, in 1942, the British Council of Churches was founded. Today, twenty-seven denominations are represented and the Roman Catholic Church has observer status. Associated with the World Council of Churches, the Council defines itself as 'a fellowship of Churches in the United Kingdom and in the Republic of Ireland'. The uniting bond of member Churches is the confession of 'the Lord Jesus Christ as God and Saviour according to the scriptures' and their aim is to 'seek to fulfil together their common calling to the glory of the one God, Father, Son and Holy Spirit'.

The Assembly, consisting of 150 representatives, appointed by the member Churches and other organisations, is the governing body and meets twice a year. The Assembly's decisions are worked out in detail by the 31 members of the Executive Committee and five Divisional Boards. The General Secretariat coordinates the work of the five Divisions and is responsible for publications, finance and the Council's property.

The Five Divisions are:

International Affairs
Maintains relations with those responsible for foreign policy in Britain and Ireland, Churches throughout the world, and international Christian bodies. It consults with specialist advisers to provide Christian comment on international issues. This division administers the Human Rights Forum, the Peace Forum and the Committee for Southern Africa. It is served by specialist committees on Western Europe, South Africa and the Middle East.

Ecumenical Affairs
Relates to local Councils of Churches and local ecumenical projects. Promotes and explores the theological basis for a growing ecumenical relationship. Encourages the partnership project between black-led and white-led churches and the cultivation of an ecumenical interest and activity among young people.

Community Affairs
This division emphasises the Churches' role in cultivating community awareness. It distributes money on behalf of the DHSS to support voluntary social work. Produces briefing papers for the Churches on topical issues, such as Sunday trading, etc.

Conference for World Mission
Provides a meeting place for forty-one missionary societies and boards to consult and work together in joint action for mission. Seeking cooperation both with the Roman Catholic National Missionary Council and the Evangelical Missionary Alliance. Brings overseas Church leaders to Britain to share in mission.

Christian Aid
Founded after the last War to help displaced people in Europe. Christian Aid is now the British Council of Churches' overseas development and relief agency. It supports hundreds of development projects in the world's poorest countries, helping the poor to help themselves.

The General Secretary of the British Council of Churches is Rev. Dr Philip Morgan; the Council's offices are at Edinburgh House, 2 Eaton Gate, London SW1V 9BL, where forty-six members of staff are employed.

Member Bodies of the British Council of Churches

Baptist Union of Great Britain & Ireland
Baptist Union of Scotland
Church of England
Church of Ireland
Church of Scotland
Church in Wales
The Congregational Federation
Congregational Union of Scotland
Archdiocese of Thyateira & Great Britain
Independent Methodist Church
Lutheran Council of Great Britain
Methodist Church
Methodist Church in Ireland
Moravian Church
Presbyterian Church in Ireland
Presbyterian Church of Wales
Russian Orthodox Church (Patriarchal Diocese in the UK)
Salvation Army
The Scottish Episcopal Church
Union of Welsh Independents
United Free Church of Scotland
United Reformed Church

Associate Members
The African Methodist Episcopal Church
Cherubim and Seraphim Council of Churches (UK)
Religious Society of Friends
Shiloh United Church of Christ (Apostolic) Worldwide
Unitarian and Free Christian Churches

Bodies in Association
Council of African and Allied Churches
Council of Churches for Wales
The Free Church Federal Council
Industrial Mission Association
International Ministerial Council of Great Britain
Irish Council of Churches
Scottish Churches' Council
Student Christian Movement
United Society for Christian Literature
Young Men's Christian Association
Young Women's Christian Association

Consultant Observers
British Bible Societies
The Roman Catholic Church (in England, Wales and Scotland)
Seventh-Day Adventists

The World Council of Churches

A Brief History

Toward the end of the last century, growing dissatisfaction with divisions in the church led people from many Christian traditions – missionaries and Sunday school workers, young people and university students – to begin meeting together across denominational lines.

An ecumenical vision was taking form – the vision of a fellowship that could overcome divisions and move towards unity. Following a world missionary conference in Edinburgh, Scotland, in 1910, that drive towards unity started to take organisational shape.

Three related movements were founded in the 1920s. The International Missionary Council (1921) brought together foreign missionary societies and national Christian councils for study and common action on Christian witness. The Life and Work Movement

(1925) explored Christian responsibility in the face of burning issues facing society. And the Faith and Order Movement (1927) confronted thorny controversies and differences over doctrine and authority which spawn or strengthen church divisions.

Those movements lay behind the decision in 1937 to form a World Council of Churches (though the actual formation was delayed for eleven years by World War II). The concerns which motivated those movements – as well as those of the World Council of Christian Education, which merged with the WCC in 1971 – remain at the centre of the Council's agenda today.

Under the able chairmanship of Dr Visser 't Hooft, the first general secretary, the first Assembly of the World Council of Churches met in Amsterdam in 1948. Never before had so many Christians from so many different traditions and countries prayed the Lord's Prayer together. Their shared enthusiasm gave rise to the slogan 'We intend to stay together'. There has been continual growth since 1948. Then there were 146 member churches, today there are 306. Although the Roman Catholic Church is not a member of the WCC, there are several important ways in which it is working together ecumenically with the Council.

Churches have also banded together in councils and conferences to work on common problems, common needs and common witness not only worldwide, but also regionally, nationally and locally. Many of these ecumenical bodies are officially related to the WCC, including the British Council of Churches. A number of international organisations bring together churches which share a common confessional tradition.

Worldwide ecumenical activity also goes on in organisations which focus on the needs of a particular group of people or which promote the translation and distribution of the Bible.

How it works

Situated in Geneva, close by the United Nations building and the World Health Organisation, the WCC building comprises a complex of offices, conference-rooms, exhibition area and chapel. The council employs 308 staff, representing 47 different countries and many more Christian traditions. Coordinating the work of the programme units and giving leadership to the World Council as a whole is the work of the General Secretary, Dr Emilio Castro, a Methodist from Uruguay.

The World Council 'is a fellowship of churches which confess the

Lord Jesus Christ as God and Saviour according to the Scriptures and therefore seek to fulfil together their common calling to the glory of the one God, Father, Son and Holy Spirit'. The Council claims to be no more. Its membership is open to any Church which can accept the basis of the Council, stated above. The Council's authority rests entirely on its members' acceptance. This was put well by one of the founding fathers of the Council, Archbishop William Temple: 'any authority the Council will have will consist in the weight which it carries with the churches by its own wisdom'.

The work of the WCC is divided into what are called Programme Units. There are three of these, and their headings and sub-units are as follows.

Programme Unit 1	*Faith and Witness*
	Faith and Order
	World Mission and Evangelism
	Church and Society
	Dialogue with People of Living Faiths
Programme Unit 2	*Justice and Service*
	Churches' Participation in Development
	International Affairs
	Programme to Combat Racism
	Inter-Church Aid, Refugee and World Service
	Christian Medical Commission
Programme Unit 3	*Education and Renewal*
	Education
	Women in Church and Society
	Renewal and Congregational Life
	Youth
	Theological Education

Presidents and Executive Officers of the Council

Presidents
Dame R. Nita Barrow, Barbados
Dr Marga Bührig, Switzerland
Metropolitan Dr Paulos Mar Gregorios, India
Bishop Dr Johannes W. Hempel, German Democratic Republic
His Holiness Ignatios IV, Syria

Most Rev. W. P. Khotso Makhulu, Botswana
Very Rev. Dr Lois M. Wilson, Canada

Executive Officers
Dr Heinz-Joachim Held, Federal Republic of Germany (Moderator)
H. E. Metropolitan Chrysostomos of Myra, Turkey, and Dr Sylvia Talbot, USA (Vice-Moderators)
Rev. Dr Emilio Castro, Uruguay (General Secretary of the WCC)

Periodicals of the World Council of Churches

On a subscription basis:
The Ecumenical Review: The quarterly journal of the WCC in which the major theological, ethical and other issues relating to the work of the Council in particular and the ecumenical movement as a whole, are discussed and debated.
Ecumenical Press Service: Aims at keeping its readers informed of trends of thought and opinion in and about the churches and Christian movements.
International Review of Mission: The quarterly journal on mission and evangelism in six continents, published by the Commission on World Mission and Evangelism.
One World: A popular, well-illustrated monthly magazine (published ten times a year) bringing first-hand information of general interest about the World Council and the Churches around the world.
Risk: A book series published four times a year, each issue is devoted to exploring less well-covered ecumenical themes in greater detail.

Most of the sub-units publish a newsletter. The complete list of these newsletters (which are supplied free of charge), as well as the following books, all published by the WCC, are available from WCC Publications, 150 route de Ferney, 1211 Geneva 20, Switzerland.

Selected reference books

Gathered for Life, report of the Sixth Assembly of the WCC, Vancouver, 1983, ed. David Gill, 1983 (co-published with Eerdmans, Grand Rapids, USA).

The Genesis and Formation of the World Council of Churches, Willem A. Visser 't Hooft, 1982.
Faith and Faithfulness: Essays on Contemporary Ecumenical Themes, a tribute to Philip A. Potter, ed. Pauline Webb, 1984.
Handbook of Member Churches, ed. Ans J. van der Bent, 1985.
Directory of Christian Councils, 1985.
Major Studies and Themes in the Ecumenical Movement, Ans J. van der Bent, 1981. A reference book dealing with some 80 major study projects of the WCC since 1948.
Vital Ecumenical Concerns: Sixteen Historical, Analytical and Documentary Surveys, Ans J. van der Bent, 1986. Official statements of WCC Assemblies, Central Committees, major ecumenical conferences, and records of consultations on vital concerns such as Christianity and culture, mission and evangelism, church unity, the Bible, peace and justice, ideology, human rights, development, spirituality etc., since 1948.
Apostolic Faith Today: a Handbook for Study, ed. Hans-Georg Link, 1985. A collection of essential documents in the area of faith and order: creeds of the ancient Church, confessions of faith from the sixteenth and seventeenth centuries, statements coming out of the ecumenical movement of the twentieth century.
Guidelines on Dialogue with People of Living Faiths and Ideologies, 2nd printing 1982.
Mission and Evangelism: an Ecumenical Affirmation – a Study Guide, compiled by Jean Stromberg, 2nd printing 1985, WCC Mission Series 4.
Baptism, Eucharist and Ministry, Geneva, WCC, 1982. Statement resulting from a fifty-year process of study and consultation and representing the theological convergence achieved through decades of dialogue. Now being studied by the churches, whose response will be a vital step in the ecumenical process of 'reception'.
Towards a Church of the Poor: the Work of an Ecumenical Group on the Church and the Poor, ed. Julio de Santa Ana, 1979. Emphasises that Churches must express their solidarity with the poor and the oppressed, because development is not for the poor, but can be achieved by them and with them when they become full participants in the processes which lead to justice and liberation.
A History of the Ecumenical Movement, Vols I and II, reprinted 1986, Vol. I: 1517–1948, eds Ruth Rouse and Stephen Neill. Vol. II: 1948–1968, ed. Harold E. Fey.
Faith and Science in an Unjust World, report of the WCC conference on 'Faith, Science and the Future', Massachusetts Institute of

Technology, Cambridge, USA, July 1979. Vol. I: Plenary Presentations. Vol. II: Reports and Recommendations. 1980.
The Community of Women and Men in the Church: the Sheffield Report, ed. Constance F. Parvey, 1983. Traces the four-year development of the community programme: its beginnings in local study/sharing groups throughout the world, its clarification and maturation in regional and specialised consultations, and its culmination at Sheffield, to consolidate initial findings and formulate recommendations for follow-up activities.
Churches Respond to BEM: Official Responses to the 'Baptism, Eucharist and Ministry', Text, Vol. I, ed. Max Thurian, 1986.
Hope in the Desert, ed. Kenneth Slack, 1986. A collection of essays on the work of the WCC's Commission on Inter-Church Aid, Refugee and World Service, which has celebrated its fortieth anniversary.

Further, more detailed information about the World Council of Churches, its projects and publications can be obtained from:

The World Council of Churches
Communication Dept.
150 route de Ferney
1211 Geneva 20
Switzerland.

Christian Unity Fellowships

The Bible Reading Fellowship

The Fellowship was founded in 1922 to promote growth in the knowledge of God through intelligent and devotional reading of the Bible. It provides daily readings, material for group study and Bible Aids for Religious Education. It also produces sound strips and cassettes.

President:
Rt Rev. Lord Coggan
Chairman:
Rt Rev. J. M. Bickersteth
Director:
Rev. David Rhodes

General Secretary:
Christopher Bayne
St Michael's House
2 Elizabeth St
London SW1W 9RQ
Tel: 01 730 9181

An Ecumenical Fellowship of Prayer for Unity

This is the description of the Farncombe Community which believes that the movement towards Christian unity should be rooted in prayer. It aims at binding together, across the frontiers of our human divisions, a body of men and women who desire to pray and work together.

Situated at Godalming, near Guildford, the Community house does not just have a resident community but acts as the hub of a fellowship of prayer. The residents, the Companions and the members of the Fellowship of Prayer are all from different Christian traditions. The Companions, of whom there are now about one hundred, promise to keep a simple rule of prayer and to work for unity in whatever ways lie open to them. They visit the Community as often as they can and keep in touch with resident members. The members of the Fellowship of Prayer receive a regular newsletter and promise to pray with and for the Community.

If you would like to know more about the Community and what is involved in membership of any of the groups, or if you think the Community can help you in any ecumenical venture, please write to:

The Head of the Farncombe Community
5 Wolseley Rd
Farncombe
Godalming
Surrey GU7 3DX

enclosing a stamped addressed envelope.

Maranatha – unity through Renewal

The members of the Maranatha Community are convinced that God is calling the Churches in England to renewal.

This ecumenical community lays great stress upon loyalty to the institutional church, but they are equally convinced that God is determined to break down the denominational barriers which divide Christians, hinder the proclamation of the Gospel and constitute a major stumbling block to renewal movements.

The community came into existence a few years ago when Methodists who supported the statement 'Methodism and the Future Church' came together with Roman Catholics who were concerned with renewal in their Church.

Since the first meeting when 300 Methodists and Catholics joined together, a common spirituality between the two traditions has been discovered. Typical of this was the coming together of Monsig-nor Michael Buckley, a former member of the Secretariat for Church Unity in Rome, with Mr Dennis Wrigley, a Methodist layman from Manchester, the joint founders of the community. Since its formation, Maranatha has mushroomed into a large and growing community embracing virtually all the main Churches in Great Britain.

Although consideration is being given to the opening of community houses, Maranatha is essentially a scattered community. Its members come together for one-day gatherings in various cities and towns in different parts of Britain and in a number of places local Maranatha groups are springing up.

There is no centralised organisation which runs the community and it steadfastly avoids any form of hierarchy. Those who take on specific responsibility are referred to as 'servers'.

Its full-day gatherings, usually held in large modern churches, have a high content of prayer and teaching. Great emphasis is placed upon openness and sharing, particularly when the members go into groups.

This openness has paved the way for healing, and healing takes place at all Maranatha gatherings. The experience of healing of relationships has led many members of the Maranatha Community into community work.

Maranatha Community members are encouraged to make use of the growing number of Maranatha cassettes. These are designed for use by house groups. The subjects covered include 'Christian Renewal', 'Christian Faith', 'Christian Hope', 'Christian Love', 'Christian Healing', 'Christian Mission', 'Christian Community', 'Christian Growth', 'Christian Prayer', 'Jesus – Disturber of our Peace', 'Our Search for Peace', and 'Christian Peace and Reconciliation'.

In their booklet *Maranatha – A Pathway to Christian Renewal* they state: 'Within Maranatha there has been a great emphasis upon exploration. We have become a community of Christians who are experiencing together the full significance of the Resurrection. We have discovered that we cannot be renewed in isolation.'

Concerning the future development of Maranatha, which has held gatherings in many different parts of Great Britain including London, Nottingham, Sheffield, Liverpool and Manchester, their booklet states:

We simply do not know the paths along which God will lead us but we do know the direction in which we are going. We are totally convinced that God is with us in what we are doing and already he has given us abundant evidence of this. But we claim nothing original and we have a great love for and loyalty to the Church of Christ.

There are always temptations for those who are concerned with renewal to withdraw and form separate groups which may even become exclusive. Within this community Christian people gather together to share prayer and experience, and in the power of Christ, they enrich one another's lives and, therefore, the life of the Churches.

With the growth of Maranatha its membership lists have had to be computerised and already an experimental Maranatha video programme has been recorded. Later, a range of Maranatha video tapes will be available.

At their gatherings members of the community draw on all the main Christian traditions, with Roman Catholics enjoying the hymns of Charles Wesley and Methodists sharing in the meditations of Catholics such as Charles de Foucauld and Carlo Carretto.

Speaking at a recent Maranatha gathering, Monsignor Michael Buckley said:

In so many of our churches today our faith is limited and our lives are bound by fear. We are prone to fear and it is one of our greatest enemies and we are afraid because we don't trust God enough.

In our churches and in our personal lives we need to acknowledge that God is our father and that he knows what he is about even though his purpose may be temporarily hidden from our understanding. Organised religion can easily become a substitute for faith and the Gospels warn us of the dangers of a narrow religious attitude which conflicts with the liberating power of Christ. In the Maranatha Community we are discovering again that the task of Christ's church is one of liberation.

Further details from:

The Maranatha Community
c/o Renewal Publications
Westway
Western Road
Flixton
Manchester M31 3LE

Ecumenism – some useful addresses

Bible Society
146 Queen Victoria Street
London EC4V 4BX
Tel: 01 248 4751

also

Stonehill Green
Westlea
Swindon
Wilts. SN5 7DG
Tel: 0793 486381
The Society produces and publishes
Scriptures and Scripture-related
materials for distribution at home and
overseas.

*Catholic Biblical Association of Great
Britain*
1 Malcolm Road
Wimbledon
London SW9
Secretary:
Fr O'Reilly
To promote the biblical apostolate
through published works, study groups,
courses, Bible study, Bible weeks,
Bible prayer groups, devotional
reading, teacher study weekend.

Catholic League (Anglican)
205 Merlin House
Napier Road
Enfield EN3 4QN
Secretary: Geoffrey Wright
Objects are: the promotion of
fellowship among Anglo-Catholics in
communion with the See of
Canterbury, the Union of all Christians
with the Apostolic See of Rome, the
spreading of the Catholic faith, and the
deepening of the spiritual life.

The Council of Churches for Wales
Correspondence to the General
Secretary
Room 7
Ty John Penry
11 St Helen's Rd
Swansea SA1 4AL
There are eight member churches; the
Society of Friends has 'observer' status,
and the Roman Catholic Church has
'consultant observer' status.

*Church of Scotland Board of World
Mission and Unity*
121 George Street
Edinburgh EH2 4YN
Tel: 031 225 5722
The Board, whose remit is mission and
unity in a world setting, supports
partner churches overseas in their
concern for the wholeness of their
people, a concern which includes social
justice.

Focolare Movement
3 Abbeville Road
London SW4 9LA
Tel: 01 673 3222

or

34 Earls Court Square
London SW5
Tel: 01 373 9808
An international movement to bring
about the fulfilment of Christ's prayer
'that all may be one'.

International Ecumenical Fellowship
3 Water Farm
Elham
Canterbury
Kent CT4 6TW
Tel: 0303 84 626
Secretary: Mrs M. Hall

The Irish Council of Churches
Interchurch Centre
48 Elmwood Ave
Belfast BT9 6AZ
Tel: 0232 663145
General secretary:
Rt Hon. D. W. Bleakley
There are eight member churches
represented by 65 members.

Scottish Churches' Council
Scottish Churches' House
Dunblane
Perthshire FK15 0AJ
Tel: 0786 823588
General Secretary:
Canon Kenyon E. Wright
Reconstituted in 1964, the Council
comprises representatives from
fourteen churches and organisations in
Scotland. The Roman Catholic Church
has 'observer' status.

*Soldiers' and Airmen's Scripture
Readers Association*
75–9 High Street
Aldershot
Hants GU11 1BY
Secretary:
Lt-Col. K. W. Sear
Lay evangelism in Army and RAF on a
non-denominational basis. Promoting
interdenominational evangelical
fellowship.

CHAPTER THREE

World Faiths

The Jewish Faith

The Common Spiritual Patrimony

Pope Pius XI, in a memorable sentence, summed up the declaration to be made much later at the Second Vatican Council, when he said, 'spiritually we are all Semites'.

'Since the spiritual patrimony common to Christians and Jews is thus so great, this sacred Synod wishes to foster and recommend that mutual understanding and respect which is the fruit above all of biblical and theological studies, and of brotherly dialogues.' (Second Vatican Council – Relationship of the Church to Non-Christian Religions §4)

The famous Rabbi, Moses Maimonides, put together in the twelfth century AD, thirteen principles of Jewish faith, which are still used today.

1. I believe, with all my heart, that God who
   Made the world (blessed be his name) is the
   Maker and the guide of every creature;
   He alone has made, does make, and will make all things.

2. I believe with all my heart, that God who
   Made the world (blessed be his name),
   Is one God.
   There is no other God: our God is one, and the only God.
   He is our God.
   There is no other; there never was, and there never will be.

3. I believe with all my heart, that God
   Who made the world (blessed be his name),
   Is not a person, as we are;
   He is not affected by the things that happen in human life,
   He doesn't have a shape, or any kind of form.

4. I believe with all my heart, that God
   Who made the world (blessed be his name),
   Was the first life, and will live for ever.

5. I believe with all my heart, that God
   Who made the world (blessed be his name),
   Is the God to whom I should pray:
   Only to him.
   It is not right to pray to any being
   Except God.

6. I believe with all my heart,
   That all the words of the prophets are true.

7. I believe with all my heart,
   That the prophecy of Moses, our teacher
   (Peace be on him),
   Was true.
   I believe that he was the chief of the prophets:
   Of those who came before, and those who followed him.

8. I believe with all my heart,
   That the whole of our Law, that we possess,
   Is the same as that which was given to Moses, our teacher
   (Peace be on him).

9. I believe with all my heart,
   That the Law will not be changed,
   And that there will never be any other Law
   Given to us by God.

10. I believe with all my heart,
    That God knows everything that
    His children do,
    Everything that they think.
    As it says: He made all their hearts,
    He knows all their deeds.

11. I believe with all my heart,
    That God
    Rewards those who keep his Laws.
    And punishes those who break them.

12. I believe with all my heart,
    That the Messiah will come,
    And although he may not come soon,
    I will wait daily for him to come.

13. I believe with all my heart,
    That we shall rise from the dead,
    At a time that pleases God,
    (Blessed be his name)
    May his memory live for ever.

Festivals of the Jewish Year

Rosh Hashana

The first two days of the Jewish year are Rosh Hashana, 'the head of the year'. In the synagogue the shofar, the curved lamb's horn, is sounded. Its harsh timbre, ranging from high quavering notes to strong, deep ones, is meant as a clarion call to the conscience. These are intended as days of spiritual stocktaking and reconsideration of one's relationship with God. One should seek to put right any wrongs one may have committed. The first ten days of the year are known as the 10 Days of Repentance, culminating in:

Yom Kippur

The climax of these ten days of penitence comes on the last day, Yom Kippur, the Day of Atonement. Most synagogues are packed out for it and there sometimes have to be overflow services in halls.

Traditional practice is to fast for the whole 24 hours. (Typically, however, Jewish law has an injunction to eat a good meal beforehand.) In the synagogue, an Orthodox Jewish man wears his kittel, which is his actual shroud – a long white garment – in which he will one day be buried. The Day of Atonement is the only occasion on which a Jew kneels in worship. At the conclusion of the day-long service a pious Jew feels that, spiritually speaking, he has been reborn.

Succoth and Simchat Torah

Five days after the Day of Atonement comes Succoth, the Feast of Tabernacles, which lasts for a week. The tradition is still to some extent maintained that during it a Jew should live, or at least eat, in a fragile wooden hut. Orthodox Jews still erect them in their gardens. This is a remembrance of the biblical story of the Jews wandering for 40 years in the wilderness. The stars which are visible at night through the roof emphasise the transience of life.

Next comes Simchat Torah, the Rejoicing of the Law. Saturday by Saturday during the year the whole pentateuch is read, in instalments, in the synagogue. At the Feast of the Rejoicing, the cycle is completed by the reading of the last verses of Deuteronomy and restarted by reading the opening of Genesis. This is a particularly joyful service and children are sometimes given miniature scrolls to carry and flags to wave.

Chanukah
At about the time of the Christian Christmas comes Chanukah, the Feast of Lights, and the custom has grown up of giving children presents for it. It lasts for eight days and traditionalist Jews light candles in their homes, on the first day one candle, on the second two, on the third three and so on. Commonly the lighted candles are placed in a window. Historically, the feast commemorates the rededication of the Temple in Jerusalem, after it had been desecrated by pagan rites.

Purim
The jolliest festival of all is Purim, which comes in about March. This celebrates the story of Esther, who has a book to herself in the Bible. It tells of a plan, by the wicked Haman, to commit genocide against the Jewish community in the Persian Empire some 2,300 years ago. Thanks to Esther the plan is foiled and Haman himself is hanged. The Jewish way of life is strongly antipathetic to the abuse of alcohol: a person should not drink so much as to lose control of himself. But it is permissible or even laudable to get a little tiddly for Purim. There is also special duty at this time to give to the poor.

Pesach
Next comes the best known Jewish feast, Pesach, the Passover, at about the time of the Christian Easter. For eight days a pious Jewish family has no leavened bread in the house. There is a charming custom in some families that it is the children's task to search the house before the Passover season to make sure there is no leaven in it. Of course leaven is specially concealed in some dark corner, ready to be found. Instead of bread the family eats biscuit-like matsah. This is to commemorate the 'bread of affliction' of the Jews as slaves in Egypt.

Shavuot
Shavuot or Pentecost itself celebrates the giving of the commandments from Mount Sinai and also the first-fruits of the harvest: it is customary to decorate the synagogue with flowers and plants.

Christian Jewish Relations

The following extract from a communication by Archbishop William Temple to Chief Rabbi Joseph Hertz written in 1942 is the basis of today's policy and procedure for the Council of Christians and Jews:

My own approach to this matter is governed by the consideration that the effectiveness of any religious belief depends upon its definiteness, and neither Jews nor Christians should, in my judgement, combine in any such way as to obscure the distinctiveness of their witness to their own beliefs. There is much that we can do together in combating religious and racial intolerance, in forwarding social progress and in bearing witness to those moral principles which we unite in upholding.

Originally concerned with antisemitism stemming from the Nazi regime, it was felt that antisemitism was one symptom of a general malaise. Today, Christians and Jews use their skills in the broader field of community relations and fighting all forms of prejudice.

The encouragement of Jewish/Christian relations is of paramount importance when considering today the multi-ethnic, multi-religious and multi-cultural society in which we are living. The fact that Jews can live in religious freedom thus being able to practise and adhere to the fundamentals of Judaism is a situation for which to be appreciative and thankful.

The strength of our multi-racial society is dependent on sound personal knowledge and practice, and similar understanding of each other, not only for Jews and Christians but for all peoples that are living in Britain. One only has to remember that ignorance leads to prejudice, and thus by eliminating the ignorance as far as possible and replacing it with knowledge then perhaps understanding and cooperation will ensue.

At the heart of Judaism lies unbounded optimism. It is nourished week by week in the synagogue by readings from the ancient prophets, of whom the greatest was the author of the second part of Isaiah: 'The Glory of God shall be revealed and all mankind shall see it; for the mouth of God has spoken.'

The Council of Christians and Jews is involved in the fight against racial and religious intolerance, but refuses to allow the enemy to have the initiative, working in a positive way to clear the grounds from which prejudice and intolerance spring.

Israel is part of the Council's agenda. Jews can explain to Christians why and how world Jewry and Israel are so inextricably linked, and Christians in turn can explain to Jews why Christians of different traditions adopt different stances politically, diplomatically and theologically towards the State of Israel. The main aim of the Council remains, nevertheless, that of promoting the Judaeo-Christian ideals of freedom, justice and responsibility, under the one True God.

S.P.

Useful addresses

Council of Christians and Jews
48 Onslow Gardens
London SW7 3PX
Tel: 01 589 8854/5
Chairperson:
Rt Rev. Lord Coggan.
Establishing true relationship between Christians and Jews. Teaching and preaching so as to eliminate prejudice, misunderstanding and eliminating antisemitism and anti-Judaism.

Secretariat for Catholic Jewish Relations
17 Temple Fortune Lane
London NW11 7UB
Tel: 01 458 4681
Secretary:
Rev. Graham Jenkins
To implement the Vatican documents, *Nostra Aetate*, to improve relations between Catholic and the Jewish Community.

Festivals of Other World Faiths

Hinduism

The name, Hindu, is a Persian invention for the religion of the majority of the inhabitants of the Indian subcontinent. Hindus call their religion Sanatan Dharma, 'eternal truth'. There is no church and little organisation. The major festivals are as follows.

Makara Sankranti (14 January)
The only festival which falls on the same day every year. On this day people distribute *til ladoos* (balls of sesame seeds made with sugar) to all as a token of peace. Children have fun flying kites.

Vasant Panchami (January–February)
A Spring festival in North India, held on the fifth day of the bright fortnight of the month of Magha. (The Indian calendar works on the lunar month and is divided into two fortnights, bright and dark respectively, depending on the quantity of moonlight.)

Maha Shivaratri (January–February)
This is held on the fourteenth day of the dark fortnight of the month of Magha. People fast on this day and worship the Lord Shiva in his emblem of day and night, offering him milk, water and bilva leaves.

Holi (March–April)
The most popular of all Hindu festivals. It is on the fifteenth day of
the bright fortnight of the month of Falgun. It is the Hindu harvest
festival, celebrated by fires in the villages and fun and games.

Rama Navami (April–May)
On the ninth day of the bright fortnight of Chaitra, people fast and
worship the Lord Rama.

Guru Purnima (July–August)
On the fifteenth day of the bright fortnight of the month of Ashadh
is celebrated a special day of worship of Guru, or spiritual guide.

Raksha Bandhan (August–September)
The fifteenth day of the bright fortnight of Shravana sees the ceremony of the changing of the sacred thread, or Rakhis. A sister ties a
rakhi on the right wrist of her brother, male cousin or adopted
brother, as a protection from evil.

Janmashtami (August–September)
The birthday of the Lord Krishna. After fasting all day and singing
hymns Hindus celebrate the birthday at midnight by ringing bells.
This is on the eighth day of the dark part of the month of Shravana.

Ganesha Chaturthi (September–October)
The idol of the Lord Ganesha is brought into the home and worshipped with special prayers, for his incarnation day; the fourth day of
the bright fortnight in the month of Bhadrapad.

Nava–Ratri (October–November)
A festival of nine nights, starting with the first day of the month of
Ashvina. The goddess Durga is worshipped with great enthusiasm
and gaiety.

Dashera (October–November)
Celebrated in various ways, it is the 'victory of the Lord Rama' day.

Diwali (October–November)
Observed on the fifteenth day of the dark fortnight of the month of
Ashvina. The derived word 'Diwali' means 'rows of light', and this
is a festival of light, a joyous time of illumination, firework displays
and a festival of sweets.

Islam

Islam means peace and also submission to God. A Muslim is one who submits to the will of God. There are about 800 million Muslims of different ethnic, linguistic and national origins spread across the globe. Historically, therefore, Islam represents a broad diversity of cultures and interpretations within the basic unity of the faith. All Muslims are united in their adherence to the fundamental principles of Islam, which include the belief in oneness of God, Muhammad as the last and final Prophet through whom the Quran was revealed, and man's ultimate accountability to God.

The Quran repeatedly urges the importance of learning and reflecting upon the wonders and mysteries of nature. This primacy of knowledge also finds expression in many of the Prophet's sayings. The seeking of knowledge is obligatory upon every Muslim man and woman, the Prophet is reported to have said, while his urging Muslims to seek knowledge – even if it be in China – emphasised the universality of knowledge. These teachings encouraged a spirit of inquiry and provided an impetus to cultural and scientific developments which also inspired the intellectual endeavours during the Renaissance in Europe.

As with knowledge, so the Quran and the Prophet's traditions also encouraged a respect for other faiths and beliefs. Thus the Quran refers to the Jews, and Christians and the Muslims as *ahl al-Kitab*, the people of the Book. Indeed, the Muslims recognise that the essential message of Islam is fundamentally identical to that of the Old and the New Testaments.

This emphasis on the universality of knowledge, and respect for other religions, inspired a creative interface of Islam with other faiths and a great flowering of its culture into a global civilisation, which, within three centuries of the death of the Prophet in 630, came to stretch from Spain to Indonesia and from the steppes of Central Asia to the forest lands of Africa.

Muslim Festivals

Muslims celebrate a number of festivals. Among these are the following:

Id al-Adha, a central festival of Islam, commemorates Prophet Abraham's readiness to sacrifice his son, Ismail, at the command of God. The festival begins with congregational prayers and is accompanied with much rejoicing, giving of presents and acts of charity.

Id al-Fitr is observed at the end of the fasting period in the month of Ramadhan and lasts for three or four days. The festival involves congregational prayers in every town and village in the Muslim world, followed by feasting, public entertainment, exchange of gifts and almsgiving.

Mi'raj commemorates Prophet Muhammad's spiritual ascension to the presence of God and symbolises the supreme goal which all Muslims seek to attain. The observance of Mi'raj usually takes the form of special prayers and meditations.

Sikhism

The word Sikh literally means 'disciple', a follower of Guru Nanak, the founder of Sikhism. Nanak was followed by nine other Gurus, of whom the fifth, Arjan, compiled the basic scripture, *Adi Granth*. The festivals are as follows.

Baisakhi (April)
This is the only fixed festival, falling on 13 April and marking the beginning of the Sikh religious year. On this day in 1699 Guru Gobind Singh brought into being a new brotherhood of saint-soldiers – the Khalsa – to fight against political and social injustice and to uphold the freedom of worship and religious liberty. New converts are received into Sikhism on this day.

Diwali (October/November)
A festival shared in common with the Hindus. It is a time of spring cleaning and decoration. People buy new clothes and children have fun with fireworks.

Hola Mohalla (March)
Related to the Hindu festival of Holi. The celebration is marked by a good deal of horse-play and ribaldry.

Gurupurbs
Purely Sikh festivals, holy days in honour of the Gurus. Sikhs all over the world celebrate the birthdays of Guru Nanak and Guru Gobind Singh.

Buddhism

The name Buddhist is derived from Buddha, a title which means 'enlightened'. It is applied properly to Gautama, the founder of Buddhism. There are two major forms, the Theravada who believe in relatively few Buddhas, and the Mahayana who believe in countless Buddhas.

The festivals of Buddhism are not included here because Buddhism presents a peculiar problem. Western Buddhists follow the teachings of Buddha but, on the whole, not the festivals and outward observances common to Buddhists in other parts of the world.

Recommended reading

Comparative Religions: a modern textbook edited by W. Owen Cole, and published by Blandford Press, Poole, Dorset. Written by practising members of each world religion.
Community Festivals Handbook. Community Projects Foundation, 60 Highbury Grove, London N5 2AG.

Useful addresses

Anglican Inter-Faith Consultants
c/o Lambeth Palace
London SE1 7JU
Secretary:

Specialist consultants appointed by the Archbishops of Canterbury and York to advise on inter-faith relations.

Multi-Faith Resource Unit (MFRU)
1 College Walk
Selly Oak
Birmingham B29 6LE
Tel: 021 472 0139
An international centre established 1980 to provide workshops and programmes for groups from different faiths and cultures.

World Congress of Faiths
28 Powis Gardens
London W11 1JG
Tel: 01 727 2607
Secretary:
Miss P. Morrison
To encourage understanding between members of all religions.

Housetop Trust and the Sects

Many young people in the West are attracted to oriental sects and so-called Human Potential cults. About seventy such new religious movements are actively recruiting in England. Since no other Catholic agency or institute was addressing itself to this problem, Housetop built up a library of information on these religious movements and began to distribute relevant information to pastors, teachers, families of persons involved, and so on. Its advisory leaflet *Advice to Relatives and Friends* found a wide response throughout the country.

At the request of the Catholic Bishops' Conference of England and Wales, Sister Deirdre Ford of the Housetop team has compiled a 150-page report on *The New Religious Movements in England and Wales* (obtainable from the Housetop Trust). It formed the basis for new pastoral recommendations made by the Bishops' Conference during their meeting in November 1984.

Housetop is an apostolic centre established with the sole purpose of promoting and supporting missionary apostolate throughout the world.

Housetop Trust
39 Homer St
London W1H 1HL
Director:
Fr John Wijngaards MHM

PART FOUR

Church and Society

CHAPTER ONE

Politics and Government

How to get the best out of your MP

Members of Parliament are seen by most people as the links between the individual and the government. They exist to be used! They are the persons to complain to. Naturally the way members go about their duties, the way they represent a constituency, depends upon individual personality. However it is possible to give a general guide of how to get the best out of your MP.

The first step is to find out which constituency you live in; you can waste valuable time and effort writing to the wrong MP. If you are unsure who represents you in Parliament, telephone the local Town Hall and their information department will help you.

There are a number of ways in which MPs can help you with a problem. First, you can write: simply address your letter to your member at The House of Commons, Westminster, London SW1, and he or she will get it. It is always worth remembering that an individually-written letter will be much more impressive than a photocopied or duplicated letter prepared by a pressure group. (Do remember to sign your letter; it really is surprising how many people forget.)

Secondly, you can telephone your MP at the House of Commons; the number is 01 219 3000. A message left will be passed on to the MP or the staff and your call will be returned.

Thirdly, MPs can present petitions to the House of Commons. They have the advantage of having no doors closed; they can really talk to the person at the top. Contacting the relevant authority on your behalf may not necessarily solve your problem; on the other hand it might speed up a bureaucratic process. Most MPs hold constituency surgeries on Friday evenings, or Saturday mornings; usually on a fortnightly basis. If you would like to bring a problem to one of these sessions, telephone the Town Hall and they will tell you when and where they are.

There are other ways your Member can help: by asking questions, initiating Adjournment Debates and tabling Amendments to Bills. Your point of view can find expression in relevant debates on Bills or on general subjects. Approaches can be made, privately or publicly, to Ministers and the Member can lead delegations to call on Ministers.

MPs react to reasonable and sensible pressure but they expect reasonable notice of meetings, etc. For example, never just turn up at the House of Commons expecting to see your MP without prior arrangement; he or she could be involved in a long meeting or away in the constituency. The public seem to think that their MP has magical powers to solve problems. It should be remembered that an MP represents 70,000 people and is incredibly busy. He or she is often only supported in the work by one or two part-time assistants. But having said that, the value of the British democratic system lies in the usefulness of the Member of Parliament; using the above guidelines you can get the best out of your MP, who can be a life-line in time of trouble.

D.A.

Principal British Political Parties

Conservative and Unionist Central Office
32 Smith Square
London SW1P 3HH
Tel: 01 222 9000

Labour Party
150 Walworth Road
London SE17 1JT
Tel: 01 703 0833

Liberal Party Organisation
1 Whitehall Place
London SW1A 2HE
Tel: 01 839 4092

Social Democratic Party
4 Crowley St
London SW1
Tel: 01 222 7999

Communist Party of Great Britain
16 St John St
London EC1M 4AD
Tel: 01 251 4406

Other useful addresses:

Conservative Action for Electoral Reform
6 Queen St
London W1X 8JT

Tory Reform Group
9 Poland St
London W1V 3DG

Local Government – how it is structured

England and Wales

Relationship with Central Government
The powers of local authorities and their responsibilities are defined by Parliament. While the authorities have to give an account to their electorates for the way in which they discharge their duties, central government is answerable to Parliament for policies concerning the services administered by the local bodies. Legislation from Parliament governing local authority services divides broadly between Mandatory (which imposes duties) and Permissive (which empowers the authorities). The first is usually expressed in very general terms, allowing wide scope for local interpretation.

There is also legislation which gives specific powers to central government to control the work of local authorities in relation to certain services. These powers exist basically to ensure a degree of uniformity in the standards of service: they are considered to be supervisory and advisory. They can be summarised as follows.

Financial control Local authorities can only spend money on items authorised by Acts of Parliament. Approximately three-fifths of the income available comes from general taxation, through central government, which controls the size of grants and sets limits to amounts paid.

Planning control Matters like housing and employment are affected by major planning procedures issuing from central government.
Inspectorates and advisors Some social services are subject to scrutiny by inspectors appointed by a government department. For example, the education service, the police service, and the probation and after-care services are so covered.
Government circulars All departments of central government issue circulars, which can be mandatory or merely advisory, defining the ways local authorities are expected to carry out their duties.

Organisation of local government
The basic unit in England and Wales is the county, of which there are fifty-three. Each area has an elected council of part-time (unpaid) representatives and a staff of full-time (paid) officials. Each county is divided into districts, which range in number from two to fourteen. Altogether there are 369 district councils in England and Wales. Greater London is treated quite separately and is divided into the thirty-two London boroughs and the City of London.

The county authorities provide those services which require wider areas of administration; the district councils are responsible for local services. In the countryside and small towns there is a third tier of local government, the parish councils. They have very limited power.

Administration
The elected members of the council (county, district or parish) are responsible for local authority services. However, services are administered and delivered to the public by local authority employees.

Relationship between Statutory and Voluntary and non-statutory services
The local authority provides services by statute of Parliament; these are therefore known as the Statutory services. Long before many of these services were provided by law, voluntary bodies were meeting the many and various needs. Their pioneering work was first recognised in 1914 with financial support from central government.

Voluntary and non-statutory bodies still provide valuable service, acting as pressure groups for social, reform, providing supportative services for the professional worker and filling in the gaps in the Statutory services.

Local Government – Scotland

Scotland has always developed its local government in a distinct way from that of England and Wales. The Minister responsible for Scotland is the Secretary of State, who works through the Scottish Development Department and the Scottish Home and Health Department. Their headquarters are at:

New St Andrew's House
St James Centre
Edinburgh EH1 35X.

Personal social services
These services in Scotland were reorganised before those of England and Wales. Under the provisions of the Social Work (Scotland) Act of 1968, the local authorities appointed social work departments administered by directors of social work. The new departments took over the work formerly done by the welfare and children's departments, by local authorities mental health service,

and the probation service. Juvenile courts were virtually abolished by part of the same Act, replacing them with a system of children's hearings.

Personal health services
These services were reorganised by the National Health Service (Scotland) Act of 1972 along similar lines to those of England and Wales. Administration is the main area of difference. In Scotland there are fifteen Area Health Boards who are directly responsible to the Secretary of State for Scotland; the Common Services Agency carries out some of the functions performed by the regional authorities in England. The health and social work authorities of Scotland are not obliged to establish joint consultative committees, but the social work departments are required to consult the appropriate Area Health Boards on matters of common interest to patients, while the public interest is represented by local health councils.

CHAPTER TWO

Health Care

The National Health Service

As a result of the National Health Service Reorganisation Act of 1973, the administration of personal health services in England and Wales was given a new structure (see page 405 above for Scotland). The Act placed responsibility for managing the service at three different levels – the Secretary of State, Regional Health Authorities and Area Health Authorities. As the result of a later Act, The National Health Service Act 1977, the Area Authorities were replaced by District Health Authorities. There are now 192 District Authorities which have been given more autonomy as to staffing and deployment of resources.

The Secretary of State

National objectives and priorities, with the allocation of resources, are determined by the Secretary of State for Health and Social Services. He does not work alone but in conjunction with the Secretaries of State for Wales and Scotland. Together they are advised by their own departments and the Central Health Services Council for England and Wales, and its Scottish equivalent. The Department of Health and Social Security is the government department responsible for the NHS in England. The actual administration, however, has been delegated to regional and district level.

Regional Health Authorities

The chairman and members of each of England's fourteen Regional Health Authorities are appointed by the Secretary of State. The RHAs are responsible to the Secretary of State for the development of long-term strategies for the District Authorities and for allocating resources to them. The RHAs also organise a few direct services, which are more appropriate on a large scale, for example, the Mass X-Ray service.

District Health Authorities

District Health Authorities (DHAs) are responsible for the planning, development and management of health services for a total of 192 districts with populations of up to 860,000. Within the resources available, the DHA will be responsible for administering the health services in their district, including general hospital services, maternity, child care, services for the elderly, the mentally ill and the mentally handicapped. While each DHA is accountable to the RHA for the performance of its responsibilities, each has a Community Health Council to represent public opinion.

Community Health Councils

Each English district has a Community Health Council, and there are 22 in Wales. Half the members of a council are appointed by the local authority, one-third by voluntary organisations which have a particular interest in health matters, and the remainder by the Regional Health Authority. They exist to represent the interests of the user of the health services and are able to comment on present adequacies and future plans.

Health Service Commissioner

Complaints, which do not seem to have been resolved through the usual channels, concerning hospital treatment and community health services, can be referred to the Health Service Commissioner. He does not deal with complaints about family practitioner services (see below). He can be contacted directly in writing by the public (provided the matter has already been referred to responsible authorities) at:

Health Service Commissioner for England (or Wales, or Scotland)
Church House
Great Smith St
London SW1P 3BW
Tel: 01 212 8776.

Family Practitioner Committees

There is approximately one Family Practitioner Committee for each of the District Health Authorities. Their responsibility is to the DHSS for the provision of general management of family practitioner services – including dentists, chemists, and opticians as well as family doctors – and to investigate any complaints against them.

Health and Health Education

Self-help organisations

There are so many self-help organisations that it is impossible to list more than a selection of the larger ones. The groups are listed under general headings because some of the organisations cater for more than one type of problem and fit into more than one category.

Medical

Association to Combat Huntington's Chorea
34A Station Road
Hinckley
Leicester LE10 1AP
Tel: 0455 61558
This organisation was formed to instigate and help raise funds for research into the disease.

British Migraine Association
178A High Road
Byfleet
Weybridge
Surrey KT14 7ED
Tel: 0932 52468
Information is given to members about specialist clinics and research news.

Cancer After-Care and Rehabilitation Society (CARE)
Lodge Cottage
Church Lane
Timsbury
Bath BA3 1LF
Tel: Timsbury 70731
A society conducted by people who have had cancer and who now seek to help others.

Chest, Heart and Stroke Association
Tavistock House North
Tavistock Square
London WC1H 9JE
Tel: 01 387 3012
The association aims to reduce the incidence of chest, heart and stroke illness and to help those who suffer from them. It carries out research, health education, rehabilitation, welfare and counselling services.

Coeliac Society
PO Box 181
London NW2 2QY
Tel: 01 459 2440
The society promotes research into the condition and provides holidays and other social activities.

Colostomy Welfare Group
38–9 Eccleston Square (2nd Floor)
London SW1V 1PB
Tel: 01 828 5175
A welfare service provided for patients who have had, or are about to undergo, colostomy or other similar operations.

Cystic Fibrosis Research Trust
5 Blyth Road
Bromley
Kent BR1 3RS
Tel: 01 464 72111/2
The Trust finances research into the nature and treatment of the disease.

The Mastectomy Association
26 Harrison Street
London WC1H 8JG
Tel: 01 837 0908
This is a non-medical service by and for women who have had or are about to have a breast removed.

The National Eczema Society
Tavistock House North
Tavistock Square
London WC1H 9SR
Tel: 01 388 4097
The society encourages research into eczema, giving counselling and information to sufferers and their families.

National Society for Cancer Relief
30 Dorset Square
London NW1 6QL
Tel: 01 402 8125
The Society provides financial assistance to cancer patients in the form of grants: to help any heavy debts, nursing and convalescent home fees, days or night nursing, etc.

Parkinson's Disease Society
36 Portland Place
London W1N 3DG
Tel: 01 323 1174
The society aims to help patients and their relatives with problems in the home, to collect and disseminate information and to sponsor research.

Psoriasis Association
7 Milton Street
Northampton NN2 7JG
Tel: 0404 711129
This Association promotes research and understanding of psoriasis and other skin conditions.

The Renal Society
64 South Hill Park
Hampstead
London NW3 2SJ
Tel: 01 794 9479
Gives encouragement and information to kidney sufferers.

The Self-Help Information Bank
177 Battersea High Street
London SW11 3JS
Tel: 01 223 0924
This Bank acts as a national information exchange and a referral and guidance centre for self-help practitioners and other interested individuals or organisations.

The Society of Skin Camouflage and Disfigurement Therapy
Wester Pitimenzier
Auchtermuchty
Fife
Scotland
A self-help organisation which seeks through discussion and counselling to cover the problems and fears associated with disfigurement.

Physical disability

Arthritis Care (The British Rheumatism and Arthritis Association)
6 Grosvenor Crescent
London SW1X 7ER
Tel: 01 235 0902
The Association provides basic information about welfare services, allowance aids for the disabled, holidays, fund-raising and publicity.

Association of Crossroads Care Attendant Schemes
94A Coton Road
Rugby
Warwickshire CV21 4LN
Tel: 0788 61536
The Association's aims are to prevent disabled people being admitted to residential or hospital care by providing the practical assistance necessary to enable them to remain in their own homes.

Association of Disabled Professionals
The Stables
73 Pound Road
Banstead
Surrey SM7 2HU
Tel: Burgh Heath (07373) 52366
A self-help group concerned with the rehabilitation, education, training and employment opportunities of the disabled.

Disability Alliance
25 Denmark Street
London WC2
Tel: 01 240 0806
The Alliance is a federation of organisations for the disabled which aims to achieve a comprehensive income scheme for disabled people.

Disablement Income Group (DIG)
Attlee House
28 Commercial Street
London E1 6LR
Tel: 01 247 2128
DIG is a pressure group campaigning for legislative reform to provide adequate income and allowances for disabled people.

The Disabled Living Foundation
380–384 Harrow Road
London W9 2HU
Tel: 01 289 6111
This organisation provides a comprehensive information service for the disabled, run on a subscription basis.

Motability
Boundary House
91/3 Charterhouse Street
London EC1M 6BT
Tel: 01 253 1221
This is an independent charitable organisation set up to help recipients of mobility allowance, whether drivers or passengers.

National Fund for Research into Crippling Diseases
Vincent House
1 Springfield Road
Horsham
West Sussex RH12 2OA
Tel: 0403 64101
This organisation is concerned with the promotion of research into the cause, prevention, cure and treatment of all forms of crippling diseases.

Sexual and Personal Relationships of the Disabled (SPOD)
286 Camden Road
London N7 0BJ
Tel: 01 607 8851/2
This organisation is concerned with research into the sexual aspects of disability and with educating both the public and professional workers who have tended to deny sexuality of severely disabled people.

The Spastics Society
12 Park Crescent
London W1N 4EQ
Tel: 01 636 5020
Its aims are to provide care, treatment,
education and employment training for
spastics. It also has an intensive
research programme.

Blind People (see also page 164)

*National Federation of the Blind of the
United Kingdom*
20 Cannon Close
London SW20 9HA
This organisation is concerned with the
welfare of the blind.

The Partially Sighted Society
40 Wordsworth Street
Hove
East Sussex BN3 5BH
Tel: 0273 736053
Offers assistance and support to
partially sighted people.

Support Groups for Children and Families

*Association for Spina Bifida and
Hydrocephalus*
Tavistock House North
Tavistock Square
London WC1H 9HJ
Tel: 01 388 1382/5
The Association gives support and
advice, including help with holidays,
equipment, training and employment.

Down's Children's Association
Quinbourne Centre
Ridgeacre Road
Birmingham B32 2TW
Tel: 021 427 1374
Provides an advisory service for the
parents of Down's Syndrome babies.

The Family Fund
PO Box 50
York YO1 1UY
Tel: 0904 21115
The aim of this fund is to help families
caring for a severely handicapped child
(mentally or physically) under the age
of 16.

The Haemophilia Society
PO Box 9
16 Trinity Street
London SE1 1DE
Tel: 01 407 1010
The Society promotes the study of
haemophilia and allied conditions, and
support is given to sufferers from the
disease and their families.

*Invalid Children's Aid Association
(ICAA)*
126 Buckingham Palace Road
London SW1W 9SB
Tel: 01 730 9891
ICAA offers a social work service to
handicapped children and their families
in London and parts of the Home
Counties. It has an information service
providing free advice for parents.

*National Association for the Welfare of
Children in Hospital (NAWCH)*
Argyle House
Euston Road
London NW1 2SD
Tel: 01 833 2041
This is a voluntary organisation and
works to promote the welfare of sick
children in general, including the
improvement of facilities in hospitals
for children and their families.

*The National Society for Autistic
Children*
276 Willesden Lane
London NW2 5RB
Tel: 01 451 3844
This Society provides and promotes
day and residential centres for the
treatment and education of autistic or
non-communicating children.

*Voluntary Council for Handicapped
Children*
8 Wakley Street
Islington
London EC1V 7QE
Tel: 01 278 9441
This organisation aims to promote
cooperation between different
voluntary bodies and agencies
concerned with the welfare of
handicapped children and to provide
the families with advice and
information on statutory and voluntary
services.

Mental Health

Depressives Associated
19 Merley Ways
Wimborne Minster
Dorset BH21 1QH
Tel: 0202 883957
Aims to stimulate interest, awareness
and understanding of the problems of
depression by publicity and research.

*Psychiatric Rehabilitation Association
(PRA)*
21A Kingsland High Street
London E8 2JS
Tel: 01 254 9753
Promotes the rehabilitation of the
mentally ill on their return to home,
employment and society.

The National Schizophrenia Fellowship
78/79 Victoria Road
Surbiton
Surrey KT6 4NS
Tel: 01390 3651/2
A national organisation for all matters
concerning the welfare of sufferers
from schizophrenia and their relatives.

Multiple Sclerosis

Crack MS (The young arms of the
Multiple Sclerosis Society)
286 Munster Road
Fulham
London SW6 6AP
Tel: 01 381 4022/5
Aims to meet the particular welfare and
social needs of young people with MS.

*Multiple Sclerosis Action Group
(ARMS)*
11 Dartmouth Street
London SW1H 9BL
Tel: 01 222 3224
Represents the interests of sufferers.

*The Multiple Sclerosis Society of Great
Britain and Northern Ireland*
(Incorporating Crack MS for younger
members)
286 Munster Road
London SW6 5AP
Tel: 01 381 4022
The Society provides a free counselling
service, outings, holidays, social
activities and financial help to sufferers
and their families.

Health agencies and support organisations

British Red Cross Society
9 Grosvenor Crescent
London SW1X 7EJ
Tel: 01 235 5454
This is a voluntary organisation and is
dedicated to the relief of suffering
whether through war, disaster or
accident.

Health Education Council
78 New Oxford Street
London WC1A 1AH
Tel: 01 637 1881
The HEC was set up by the
government as a national centre of
expertise in health education. It
promotes and encourages healthy living
and sponsors relevant research.

Health and Safety Commission
Health & Safety Executive
St Hugh's House
Stanley Precinct
Bootle
Merseyside L20 3QY
Tel: 051 951 4000
The Commission deals with research,
provides information and advisory
services, develops policies in the health
and safety fields and submits proposals
for new regulations to and carries out
the directions of the Commission.

Hospital Saving Association
Hambledon House
Andover
Hants. SP10 1LQ
Tel: 0264 532111
This is a voluntary organisation; its
aims are to provide contributors and
their dependents with cash benefits
which supplement those of the NHS
when they are admitted to hospital,
convalescent home, etc. There are also
many other benefits.

*The National Association of Leagues of
Hospital Friends*
565 Fulham Road
London SW6 1ES
Tel: 01 385 0974
This Association was established to
provide a variety of services which
include running hospital shops and
visiting lonely patients, and is operated
in most hospitals.

The Patients Association
Room 33
18 Charing Cross Road
London WC1H 0HR
Tel: 01 240 0671
This is a voluntary organisation which
aims to give help and advice to
individual patients.

St John Ambulance Brigade
1 Grosvenor Crescent
London SW1X 7EF
Tel: 01 235 5231
This is a voluntary organisation and
helps to spread the knowledge of first
aid through training classes and
instructional literature.

*Women's Royal Voluntary Service
(WRVS)*
17 Old Park Lane
London W1Y 4AJ
Tel: 01 499 6040
This is a voluntary organisation, and
amongst its many welfare services the
WRVS provides non-medical
assistance in hospitals, e.g. trolley
shops, clubs in hospitals and mental
hospitals.

The Church and Health

*Catholic Bishops' Joint Committee on
Bio-Ethical Issues* (England, Ireland,
Scotland and Wales)
1A Stert Street
Abingdon
Oxon OX14 3JF
Secretary:
Mgr Michael Connelly
To advise the Bishops' Conference on
matters concerning medical, ethical
problems.

*Catholic Nurses' Guild of England and
Wales*
Hon. Secretary
Miss M. Baird
26 Southend Parade
Hebburn
Tyne and Wear
To promote the spiritual, professional
and social well-being of its members.
Through its membership to CICIAMS
(The International Committee of
Catholic Nurses, Midwives and Health
Visitors) gives help and guidance to
nurses in the developing countries.

*Churches' Fellowship for Psychical and
Spiritual Studies*
St Mary Abchurch
Abchurch Lane
London EC4N 7BA
Secretary:
Mr Julian Drewett
The Fellowship was founded by a group
of clergy and laymen who were
convinced that psychic phenomena had
great relevance to the Christian faith,
both in life and death. The Fellowship
can give help where a psychic problem
becomes evident in personal
counselling.

Clinical Theology Association
St Mary's House
Church Westcote
Oxford OX7 6SF
Secretary:
Rev. P.J. van de Kasteele
The Association exists for the training
of people, ordained and lay, in
Christian pastoral care and counselling;
for the deepening of Christian life and
growth towards personal maturity and
stability; and for research by
appropriately qualified persons into the
integration of psychology and
psychotherapy with the Christian faith.

The Guild of Health
Edward Wilson House
26 Queen Anne Street
London W1M 9LB
Company Secretary:
Mrs Teresa Parker
This is an interdenominational
organisation promoting the Church's
ministry of healing.

Guild of Pastoral Psychology
37 Hogarth Hill
London NW11 6AY
Secretary:
Mrs Marion Ditchfield
The Guild of Pastoral Psychology
offers a meeting ground for all those
interested in the relationship between
religion and depth psychology,
particularly the work of C.G. Jung and
his followers.

Institute of Religion and Medicine
St Marylebone Parish Church
Marylebone Road
London NW1 5LT
Secretary:
Mr C. Horace Sinclair
Serious study and sharing of
experiences across professional
boundaries by members (ministers of
all religions, registered practitioners in
all branches of medicine, etc.). By
discussion in field groups, participation
in the annual Residential Conference
and information disseminated in the
quarterly *Religion and Medicine.*

*St Marylebone Centre for Christian
Healing & Counselling*
St Marylebone Parish Church
Marylebone Road
London NW1 5LT
Counselling and Christian healing.

The Church and Social Responsibility

*British Unemployment Resources
Network (BURN)*
c/o Birmingham Settlement
318 Summer Lane
Birmingham B19 3RL
Tel: 021 359 6596
To develop and maintain self-help
groups which are concerned with
unemployment, and to create a
national information and resources
network.

Christians at Work
148 Railway Terrace
Rugby
Warwickshire CV21 3HN
Secretary:
Mr Rod Badams
Encouraging Christian witness and
fellowship in all places of work, chiefly
through forming and assisting Christian
groups of employees.

Church Action with the Unemployed
318 St Paul's Road
London N1 2LF
Director:
Norman Oliver
Helping and encouraging local
churches of all denominations to work
with unemployed people.

*Churches Community Development
Consultancy*
St Mary's Church House
Kingswood Road
Shortland
Bromley
Kent BR2 0HG
This charity assists Christian churches
and organisations with their
involvement in society.

Church of England Board of Social Responsibility
Church House
Deans Yard
London SW1P 3NZ
Tel: 01 222 9011
The BSR seeks to study issues of social concern in the light of Christian faith, to identify and investigate areas of special concern and to relate these to church life at all levels.

The Church of England National Council for Social Aid
Church House
Dean's Yard
London SW1P 3NZ
Tel: 01 222 9011
Secretary:
Rev. E. W. F. Agar
Penal affairs; delinquency; alcoholism; drug misuse; gambling. Council supplies an information service, and also publishes literature on delinquency; alcoholism; drug misuse; gambling.

Church of Scotland Board of Social Responsibility
121 George Street
Edinburgh EH2 4YN
Tel: 031 225 5722
A voluntary organisation which runs 68 social-work establishments offering care for people in need: elderly and young people, alcoholics, homeless and handicapped.

Industrial Christian Fellowship
4 Steche Road
Swanage
Dorset BH19 1NF
Secretary:
John Davis
Helping Christians who work in industry or commerce with their ministry at work.

Law Centres
The Legal Action Group
28a Highgate Road
London NW5 1NS
Tel: 01 485 1189/01 267 0048
The Federation of Law Centres
164 North Gower Street
London NW1
Tel: 01 387 8570
Law centres exist in many parts of the country. They employ full-time staff, including lawyers, and will handle a client's case from beginning to end, including representation in court or at a tribunal. These services are free unless the centre explains otherwise.

National Council for Civil Liberties
21 Tabard Street
London SE1 4LA
Tel: 01 403 3888
The NCCL gives free legal advice to protect the rights and liberties of all private citizens.

CHAPTER THREE

Social Responsibility

Church Action with the Unemployed (CAWTU)

Launched in 1982 with an introductory leaflet to 25,000 ministers of all denominations, CAWTU has moved vigorously forward, spurred on by the response of thousands of committed Christians. More than 500,000 free leaflets have been widely distributed giving suggestions and advice on the following topics:

Coping with Unemployment, a step-by-step guide to understanding feelings, applying for financial support, planning the future;
Mutual Help Groups and Resource Centre, how to set up a mutual help group, keys to its success, reports of other successful groups;
Opportunities for Adults, emphasises the positive aspects of unemployment, sponsoring a project, sources of funding.

Other leaflets in the same series are *Opportunities for Young People* and *Creating new jobs*.

There is also a pack of eight leaflets designed to focus the Churches' attention on the issues of unemployment.

CAWTU publishes a newsletter, *Beyond Unemployment*, and a video; makes grants to assist the creation of mutual help groups, and provides advice to Churches on local initiatives.

All leaflets can be obtained from

Church Action with the Unemployed
318 St Paul's Road
London N1 2LF

or from local contact people (list available from CAWTU).

This charity is promoted by a group of people from the major Christian Churches in Britain who are concerned about unemployment. It is chaired by Canon Frank Scuffham, Industrial Chaplain in Corby. It is funded by the supporting Churches and from charitable trusts, commerce and industry.

Social Responsibility: a book list

Work Today and Tomorrow, by the Industrial Affairs Advisory Group of the Church and Society Department of the United Reformed Church. From the United Reformed Church, 86 Tavistock Place, London WC1H 9RT, April, 1981. A pack of materials designed for use in house groups, church meetings, etc. To help church members to consider the theme of work in the light of present problems and future possibilities.

Our Parish and Unemployment, by Family and Social Action, World of Work Service, 106 Clapham Road, London SW9 0JX, 1981; 40 pages. Pastoral guidelines for parishes and local groups on making a positive response to the need of the unemployed.

Work, Unemployment and the Christian Faith, by Scottish Industrial Mission, From Church of Scotland, Church and Industry, 121 George Street, Edinburgh EH2 4YN, July, 1981. Nine discussion starters each based on the pattern, 'See, judge, act'. Written by an inter-denominational group of clergy in the conviction that unemployment poses questions for faith and faith provides a vision of life which our contemporaries, employed and unemployed alike, can ill afford to ignore.

The Christian and Unemployment, a parish study guide towards a new understanding of work, with Bible references and questions for group discussion, by Wendy Green, Mowbray, 1982. A 45-page pamphlet with 15 chapters and a section 'Sources of information and support'.

Making Tomorrow Work, from London Diocesan Board of Education, Education and Community Division, 7 St Andrew Street, London EC4 3AB. A set of six leaflets: *What's happening?*, *The Wider Vision*, *Tomorrow's World*, *Family Life*, *A personal view*, *A Parent's view*, and a guide to how to use these leaflets.

Unemployment and the Future of Work, Church of England General Synod Board for Social Responsibility Industrial and Economic Affairs Committee, December, 1982. A study pack with seven resource papers, the purpose of which is 'to get discussion and argument going!'

Work or What, Eric P. Forshaw, from *Work or What?* 11 Clumber Crescent North, The Park, Nottingham. This is a study pack investigating the issues and implications of unemployment in 3 parts: 1. Datamaze, 2. Simulation Game, 3. Action Notes.

Counselling People Made Redundant, notes for clergy; a 4-page A4 leaflet, produced by Coventry Industrial Mission.

A paper by the Industrial Mission Team in Hertfordshire and Bedfordshire, 1980, called 'Counselling the Redundant', is based on this paper.

Redundancy – the Last Option, from Mr F. Newman, 89 Chepstow Road, Newport, Gwent NP1 8BY. By a group of people involved in redundancies and closures in the West Country and South Wales, plus three industrial chaplains. Seeks to discover ways in which a redundancy operation can be carried through with as much dignity and humanity as the commercial and legal and other constraints surrounding a closure allow. For companies and trade unions.

Redundancy and Unemployment – New Initiative Paper No. 5., Ray Smith and Roy Allen, Birmingham Council of Christian Churches, Central Hall, Corporation Street, Birmingham 4. A fold-out leaflet.

Redundant, a step-by-step guide to help you to know what to do. Similar guides under this title have been produced by Kidderminster Industrial Chaplaincy, Redditch Industrial Chaplaincy, Industrial Mission in Kent and Croydon, Norwich Industrial Mission and others.

A Guide for the Unemployed, from the Industrial Chaplain, Birmingham Diocesan Office, Church House, Harborne Park Road, Birmingham B17 0BH. A fold-out leaflet, giving 13 steps of essential advice, information and where to get help. Many other industrial missions have similar leaflets.

Church Action with the Unemployed, from Church Action With The Unemployed, 318 St Paul's Road, London N1 2LF.

Action on Unemployment, CAWTU. Directory of 100 projects.

Four Million Reasons to Care, Peter Elson and David Porter, published jointly by CAWTU and MARC Europe.

The Response of the Christian Churches in England to the Problem of Unemployment, R. F. Elliot, available from CAWTU.

It made all the Difference, CAWTU. Study of a small grant scheme for unemployed individuals in Redcar.

In Place of Work: the Sufficient Society – A Study of Technology from the Point of View of People, David Bleakley, SCM Press, 1982.

Work: the Shadow and the Substance – A Reappraisal of Life and Labour, David Bleakley, SCM Press, 1983.

Work in Crisis – Dilemma of a Nation, Roger Clarke, The Saint Andrew Press, 1982.

Employment – Some Useful Addresses

Action Resource Centre
9 Henrietta Place
London W1M 9AG

Co-Operative Development Agency
Broadmead House
21 Panton Street
London SW1Y 4DR

Industrial Common Ownership Finance
Ltd
4 St Giles Street
Northampton NN1 1AA

Industrial Common Ownership
Movement Ltd
7/8 The Corn Exchange
Leeds LS1 7BP

Job Ownership Limited
9 Poland Street
London W1V 3DG

Manpower Services Commission
Moorfoot
Sheffield S1 4PQ

National Council for Voluntary
Organisations
26 Bedford Square
London WC1B 3HU

National Youth Bureau
17/23 Albion Street
Leicester LE1 6GD

Practical Action
Victoria Chambers
16/20 Strutton Ground
London SW1P 2HP

Scottish Co-Operative Development
Committee Ltd
Templeton Street
Bridgeton
Glasgow G40 1DA

Urban Enterprise Development
99 Southwark Street
London SE1 0JF

Youthaid
9 Poland Street
London W1V 3DG

Justice and Peace Work in the Parish

The basic unit of the Church is the parish. As a community centred on Christ, the parish is the forefront of the Church in the world. It is both a sign and an instrument of unity with God *and* the unity of the community. But for the parish to fully realise this unity, its members need to reflect constantly on the meaning of the Gospel in today's world and to discern the movement of the Spirit. As a focus for the power of God, the parish can assist in the transformation, or conversion, of the individual and the community. The Justice and Peace movement seeks to make the connection between personal and social transformation based on the Christian law of love.

The expression of love and work for social transformation are a central part of the message of the Bible. The account of Exodus, the Psalms and the Old Testament prophets speak of God's love for all people, but especially the victims of injustice: the poor and needy, the hungry, the widow, orphan, stranger, the worker denied a just wage, etc. On the other hand, God's wrath is reserved for those who exploit, oppress or ignore the poor. The God of the Bible constantly rescues the needy and oppressed. To 'know' or have faith in God is to do likewise. Indeed the prophets equate knowledge of God with work for justice (e.g. Jer. 22: 13–16). They warned that true peace, *shalom*, can only be established by the practice of true religion, which involves justice towards the poor and the powerless.

In the New Testament the poor are the first to whom Jesus' mission is directed (Luke 4: 18–21) and concern for them is proof of his authenticity (Luke 7: 20–3). It is through the eyes of the hungry, destitute and suffering people of the world that Jesus says to us: 'What you do to the least of these my brothers and sisters you do to me' (Matt. 25: 40).

For 2,000 years the love of God and neighbour has been preached and, to varying degrees, practised by Christians. But recently a new awakening is taking place in the Churches. The Good Samaritan of today is concerned not only with those he sees but with those far away.

This new awakening demands a coming to grips with injustice and violence that may be part of the structure of society. As consumers, producers and citizens, we each have a relationship with many other people. The problem is to see that our involvement in any social structure contributes to the well-being of other people. No matter how good and honest we are individually, if we are part of unjust structures we are contributing to injustice. The Church should give a counter-sign, a real expression to the oneness of the human family and of the possibility of life based on justice, love and peace.

To assist the Church in the preaching of the Gospel and the transformation of the world, more and more Christians are working in groups for justice and peace. Such groups, however, should not be seen as optional extras in the life of the parish. Nor are they the seedbed of an 'alternative church'. They are part of the universal Church and flow from the sacramental and communal aspects of parish life. Through prayer, education and action, a Justice and Peace group can help the parish and the Church be the leaven in the world. What would such a group do?

Prayer

The group can help the parish pray by
(a) assisting in the preparations for the Sunday liturgy through writing prayers, helping prepare the sermon, putting up posters, etc.
(b) organising liturgies for special occasions such as Peace Sunday, Prisoners' Sunday, Remembrance Day, etc. and
(c) organising prayer vigils, fasts, etc.

Education

The educative role of the group will help people apply the general principles of justice as found in the Bible and Church documents. Rarely would a whole parish be of one mind on what to do about a specific social issue. Through displaying materials, arranging study days and speakers, using drama and in other ways, a group could provide an opportunity for dialogue and clarification. There are a host of national and international organisations which can be tapped for information and assistance. Almost any interest can be nurtured and directed by specialists.

Action

The actions that result from prayer and education will vary depending on the style and the creativity of the group. It is at this point that often the charge of 'mixing religion with politics' is made. Such accusations are not new and can provide further opportunity to engage in dialogue and education. Organisations campaigning for social change require people, ideas and action. The Church, both as an institution and through its individual members, with their own insights and methods, is in the arena of social involvement.

In addition to the services a Justice and Peace group can provide a parish, it can promote personal growth and change. The social and personal come together in a group. It is often in small groups, especially those motivated by the Gospels, through relationships and shared experiences, that people change. It is there they find courage and strength to join with others in building God's Kingdom, on earth as it is in heaven.

Two useful books, in the series of Living the Gospel, entitled *Action for Justice and Peace* and *Working Together* are the most recent and best publications for Christian groups involved in social change. They contain in much greater detail the what, how and why of Justice and Peace groups. With extensive bibliographies and resource guides they would be of great use to both experienced and beginning groups. (Copies available from CIIR: address on page 426.)

D.M.

Some Peace Groups Working for Reconciliation in Northern Ireland

Action for Peace
7 King's Road
Belfast BT5 6JF
Tel: Belfast 655914
Chairman:
Mr William Houston.

All Children Together
Lagan College Campus
63 Church Road
Belfast BT6 9SA
Tel: Belfast 702594
Secretary:
Mrs Yvonne Gilmour
16 Marylebone Park
Belfast BT9 5HF
Tel: Belfast 669028

Columbanus Community
683 Antrim Road
Belfast BT15 4EG
Leader:
Rev. M. Hurley, SJ

Community of the Peace People
Fredheim
224 Lisburn Road
Belfast BT9 6GE
Tel: Belfast 663465
Administrator:
Mrs Ann McCann

Cornerstone Community
443/445 Springfield Road
Belfast BT12 7DL
Tel: Belfast 221649
Secretary:
Mrs Kay McGarry

Corrymeela Community
Corrymeela House
8 Upper Crescent
Belfast BT7 1NT
Tel: Belfast 225008
Corrymeela Centre
Ballycastle
Co. Antrim
Tel: Ballycastle 62626
Hon. Secretary:
Mr Douglas McCulloch

Corrymeela Link
PO Box 118
Reading
Berkshire RG1 1CL
Tel: 0734 589800

The Cross Group
6a Cumberland Park
Dundonald
Belfast BT16 0AY
Tel: Dundonald 3952
Secretary:
Maura Kiely

Fact (Friends of Armagh Coming Together)
31 Desart Lane
Armagh
Tel: Armagh 525260
Secretary:
Mrs K. McAneney

Fellowship of Reconciliation in Ireland
25 Belfast Road
Holywood
Co. Down
Tel: Holywood 3261
Secretary:
Mr Robert Ballagh

Harmony Community Trust
123 Scottish Provident Buildings
7 Donegall Square West
Belfast BT1 6JL
Tel: Belfast 243223
Chairman:
Mr D.F. Harrison

Inter-Church Emergency Fund for Ireland
Inter-Church Centre
48 Elmwood Avenue
Belfast BT9 6AZ
Tel: Belfast 663145
Secretary:
Dr R.D. Stevens

Lifeline
47 Lyndhurst Park
Ballygomartin Road
Belfast BT13 3TG
Tel: Belfast 718718
Chairman:
Mrs Tilly Lindsay

Northern Ireland Children's Holiday Scheme
Room 7
Bryson House
28 Bedford St
Belfast BT2 7FE
Secretary:
Mrs Margaret Courtney
Provide holidays for children from both sides of the community.

Northern Ireland Peace Forum
c/o 8 Upper Crescent
Belfast 7
Chairman:
Mrs Eileen Carragher

Oasis Youth Centre
Portmore Street
Portadown
Co. Armagh
Tel: Portadown 331257
Secretary:
Miss Helen McElroy

Peace and Reconciliation Group, Londonderry
18a London Street
Londonderry
Tel: Londonderry 269206
Hon. Secretary:
Elizabeth Zammit

Peacepoint
35 Marlborough Park North
Belfast 9
Tel: Belfast 667528

Ulster Project
St Catherine's Rectory
Hop Hill
Tullamore
Co. Offaly
Tel: Tullamore 21367
Secretary:
Canon A.T. Waterstone

Waterside Churches' Committee for Community Needs
14 Dungiven Road
Londonderry
Tel: Londonderry 42536 (office hours)
Secretary:
John Austin

Youth for Peace
Fredheim
224 Lisburn Road
Belfast
Tel: Belfast 663465
Secretary:
Miss Maggie Darragh

Peace Councils and Centres

Brighton Peace Centre
28 Trafalgar Street
Brighton

Dorking Peace Council
Hirst Cottage
Capel
Guildford
Surrey

Dorset Peace Council
6 French Mill Lane
Shaftesbury
Dorset

Manchester Peace Council
23 Marford Crescent
Sale
Cheshire M33 4DL

Norwich Peace Council
13 Constable Road
Norwich NR4 6RN

Southampton Peace Council
17 Hulse Lodge
Hulse Road
Southampton SO1 2LA

Edinburgh CND
Edinburgh Trades Council
12 Picardy Place
Edinburgh

Quaker International Centre
1 Byng Place
London WC1

Fellowship of Reconciliation

*East Anglia Fellowship of
Reconciliation*
1 Clayhall Place
Acton
Sudbury
Suffolk

*Fellowship of Reconciliation London
Union*
(see page 426)

Fellowship of Reconciliation in Wales
c/o 53 Richmond Road
Cardiff CF2 3UP

Northern Fellowship of Reconciliation
81 Grosvenor Avenue
Jesmond
Newcastle-Upon-Tyne NE2 2NQ

Justice and Peace Development

Aid to the Church in Need
3–5 North Street
Chichester
West Sussex PO19 1LB
Tel: 0243 787325
Director:
Kevin Grant
This Catholic Relief Agency exists to
give spiritual and material aid to the
Church wherever it is persecuted, and
to refugees.

Keston College
Heathfield Road
Keston
Kent BR2 6BA
Tel: 0689 50166
Keston College is a research institute
and information centre which conducts
extensive factual investigations into the
state of religious communities in
Eastern Europe and the Soviet Union.

Amnesty International – British Section
5 Roberts Place
off Bowling Green Lane
London EC1 0EJ
Tel: 01 251 8371
Scottish contact:
24 Allison Street
Glasgow
Tel: 041 424 1375
A worldwide human rights movement.
It works for the release of prisoners of
conscience (provided they have never
used or advocated violence) and
opposes torture and the death penalty.

British Refugee Council
Bondway House
3/9 Bondway
London SW8 1SJ
Tel: 01 582 6922
The Council seeks to provide relief to
refugees and their dependents who are
in need or distress and to promote their
physical and mental health.

British Council for Aid to Refugees
Bondway House
3/9 Bondway
London SW8
Tel: 01 582 6922
The Council is the recognised
coordinating body of voluntary
agencies working for refugee relief in
the United Kingdom.

Catholic Association for Racial Justice
5 Henry Road
London N4 2LH
Tel: 01 800 6148
Secretary:
Melvin Lyons
Approved by the Bishops' Conference
the association is concerned with the
promotion of racial justice in Church
and society.

*Catholic Institute for International
Relations*
22 Coleman Fields
London N1 7AF
Tel: 01 354 0883
CIIR is an independent Roman
Catholic organisation working to
promote a better understanding of
justice and peace issues.

*Christian Concern for Southern Africa
(CCSA)*
c/o British Council of Churches
2 Eaton Gate
London SW1W 9BL
Tel: 01 730 3884
CCSA gives consideration to the ethics
of investment, particularly in relation
to British-based companies in Southern
Africa.

Commission for Racial Equality (CRE)
Elliot House
10–12 Allington Street
London SW1E 5EH
Tel: 01 828 7022
The CRE is a statutory body which
seeks to promote equality of
opportunity and work towards the
elimination of racial discrimination.

CWL Relief and Refugee Committee
2 Garden Close
Stockwell Road
London SW9 9TY
Tel: 01 735 9041
Secretary:
Mrs S.C. Allen
Affiliated to *Caritas Internationalis*,
provides aid for refugees and victims of
war and persecution.

Fellowship of Reconciliation (FOR)
40–46 Harleyford Road
London SE11 5AY
Tel: 01 582 4054
FOR is an international Christian
movement which seeks to develop
peaceful and creative ways of handling
personal and political conflicts.
(See also page 425.)

International Defence and Aid Fund for Southern Africa (IDAF)
Canon Collins House
64 Essex Road
London N1 8LR
Tel: 01 359 9181
IDAF works towards free democratic and non-racial societies in Southern Africa; aids, defends and rehabilitates the victims of apartheid legislation.

International Social Service of Great Britain
Cranmer House
39 Brixton Road
London SW9 6DD
Tel: 01 735 8941
ISS offers a casework service to help those British, Commonwealth, foreign, refugee or stateless people whose personal and family problems extend across national frontiers.

Irish Justice and Peace Commission
169 Boosterstown Avenue
Blackrock
Co. Dublin
Ireland
Tel: 0001 885021
The Commission was established as an expression of the Church's concern for matters of justice, development and peace.

Joint Council on the Welfare of Immigrants
44 Theobalds Road
London WC1X 8SP
Tel: 01 405 5527/8
An independent voluntary organisation which advises and represents people with problems in connection with the immigration and nationality laws.

Latin America Bureau (LAB)
1 Amwell Street
London EC1R 1UL
Tel: 01 278 2829
LAB is an independent research, publications and resource centre on Latin America and related development issues, also involved in work with schools.

Mexicolore
28 Warriner Gardens
London SW11 4EB
Tel: 01 622 9577
Mexicolore is a multi-cultural and development education project which aims to bring Mexico – its people, history, culture and the issues behind its present underdevelopment – alive in classroom and community centres.

Minority Rights Group (MRG)
29 Craven Street
London WC2N 5NG
Tel: 01 930 6659
MRG investigates and publicises discrimination against minority or majority groups.

National Council for Civil Liberties
21 Tabard Street
London SE1 4LA
Tel: 01 403 3888
The NCCL aims to protect civil liberties and the rights of political, religious, racial and other minorities in Britain.

National Standing Conference of Diocesan Justice and Peace Groups
c/o Sr Judith Russi
3 Wind Hill
Bishops Stortford
Herts
Tel: 0279 54758
This group exists to further justice and peace work in the Catholic Church by providing a regular communication forum of diocesan groups for each other.

Ockenden Venture
Guildford Road
Woking
Surrey GU22 7UU
Tel: 04862 72012
The Venture seeks to secure a home,
health and education for displaced and
refugee children and young people at
home and overseas.

Pax Christi
St Francis of Assisi Centre
Pottery Lane
London W11 4NQ
International Catholic Peace
movement, working in many areas of
nuclear and general disarmament.

Runnymede Trust
37A Grays Inn Road
London WC1X 8PP
Tel: 01 404 5266
The Trust provides information on race
and immigration in Britain and the
EEC with a view to the elimination of
all aspects of racism and discrimination
and the promotion of social justice.

Scottish Justice and Peace Commission
28 Rose Street
Glasgow G3 6RE
Tel: 041 333 0238
Justice and Peace advises the Scottish
Roman Catholic Bishops on matters of
social justice, international peace,
human rights and world development.

*United Kingdom Immigrants' Advisory
Service*
7th Floor
Brettenham House
Savoy Street
London WC2E 7EN
Tel: 01 240 5176
An organisation which offers free
advice and assistance to a person with a
right of appeal under the Immigration
Act 1971.

*United Nations High Commission for
Refugees (UNHCR)*
36 Westminster Palace Gardens
Artillery Row
London SW1P 1RR
Tel: 01 222 3065
UNHCR has a mandate from the
General Assembly of the United
Nations to protect refugees and seek
permanent solutions to their problems.

Peace And Ecology

*Campaign Against the Arms Trade
(CAAT)*
5 Caledonian Road
London N1 9DX
Tel: 01 278 1976
CAAT works for an end to British
involvement in the arms trade and for
the conversion of military industries to
peaceful socially useful production.

Campaign Coffee Scotland (CCS)
29 Nicolson Square
Edinburgh EH8 9BX
Tel: 031 667 0129
CCS sells coffee from Tanzania and
Nicaragua and campaigns for justice in
world trade.

Centrepeace
143 Stockwell Street
Glasgow G1 4LR
Tel: 041 552 8357
A resource centre for peace and justice
which includes a shop selling world
crafts, Campaign Coffee, etc.

Christian CND
22–24 Underwood Street
London N1 7JG
Tel: 01 250 4010
Christian CND is a specialist section of CND. It works in parishes and with other Christian groups.

Christian Ecology Group
58 Quest Hills Road
Malvern
Worcs.
Tel: 06845 2630
An informal network of people concerned about the effects on the environment of technological and other developments today.

Friends of the Earth (FoE)
377 City Road
London EC1V 1NA
Tel: 01 837 0731
FoE is a campaigning organisation promoting policies to protect the natural environment.

Ecology Party (ECO)
36 Clapham Rd
London SW9
Tel: 01 735 2485
Fields candidates in local and General elections.

Glasgow Development Forum (GDF)
30 Hillhead Street
Glasgow
Tel: 041 339 6914
GDF keeps organisations and individuals in the Glasgow area who have an interest in world development in touch with each other.

Greenpeace
36 Graham Street
London N1
Tel: 01 251 3020
One of the most active and well known of the ecology/conservation groups.

The Life Style Movement
The Little Gidding Community
Little Gidding
Huntingdon
Cambs. PE17 5RJ
The movement exists to encourage people who are trying to live more justly.

One World Week
240 Ferndale Road
London SW9 8BH
Tel: 01 733 5500
One World Week, each October, is a locally-based informal education programme about justice, peace and development, promoted by the Churches Committee of the World Development Movement.

Peace Pledge Union (PPU)
6 Endsleigh Street
London WC1N 0DX
Tel: 01 387 5501
PPU is involved in war resistance and working for a non-violent society in which war will have no place.

Quaker Peace and Service
Friends House
Euston Road
London NW1 2BJ
Tel: 01 387 3601
Quaker Peace and Service works nationally and internationally to channel and serve the witness for peace, international service and disarmament.

World Disarmament Campaign (WDC)
238 Camden Road
London NW1 9HE
Tel: 01 485 1067
WDC seeks to activate governments to take positive and decisive action to bring about an end to the arms race.

Summary of the Brandt Report on Justice and Peace

Given the decline in the world's economic system, the prodigious waste of its limited resources and the proliferation of weapons of mass destruction, some far-reaching changes are needed if we are to survive. That is really the starting point for the Brandt Report. It presents an analysis of the divisions between rich North and the poor South and urges a programme of immediate action to be pursued by striving for agreement at the highest level.

The Report's main argument is based on mutual interest. It is in the interest of the poor South for a massive transfer of resources from the North to take place – that is clear enough. But the Report is also saying what is much less obvious: that it is in the interest of the North to enable the South to develop – because that implies 'international political stability, expanding export markets, the preservation of the biological environment, the limitation of population growth'. The programme is presented, not on a basis of idealistic philanthropy, but with hard-headed self-interest in mind. It is in general a plea for change, bringing together the key international social issues of our time: peace, justice and jobs.

The Report was published in 1980 and some 180,000 copies were sold in the UK – far more than in any other country. In May 1981 there was a mass lobby of parliament by 10,000 people which forced the Government to give a more considered response. But the Report has failed in its attempt to produce any fundamental change in the position of leading politicians in the rich world. A sequel was published in 1982, called *Common Crisis*, dealing mainly with the increasing debt crisis by Third World countries and the worsening of the trends already identified 2 years earlier.

Gospel demands

The real causes of poverty and injustice are so often to do with power and vested interests within countries. Development programmes over the years have often left internal structures of injustice undisturbed. There is nothing in the Brandt Report to suggest this should be tackled. In many parts of the world, people are poor and oppressed because those in power ensure that the system is maintained which keeps each of them in their place. For the Christian, it is not so much the economic argument that makes this division intolerable, as a preferential option for the poor based on the clear message of the Gospel, together with human solidarity founded on a recognition that we are members of the same body. Perhaps Brandt, in spite of its shortcomings, will help us to see how radical the demands of the Gospel really are.

B.D.

Materials on Brandt

North-South: A Programme for Survival – The Brandt Report, Pan Books, £1.95.
Handbook of World Development: The Guide to the Brandt Report, Longmans, £1.95.
Programme for Survival (sheet summary of the Brandt Report), £0.12.
Facing up to Change: Britain and the Brandt Report, slide-cassette, 21 minutes, 72 frames. Cassette/slides, booklet, script and discussion notes on some of the main themes, especially related to trade and employment. Also available as filmstrip with cassette. Hire charge £4.00. + VAT. Purchase price £20.00. + VAT and postage.
Barbara Ward on Brandt: 15 minute video-cassette in which Barbara Ward speaks about the significance of Brandt. Available VHS or Umatic. Hire charge £4.00. + VAT and postage. All available from: Centre for World Development Education, 128 Buckingham Palace Road, London SW1.
Talking of Brandt, slide-cassette, 23 minutes, 80 frames. Cartoon-style conversation between a redundant British textile worker, and the head of an African Government Planning Bureau. Provides basis for stimulating discussion on key issues that link up workers internationally. Hire charge £7.00. + packing and postage. Purchase price £50.00. + postage and packing. Available from: Trade Union International Research and Education Group, Ruskin Hall, Dunstan Road, Old Headington, Oxford OX3 9BZ.
North-South: Our Links with the Poorer Countries of the World (6 sided A4 size), price £0.18.
Three Cartoon Sheet Discussion Starters, No.1 *Trade*, No.2 *Employment*, No.3 *Water*. Each focuses on a particular topic, using quotes from the Brandt Report and background information as an introduction. All at £0.18 each.
Peace and Justice in the World, an illustrated pamphlet by Barbara Ward, emphasising Christian response to Brandt. This is strongly recommended as the most readable introduction to the issues raised by the report. Price £0.50 plus postage. Available from: CAFOD, 2 Garden Close, Stockwell Road, London SW9 9TY.

CAFOD and its Relationship with the Catholic Community

CAFOD, the Catholic Fund for Overseas Development, is the official agency of the Bishops' Conference in England and Wales for Overseas Development. Established officially in 1962, CAFOD embraced the work that had already been initiated by the National Board of Catholic Women through the Family Fast Day scheme. Today, Family Fast Day is a central dimension of community response to the suffering and poverty faced by millions throughout the Third World. Over half the annual CAFOD general income is raised from Family Fast Day contributions each Lent and October.

CAFOD's income at the end of its first year was £25,000. At the end of the 1984 financial year the total income had reached £6.2 million and in 1985 it was nearly £12 million. Much of this has been the result of the response to the African famine. At the present time CAFOD is also supporting 400 self-help development programmes in 70 countries.

The relationship with the Catholic community has also grown in recent years. Increasingly people are asking serious questions about the causes of poverty and are seeking to make a more informed and long-term commitment.

CAFOD has responded to this interest and commitment in two main ways. First, through the type of relationship it aims to foster between communities here and in the Third World. In June 1984 CAFOD launched a 'Partnership' scheme, which says something immediately about the nature of the relationship with our sisters and brothers in the wider world. Real partnership begins with the recognition that all humanity has a common origin in God. It implies a fairer distribution of the world's resources and invites us to be with those who suffer.

Through the partnership scheme, CAFOD forges real links between parishes, schools and individuals in this country and our sisters and brothers in Africa, Asia and Latin America. Those taking part in the scheme for a CAFOD group link up with a CAFOD programme in a particular region. They learn about life in that country, the problems facing its poor, and they raise funds to support CAFOD's self-help projects there. The active participation of the whole parish and community is encouraged. A small group or committee of parishioners will probably act as the link between CAFOD and the whole parish. Groups in parishes or schools who support the scheme are provided with a pack of materials on a particular country. This gives them an insight into the social, political and economic situation of the country, identifies the development needs and looks at a range of self-help programmes supported by CAFOD. The intention is that the whole pack should be used as a focus for learning and discussion as well as fund raising.

As part of the scheme, CAFOD emphasises the call of our Lord to prayer, fasting and almsgiving (Matt. 6: 1–18) and urges people to give up something each week as a regular act of self-denial. By doing without in this country we can directly help communities in the Third World. Many people choose to give up a meal and so experience something, even if only a little, of what hunger and deprivation means. Fasting is an opportunity to show commitment to the poor.

The second response has been through a programme of development education. This has been in operation for the past seven years. As CAFOD's policy statement says, 'this programme is to enable people in this country to understand the nature and causes of underdevelopment and the Christian response to it in the light of the Church's teaching'. The main thrust of this work, for the adult community, has been through a yearly campaign. This began in 1980 when a number of dioceses were invited to take part in an education programme focusing on the Philippines. Diocesan and parish groups were encouraged to make the campaign a focus for their Lenten reflection. They study the problems faced by the Filipino communities, explore ways to respond and, through liturgy and prayer, express concern, as a Christian community, about injustice in the world.

In an attempt to widen the campaign, CAFOD now have a two-year cycle to enable groups to become more familiar with the issues presented and allow more time for dissemination and action.

CAFOD also makes contact through formal education, particularly in secondary schools, colleges and chaplaincies. The 1971 Second General Assembly of the Synod of Bishops on 'Justice in the World' spoke of education for justice as a means of preparing people for a way of life that is utterly human. Such an education is meant to awaken a critical sense towards the way in which men and women live and the values they adopt. Education should prepare us to abandon values which fail to favour justice for all. Although this says something about the educational process which we are all involved in for the whole of our lives, it has something special to say to Catholic schools.

Through work with teachers and older pupils, CAFOD aims to encourage reflection on the witness schools give concerning justice.

This involves looking at how the school is run, the quality of the relationship within the school and the teaching methods adopted, as well as the content of what is taught. CAFOD staff work with teachers to prepare programmes on justice and peace, look for ways in which Third World issues can be integrated into the curriculum and review materials produced for use in schools.

The Catholic youth network is a new area of work. Spurred by an interest in International Youth Year, many youth workers are seeking ways of introducing an international dimension into their work. CAFOD's contribution to the Year is to provide training and material support for youth events and programmes.

The framework for all the education work is based on the pastoral cycle. This is made up of four elements, each of equal importance and essential for the support of the other. The elements are:

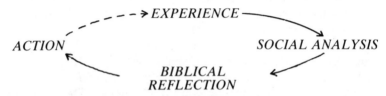

The model begins with the knowledge and life experience each person can bring to an issue. This is then used as a base for deeper analysis and questioning. If we are to be successful in our work for change as Christians, then all we do must be firmly rooted in the Gospels and the social teaching of the Church. What do the Gospels have to say to the modern world? How do they challenge us to respond to injustice? From this understanding and reflection in faith we should see more clearly what action can be taken. Finally, action leads to new experiences and learning thus taking us back round the cycle.

This model for action and reflection can be applied to any of the groups with whom CAFOD is working. It is a model which can be enabling and empowering no matter what a group's level of involvement. Attempting to operate in isolation, without support and inspiration from others, can be frustrating and destructive. Pope John Paul II, speaking of CAFOD and the work of its supporters, urged them always to keep alive their 'Gospel tradition of loving concern and service to others in the name of Jesus'. Through the various means proposed, CAFOD enables communities in Britain to work in partnership with communities throughout the Third World.

CAFOD is a way of being with Christ who is hungry, thirsty and in need: it is a way to distribute resources more fairly; an opportunity to enter into partnership with people in development projects; a means by which we can translate our weekly act of self-denial into positive action; a source of hope for the poor in small community initiatives.

B.D.

CAFOD
2 Garden Close
Stockwell Road
London SW9 9TY
Tel: 01 733 7900

Assistance to Parishes Overseas

For a long time parishes in this country have assisted the younger churches in other parts of the world chiefly through the regular annual appeals of the missionary societies, the CAFOD Family Fast Day collections and the Association for the Propagation of the Faith (APF). An increasing number of parishes (nobody knows just how many) now provide direct assistance to the younger churches. This is usually in addition to the regular appeals.

They may follow up on a national appeal for say, famine or drought. They may take on specific projects provided by CAFOD, SURVIVE, or the missionary societies. They may support missionaries from the parish. Or they may adopt a parish on a twinning arrangement.

Each of these, in bringing a personal touch to the help given, might seem preferable to the more impersonal aspect of the APF or the different missionary society that comes round each year. Personal involvement is a good thing so long as others are not left at a disadvantage. A parish in an African or Asian country may benefit considerably from adoption while a neighbouring parish is in dire straits. This is where the impersonal help through the APF, for example, ensures that everybody gets a slice of the cake. Since the desirable aim is a balance of both kinds of assistance, the more personal kind of help should not become the alternative to the other.

J.B.

Overseas Aid and Development

CAFOD
The Catholic Fund for Overseas
Development
2 Garden Close
Stockwell Rd
London SW9 9TY
Tel: 01 733 7900

Christian Aid
PO Box 1
London SW9 8BH
Tel: 01 733 5500
Scottish Office:
41 George IV Bridge
Edinburgh
Tel: 031 225 5254
Welsh Office:
Bangor
Gwynedd LL57 1TD
Christian Aid is a division of British
Council of Churches. It raises money in
Britain for development projects
overseas and does extensive
development work in Britain.

Community Service Volunteers (CSV)
237 Pentonville Road
London N1 9NJ
Tel: 01 278 6601
CSV involves people in community
service, as full-time volunteers for 4–12
months or part-time locally. Over 2,000
unemployed young people work on
MSC funded social service projects
nationwide.

EEC Commission Information Office
8 Storey's Gate
London SW1P 3AT
Tel: 01 222 8122
7 Alva Street
Edinburgh EH2 4PH
Tel: 031 225 2058
4 Cathedral Road
Cardiff CF1 9SG
Tel: 0222 371631
The Office can answer all queries about
EEC policies including social welfare
and relations with the Third World.

Help the Aged
16–18 St James Walk
London EC1R 0BE
Tel: 01 253 0253
Help the Aged is an international
organisation which aims to relieve the
distress of the world's aged caused by
poverty, sickness, bad housing,
loneliness, natural disaster or political
upheaval.

Intercare (African Catholic Sisters)
49 Melton Road
Leicester LE4 6PN
Tel: 0533 667326
This is a registered charity sending free
medical supplies to qualified Sisters in
former British colonies together with
books to help train village health care
workers.

International Broadcasting Trust (IBT)
2 Ferdinand Place
London NW1 8EE
IBT is a consortium of voluntary
organisations concerned mainly with
development education.

Little Way Association
Sacred Heart House
119 Cedars Rd
Clapham Common
London SW4 0PR
Tel: 01 622 0466
Registered charity for Aid to
Missionaries

Overseas Development Institute (ODI)
Regent's College
Inner Circle
Regent's Park
London NW1 4NS
ODI is an economic research institute
which studies different aspects of
development in the Third World and
the relationship between the EEC and
developing countries.

Oxfam
274 Banbury Road
Oxford OX2 7DZ
Tel: 0865 56777

The Pattaya Orphanage Trust
Dept UN
16/11 Freepost
London W14 0BR
Caring for orphan, crippled children,
unwanted by their families and villages,
refugee and orphaned children from
Vietnam and neighbouring territories.

Returned Volunteer Action (RVA)
1 Amwell Street
London EC1R 1UL
Tel: 01 278 0804
RVA is the British organisation of ex-
overseas volunteers: it aims to improve
the contributions of volunteer
programmes and to channel ex-
volunteers into local development
education work.

Save the Children Fund
17 Grove Lane
Camberwell
London SE5 8RD
Tel: 01 703 5400
An independent, professionally staffed
international organisation, whose
purpose is the rescue in disaster and
longer term welfare of needy children,
irrespective of nationality, race, or
religion.

*SCIAF (Scottish Catholic International
Aid Fund)*
43 Greenhill Road
Rutherglen
Glasgow G73 2SW
Tel: 041 647 2113
SCIAF is the official Third World
agency of the Church in Scotland. It
finances development projects
overseas, carries out a development
programme in parishes and schools.

*Scottish Churches Action for World
Development (SCAWD)*
41 George IV Bridge
Edinburgh
Tel: 031 225 5254
SCAWD is the Scottish Churches' own
ecumenical development education
agency. Apart from direct educational
work with church congregations and
groups, policy research is carried out
and educational materials prepared.

*Scottish Education and Action for
Development*
29 Nicolson Square
Edinburgh
Tel: 031 667 0129
SEAD exists to develop Scottish
awareness of the challenge and
problems of world development.

SPICMA
Grove Cottage
Nayland Road
Great Horkesley
Essex CO6 4AG
Tel: 0206 271098
A voluntary organisation engaged in
medical assistance and general aid
projects, working through missionary
personnel overseas.

Third World First (3W1)
232 Cowley Road
Oxford OX4 1UH
Tel: 0865 245678
3W1 works mainly with students
explaining and campaigning against the
causes of world poverty and hunger,
economic exploitation and the violation
of human and democratic rights.

Third World Publications
151 Stratford Road
Birmingham B11 1RD
Tel: 021 773 6572
Third World Publications promotes
and sells books and pamphlets from
and about the Third World.

Tools for Self-Reliance
1 Little Anglesey
Gosport
Hants.
Tel: 07017 22179
A non-commercial company which collects and refurbishes hand-tools and despatches them to working people in developing countries.

United Nations Association (UNA)
3 Whitehall Court
London SW1A 2EL
Tel: 01 930 2931
UNA works to secure the support of the public for the principles of the United Nations Charter, increase awareness of the UN's role in promoting peace, economic and social justice and human rights.

Volunteer Missionary Movement
HQ VMM Centre
Shenley Lane
London Colney
Herts AL2 1AR
Tel: Bowmans Green 24853
Sends lay missionaries, with professional or technical qualifications, to the Third World; also recruits and trains them.

War on Want
3 Castles House
1 London Bridge Street
London SE1 9SG
Tel: 01 403 2266
War on Want is a campaign against world poverty which combines funding development projects with campaigning, research and education.

World Development Movement (WDM)
Bedford Chambers
Covent Garden
London WC2E 8HA
Tel: 01 836 3672
WDM seeks to tackle the cause of world poverty by helping to remedy decisions taken in Britain which deprive people of their basic needs and exploit the weak.

United Nations Universal Declaration of Human Rights

Article 1

All human beings are born free and equal in dignity and rights. They are endowed with reason and conscience and should act towards one another in a spirit of brotherhood.

Article 2

Everyone is entitled to all the rights and freedoms set forth in this Declaration, without distinction of any kind, such as race, colour, sex, language, religion, political or other opinion, national or social origin, property, birth or other status. Furthermore, no distinction shall be made on the basis of the political, jurisdictional or international status of the country or territory to which a person belongs, whether it be independent, trust, non-self-governing or under any other limitation of sovereignty.

Article 3

Everyone has the right to life, liberty and the security of person.

Article 4

No one shall be held in slavery or servitude; slavery and slave trade shall be prohibited in all their forms.

Article 5

No one shall be subjected to torture or to cruel, inhuman or degrading treatment or punishment.

Article 6

Everyone has the right to recognition everywhere as a person before the law.

Article 7

All are equal before the law and are entitled without any discrimination to equal protection of the law. All are entitled to equal protection against any discrimination in violation of this Declaration and against any incitement to such discrimination.

Article 8

Everyone has the right to an effective remedy by the competent national tribunals for acts violating the fundamental rights granted him by the constitution or by law.

Article 9

No one shall be subjected to arbitrary arrest, detention or exile.

Article 10

Everyone is entitled in full equality to a fair and public hearing by an independent and impartial tribunal, in the determination of his rights and obligations and of any criminal charge against him.

Article 11

1. Everyone charged with a penal offence has the right to be presumed innocent until proved guilty according to law in a public trial at which he has had all the guarantees necessary for his defence.
2. No one shall be held guilty of any penal offence on account of any act or omission which did not constitute a penal offence, under national or international law, at the time when it was committed. Nor shall a heavier penalty be imposed than the one that was applicable at the time the penal offence was committed.

Article 12

No one shall be subjected to arbitrary interference with his privacy, family, home or correspondence, nor to attacks upon his honour and reputation. Everyone has the right to the protection of the law against such interference or attacks.

Article 13

1. Everyone has the right to freedom of movement and residence within the borders of each State.
2. Everyone has the right to leave any country, including his own, and to return to his country.

Article 14

1. Everyone has the right to seek and to enjoy in other countries asylum from persecution.
2. This right may not be invoked in the case of prosecutions genuinely arising from non-political crimes or from acts contrary to the purposes and principles of the United Nations.

Article 15

1. Everyone has the right to a nationality.
2. No one shall be arbitrarily deprived of his nationality nor denied the right to change his nationality.

Article 16

1. Men and women of full age, without any limitation due to race, nationality or religion, have the right to marry and to found a

family. They are entitled to equal rights as to marriage, during marriage and at its dissolution.

2. Marriage shall be entered into only with the free and full consent of the intending spouses.

3. The family is the natural and fundamental group unit of society and is entitled to protection by society and the State.

Article 17

1. Everyone has the right to own property alone as well as in association with others.

2. No one shall be arbitrarily deprived of his property.

Article 18

Everyone has the right to freedom of thought, conscience and religion: this right includes freedom to change his religion or belief, and freedom, either alone or in community with others and in public or private, to manifest his religion or belief in teaching, practice, worship and observance.

Article 19

Everyone has the right to freedom of opinion and expression: this right includes freedom to hold opinions without interference and to seek, receive and impart information and ideas through any media and regardless of frontiers.

Article 20

1. Everyone has the right to freedom of peaceful assembly and association.

2. No one may be compelled to belong to an association.

Article 21

1. Everyone has the right to take part in the government of his country, directly or through freely chosen representatives.

2. Everyone has the right of equal access to public service in his country.

3. The will of the people shall be the basis of the authority of government: this will shall be expressed in periodic and genuine

elections which shall be by universal and equal suffrage and shall be held by secret vote or by equivalent free voting procedures.

Article 22

Everyone as a member of society, has the right to social security and is entitled to realisation, through national effort and international cooperation and in accordance with the organisation and resources of each State, of the economic, social and cultural rights indispensable for his dignity and the free development of his personality.

Article 23

1. Everyone has the right to work, to free choice of employment, to just and favourable conditions of work and to protection against unemployment.
2. Everyone, without discrimination, has the right to equal pay for equal work.
3. Everyone who works has the right to just and favourable remuneration ensuring for himself and his family an existence worthy of human dignity, and supplemented, if necessary, by other means of social protection.
4. Everyone has the right to form and to join trade unions for the protection of his interests.

Article 24

Everyone has the right to rest and leisure, including reasonable limitation of working hours and periodic holidays with pay.

Article 25

1. Everyone has the right to a standard of living adequate for the health and well-being of himself and of his family, including food, clothing, housing, and medical care and necessary social services, and the right to security in the event of unemployment, sickness, disability, widowhood, old age or other lack of livelihood in circumstances beyond his control.
2. Motherhood and childhood are entitled to special care and assistance. All children, whether born in or out of wedlock, shall enjoy the same social protection.

Article 26

1. Everyone has the right to education. Education shall be free, at least in the elementary and fundamental stages. Elementary education shall be compulsory. Technical and professional education shall be made generally available and higher education shall be equally accessible to all on the basis of merit.
2. Education shall be directed to the full development of the human personality and to the strengthening of respect for human rights and fundamental freedoms. It shall promote understanding, tolerance and friendship among all nations, racial or religious groups, and shall further the activities of the United Nations for the maintenance of peace.
3. Parents have a prior right to choose the kind of education that shall be given to their children.

Article 27

1. Everyone has the right freely to participate in the cultural life of the community, to enjoy the arts and to share in scientific advancement and its benefits.
2. Everyone has the right to the protection of the moral and material interests resulting from any scientific, literary or artistic production of which he is the author.

Article 28

Everyone is entitled to a social and international order in which the rights and freedoms set forth in this Declaration can be fully realised.

Article 29

1. Everyone has duties to the community in which alone the free and full development of his personality is possible.
2. In the exercise of his rights and freedoms, everyone shall be subject only to such limitations as are determined by law solely for the purpose of securing due recognition and respect for the rights and freedoms of others and of meeting the just requirements of morality, public order and the general welfare in a democratic society.
3. These rights and freedoms may in no case be exercised contrary to the purposes and principles of the United Nations.

Article 30

Nothing in the Declaration may be interpreted as implying for any State, group or person any right to engage in any activity or to perform any act aimed at the destruction of any of the rights and freedoms set forth herein.

INDEX OF SUBJECTS

INDEX OF NAMES, ORGANISATIONS AND SUPPLIERS

Presbyterian Church of Wales 304
Prinknash Abbey 329
Priory, The, Binfield 322
Priory of Our Lady, Sayers Common
321
Prison Fellowship 194
Prisoners' Sunday Committee 196
Prisoners' Wives and Families Society
196
PROP (The National Prisoners'
Movement) 196
Protestant Evangelical Church of
England 304
Psoriasis Association 409
Psychiatric Rehabilitation Association
412
Publishers' Association 87
Pueri Cantores 76, 314

Quaker International Centre 425
Quaker Peace and Service 429
Quarr Abbey, Isle of Wight 323

RADAR 177
Raymond Cook Holidays 36
Regional Councils on Alcoholism 186
Release 187
Religious and Moral Education Press
124
Religious Society of Friends (Quakers)
305
Renal Society 409
Renewal 129
Renewal Publications 385
Restoration Magazine 129
Retreat House, Chester 333
Returned Volunteer Action (RVA) 437
Richmond Fellowship 8
Ripon Diocesan House 332
Risk 380
Rock Youth Centre 226
Roman Catholic Feminists 317
Romanian Orthodox Church in London
374
Royal Commonwealth Society for the
Blind 168
Royal Foundation of St Katherine,
London 325
Royal Incorporation of Architects in
Scotland 138

Royal Institute of British Architects 138
Royal National Institute for the Blind
(RNIB) 168
Royal National Institute for the Deaf
171
Royal School of Church Music 54, 55,
77
RP Bookservice 114, 115, 122
Runnymede Trust 428
Russian Orthodox Church 374
Russian Orthodox Church in Exile 374
Rydal Hall Conference and Youth
Centre 227, 333

St Agnes Retreat and Conference
House, Bristol 324
St Andrew's Bookshop, Maidenhead
119
St Andrew's Bookshop Ltd,
Wheathampstead 119
St Andrews Children's Society 254
St Andrew's House, London 326
St Augustine's Abbey, Ramsgate 321
St Beuno's, Clwyd 330
St Cassian's Centre, Newbury 322
St Catherine Air Ltd 35
St Cecilia's Guild for the Blind 168
St Cecilia's Guild Quarterly 166
St Columba's House, Woking 323
St David's Priory 331
St Dominic Savio Apostolate for the
Young 225
St Dunstan's for Men and Women
Blinded on War Service 169
St Francis Children's Society,
Bedfordshire 251
St Francis' House, Hemingford Grey
327
St Gabriel's Retreat and Conference
House, Westgate-on-Sea 321
St Hilda's Retreat House, Horsbury
332
St Joan's International Alliance 317
St John Ambulance Brigade 414
St John in the Vale (residential centre)
227
St John's Priory, Castle Cary 324
St Joseph's Retreat and Conference
Centre, Malpas 334
St Julian's, Coolham, Sussex 320

A MAJOR NEW PRESENTATION OF THE CATHOLIC FAITH BY

THE  UNIVERSE
The Catholic Newspaper

FAITH ALIVE

Course patron:
Michael Bowen
Archbishop of Southwark

6th SEPTEMBER 1986 – 31st JULY 1987

Faith Alive is a unique venture in modern religious education.

A 48-part course, it will be published every week from September 6th, as a supplement to The Universe newspaper.

There are three basic blocks:
>   Section One: The Good News
>   Section Two: Living in the Church
>   Section Three: Ministry in the World

Week by week, every aspect of the Catholic faith will be examined, with major theological articles, life experiences, pieces on aspects of the spiritual life, full summaries of essential points, essay questions and bibliography.

Faith Alive is equally relevant to committed Catholics and to enquirers. Its structure affords great flexibility, catering for individual readers, students, fifth and sixth formers, youth groups and prayer or parish groups. Those who present essay assignments will have their work read and assessed by course tutors.

Nobody with an interest in the Catholic faith can afford to ignore this course.

COULD FAITH ALIVE WORK FOR YOU?
For full details and enrolment, see the Universe every week or contact:
FAITH ALIVE, THE UNIVERSE
33-39 BOWLING GREEN LANE, LONDON EC1R 0AB
TEL: 01-278 7321

THE  UNIVERSE
The Catholic Newspaper

Britain's best-selling Christian newspaper

HEYTHROP COLLEGE, UNIVERSITY OF LONDON
AN INSTITUTION FOR RESEARCH AND TEACHING

Postgraduate Diploma in Pastoral Theology

This full-time College-based course lasts one academic year and is a combination of academic study, pastoral experience and reflection. It provides professional preparation or sabbatical opportunities for those engaged in ministries in the Church, whether lay or ordained and centres around 18 course units to be selected from:

The Church	Pastoral Psychology
Canon Law	Religious Education
Moral Theology	Liturgy
Sacramental Theology	Spirituality
Study of Religions	Counselling skills

In addition it is possible for students with a first degree in Theology or Religious Studies to strengthen their knowledge with a *Master of Theology* degree in *Pastoral Theology*, as well as in Biblical Studies, Christian Doctrine, Church History, Christian Ethics and Philosophy of Religion. Students with a first degree in Philosophy can go forward to the Master of Arts in Philosophy.

The College continues to expand its undergraduate programmes which consist of the well-established BD and BA (Philosophy and Theology) and now the new BA in Biblical Studies.

Also part of this centre of learning is the **Institute of Spirituality** established to facilitate the study of spirituality as a theological discipline through a wide range of activities. Members of the Institute edit two international journals of spirituality, *THE WAY* and *SUPPLEMENTS TO THE WAY*, as well as teaching in the **Pastoral Department of the College**.

The College is also well known for its Library which has one of the finest collections of philosophical and theological works in the country.

For further information about any of the above facilities, WRITE to the Information Office,

HEYTHROP COLLEGE, 11–13 CAVENDISH SQUARE, LONDON W1M 0AN

Whitechapel bells
'Speaking to people everywhere'

Electronic 'Daisywheel' Typewriter/Printer

Office Equipment Selection Ltd have for many years supplied Churches with the most up to date electronic typewriters and printers. Hundreds of churches have saved a great deal of money by using the scheme, which was the brain-child of OES Ltd; they suggested to Brother, the manufacturers, that all the individual churches in the U.K. should be treated as one corporate unit and thereby be entitled to the same massive discounts which are available to Local Authorities for bulk purchasing.

Churches are using electronic typewriters more and more in order to produce the most attracive and interesting magazines. All models have interchangeable daisy-wheels which allow a wide variety of typestyles from the same typewriter. Some have built-in memories which can store extracts of text for automatic typing whenever required. All models have a correction facility which conveniently amends any errors automatically. Wide carriages and stencil facilities are also available. The typewriter may be connected to a computer by means of an interface which allows it to double as a printer. Alternatively, daisywheel printers are available, as part of the scheme.

Those who contact OES Ltd. are immediately sent more detailed literature. This is followed by a telephone call to answer any questions and provide experience advice on the wide range of products available. Orders may be placed over the telephone, and delivery is guaranteed the following day by means of a nationwide carrier service.

The schedule is fully backed by the network of Brother main dealers who provide local engineering backup if necessary.

	Normal Price	Special CPS Price
CE51 Electronic Typewriter	£305.00	£215.00
CE70 8k memory display typewriter	£595.00	£349.00
*EM501 electronic typewriter	£499.00	£325.00
*EM511 electronic typewriter	£575.00	£390.00
*EM701 electronic typewriter	£650.00	£425.00
*EM811 20k memory display typewriter	£849.00	£559.00
HR15XL daisywheel printer	£445.00	£356.00
1509 Dot matrix printer	£495.00	£408.00

*Made in the UK All prices subject to V.A.T. 15%

Please cut out this advert and keep for future reference.

Office Equipment Selection Ltd
Sales Manager, Silverbirch, Camperdown Industrial Estate,
Killingworth, Newcastle-upon-Tyne, NE12 0RF. Tel: Tyneside
091–268 3333, 8 lines.

Relevant, rewarding and accessible music for parish celebration

Clear, professional music setting with all words underlaid

Full accompaniment and SATB given in the choir book

Melody line given in the congregation book

Printed and bound to a high quality specification to ensure maximum legibility and durability in use

Choir Edition (with full music)
Sewn paperback 336 pages £7.95

Congregation Edition (with melody line)
Sewn paperback 128 pages £2.25

Published by **Geoffrey Chapman,** 1 Vincent Square, London SW1 2PN

Music for the Mass

Books for Parish and Church

Two new parish-based sacrament programmes that facilitate the involvement of parish, school and especially of parents in children's preparation for the sacraments.

Living the Eucharist

A Preparation for First Communion

Colourful, attractive and lively preparation through an understanding of the Mass with stories, cartoons, prayers and activities.
Child/Parent Book *64 pages + 16 page*
Parents Guide *£3.95*
Catechist Guide *40 pages £2.25*
Programme Director Guide *40 pages £2.25*

Living Reconciliation

A Preparation for Celebrating Forgiveness

Prepares 7–9 year olds by teaching them to reflect on the consequences of their actions and helping them to make loving choices.
Child/Parent Book *64 pages + 16 page*
Parents Guide *£3.95*
Catechist Guide *32 pages £2.25*
Programme Director Guide *40 pages £2.25*

Christian Ministry to the Sick

Edited by Tom Coyle

"Most highly recommended. This is the book for the chaplain and pastoral worker involved in the care of the sick." **Catholic Herald**
A valuable aid and companion to the rites for the Pastoral Care of the Sick.
Paperback 194 pages £6.95

"All that the Sunday mass-goer could desire" Mgr Crichton

The New Sunday Missal

Recognised as the outstanding Sunday Missal, this edition incorporates the textual changes and additions from the revised Lectionary: over 100,000 copies now in print

"Beautifully presented and well bound" **The Universe**

All editions 1056 pages, illustrated
Standard Edition *Red or blue binding £6.95*
De Luxe Edition *White binding, gold edges and white slip case £12.50*

Three beautiful and practical books for church readings and altar use
All texts in accordance with the revised Lectionary (see below).

The Gospel Passions

The passion narratives of the four evangelists, set out in voice parts for dramatised readings at Eastertide.
Hardback Gold-blocked 32 pages £5.95

Jointly published with Collins Liturgical Publications
Book of Gospels

A richly bound, large size volume, arranged for ease of use in liturgical celebrations.
Hardback Gold-blocked 672 pages £75.00

Jointly published with Collins Liturgical Publications
Lectionary

Revised Edition in three volumes

Approved for use in England and Wales, Scotland, and Ireland. Based on *Ordo Lectionum Missae, editio typica altera, 1981.*

Volume I *The Proper of Seasons, Sundays in Ordinary Time 1116 pages £67.00*
Volume II *Weekdays in Ordinary Time, Proper of Saints, Commons 1628 pages £86.00*
Volume III *Ritual Celebrations, Masses for Various Needs and Occasions, Votive Masses, Masses for the Dead 936 pages £62.00*
Three volume set *Hardback Gold-blocked £195.00*

For further details and our full list of titles contact
Geoffrey Chapman, 1 Vincent Square, London SW1P 2PN. Tel: 01–630 7881

INDEX OF ADVERTISERS